"*They say you can't take it with you, but you can. When you die, all the stories in your head go, too.*"
Billie Snyder Thornburg

"*We tell the stories of our families, our family histories; we write autobiographies and memoirs; we write as survivors. We are the ones left alive to tell the story.*"
Dr. Emily Jane Uzendoski

"*One of my favorite stops was the tiny town library. I'd never gotten over my addiction to reading. Books were nearly as important to me as food. I would always be able to nose out a library in a strange town as quick as an alcoholic could a liquor store.*"
Maxine Bridgman Isackson

"*Nebraska was a soldier state: that is, the old soldiers were practically in control of its policies and its politics.*"
O.A. Abbott from his 1929 book.

He wrote considerably about his claim that the key to the symbolism of the Mayan hieroglyphics was based on the numbering system of nine. *"The Dictionary of International Biography credited Nichols in 1975 with founding Psycho Symbolic Investigation Archeology based on his discoveries."*

Dale W. Nichols

"Children learn to read by reading-not by looking at pictures. We want them to learn to read. Here are stories with action, plot and climax. They stimulate imagination. Children catch on that exciting things can be found on a printed page. This discovery is the key that opens the door into a literate world."

George Jackson from his 1962 book.

Nebraska Authors
Volume One

Nancy Sue Hansen
Barbara Ann Dush

Nebraska Authors Project®
D & H Adventures Publishing
PO Box 112, Fullerton, NE 68638

Nebraska Authors Project®
Nebraska Authors Volume One. Copyright 2013 by Nancy Sue Hansen and Barbara Ann Dush. All rights reserved. Printed in the United States of America.

D & H Adventures Publishing books may be purchased for educational, business or sales promotional use. For information please write D & H Adventures Publishing, P O Box 112, Fullerton, NE 68638.

First edition October 2013
Printer: Service Press, Henderson, NE USA
Nancy Sue Hansen and Barbara Ann Dush
Nebraska Authors Volume One
ISBN 978-1-4675-8015-1

Library of Congress Cataloging-in-Publication Data
1. Nebraska-State-History-Authors-Books.
2. Kansas-Nebraska Territory-Great Plains-frontier-statehood.
3. Newspapers-magazines-publishers-writing-biographies.
4. Pioneers-ranchers-farmers-cowboys-homesteaders-Kinkaid Act-sod houses-orphan train.
5. Weather-drought-grasshoppers-blizzards-heat-trees-water-rivers.
6. Railroads-entrepreneur businesses-bank crashes-unemployment-scams-crimes-criminals-social unrest.
7. Politics-regionalism-nationalism-Bourbon Democrats-Bryan Democrats-Republicans-Populists-Fusionists-Nebraska Farmers Alliance-North Platters-South Platters-urban vs country.
8. Churches-religions-Christians-spiritualism-mysticism-magic-lawyers-education-teachers-schools-colleges-universities-legislature-family life.
9. Federal Writers Project-Nebraska Writers Project-Artists-Poets-Native Americans-Sandhills-Nebraska State Historical Society.
10. Nebraska military-Indian scrimmages and War, Civil War-Spanish American War-Cuba-World War I-World War II-Korean War-Vietnam War-military families.
11. Entertainment-amusements-movies-historic markers and memorials-travel.
12. President Grover Cleveland-President Abraham Lincoln-Presidents Roosevelts, Wilson, and Nixon.

Table of Contents

Preface

The idea for this book came about as I was reading "Winter Moon Deer," a poem written by the late Emily Jane Uzendoski who grew up in Nebraska. I was seeking a deeper meaning to its content, and called Nancy to meet at a fast-food place for some contemplative conversation over chicken nuggets and a soda.

As we discussed the poem, which was reflective of Nebraska's rural scenery, the conversation led to the works of other talented writers in the area. One brainstorm led to another, and soon the plan for writing a book about Nebraska authors emerged. We were also inspired by the fact that, not only do the two of us have a passion for Nebraska and our farming roots, we have an insatiable love for the written word and the fresh revelation and knowledge that comes from opening the pages of a newly-discovered book.

Soon we were on the road to writing our first volume. We pulled up our traveling boots and began mapping the dusty roads and scenic highways of Nebraska. It was no small task – both of us interviewing, writing, and researching in between our jobs and family duties. However, after two years of this labor of love, we now present to you fifty-two of Nebraska's authors, with more to come in the next volume(s).

It is our sincere wish that as you open the pages of <u>Nebraska Authors Volume One</u>, you will become as excited and inspired as we were as the stories of these writers unfolded. We also hope it will cause you to run to your nearest bookstore or library where you can dive into one of their books. We are certain you will be met with surprise, as we were, in meeting some of these featured authors for the first time.

– Barbara Ann Dush

Introduction

Once it was decided that our venture into Nebraska history was going to be from the view of Nebraska authors, we set to work accumulating lists of Nebraska authors that had been compiled over the years. The first list was Dr. Emily Jane Uzendoski. Since she had followed the standard of those before her in determining that a Nebraska author was either born in the state or had lived in the state for at least ten years, we decided to use the same concept for our list. We set up our A-Z system and began the task of identifying where the author was born, their birth date (and death date if applicable), and list as many of their publications as could be found. We decided to concentrate on book authors and leave newspaper, magazine and other types of authorship of written materials to others.

A trip to the Jane Pope Geske Heritage Room of Nebraska Authors in the Bennett Martin Lincoln Public Library provided us with a list of over nine thousand books and Nancy matched their list with the Uzendoski list. There were others that had written about Nebraska authors, too, they will be highlighted as the volumes continue. As we found other such collections of authors and titles of books, we added the authors to our list and will continue to add Nebraska authors to our list. If you know a Nebraska author or are a book published author, see the appendix to see how to add your name and book(s) to our list. Some point prior to 2015 the compilation will be published.

In the meantime, we decided to pick one person on the A-Z list and write about them as authors. We would not write a book report or a complete biography about them, but would highlight their expertise in writing the subject they wrote about. The major questions would focus on what was going on around them as they wrote and why did they write in Nebraska. Fifteen questions were considered for each author's work. Although every story would be different, the fifteen questions kept us on target to remember it wasn't a book report or a complete biography. The information collected for each author might inspire someone to write a more complete work about an author using our research or firsthand interview as a stepping stone.

Our task was to interest our readers to read the books of the authors we were writing about and to understand more about the person and the times in which the book(s) was written. How did writers see Nebraska history, United States history or world history in relation to their work? Was their book to present the past as they remembered it or to present ideas to shape the future? Was their work for education or entertainment, poetry or pictures, propaganda for a cause or research they had done on a court case, a novel with a combination of historic facts and imaginary characters or another issue? We decided we would not make a determination on the quality of the writing or subject matter, but present each as we found them as part of Nebraska History.

Our work was to be presented in volumes and in the beginning we expected that there would be twenty-six authors in each volume, one for each letter of the alphabet. We wanted to be sure they were spread out across the state and not all the same type book; but other than that, no author was too small or too popular for our research or interviews. Looking at the history of Nebraska through the eyes of the authors that wrote during different eras of Nebraska history should be a new way to view Nebraska history. It would also be of interest, we thought, to see how an author who was born in the state or lived in Nebraska at least ten years and had ventured away from the state, or who came into the state, saw the world from their new location.

Since we had not accumulated many names of the authors when we started, Nancy randomly picked an "Abbott" since there were several on the list. O.A. Abbott was from Grand Island, according to the notes. That meant that Grand Island was now represented and we had our "A." At this point we did not know if the person was still living or not, or even what they had written. We moved to "B." As we moved to each new letter of the alphabet, if we came to a person that was from a town we'd already picked, we put that person aside for a future volume and picked another person from that alphabet letter until all the slots were filled. Then we went back to see how many were poetry, government, frontier and other identifiable subjects so we would have a mix. We were pleasantly surprised to find that not only were the picks about half-mixed evenly male and female, they were about half still living, which meant personal interviews and the other half research. While Nancy continued to collect and alphabetize names, locate birth and death dates and updated lists of publications, we started to write for volume one.

It was decided that since Barb was a seasoned interviewer, as she currently works in the newspaper publishing business, she would take the majority of those with whom interviews could be completed. Nancy operated a video camera, when acceptable, and preserved the interviews on video as well as through tape recordings and transcripts. It was decided that with each interviewed author, a draft would be sent to them to review for corrections and additions and a form would be signed as an agreement to publish. When an author's family was found and interviewed regarding an author that had already passed away, a draft could be sent for any corrections or additions; however, no signature would be necessary to publish. Barb and Nancy would be assured the work would be as correct and as firsthand as possible, using that method. Nancy's day job involved travel so she took those authors who had passed on and incorporated the research needed as she traveled. Many interlibrary loan requests from the staff at the Alice Farr Memorial Library in Aurora assisted her in identifying needed research information. Much thanks goes to Jan for her patience when not much information was known about a book that was needed.

Volume One was taking shape. We both had a couple of stories yet to write and our process seemed to be working well. Nancy had J. Sterling Morton and Ruth Van Ackeren left to write. She planned a trip to Arbor Lodge. She figured that the information about the books he'd written would be available there. As she prepared for her visit with the curator, Laura Steinman, Nancy realized that Morton's books were actually published after his death. Not just one year or so after his death, but several years after his death so now there were new questions. The biographies on Morton, she had reviewed, did not shed light on his books which added even more questions. By the time Nancy arrived in Nebraska City for the interview, the normal fifteen questions about an author had multiplied. Surely there was a quick answer and the story could be written the next day, leaving only one story to be finished before going to publication. While the curator had done a wonderful job reviewing Morton's personal collection and provided the Nebraska Authors Project® with a copy of the grant proposal she had written, she did not have the needed information about the books he had written. This meant a trip to the Nebraska State Historical Society and their archives where a collection of the Morton papers are deposited. So much for a quick story! Six months later the concept of the Nebraska Authors Project® Volume One had to be revised and an interesting view of what was going on in Nebraska history thirty-five years after Statehood emerged.

Nancy discovered during her research there were several additional editors for the Morton books who were called into full service on the book(s) he was writing and editing after his unexpected death. Editor-authors James Beattie, Augustus O. Thomas, and Arthur C. Wakeley could be written about in other volumes and simply refer back to their work on the Morton books. Four other editors: Albert Watkins, Dr. George Miller, C.S. Paine and Grant L. Shumway had a vital part in seeing that these books were published. In looking at each of the additional editors, three of them would not have appeared on the Nebraska Authors list as they did not have other books they had written. Two of them, Watkins and Miller, were newspapermen and Paine had business and history interests. Shumway was a newspaperman, but had a book written about the Nebraska Panhandle counties to his credit. Now Barb and Nancy had a decision to make. The story about Morton's books would not be understandable if the work of the other four were not included in the Nebraska Authors Volume One book; however, that meant more than one of a specific letter. The neat A-Z twenty-six stories suddenly became fifty-two stories. It was decided to make Volume One a double volume to accommodate the Morton history makers.

Barb and Nancy went back through the authors' list and filled in some of the slots for additional authors. The new authors were picked just as the first set had been, nearly random without knowing anything about them when they were selected except where they were born or their attachment to Nebraska. Writing on the new authors began and pushed the publication date back.

Barb finished the details of a couple of her original stories. She had several events in her travels that made this volume especially meaningful. One such incident was Dorthy Koepke's story. When Mrs. Koepke's daughter, Lana Johnson, contacted the Nebraska Authors Project® with the news that her mother had passed on, the Project sent a long-stemmed yellow rose bouquet to the funeral service, simply because yellow represents peace. When Barb arrived at the service, she was quite surprised when she opened the funeral folder to find a poem titled "Let It Be Spring" written by Mrs. Koepeke about her wish that yellow roses be planted in her remembrance. Barb had never laid eyes on that particular poem. Then during the service, Mrs. Koepeke's daughter shared that her mother had said she always wanted to be recognized in a book about Nebraska authors. It was with continuing discoveries like this experience that we knew this project was an assignment we had to complete.

Nancy went to Alliance to finish the last of her original stories looking at author Van Ackeren who wrote from the Sandhills. Once again, there was a twist. While Mrs. Van Ackeren had passed away in 2002, the co-author of her last book was still living and had just moved into a care facility. Nancy was encouraged by Becci Thomas, of Knight Museum and Sandhills Center in Alliance, to visit him on her trip; and although it was not in the original plan, she did meet and briefly interview Mr. Robert Howard. He was interested in the project and agreed to have his story told about his own book(s) as well as the co-authorship with Mrs. Van Ackeren. He became the second "H." Nancy was internally impressed to return to Alliance to visit with Mr. Howard within a few days of her first visit and to talk to him by phone within the next week to complete the story. She went again exactly one month after the first interview to pick up photos and have the agreement to publish signed. He was not in his room. Nancy returned home and within twenty-four hours of sending a note to him about 'sorry I missed you', she found he had passed away. His family provided the photos; and Nancy and Barb are pleased that his story, as interviewed, is included.

The *coincidences* of meeting Mr. Howard included that he had written the introduction to one of Billie Thornburg's books and Thornburg was the publisher of Barb's book, Listen With The Heart. Barb had already written both Thornburg and Caroline Sandoz Pifer's stories when we found that Pifer had written the preface for Van Ackeren's book. It is also interesting that the Bartlett Richard book that Mrs. Van Ackeren completed had to pass through James Rawley before the Nebraska State Historical Society would publish it. It was also interesting that it was A.E. Sheldon, best known as working with the Nebraska State Historical Society, (who had been a house of representatives member working with author Yeiser), wrote a children's textbook on the history of Nebraska that added a chapter to his book about "Old Jules" and Mari Sandoz. That chapter taught hundreds of Nebraska children about the conflict discussed in the Van Ackeren-Richards-Howard books. Mari Sandoz had worked for Sheldon after working with Rudi Umland, before her first book became popular and she moved to New York [Mari Sandoz will be in a future volume]. Each of the authors: Rawley, Sandoz-Pifer, Thornburg, Yeiser, Umland, and Van Ackeren had been picked randomly for volume one [Sheldon will in in a future volume]. Nancy and Barb had made one nonrandom decision when they decided to include Barb in the Nebraska Authors Volume One and the story about Nancy will be included in a future volume.

The twists in the Morton and Howard stories were just the beginning of interesting threads among the authors with their backgrounds and how one life affected another. There are many dots to connect in the stories which the Nebraska Authors Project® authors did not know about until the stories were written and placed together. Some of the stories were so intertwined, in theory, that the Authors Project wonders if they knew each other's work or if circumstances were coincidental. For example: Mr. Yeiser wrote about labor, wages and the national debt just prior to becoming a State House Representative, and a new graduate named Fred Fairchild had the same topic as he appeared before Congress a few years later. More research would need to be done to see if Fred's book(s) used any part of Mr. Yeiser's plan. We will leave that for other writers to uncover, but we are curious.

Other examples: authors Babcock and Lawrence worked at the same place, the Lincoln Newspaper, years apart, as they went to college. Lawrence had a good experience with his boss and came back to eulogize him, while author Rudi Umland did not have such a good experience with Lawrence's boss as Rudi wrote from another setting. Lawrence's boss used his connections with Senator Norris in Washington against the best interests of Umland and his co-workers. Babcock was used as the model for the newspaper reporter in a television presentation of Senator Norris's return to Nebraska declaring his wish that the United States would not enter World War One. Darryl Zancuk produced a positive movie about President Wilson and the entry into World War I and made Omaha the site of the world premiere of the movie. The examples continue: Babcock's father was instrumental in the initial work to get water and power to the Columbus, Nebraska, area about the time Rex German's father was inventing plastic tubes for irrigation, working his business near Cozad. Both fathers intense work provided water assistance to thousands of Nebraska families over time. German stayed working with the family business and wrote about local history that was a major part of the growth in mid-Nebraska. Babcock traveled the world for *The Chicago Tribune* as the Travel, and later Books Editor, providing education about the world as he saw it. Lawrence, Babcock, Umland, Zanuck, German, as all the others, were randomly selected. Enjoy the dots you can connect as you take a new look at history through the eyes of Nebraska authors.

The writing of the A-Z Volume One was coming to a conclusion with the decision of what to do with "X." In all the collection of names of Nebraska authors there was not a last name with "X." Barb and Nancy decided to use this space to highlight someone who wrote about Nebraska, but may not have lived in the state. The first story is Malcolm X who was born in Nebraska; however, "X" was not a real last name. The "X" was part of his story so he was added as the first in the "X" section. The second selection was Luna Kellie. Kellie was from the Hastings area; however, the author that brought her story to light is from Iowa. In the collection of names of authors there are several other letters of the alphabet that have limited authors that meet the criteria of 'Nebraska author' so future volumes may use the space for specialized topics and authors writing about Nebraska.

As Barb and Nancy wrapped up Volume One, they decided they wanted to encourage readers to participate in Nebraska life as the authors had done. Remembering the past culture(s) in the state as well as participating and building its future through understanding, Nebraska history seemed to be the topic of numerous conversations between the two Volume One authors. It was decided that at the end of each story there would be an autograph box. Book signings will be scheduled and readers can bring their book to a signing and each author can sign the box after their story. The autograph boxes also include activities which represent some interest of that author. Traveling to the area where a particular author called home for at least part of their life would provide readers the option to see where history took place as well as participate, in some cases, in history being made. When all the boxes are signed and dated or have the activities completed, follow the instructions in the appendix. The Volume One authors and the Nebraska Authors Book and Travel Club look forward to meeting you.

How can a reader use this book? The stories are arranged so they are relatively short and can be read on an airplane, in a waiting room, or with a cup of your favorite beverage taking a break. Teachers of all subjects may find it interesting to have students read a story or two and present the information to a class on the various topics found in the book. Persons interested in deeper understanding will find the footnotes-endnotes-sources all together at the end of a story for clarification of specific terms or situations that make the story more interesting, if they are needed. Other readers may be interested in taking the facts listed at the top of each story and researching more about an author for a complete biography or research paper they author themselves.

Quoting Volume One information is acceptable without being considered plagiarism if there is appropriate documentation listing the <u>Nebraska Authors Volume One</u> and the appropriate section in the book as your source, Chicago style is suggested. Neither the Nebraska Authors Project® nor D & H Adventures Publishing have the rights, in most cases, to authorize use of photos we did not take ourselves; so for use of photos, please contact us prior to use so appropriate citing can be included in your work. Although Barb and Nancy consider this book a joint work, each story has been 'signed' with their first initial at the end of the story for those who are curious who wrote a specific story.

Discover United States and world history through the pen of Nebraska authors. It takes each person to build a nation. *Write* ~~What's~~ʌ your story?

DAVID P. ABBOTT

Date of birth: Sept. 22, 1863
Location of birth: Falls City, NE
Education: elementary
country school;
final year, Falls City High School
Date of Death: June 12, 1934
Location of Death: Omaha, NE
Buried at West Lawn cemetery
in family plot

David P. Abbott on the cover of Sphinx Magazine, October 1906.[1]

Known publications:

Abbott, David P. wrote numerous articles in <u>The Open Court</u>, a monthly magazine founded by Edward C. Hegeler. Devoted to the Science of Religion, the Religion of Science and the Extension of the Religious Parliament Idea.

Abbott, David P. <u>Cagliostro</u>. Sheet music. Quickstep. Published by W.H. Boner & Co., Philadelphia, 1885 [to F.A. Harrison printed on face page].

Abbott, David P. <u>Behind the Scenes with the Mediums</u>. Chicago: Open Court Publishing Co, 1907. vi+328pp. reprinted 1926.

Abbott, David P. <u>The Marvelous Creations of Josefy</u>. 1908.

Abbott, David P. <u>The History of a Strange Case</u>, 1908.

Abbott, David P. <u>Gene Dennis Von Herberg Wonder Girl</u>, unknown date.

(Abbott, David P.) Graham, Walter. David P. Abbott's Book of Mysteries. Published posthumously, 1977.

Teller and Todd Karr, Eds. House of Mystery: The Magic Science of David P. Abbott. The Miracle Factory: Los Angeles, two volumes, 2005. Vol 1 Behind the Scenes; Vol 2 The Book of Mysteries. [All known works of David P. Abbott are in these two volumes, including the Graham book. They are available through the Penn and Teller show in Las Vegas.]

It was the stroke of the pen and the signatures of Presidents on several documents that provided the Eastern states of the United States with a new frontier. Pioneers, homesteaders and business tycoons brought their social morality, educational basics, political agendas, occupational trades and their religions to the new land. The Nebraska-Kansas territory beckoned every personality of the human species to create a new life for themselves and their families. The migration routes started with fur traders before the Lewis and Clark Exploration of 1804. The beginnings of part of the Oregon Trail, in Nebraska, can be traced back to 1813.[2]

It was 1856 when the first settlers arrived in Richardson County, Nebraska. There were already over 5,000 settlers in various parts of the North and South Platte territories.[2] About this time, George Asahel and Sarah Francis Abbott began their married life near Falls City, in Richardson County.

Some of the new settlers from the East who came to Nebraska had already been in political fights for women's suffrage and the abolition of slavery. Among the religious beliefs that came with some them was the practice of Spiritualism.[3] They brought their emotion and endurance with them seeking converts as they came west.

According to the Nebraska State Historical Society (NSHS), Spiritualism was imported from Europe and began in New York as early as 1848. The system was well entrenched in the Eastern States at the time of the Civil War with séances in the White House and practices common among many of the elite Americans.[4, 5] By 1897, the belief system claimed more than eight million followers in the United States and Europe.[3] "*Both Lincoln and Omaha City Directories indicated spiritualist churches were in operation at the turn of the twentieth century."*[4]

The belief system or religion of Spiritualism has the foundation that spirits of the dead reside in a spirit world. To believers, these spirits have the ability and desire to communicate with the living. Practitioners are led by mediums who receive messages from the dead to pass on to the living. The most popular information sessions are the formal séances, trance-channeling, clairvoyance, remote viewing and consulting an Ouija board.[3,4] Many of the techniques used in Spiritualism, such as certain playing cards or some memory guessing games, were common as parlor games and remain entertainment in many Nebraska homes.[6]

A large industry grew up around the Spiritualism religion. Professional mediums made a good living whether reputable or not. Nebraska had several practitioners and their advertisements were published alongside articles about the new state constitution as noted by the *Lincoln Daily State Journal,* October 14, 1875.[2,4] It was into this ever changing political and religious atmosphere that George and Sarah Abbott's first child, David, celebrated his twelfth birthday. Young David grew up deciphering what was right and wrong. He took the side of not liking to see new settlers from all over the world become 'duped' and manipulated because a concept was new to them. He realized that 'tricks' of magic were different than true spiritual contacts. He honed his magic skills to prove his point. His modest beginnings and family life gave him the tools he used with people for the rest of his life.

David P. Abbott was born September 22, 1863, in a *"rude log cabin a short distance east of the old Muddy mill on the Rulo road"* near Falls City, Nebraska. The *Falls City Journal* on June 13, 1934, had a lengthy front page story about David's death the previous night. They wrote about their native son by saying, *"When he was a young man Mr. Abbott displayed an aptitude toward music and composed several selections some of which became well known. He played the piano and several other instruments and taught music for some time while a young man here. He began development of his tricks in magic while living here."*[7] The reading audience was reminded that he had often given free magic entertainment to citizens of Falls City.

As David grew up he had farm chores and learned business. He also learned that it was acceptable not to do what everyone else does. His father, George Abbott, was a progressive farmer that "wanted to do things in the area that others didn't want to do. He was known as a 'character,' " said Richard Zentner, Falls City volunteer historian, in an interview with the Nebraska Authors Project.⁹ According to the census reports for the area, the George Abbott family lived at various locations until 1880 when the family moved to the Stanton Lake area. "George owned the land from the railroad to the lake and wanted to make it a family park for picnics and the like. He had rodeos and other events there," Zentner continued. In the winter, George Abbott took on the job as the ice-man, cutting blocks from the frozen lake and selling the ice before refrigeration. Eventually a street in Falls City was named for George Abbott. George and Sarah had six children.

David Abbott became a postal clerk in the small town post office of Preston around 1885, according to the census reports. He married the daughter of one of the earliest settlers of the county, Fanny Miller, in Beatrice in September 1887. Meantime, Abbott became skilled enough with magic tricks to identify genuine and quality performers.[8] *"Abbott built his work of magic and deception on the devious principles he learned from spirit mediums, who could not afford to get caught. Abbott, fascinated with the concept of contacting disembodied souls from the departed, decided to study and research the phenomena."* [13] Halloween wasn't his only investigation day. He began investigations into paranormal claims, mystics, magic tricks and fraud before he and Fanny moved to Falls City in 1900.

Abbott was aware that some of the citizenry who placed a lot of money on the table of mediums and occultists, clairvoyants and high priests (priestess) of strange religions was to "satisfy the longing of the human heart." [8] While Abbott understood the pain in looking for a lost loved one or to resolve another issue, he also knew that many people were emotionally led down a path of fraud and deception. He wanted to be sure everyone had the understanding that most magic performed was a 'trick' and not a real spirit connection, just a loss of money for the helpless living soul. While Abbott refined his hobby into masterful tricks and his investigations exposed frauds, he kept open the idea that some phenomena, regardless of skepticism, had the possibility of being genuine.

In one of his investigations, he reviewed a pair of mediums, known as the Bang Sisters, who were performing a trick advertised as a genuine phenomenon. The 'trick' consists of a 'spirit portrait painting' where an image appears as you think of it. Abbott gained notoriety when he exposed their 'trick' and then duplicated it as "Spirit Paintings." The trick can be very eerie to watch as an image slowly appears on a canvas. This "mysterious and beautiful effect" is still performed by many magicians today.[8, 13] Abbott declared his actions as a 'trick' (not a genuine phenomenon) and even professionals could not figure out his methods. Finally, he told a Dr. Wilmar and the doctor immediately sold the information to Selbit and Kellar for their performances. However, nothing could quite match the stage presence of David P. Abbott.

Abbott wrote articles on psychic subjects, most notably in the columns of *The Open Court* magazine, where he answered citizen questions in a scientific manner. While Albert Watkins, C.S. Paine, and Dr. George Miller put the finishing touches on the J. Sterling <u>Morton Illustrated History of Nebraska</u>, [15] there was another book published presenting the darker side of Nebraska. In 1907, David Abbott published his first book <u>Behind the Scenes with the Mediums</u>.[8] It exposed techniques of fake spirit mediums. Most of them were located in eastern Nebraska. A portion of the book includes a séance that Abbott attended in Lincoln and his scientific reasoning for the strangeness involved. He exposed 'slate writing' and 'billet tests' among other phenomena. According to Abbott, any trick that needed to have the lights out was a very poor and cheap trick and must require very little skill to perform since it had to be hidden.

In his book, Abbott admitted that some people would find out someone or something was fake, go to someone else, and be duped again. Many prominent Nebraskans were part of the spiritualist movement and shared information with each other. Bits of information from conversations were collected by one woman and placed in a book. Her 'trick' of knowing so much about a person was exposed and her little book was turned over to the police. It became known as the *Omaha Blue Book* which included names, dates and events. Even being confronted with the book, some people would not believe she was a fraud.[8]

Abbott was curious about Josefy, an engineer by trade, who did magic. He wrote an expose of <u>Josefy</u>, 1908. He was also intrigued by a woman from Kansas who came to Omaha to work her magic. Gene Dennis Von Herberg was called "Wonder Girl," but over the years she became less effective and, according to reports, 'lost her touch' for no known reason. Abbott wrote about her skill and mystic in <u>Wonder Girl</u>. He continued to investigate and write all of his life.

Reports show Abbott and his wife moved to Omaha by 1910, and in 1914 they were living in a large home David had specially built on

Center Street to accommodate his hobby. The spacious front room was where he held all his magic shows.

Abbott was a businessman: a money lender in the brokerage trade. His office was at 17th and Farnam in the Patterson Building, but Abbott's passion remained mathematics, science and philosophy. By the time he moved to Omaha, the amateur magician was inventing many feats of magic. His amazing skill drew the likes of magicians Harry Houdini, Selbit and Kellar, Thurston, Horace Goldin, Theo Bamberg and Ching Ling Foo "to be baffled and to learn" new tricks for their profession.[13]

Abbott on left and Houdini on right in downtown Omaha while visiting with Abbott at his home.[14]

Abbott's hobby presented several lasting contributions to the fields of spiritualism and magic. He created effects such as the floating ball which was later made famous by Okito[3] and by Bamberg as he traveled the world.[13] He invented the "Talking Teakettle" which could be shown empty *yet when the spout was held to a spectator's ear it would answer a question of which the spectator had been thinking; this effect was performed well before the advent of radio.*"[1,13]

In 1931, as Professor-Scientist Albert Einstein's theory of relativity was front and center in the news of the world, the *Omaha World Herald* interviewed Abbott about the discovery. The interview was intended to provide those readers who were from the nonscientific population with a layman's view of the Einstein theory. With his emphasis in his understanding of math and science he provided his version of an explanation for the readers for the newspaper published as "Magician-

Abbott performing teakettle trick on his living room stage.[14]

Philosopher Interprets Einstein's Theory of Relativity."

Abbott's first book was *"considered to be one of the best exposure of methods used by psychics"* worldwide. He *"wrote a second book, which included descriptions of many magical feats which had astounded top professional performers. He died before it could be published."* [9]

According to the 1934 *Falls City Journal* news article, David Abbott had Bright's disease (also known as nephritis) and diabetes. He and his wife Fannie were both seriously ill and at the Omaha Lord Lister hospital. They were able to return to their home for a week before both were re-admitted. The couple had no children. It was the front room of the Abbott home that hosted David's funeral. He is buried in Omaha.[7] Fannie (1868-1936) joined him two years later.

David P. Abbott's death was a blow to the international magic community. Abbott's attorney Edith Beckman bought the home and auctioned off most of the Abbott possessions, but Abbott's final manuscript, complete with photos, became misplaced to the magic community until 1974. The unintended vanishing trick lasted thirty years. Walter Graham, amateur Omaha magician, decided to look for it. His efforts paid off and he published it in 1977 as <u>David P. Abbott's Book of Mysteries</u>.

In March 26, 2013 the Nebraska Authors Project® interviewed the 90 year old Walter Graham at his Omaha home. Graham noted his own interest began when he was about 12 when he and a friend decided to learn some tricks and make money 'during the hard times'.[14] After he returned from WWII he purchased a box of papers that belonged to Abbott and found fragments of an unfinished manuscript. Without photos in their appropriate places the manuscript may be an artifact, but not for publication reasoned the professional editor friend he asked for help to review the paperwork. The mystery papers went back into the box, but the contents were not forgotten. Over the years people have given him Abbott memorabilia which he proudly shared during the interview.

It was in 1974 when Graham decided he needed to see the inside of the Abbott home so he called the current owners. They revealed there were items at the house that belonged to Abbott. Graham made his first of several visits to the home. It would take another few months before Graham could negotiate a sale of the historic materials, including what he recognized as the missing manuscript and his paper-mache 'talking' skull. Graham, the owner of the Modern Litho Printing Company in Omaha, self-published the Abbott manuscript in 1977, and ran ads in magic publications to generate sales. One person that responded to the ad was a budding magician working as a Latin teacher from New Jersey.

After the book was published, Graham continued sharpening his skills and preforming magic shows as a hobby and he continued to correspond with the Latin teacher. It took about twenty-five years before Graham got a call from the Penn and Teller show in Las Vegas wanting to schedule a meeting. The Latin teacher had made it in the big time. An article in the October 2003 *Omaha World Herald*, "Magic Draws Teller to Omaha," announced his mission.[16] A trip, in 2004, provided another visit to the Abbott home as well as visits to Abbott family members. On June 2, 2013 the *Omaha World Herald* published a story "In This Illusionist's House of Mysteries, Secrets Didn't Vanish"

Walter B. Graham October 2003 with Abbott screens.

by Casey Logan. Details of the relationship between Graham, Lenora Schrat, owner of the former Abbott home, and the Teller (known as the little magician) were highlighted.

David P. Abbott's memory is still alive in Omaha and throughout the magic industry. Fans and practitioners, such as Walter Graham and the Penn and Teller show, continue to amaze audiences with their tricks. Many of these tricks invented or perfected by Abbott.

Teller worked with Editor Todd Karr to locate all the known works of David P. Abbott and publish them into a two volume set, including the manuscript Graham had published. In 2005, House of Mystery: The Magic Science of David P. Abbott was complete and published.

David P. Abbott invented magical effects that are still used today. He mastered a hobby using mathematics, science and philosophy, a keen sense of observation and a gift of presentation. When Abbott's book(s) were published, the worlds of spiritualism and magic were presented with the opportunity to provide entertainment declared to be human skills of magic or to continue to conjure money from people's wallets with false promises of disembodied spirits revisiting earth performing the same 'tricks'. Abbott did not seek to vilify the Spiritualism Movement, but to separate the 'tricks' from what might be 'real'. Are you able to detect the differences in mental and physical 'tricks' around you today?

If you choose to spend your money for magical illusionist entertainment, remember that much of what the performer presents may have been the invention of Nebraskan David P. Abbott. N

Endnotes, Footnotes & Sources:

*During the course of this research two middle names were found in the records. The most common was Phelps; however, Patterson was also used in an early census.

[1] Abbott, David. MagicPedia, Genimagazine.com the free online encyclopedia for magicians by magicians. Reviewed 3/15/2013. Opening Photograph was given with permission to publish from Walter Graham. Details of when photo was taken was found at www.geniimagzine.com.

[2] Sheldon, Addison Erwin. Nebraska Old and New History, Stories, Folklore. Lincoln: The University Publishing Company. 1937. 470 pp.

[3] www.wikipedia. *Spiritualism.* Reviewed 3/16/2013.

[4] Bacon, Dale. *Spiritualism: Messages from the Great Beyond.* Nebraska State Historical Society, Assistant Curator. www.nebraskahistory.org. Reviewed 3/16/2013.

[5] The Copperhead Chronicle Volume Two, Number Three, Fourth Quarter, 1999, www.csa-dixie.com. Reviewed 3/16/2013.

[6] www.wikipedia. *Helena Blavatsky.* Reviewed 3/16/2013.

[7] "David Abbott is Taken by Death: Born in County." *Falls City Journal*, front page, June 13, 1934.

[8] Abbott, David P. Behind the Scenes with the Mediums. Open Court Publishing Co, 1907. vi+328 pp. Reprinted 1926.

[9] Abbott, David P. *Nebraska State Historical Society (NSHS).* www.negov. Reviewed 2/1/2013.

[10] Abbott, David (magician). www.wikipedia.com Reviewed 2/1/2013.

[11] Abbott, David P, Master Magician. *Nebraska State Historical Society's website Blog.* — Patricia C. Gaster, Assistant Editor for Research and Publications October, 2010. Reviewed 2/1/2013.

[12] Abbott, David P(helps) (1863-1934). Encyclopedia of Occultism and Parapsychology. 2001. *Encyclopedia.com.* (March 15, 2013). http://www.encyclopedia.com/doc/1G2-3403800013.html. Reviewed 3/15/2013.

[13] Abbott, David. www.thedailydeception.com. Reviewed 3/15/2013.

[14] Interview with Walter B. Graham, March 26, 2013, notes located in Nancy Hansen's files. Photos courtesy of Walter B. Graham. For more information about Walter B. Graham see his story in the forthcoming military volume written by Barbara Ann Dush and Nancy Sue Hansen. At the time of this publication he can be contacted through magigraham@aol.com

[15] Hansen, Nancy Sue and Dush, Barbara Ann. Nebraska Authors Volume One. "J. Sterling Morton." "Albert Watkins." "George L. Miller." "C.S. Paine." "Grant L. Shumway."

[16] Palmer, Jane, "Magic Draws Teller to Omaha," *Omaha World-Herald*, October 2003.

Erickson, Howard. "Magician-Philosopher Interprets Einstein's Theory of Relativity." *Omaha World Herald*, January 4, 1931.

Logan, Casey "In this illusionist's house of mysteries, secrets didn't vanish," Omaha World Herald, June 2, 2013.

Thank you to:
Walter B. Graham for the use of his photographs and interview about Abbott. Graham's own story is to be published in a separate volume.

Richardson County Historical Society, Inc.: Richard and Ann Meinzer, Ramona Godemann and Jo Ann Auxier, Curator.

Fall City Public Schools staff: Vicky Zoeller, Jenny Herling and Norma Thompson.
Fall City Library front desk staff

Special thanks to Richard Zentner for his time and knowledge of the history of Richardson County, the Abbott family and his mastery of the computer programs needed to verify our research.

OTHMAN ALI "O.A." ABBOTT

Date of birth: Sept. 16, 1842
Location of birth: Hatley, Canada, Providence of Quebec
Education: Belvidere, Ill.
Moved to Nebraska: 1867
Veteran: Civil War – 9th Ill. Cavalry
NE first Lieutenant Governor: 1877-1879
Date of death: June 25, 1935
Location of death: Grand Island, NE

Othman Ali (O.A.) Abbott[1]

"Responding to the urgent appeals of his children and his friends to put his personal recollections of the mighty drama of human life on the American continent in which he has had part for over 80 years. Mr. Abbott has prepared this manuscript. The Nebraska State Historical Society is glad to print..." wrote Editor Addison Sheldon.

Abbott, Othman Ali. <u>Reminiscences of a Pioneer Lawyer/ Recollections of a Pioneer Lawyer</u>, A special publication of the Nebraska State Historical Society, (Lincoln). Edited by Addison E. Sheldon, 1929, 178 pages.

Reminiscences and recollections of a boyhood in Canada and Illinois provide a glimpse into North American history prior to Nebraska Statehood. The Gold Rush, the Civil War, the life and times of growing up and becoming educated in world affairs were placed on paper from the view of an aging country pioneer lawyer. Othman Abbott ended his manuscript reminiscences by stating that he wrote the book to record his own early experiences and not to attempt to write a history of Nebraska. He noted that he had been already admitted to practicing law before he started to Nebraska in a covered wagon and his heart was in law, not history. He covered his major interests of the new state of Nebraska's constitutional struggles; bills that were introduced, including church taxes; the railroad; homesteading; timber culture; pre-emption land; and supporting the unpopular women suffrage. This manuscript stopped about the time he was elected as the first Lieutenant Governor. He completed his mission to write about his early years, not his political career.

Othman Ali (O.A.) was the second son of Abiel and Sabrie (Young) Abbott of German ancestry. His father Abiel was the son of William Abbott and grandson of Williams' parents: George Abbott and Hannah Chandler of Andover, Massachusetts. William married Elizabeth Gray, the granddaughter of James and Mary Chilton, of Plymouth, Massachusetts. James Chilton was the twenty-third signer of the Mayflower compact.

Othman was a farm boy with all the chores and memories of early farming traditions. He wrote that buckskin coats and breeches were common and he agreed with the common saying of the day: "Buckskin clothes be they ever so dry and warm, are always wet and cold." He noted that boots and shoes were made by the village shoemaker and said, "I remember my first pair of boots with red leather tops. My pride in them induced me to wear my pants inside so the tops would show."[2]
(p 9-10)

It was his love of astronomy, bird watching and reading the latest books about them that encouraged his love of reading. He read about the world beyond the United States borders in stories about the Crimean War which began in 1854, and works of Alfred Lord Tennyson.

He told about the 'schools' of the day as being specialized events. He said music schools were in vogue, but it was the 'spelling' schools that all students attended. The spelling schools were events where children were on teams and spelled words as given to them. Usually when the spelling events were ended for the day there was time for recitations and 'speaking pieces'.

Othman wrote about his love of reading and orations, but also about an author he did not like when he was a child: Charles Dickens. He stated it wasn't until he was in the Civil War when he picked up a book, liked it, and when he found out Dickens wrote it decided to re-read all the books he had disliked as a child. He became a devoted admirer of Dicken's works.

Abbott remembered walking long distances to hear speakers that came to his area. He missed Douglas and Lincoln, but did walk ten miles to hear Wendell Phillips, the great anti-slavery orator. He loved these events even if his physical body exhibited pain, especially his feet and legs. He heard orations about the Kansas-Nebraska Act and the Civil War long before he became a soldier or a Nebraska lawyer and politician. Another future Nebraska resident, Mrs. O.C. Dake, also of Illinois, described her regret at missing hearing Lincoln when she was young. Orations were major events in the lives of many.[4]

A vivid memory as a youth was of the banking system in Illinois. This experience carried through to his political years on the plains of Nebraska in future years. He wrote, *"Banks were unregulated by state or national law and any man or set of men who had money to rent an office and put out a sign, opened a bank and issued currency without let or hindrance; and the money so issued was the only medium of exchange aside from gold and silver. As a rule Eastern money was the safer medium, but money issued by these irresponsible banks was not a good tender for debts, would not buy postage stamps, nor could it be used to pay taxes, or fare on railroads or canal or lake boats. Every merchant kept a bank note detector about the size of a modern Sears-Roebuck catalogue. In some states, banks were given charters by the State, the state in some cases being a partner in the banking business or attempting to guarantee the payment of the notes or currency so issued. But these expedients were of doubtful value and farmers preferred to exchange his produce for goods when it could be done. Men suffered from this medium of exchange at all times. I remember that we had a wood box papered with worthless currency."*[2]

Abbott discussed many events that he remembered vividly while writing his memoirs. He considered the Dread Scott case and the youth club he joined: The Wide-Awakers. One event he remembered distinctly that changed the nation was the attack on Fort Sumter on April 11, 1861.

"...patriotism in the North ran high. Certainly there was great excitement in northern Illinois. There were flags on all the churches and the pulpits and men and women everywhere wore the symbol of the union. And when flags could no longer be bought women sat up all night making them without sewing machines, and the supply of red and blue cloth was soon exhausted." [2(p 29)]

"The first call for 75,000 volunteers was answered more largely from the cities where militia companies were already armed….there were more volunteers than the government could uniform, shelter, or equip with arms. As I recollect, the sentiment of the North was not demanding the abolition of slavery. The overwhelming majority were demanding that the union be saved, that the attempt to destroy the government of the fathers be stopped that the South must obey the laws and uphold the Constitution; that the South was simply an organized rebellion against the best government in the world and that rebellion must be overthrown regardless of cost in blood or treasure."[2] (p29)

The young Abbott did not ask permission to enlist, nor did he discuss it with his parents or siblings… "it was generally understood that we were to become members of the First Western Calvary and that Colonel Brachett of the regular army was to command the regiment…"[2] It was concern of the new recruits if the leadership would be a regular army man or someone less qualified. Abbott was grateful he had a man with experience at the top as he enlisted. The First Western Calvary became the Ninth Illinois Calvary, Company I, which was one of twelve companies presented by Illinois in the Civil War. The enlistment requirement was three years or during the time of war. Military experienced Nebraska territory resident Victor Vifquain was requested to assist the Ninety-seventh Illinois Volunteer Infantry and became Adjutant in the summer of 1862 .[4]

Othman wrote his impressions and experiences of his enlistment. His memories included their first enemies as ticks and bedbugs and the wild hogs that would dig in the graves of the dead. The military marching by would see the white bones coming up through the ground. The memories of being in the Civil War and the times were written vividly in his book. Abbott was wounded twice in the war and had a nearly fatal case of what they called pneumonia. In the Battle of Nashville he was injured, helped others who were wounded, and then went back with his men. Later he was handed a mashed bullet that had hit his diary first before bouncing into a rib. Abbott wrote that he had the bullet and the diary with the dent in his office desk for years. He noted that the bullet was lost or stolen at some point, but the diary was among his effects.[5] One injured man Abbott helped at the Battle of Nashville later spent his life in Chapman, Nebraska, not far from where Othman began his law practice.

Abbott described finding out about the end of the war. *"While we* *were in camp at East Point, we received the news of the surrender of Lee's forces at Appomattox on April 9, 1865. We did not learn of it for some days after its occurrence, but when the news arrived we indulged in a general holiday. It foretold the end of our long service. We had scarcely finished our jubilation over Lee's surrender before the sad news of Lincoln's assassination on the 14th of the same month. This was really like a personal bereavement to every soldier. I did not know a single man who did not take it as personal sorrow to himself. Many refused to believe it until the news was confirmed in all of its heart sickening details. A desire to avenge his death at first filled the minds of all of us, until we realized that it was only a Northern Copperhead who dealt the final fatal blow, and not the last desperate deed of a defeated former who risked his life in the cause of the Confederacy...*[2] (p85)

A photo of Othman Ali Abbott in military uniform in his book is displayed in a glass case at the Edith Abbott Public Library in Grand Island, Nebraska.[3]

When the war came to an end the soldiers didn't automatically get sent home. For Abbott, now a first lieutenant, they had clean-up work to do. He recalled several stories of keeping new law and order in the southern states as they headed north. One story included the closure of an Episcopal church because they refused to pray for the new country and its leaders. When he was finally mustered out of his unit he wrote:

"I shall never forget the peculiar sensation of riding through those wooded hills unarmed without wearing my arms almost night and day for so long. At the sound of approaching footsteps ahead or from the side, I would instinctively feel for my revolver or carbine, only to wake up mentally, so to speak, at finding myself unarmed. The sensation was very

peculiar and wore away very slowly"[2] (p86-87).

Abbott had decided to study law while in the military as it was obvious to him that his injuries would keep him from the hard labor of a traditional farmer. On his way back through Montgomery: *"I took the first step toward preparation for post-war work for I knew there would be no more fighting and I thought it would be a good plan while we were waiting to be ordered home. I had freely made up my mind to take up the practice of law after our discharge from the service and to that end I bought my first law books: "Blackstone's Commentaries", Chitty Edition in two volumes, to spend my leisure time getting an idea of the law, discarding army regulations and war studies."*[2]

He found that the Latin he had in high school helped in the reading of his books. He noted that they were among the first books he brought to Nebraska for his law library.

Those books were valuable in getting him into school with a Mr. Moore. Mr. Moore was in the process of writing "Civil Justice" which would later be used as the text book in Illinois law. The legal system was a type of apprentice system and Abbott had shown initiative by purchasing the books while still in the military and actually reading them, which gave him the nod to become one of the famous man's students.

While studying with Mr. Moore, Abbott supported himself as a country school teacher. He described his experiences trying to keep order with older students as well as instruct all grades. He later started a new school in the Grand Island area and taught when teachers were not available.

He describes two of his uncles heading from the farmland where they all worked and lived in Illinois, to California as 49'ers when gold was found. He told of heading to Nebraska through Omaha and on west of Grand Island (Wood River) to where an uncle lived before he set up his first law office. "When I drove our covered wagon into Grand Island, Nebraska that early spring day in 1867…there were a half dozen small houses and a couple of businesses."[2] To support himself while his law practice grew, he sold insurance for Mutual Life of New York: "The hardest part of an insurance agents job was to persuade the man's wife."[2-p116] He was the first practicing attorney in Grand Island.

He returned to Illinois on February 9, 1873, to marry and returned with his new wife to Grand Island. He wrote of Mrs. Abbott: Elizabeth M. Griffin. She was a teacher in Iowa for a time before their marriage.

She became very active in the Nebraska Woman's Suffrage Society, including an officer in the organization. As the suffrage movement lost votes and steam, the women turned to other community work. Mrs. Abbott turned to starting a public library. The couple's daughter Edith was seven when the library work began. She picked up the interest as her own with the current Grand Island Library named after her.

Abbott wrote, "Nebraska was a soldier state: that is, the old soldiers were practically in control of its policies and its politics. Hall County had never had a representative in a Republican State Convention…" [2-p134] and when his fellow countrymen chose him to be a delegate and chipped in to pay his traveling expenses, his political career took a new turn. He later became known as one of the nine men of the state who were members of the two Nebraska Constitutional Conventions of 1871 and 1875. He did not write a book about his political experiences, but Abbott's papers can be found at the Stuhr Museum and in a special section at the Edith Abbott Public Library in Grand Island, called the Abbott Sisters Research Center.

Mr. and Mrs. Abbott[1] on the grounds of the Abbott house in Grand Island after 1884-1887.

Mr. and Mrs. Abbott had a home built for themselves, but according to the *Nebraska State Journal* of March 17, 1977, the house was burned down by the Grand Island Fire Department to make way for expansion of a firm which purchased the property. Abbott wrote about friends that stayed at their home as they passed through the area including Susan B. Anthony.

Each of the couple's four children had visible careers of their own. Both girls, Edith and Grace, became famous for their social work with Grace Abbott being appointed in 1921 by the President of the United States to the position of Chief of the U.S. Children's Bureau. The oldest son, known as "Ottie" (O.A. Abbott Jr. 1874-1954), became a court reporter of the 11th Judicial District, and was four-term mayor of Grand Island three consecutive terms 1927-1932 and again 1939-1940. Arthur G. Abbott (1880-1969) also chose the legal profession.

"It has been no part of my plan to prepare a history of Nebraska. Others have done that and, in passing, I must refer to the attempt of my old friend J. Sterling Morton of Nebraska City, to provide a history of this state while its sources were still known to the writers. J. Sterling Morton was a democrat until he became a devoted supporter of 'Sound Money' and an opponent of what was called 'Bryanism.' Although he was a democrat, J. Sterling Morton had many friends among those of us who belonged to the other party and among those of us who lived in the other part of the State."[2-p175, 4]

Why did Mr. Abbott stay in Hall County, Nebraska? In his reminiscence, he answered that question: *"my imagination had perhaps been fired by the vast expanse of the surrounding prairie country, and I had begun to see visions and dream dreams."* [2] Throughout the book Othman Abbott shows his love for Nebraska. N

Endnotes, Footnotes & Sources:

[1] Nebraska State Historical Society photo files. Lincoln, Nebraska. Received by Nancy Sue Hansen with permission to publish. 2012.

[2] Abbott, Othman Ali. Reminiscences of a Pioneer Lawyer/Recollections of a Pioneer Lawyer, A special publication of the Nebraska State Historical Society, (Lincoln). Edited by Addison E. Sheldon, 1929, 178 pages.

[3] Photo by Barbara Ann Dush taken at Edith Abbott Library, Grand Island, Nebraska. 2012.

[4] Hansen, Nancy Sue and Dush Barbara Ann. Nebraska Authors Volume One. "Jean-Baptist Victor Vifquain.," "O.C. Dake," "J. Sterling Morton," "Albert Watkins," "George L. Miller," "C.S. Paine," "Grant L. Shumway." Fullerton: D & H Adventures Publishing, 2013.

[5] Mr. Abbott's diary is among his material collection held at the Stuhr Museum of the Prairie Pioneer, Grand Island, Nebraska. As this book goes to publication it is the national memorial events of the Civil War around the nation. The Abbott diary is on loan to the exhibits where he served. Kari Stofer, curator of the Stuhr Museum of the Prairie Pioneer, suggested it would be at least two years before the diary would be returned to Nebraska.

Nebraska Authors Book & Travel Club

Visit Pioneers Park in Grand Island between Hwy 30 (West 1st Street) and West Second Street at North Elm. In the summer a water fountain and flowers will make your visit to the block-size park near downtown welcome. It was the site of the first Hall County Court House where Abbott, as a lawyer, would have spent some time.

FREDERIC L. BABCOCK

Date of birth: Oct. 31, 1892*
Location of birth: Ord, NE
Education: Columbus High
School, 1911
University of Nebraska grad
1917 (1913-1917)
Military: WWI, Army, six
months 1918 at Camp Lewis
and Camp Hancock
Date of Death: May 13, 1979
Location at Death: Winter
Park, Florida
Buried in Wheaton, DuPage
Co., IL

Frederick "Fred" L. Babcock

Known Publications:

Babcock, Frederic. <u>Blood of the Lamb</u>, publisher: Mohawk, 1932.

Babcock, Frederic: city editor for the *Cheyenne Wyoming State Tribune*, drama editor for the *Denver Post* and member of editorial staff of the *Seattle Times* and *Minneapolis Journal*. He is best known for his work for the *Chicago Tribune* as travel editor and then later as editor of the magazine of books.

Babcock, Frederic. <u>Hang Up the Fiddle</u>. Garden City, N.Y.: Doubleday and Co., 1954. 320 pp. Novel.

Babcock, Frederic. *All Florida Magazine*, numerous articles 1965-1967.

Henry Ernest "H.E." and Jeannie Powell Babcock married December 24, 1885, while Henry was attending law school at Ann Arbor,

Michigan. The couple moved to Ord, Nebraska, in 1886 after graduation where Henry began a law practice. His practice work load soon overwhelmed his health and he was forced to change the direction of his interests. He chose to concentrate on a major interest of his: promotion of irrigation projects. His obituary declared "H. E. Babcock, the man who conceived the Columbus [Nebraska] power canal project and labored long in effort to interest capital to develop it."[1]

The couple raised six sons: H.E. Jr., Herman, John, Frederic, Earl and George, and one daughter, Dora. Frederic was born at the Ord home on October 31 according to all records. *What is in dispute is the year he was born. One historical story[2] that includes his family in the community record declares the year he was born to be 1894; and The Howard Gotlieb Archival Research Center [3] and his tombstone say 1896. The 1900 census shows him at age seven with the birth year as 1892. The 1910 census lists him as age seventeen in 1910, and the Social Security Death Index says he was born in 1892.[1]

H.E. concentrated on water. Droughts plagued Nebraska farmers and retarded the growth of villages, towns and cities. Between 1895 and 1897, H.E. moved his family to Platte County, *"Monroe, Neb., and undertook to form an irrigation system that would supply water for thousands of acres of land in the Loup and Platte valleys from Genoa eastward almost to North Bend. He carried the water from Beaver Creek above Genoa by canal across to Lost Creek, near Platte Center, using the bed of that creek as a natural canal from which the laterals could be run. The project was a success during the dry spell which lasted about two years, but when the rains came again the land owners felt no further need for it."[4] H.E. moved his family to Columbus in 1898, and set about integrating his irrigation plan with needed power options for the Platte and Loup Valley.

As the family settled into their new home, the Trans-Mississippi and International Exposition committee was finishing their plans for the Omaha event scheduled for 1899. The drought, devastated economy, and labor market were on the rebound and it seemed that times in Nebraska were looking up.

In Columbus, the local chapter of the Grange had proposed a plan for five hundred farmers of the Loup and Platte Valleys to purchase shares of stock for two hundred dollars each to create a public power and irrigation system, but the grasshopper plague of 1874 destroyed the dream. The Columbus newspaper continued to encourage and remind the citizens that trade and growth was dependent on water and power. Other plans were made over the years, but each failed for different reasons, including the plans during the most recent drought and devastated economy of 1895.[4] Bolstered with success in the Monroe area, H.E. Babcock became a leader in the irrigation movement in Columbus, Platte County.

In 1910, he "spent many months in New York City negotiating the proposed power canal." The plan included Swiss businessmen and other interested parties outside of Nebraska. It, too, failed. Again in 1912, H.E. Babcock proposed a plan acting for the "Great Eastern Company" with more interest from Lincoln. It was in the plan of the 1930's that the canal would eventually be completed, *the fact that the giant basin originally designed by Engineer W. L. McEathron as the reservoir for the dreamed-of dam in 1902, was located on almost the identical site of Lake Babcock, the regulating reservoir of the Loup River Public Power District, north of Columbus."* [4]

H.E. Babcock and his wife did not live long enough to see the work begun. According to H.E.'s obituary, his wife Jeannie died in Columbus in April 1914, toward the end of Frederic's freshman year in college. H.E. married Miss Beryl Martin of New York, who survived him when he passed away in December 1917 in Los Angeles while recuperating from a business trip to Salt Lake City.

Frederic had grown up through drought and a devastated Nebraska economy. His father was absent from the home on irrigation business trips for much of his growing up years. When he was sixteen, just before his seventeenth birthday, Frederic took a position as a printer's devil. It was a good starting level errand boy type job giving him experience in the workings of the newspaper industry. He graduated from Columbus High School in 1911. His studies began in Journalism at the University of Nebraska in 1913. According to UN-L yearbooks, Frederic belonged to Alph Sigma Phi and Sigma Delta Chi in 1914 and was listed as a junior in 1915. He had worked his way through the University as a reporter at the *Nebraska State Journal/Lincoln Journal* and graduated in 1917.[1]

It was in the waning months of World War I when Babcock joined the United States Army. He served at Camp Lewis and Camp Hancock before the war ended. He was listed in his father's December 1917 obituary as being from Landers, Wyoming.[1] After his military service he accepted a position as the city editor for the *Cheyenne Wyoming*

State Tribune where he worked until 1924. For the next two years he worked as drama editor for the *Denver Post*. He became a member of the editorial staff of the *Seattle Times* and later the *Minneapolis Journal*.

His goal was to work for the *Chicago Tribune,* so in 1927 he settled in Chicago. He found that he needed some local news experience before the *Tribune* would hire him so he took a job with the *Herald Examiner*. In four months he got a job as a copy editor at the *Tribune*. He began writing his first book, <u>Blood of the Lamb</u>, which was published in 1932. In the same year, Babcock's work at the copy desk paid off and he received a promotion to Travel Editor. During the drought, dust bowl, and international economic depression and the beginning of World War II, Babcock traveled to over fifty countries posting stories. He held the position for more than ten years.

On October 20, 1935, he was married to Helen Reber at Glen Ellyn, Illinois. They raised two children. According to the information on the inside flap of his second book, Babcock was asked to organize the *Chicago Tribune Magazine of Books*. In October 1942, he became its first editor and remained at the post until his retirement in 1960. The *Columbus Telegram* [Nebraska] newspaper published an article about Babcock and his thirty years at the *Chicago Tribune* in the January 8, 1958, issue.[6]

Babcock's style was said to be a "shrewd and fair critic." [3] But he did have one headline-making decision which for many fans, in retrospect, was an error in judgment. In 1950, he wrote that Vladimir Nabokov's novel <u>Lolita</u> "is pornography and we do not plan to review it." [3] Despite the later acclaim of the novel, Babcock did not publicly change his mind. In his collection of materials left to the Gotlieb Archival Research Center, there are several items pertaining to Charles Dickens. During the years 1944-1946, he corresponded with Wiley T. Dickens (nephew of Charles Dickens, son of Charles Dickens brother Augustus). Babcock had published four stories related to Dickens during those years and had printed the reader's responses. These and many other materials are available as research at the Gotlieb Archival Research Center.[3]

Babcock maintained membership in the Authors' League of America, the Society of Midland Authors, the Thoreau Society, the American Legion and the Masons. He was also a member of the Society of Friends (Quakers) church and considered himself politically Independent. His favorite pastimes were chess and reading. He and his family spent their time between their farm in Vermont and their log cabin forty miles from Chicago. He also lived for a time in Florida. Babcock lectured throughout the Midwest and was often a guest on radio programs. For two years he served as one of the three judges for the Pulitzer Prize in fiction.

Chicago had four newspaper book editors and three of them called themselves "Bug-eaters." The three were Nebraskans who remembered when the football team nickname of 1900 was called the Bug-eaters. Frederick Babcock, *Chicago Tribune* editor, was joined by Emmet Dedmon of the *Chicago Sun-Times* who had been born at Auburn, Nebraska, and Van Allen Bradley of the *Chicago Daily News* "who qualified through heading the copy desk of the *Omaha Bee-News* from 1935-1937," noted the *Lincoln Star* article of 1961.[7]

Besides identifying with the Bug-eaters during lighter moments, Babcock also identified two Nebraska authors for honors when he was asked by the Books Across the Sea committee of the English-Speaking Union to nominate books for exhibit in Ottawa, Canada, in 1959. The committee had asked the question: "Which books best interpret the life and thought of the Midwest to the rest of the country and to other nations? According to a *Lincoln Journal Star* article he nominated Willa Cather, a longtime resident of Red Cloud, for <u>My Antonia</u> and Virginia Faulkner, the assistant editor of the University of Nebraska Press, for the <u>Roundup : A Nebraska Reader</u>.[8]

Babcock finished his second book in 1954. Published on the back cover Carl Sandburg wrote: "With rare compassion and love of decency, Mr. Babcock in <u>Hang Up the Fiddle</u> gives his readers a small Midwest town, tangles of passions and politics, murder in the first degree, unspeakable treachery in a city news room, and a curious thread of belief in a 'inner light' guiding some good people."[5]

It was Babcock's newspaper experiences that made this portrait of the newspaper business so alive. The novel takes place in a small town before WWI. The *Lincoln Journal Star* headlined their article about the book as "Nostalgia Marks Tale by Editor, Babcock Uses Lincoln Scene." While describing the plot for the readers, author Helen Mary Hayes notes that the fiction involves characters resembling people he worked with while working in Lincoln. In a book note by Raymond A. McConnell, Jr. in the *Lincoln Evening Journal, Nebraska State Journal,* he quotes Babcock: "While all of the characters are drawn from imagination…you and your co-workers may find enjoyment in noting the slight resemblances of three characters to George Norris, Frank Williams (late *Journal* editor), and Edgar Howard." [9,10]

Babcock's connections with George Norris did not end with the fictional disguise in his book. In 1985, NBC-TV produced a series titled "Profiles in Courage." One of the segments profiled Nebraska Senator George Norris. Tom Bosley portrayed Norris presenting his opposition to President Woodrow Wilson's armed ships and entry into World War I. Norris was nationally denounced as a traitor for his position. During an episode, Norris is shown returning to Nebraska in 1917 to defend his anti-war position. He was interviewed by a *Nebraska State Journal* reporter patterned after Frederic Babcock. [11]

Babcock died suddenly while visiting in Florida in 1979. From Ord, Monroe, Columbus, and Lincoln, Frederic Babcock took the Nebraska life, enriched it and shared it from Chicago. N

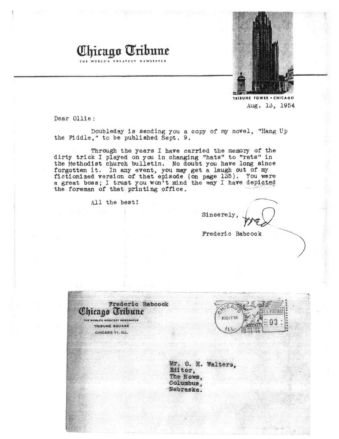

Letter with envelope of trick played while in newspaper office.[12]

Endnotes, Footnotes & Sources:

[1] E-mail of May 3, 2013, to Nebraska Authors Project® from Cheri, Platte Co. Museum, H.E. Babcock obituary, December 14, 1917, and Frederic birth date controversy. Correspondence on file with Nancy Sue Hansen.

[2] Margaret Curry's "History of Platte County," published in 1950. On-line, reviewed 5/4/2013. http://www.usgennet.org/usa/ne/topic/resources/OLLibrary/Platte/pages/bios/hpcn0108.htm.

[3] Howard Gotlieb Archival Research Center. Reviewed 5/4/2013 http://www.bu.edu/phpbin/archives-cc/app/details.php?id=7364&return=http%3A%2F%2F www.bu.edu%2Fphpbin%2Farchives-cc%2Fapp%2Fbrowse.php%3Fletter%3DB.

[4] Platte County, Columbus: Power, Chapter Twenty-one, NEGenWeb Project Resource Center On-Line Library reviewed 5/2013 http://www.usgennet.org/usa/ne/topic/resources/OLLibrary/Platte/pages/hpcn0071.htm.

[5] Babcock, Frederic. Hang up the Fiddle book cover viewed 2/1/2013.

[6] Columbus Telegram [Nebraska] newspaper published an article about Babcock and his thirty years at the Chicago Tribune in the January 8, 1958, issue.

[7] Lincoln Star. "Three Ex-Nebraskans Prefer To Be Known as 'Bug-eaters.'" Lincoln, Nebraska, July 23, 1961.

[8] Lincoln Journal Star. "Books by 2 Nebraskans Nominated for Ottawa Show." Lincoln, Nebraska, June 22, 1958.

[9] Lincoln Journal Star. "Nostalgia Marks Tale by Editor Babcock uses Lincoln Scene." Helen Mary Hayes, Sunday Staff Writer. Lincoln, Nebraska, September 5, 1954.

[10] Lincoln Journal Star. "Frederic Babcock." Raymond A. McConnell, Jr., Lincoln, Nebraska. August 1954.

[11] Lincoln Journal Star. "Sen. Norris Profiled." Lincoln, Nebraska, March 28, 1985.

[12] Letter and envelope from files at the Lincoln Journal Star.

Special thank you to:
Michelle Cruise, Communications Coordinator, Columbus Public Schools, and Cheri Schrader, Platte County Historical Society, museum@megavision. com.

Nebraska Authors Book & Travel Club

Keep a journal of your travels around Nebraska as you participate in the Nebraska Authors Book and Travel Club. Record the sights, smells and sounds as well as your emotions about your travels. What did you learn or unlearn about your trip(s). You might read some old newspapers to see how articles have been written in the past. Authors in this volume such as George L. Jackson and Dale Nichols wrote travel articles. Try your hand at writing a travel article about your Nebraska Authors Travels, as Babcock would have done. See Nebraska Authors Travel & Book Club policies for more information. Enjoy your travels.

BONE CREEK MUSEUM
OF AGRARIAN ART
Amanda Mobley Guenther
Associate Curator, Author

Amanda Mobley Guenther
Date of Birth: July 1, 1986
Location of Birth: Citrus Heights, CA
Moved to Nebraska: fall of 2004
Education: Bachelor of Arts in Art,
University of Nebraska-Lincoln, 2008
Guenther currently lives in Lincoln

Amanda Mobley Guenther

Known Publications:

Guenther, Amanda Mobley. The Canopy Overhead, the Later Years of Dwight Kirsch, Lincoln: Great Plains Art Museum, Center for Great Plains Studies, University of Nebraska, 2008, 28 pp.

Guenther, Amanda Mobley. Dale Nichols: Transcending Regionalism, Lincoln: Great Plains Art Museum, Center for Great Plains Studies, University of Nebraska, 2011. 197 pp.

Amanda Mobley Guenther has cataloged the work of one of Nebraska's most famous artists in her intriguing book, Dale Nichols: Transcending Regionalism. Her talents were duly noted when the catalog won first place in the 2011 Mountain-Plains Museum Association book competition.

Guenther's love for art began in the beautiful surroundings of her native Grass Valley, California. In 2004, she decided to move to the Midwest and attend the University of Nebraska-Lincoln.

She is often asked why she chose Nebraska. "We lived in a rural area, so I thought going to San Francisco or LA might not be a good thing for me," Guenther explained. "My parents grew up in Iowa. We have always come back to visit for the summers, so I felt really familiar and comfortable with Nebraska."

The "great tradition" the University of Nebraska-Lincoln offers on and off campus, and the campus architecture, lured her to Lincoln. It wasn't until her senior year as an art major, however, that Guenther realized she wanted to go into museum work.

"That's really when it came together for me ... my skills, being interested in art, but not necessarily having the drive as an artist to produce art. To be able to a look at art, critique art, evaluate its history and meaning, then incorporate writing which I always like to do, is a good fit for me," Guenther said.

She stepped into that "fit" after graduating in 2008 and landing a job as associate curator for the Bone Creek Museum of Agrarian Art in David City, Nebraska. There Guenther was assigned the task to catalog Dale Nichols work into a book.

"This book, because it's a museum project, correlates with an art exhibition. So over the past two and a half years, I have planned both of them together and simultaneously, so that the paintings that are in the book are also on the shelf. There's a strong correlation to them. So I started by looking at his work and learning about who he was and what I could find out about him."

The research took two and a half years; however, not a long duration for a project such as this.

"I think the reason that I was able to do it so quickly was because Dale's niece, Ruth Nichols, had compiled over the years an immense amount of information and resources, so I didn't have to take the time to find all the research pieces, all of the newspaper articles, or all of what other museum art files have."

Guenther learned through her research that Nichols was determined to leave his artistic legacy to his niece, which proved invaluable in putting together Guenther's book.[3] Nichol's childhood formed the man that he became, and the landscape he grew up in formed the type of artistry for which he was known. When in his twenties, Nichols reflected on his surroundings of the plains of Nebraska: "I trod, barefoot, the two miles of the dusty country road, or 'short-cut' on the crust of frozen, glittering snow which hid the tops of four foot fence posts, to attend East Olive Township rural school."

Nichols knew from a young age that he was destined to be a great artist. Yet, few of his Nebraska images were painted in Nebraska. He largely worked from imagination and memory, and more than any other theme, his "one source of light" philosophy was a shining element in his work. All of Nichol's paintings contained three essential elements: light, order and love. He wrote of his most famous work, *End of the Hunt*: "Foundations of buildings are at eye level for cathedral effect. Female curves in snow banks, and other female symbols

Amanda Mobley Guenther displays her books, <u>Dale Nichols: Transcending Regionalism</u>, and <u>The Canopy Overhead, the Later Years of Dwight Kirsch</u>. Kirsch (1899-1981) was an artist, teacher and art administrator. He was born near Mayberry, Pawnee County, Nebraska. The Museum of Nebraska Arts holds twenty-nine works by Kirsch.[2-3]

especially in tracks and soft lines of snow on roofs and general shapes of trees ... these give the charm of female appeal which is the strength of women ... The vertical lines of the man and his rabbit, including the trunks of the trees, are the strength of men ... One source of light controls the shadows and color values. Time of day was late afternoon for long shadows to indicate where the life-giving sun was located."

Guenther was also pleased to discover that Nichols painted in the style of Grant Wood and Thomas Hart Benton, and once had a work hang in the Metropolitan Museum of Art next to a Picasso.

Dale Nichols: Transcending Regionalism contains all the images in the exhibit and five chapters. There is a biographical chapter, two chapters about his ideology of painting, and a chapter relating Nichols to the genre of art that he is known for in American art history. The last chapter is excerpts of letters written by Nichols to his niece, Ruth. "By reading the section you really get a sense of his personality because it's his voice," Guenther notes. "And it's his language and his words and the way that he wrote to her. In reading his ideas about his work, everything has a meaning. There was nothing that wasn't meant to be there. He was an extremely intentional painter and everything has a symbol. I have scarcely come across another artist that thinks of their work so seriously as he thought of his work."

Guenther's book will not only assist in the education of Nebraska artists, sales of the book will also support the museum's operations to continue providing the special niche of agrarian art to the community there and at large. B

Endnotes, Footnotes & Sources:

Interview with Amanda Mobley Guenther/photos by Barbara Ann Dush.

[1]See Dale Nichols story in this volume.

[2]WorldCat.org.

[3]http://monet.unk.edu/mona/cintemp/kirsch/dkirsch.html
Museum of Nebraska Art/Artists/Dwight Kirsch.

[4]http://see.ndrw.me/post/18346627847/dale-nichols-platte-valley-summer-1969-oil-on.

Bone Creek's Chief Curator Mark L. Moseman stands next to one of Nichol's paintings – Platte Valley Summer - 1969 – which was featured at the Bone Creek Museum of Agrarian Art.[4] Go to www.bonecreek.org to purchase Guenther's book, make a donation, or discover information.

The museum was founded in David City in 2007.

MARGARET CANNELL

Date of birth: 1902
Location of birth: Crab
Orchard, NE
Education: Lincoln High
School, NE, 1921
Bachelors Degree University of
NE, Lincoln, 1924
Masters Degree English,
Columbia U. 1931
Moved to Menlo Park, CA,
1963
Date of Death: Sept. 10, 2000
Location at death: California

Margaret Cannell[1]
UN-L English Professor

Known Publications:

Cannell, Margaret. <u>Signs, Omens and Portents in Nebraska Folklore</u>.
Lincoln: University of Nebraska, 1933. University of Nebraska Studies
in Language, Literature and Criticism, No. 13. 112 pp. Non–fiction. [2]
See digitalcommons.unl.edu

Cannell, Margaret. *The Kitchen Frontier*. (pp. 44-449). <u>Roundup:
A Nebraska Reader</u>. Faulkner, Virginia, compiler, editor, Lincoln:
University of Nebraska Press. 1957. 493pp.

Cannell, Margaret. *Graveyard Language*. Unpublished. Located at the
Nebraska Society Historical Society: Louise Pound Collection. Date
unknown.[3]

M argaret Cannell, a University of Nebraska English professor,
wrote only one book of just over a hundred pages, but readers of var-

ious types of material will find it listed in dozens of bibliographies. Quoted by peers and researchers from the day it was written, <u>Signs, Omens and Portents in Nebraska Folklore</u> remains as interesting today as it was in 1933.

Her work was a requirement to complete a course taught by Dr. Louise Pound. As a student, Margaret wrote in the preface of her work: *"For the material in the following study the writer is indebted to many informants, but especially to Dr. Louise Pound from whose collections of Nebraska folklore many beliefs were obtained."*[2]

According to obituary accounts, Miss Cannell moved to Menlo Park, California, in 1963. She was widely known as a former president of the Menlo Park Friends of the Library and as a member of several book clubs. She was also active at the Pal Alto Unitarian Church and loved singing and giving recitals.

Her family was quoted as saying, "She had a keen mind and could recite long passages from Shakespeare and many English Poets through her mid-90's…" The Phi Beta Kappa key member died at age 97.

Her book can now be read on-line at the University of Nebraska Digital Commons website. N

"A girlishness in voice and manner.
Romance and Good English; Orpehons; Writers Club; Student Standard Club."

Margaret Cannell, 1921 Lincoln High School Yearbook[4]

Endnotes, Footnotes & Sources:

[1] Photo from University of Nebraska Library Archives, with permission to publish, 2012.

[2] Cannell, Margaret. Signs, Omens and Portents in Nebraska Folklore. Lincoln: University of Nebraska, 1933. University of Nebraska Studies in Language, Literature and Criticism, No. 13. 112 pp. Non–fiction.

[3] Nebraska State Historical Society, Lincoln, Nebraska. Louise Pound Collection, Box 15, Folder 12. Reviewed 2012.

[4] Photo from Lincoln High School Yearbook, 1921, Lincoln, Nebraska with permission to publish 2012.

www.genealogybuff.com/ca/sanmateo
www. paloaltoonline.com

Thanks to Lincoln High School Multi Media, Larry Dawson, and the Library staff for assistance with the yearbook photo.

Thanks to the University of Nebraska Library Archives staff for locating the professor's photo.

Thanks to the Nebraska State Historical Society staff for attempting to locate anything they might have related to Miss Cannell.

Nebraska Authors Book & Travel Club
Attach a ticket or photo of your visit to the Nebraska Renaissance Faire or Nebraska Shakespeare Festival.

MARY CONNEALY

Date of Birth: March 20, 1956
Location of Birth: Oakland, NE
Education: Jefferson Rural
School through eighth grade;
Lyons High School, 1974
Bachelors of Science Wayne State
College 1976
Lyons native currently lives in
Decatur

Mary Connealy

Known Publications:

Connealy, Mary. <u>Petticoat Ranch</u> (Lassoed in Texas, Book 1). Barbour Publishing, 2007. 288 pp.
Connealy, Mary. <u>Calico Canyon</u> (Lassoed in Texas, Boos 2), Barbour Publishing, Inc., 2008. 288 pp.
Connealy, Mary. <u>Gingham Mountain</u> (Lassoed in Texas, Book 3). Barbour Books, 2009. 288 pp.

Connealy, Mary. <u>Buffalo Gal</u> (South Dakota Weddings, Book 1), Barbour publishing, Inc., 2008. 176 pp.
Connealy, Mary. <u>Clueless Cowboy</u> (South Dakota Weddings Book 2), Barbour Publishing, 2008. 176 pp.
Connealy, Mary. <u>The Bossy Bridegroom</u>, (South Dakota Weddings, Book 3). Barbour Publishing, Inc., 2008. 176 pp.

Connealy, Mary. <u>Nosy in Nebraska: Of Mice...and Murder/Pride and Pestilence/The Miceman Cometh</u> (Maxie Mouse Mystery Series Omnibus) (American Loves a Mystery: Nebraska), Barbour Publishing,, Inc. 480 pp.

Connealy, Mary. Cowboy Christmas, Barbour Books, 2009. 304 pp.

Connealy, Mary. Montana Rose (Montana Marriages, Book 1). Barbour Publishing. Inc., 2009. 318 pp.
Connealy, Mary. The Husband Tree (Montana Marriages, Book 2), Barbour Publishing, Inc., 2010. 320 pp.
Connealy, Mary. Wildflower Bride (Montana Marriages, Book 3), Barbour Books, 2010. 320 pp.

Connealy, Mary. Doctor in Petticoats (Sophie's Daughter's), Barbour Books, 2010. 320 pp.
Connealy, Mary. Wrangler in Petticoats (Sophie's Daughter's), Barbour Books, 2010. 320 pp.
Connealy, Mary. Sharpshooter in Petticoats (Sophie's Daughter's), Barbour Books, 2011. 315 pp.

Connealy, Mary. Black Hills Blessing (Romancing America: South Dakota), Barbour Publishing, Inc., 2010. 368 pp.
Connealy, Mary, Deep Trouble. Barbour Books, 2011. 320 pp.

Connealy, Mary. Out of Control (The Kincaid Brides). Bethany House, 2011. 336 pp.
Connealy, Mary. In Too Deep (The Kincaid Brides Book 2). Bethany House, 2012. 336 pp.
Connealy, Mary. Over the Edge (The Kincaid Brides). Bethany House, 2012. 336 pp.

Connealy, Mary. Swept Away (Trouble in Texas). Bethany House, 2013. 320 pp.
Connealy, Mary. Fired Up (Trouble in Texas). Bethany House, 2013. 336 pp.

Connealy, Mary. Winter Wedding Bells, published in A Bride for All Seasons novella collection. Thomas Nelson, 2013. 400 pp.

Mary Connealy wrote for ten years before her first book was published. Perhaps that's why one of her favorite website quotes reads: *Don't be afraid to strive and sweat and pray and fail and strive and pray some more for the desires of your heart. Because my books and this site are proof that dreams can come true. That with God all things are possible.*

When Connealy signed her first book contract, "I had twenty finished books on my computer at home," she reflected. "I had just enough encouragement through those ten long years to keep me going."

Connealy was a stay-at-home mom when she started putting words to the keyboard, and it was during those years as her children grew up that she also got a job working forty hours a week, teaching GED for the last five years.

During her third year of writing, Connealy sent a manuscript to Silhouette Romance. They responded and requested a full manuscript. "From the time I sent the three chapters in, then their request for a whole manuscript, then finally their rejection, it took a full year," she said. "So I'm starting to see just how slow the publishing world is. I sent that book in as a result of placing third in a writer's contest and I did pretty well in them. I learned a lot from the critiques. Also, when I'd final, I got judged by editors and agents."

Two years before being published, Connealy was a finalist in eleven contests with five different books. Then she discovered ACFW (American Christian Fiction Writers) and entered her manuscript, Petticoat Ranch, in the unpublished contest division. "I was a double finalist in 2004. Another book of mine, Montana Rose, was in the running, too."

When Connealy won the Noble Theme contest, she received numerous requests to send in her book, Petticoat Ranch, including a request from novel author, Cathy Marie Hake, who asked for the first three chapters.

Hake reviewed the chapters and told Connealy she thought she was 'ready.' "By this time, I had so many rejections I had a hide like a rhino," Connealy joked. "So submitting work didn't even phase me. Okay, well maybe I crawled under my computer desk and sucked my thumb for a day or two every time I got one, but other than that I was fine."

Just prior to the next year's conference, Hake told Connealy that she wanted to pitch her name to write a book as part of a three-book series set in historical Alaska.

"Every year at the conference the acquiring editor for Heartsong Presents gives a contract to an unpublished author, I was so hopeful!" she recalled. "I knew there was a chance it could be me. The Heartsong editor, Tracie Peterson, said someone else's name. So okay, I've been rejected before.

"Then she said, 'This year we're giving two contracts to first time authors. We're offering a contract to Mary Connealy.' I get chills saying that! It was a wonderful, thrilling shocking moment. I had to go up and get the contract in front of 350 other writers, all clapping. A great, great moment in my life."

She earned her first contract in 2005. Since then, Connealy's twenty-sixth book came out in March of 2013 with a contract stretching ahead of her for the next four years. She was also a Rita and Christy Award finalist, a finalist in the Inspirational Readers Choice Award and is a two-time Carol Award winner, as well as the Nebraska Press Women's Fiction Book of the Year first place award winner in 2008.

Connealy is quick to give God the credit for her talent. "I believe the ability to write is a gift from God," she noted. "I believe the hard work to learn the skills I needed to use that gift wisely comes from being raised to believe in hard work and perseverance, and that comes from both my parents and then later my husband and the rural life we live together."

She also credits the enthusiasm and imagination of her early reading years as preparation for her current success: "I remember the first time I read a Black Stallion book by Walter Farley. Just being in that book, I was in the middle of that horse race. I wondered how he'd done that, what skill did it take to drag someone so deeply into a book that they could smell the dust and hear the pounding hooves and feel those big bodies jostling against each other. I consider Farley an inspiration. Mary Higgins Clark and Clive Cussler are two others that, when I read their work, I realize just how rapt a reader can be, how compelled to keep turning the page."

Connealy's favorite reading includes romance, comedy and action. "If they're sassing each other and falling in love while they're running for their lives, then I'm happy," she added.

This Lyons, Nebraska, native who currently lives in Decatur, also has a passion for her state. "Nebraska is great cowboy country," she explained. "I love the rural life. I love the cattle and wildlife and the privacy of the country. Bess Streeter Aldrich's <u>A Lantern in Her Hand</u> is one of my favorite books of all time, and I live only about fifteen miles from the Neihardt Center in Bancroft and love his work."

Connealy shares her writing success with her husband, Ivan Connealy. "He has done a hard job for years and years running our farm and working our cattle. I was a stay-at-home mom for twenty-seven years and we both wanted it that way, but I'd have never been able to be home with our four daughters if he hadn't been working so hard. And I'd have never gotten my writing career if he hadn't taken care of us all those years."

Even with her overwhelming popularity, Connealy calls herself just a "normal" person: "The fact that I'm a published author and that publishers keep wanting more of my books is amazing to me. I would hope that people would look at me and decide to take a chance on their dreams." B

Lyons water tower and park.

Endnotes, Footnotes & Sources:

Interview via email with Mary Connealy in Barbara Ann Dush files, 2013.

www.maryconnealy.com.
Mary Connealy~Real Life Petticoat Ranch: ABOUT MARY.

Nebraska Authors Book & Travel Club
Signature or attach a photo of your shopping, camping or antiquing experience in Lyons, Nebraska.

ORSAMUS CHARLES "O.C." DAKE

Date of birth: Jan. 19, 1832
Location of birth: Portage, New York
Education: Madison Univ, Hamilton, NY grad 1849
Ordained Episcopal minister 1862
Moved to Omaha in 1863
Date of Death: Oct 18, 1875
Location of Death: Lincoln, NE
Author's pen name O.C. Dake

Orsamus Charles Dake

Known Publications:

Dake, O.C., <u>Nebraska Legends and Poems</u>. Cooper Union, NY. Pott and Amery, 1871, 165 pp
Reprinted in 2010 by Kessinger Publishing.

Dake, O.C. <u>Midland Poems</u>, Lincoln Nebraska: State Journal Co.,1873.

U sual portrayals of O.C. Dake begin with his arrival in Omaha as an Episcopal rector, work with Brownell Hall, and his church building assignment in Fremont. The short biographical information declares he was the first University of Nebraska professor of English Literature, acknowledges that he published the first known book written in the State, and that it was a book of poetry. There his bio usually comes to an end.[1,2]

For the first hours of research it seemed as this biographical story may simply highlight the first known author from the State of Nebraska presenting a couple of conflicting facts found in articles on Dake related to his best known poem. Morton's <u>Illustrated History of Nebraska</u> provided some details, but not the complete story.[3] Yet tucked away in a Nebraska State Historical Society (NSHS)[1] file in a few items the Dake family provided, including some unpublished poems, there was a reflection from daughter Anna. She had written about her mother for a celebration about mothers in 1947 in Illinois: <u>My Pioneer Mother</u>. It was a memorial snapshot, in words, about what her mother passed down to her children about their life before Nebraska that shed a new look on the professor.[4]

Anna began by writing that her mother Amanda Eaton, age sixteen of Edwardsville, Illinois, and her father, O.C. Dake, age twenty-one, were married February 9, 1853.[4] Dake had graduated college in 1849 and taught school, including becoming county superintendent of schools.[3] Dake had been chosen as the successor to Mr. Jake Terry as teacher at Edwardsville School in Illinois. The position was an important first step for the young couple.[3,4] Edwardsville was the third largest city in Illinois at the time. Dake began thinking about theological issues and the Episcopal ministry, and studied toward ordination. In a short time, both parents declared they were abolitionists.[4]

It wasn't long after the abolitionist declaration was made that another position was offered to the young Dake. He was asked to go to Lincoln, Illinois, and edit the *Lincoln Herald* there, which he did from 1859-1860: "in the interest of Mr. Lincoln's candidacy." [4]

Anna wrote that it took courage for her mother to meet each day for the rest of her life as her husband "moved from teacher, to editor, to Episcopal Rector and to professor in the University of Nebraska." [4]

Anna continued, *"It was one of her mother's chief regrets that she did not see Mr. Lincoln when she lived in Lincoln, Ill. It was at Criffields' Drug Store that Mr. Lincoln frequently talked and told stories when doing business in Lincoln. In later life, she liked to tell of Mr. Lincoln and my father driving together to Mt. Pulacki to speak, Mr. Lincoln talking on the law and my father, Mr. Dake, on the press."[4]*

Anna's mother wasn't the only one with regrets about missing some of the intellectual presentations of the day. O.A. Abbott wrote in his Illinois childhood memoirs about walking ten miles to hear speakers that came to his area. He noted he missed Lincoln and Douglas and he regretted it.[5] Hearing people speak in person impacted lives and opinions. The Dake's and Abbott's were no exceptions in carrying these experiences to the newly opened Kansas-Nebraska territory as they emigrated.

Following the November 6, 1860, election Dake accepted a "clerkship in the interior department at Washington."[3] Fast forward to 1863. Anna continued, *"Having sandwiched in with his other endeavors, studying for the ministry, Father was called to Trinity Church, now the Cathedral of Omaha, Nebraska. He went on and very shortly mother and three children followed him to Omaha by steamboat on the Missouri River. The trip took two weeks for they had to tie up to the bank almost every night on account of low water and sandbars..."* Anna wrote that the Illinois family was afraid they were going to encounter Indians. The safety concern was real, but the Dake family had an uneventful arrival at the Omaha dock.[4]

Some articles of Nebraska history note that Dake started the Brownell Hall School in Omaha; but according to Cathy Tibbels, the current Public Relations Director at Brownell-Talbot, it was not Rev. O.C. Dake that founded the school. He served as the rector of Trinity Parish in Omaha and the first principal for the school in its opening first semester, September 17, 1863; then he was "called" away from the position after Christmas.[6]

Rev. Dake moved his family to Fremont where his new assignment was to organize and build a church: St. James. It was 1864. Anna wrote "that is where I came on the scene."

Words on stain glass window to honor Dake at St. James Episcopal church in Fremont as of June 2013: "In memory of the Rev. O.C. Dake, 1865 Entered into Rest 1875, The first missionary and Rector," In the area around the entered into rest are the light impression words "By those who knew him longest and loved him best."[16]

Files show that Dake owned land in several counties, including Polk and Dodge. There are copies of Union Pacific Railroad land deeds among the papers in NSHS files. [1,4]

While Dake was completing his tasks as a missionary and building a new church, he was also involved in at least two organizations, according to Morton's Illustrated History of Nebraska. On June 16, 1865, a dispensation was issued to "open a commandery of Knights Templar and the appendant Orders at Omaha and to create …a commandery of Knights Templar. On July 14, 1865, under the dispensation, a commandery was formed…Orders of Knighthood included Orsamus C. Dake."[7] The Royal Arch Masonry had been given a dispensation on November 21, 1859, to form an Omaha chapter and recruit members. The list of members having received their Royal Arch Masonry degrees from 1859 to August 25, 1865, included Orsamus C. Dake.[8]

The Civil War concluded, President Lincoln was assassinated, and Nebraska became a state on March 1, 1867. As state government was being set up for the new state, the University of Nebraska was chartered on February 15, 1869. Dake had begun writing a book in addition to his duties at St. James and the related missionary work which provided the opportunity to travel around part of Nebraska.

In 1871 Dake was appointed the first professor of English literature at the University of Nebraska. There were five faculty members each selected from a different religious denomination.[9] Not only did Dake begin a new position in 1871, but he published the book he had been working on: Nebraska Legends and Other Poems. He published another in 1873: Midland Poems.

Anna wrote that while her father was 'chair' at the Nebraska University her "mother was an active member of the Guild and held a position in the city's administration of relief for grass-hopper suffers…"[4] According to the child's history textbook Nebraska Old and New, "Eight times between 1857 and 1875" grasshoppers swarmed into Nebraska. "The greatest of all grasshopper raids came the week of July 20-27, 1874. Along the entire frontier of Nebraska, Kansas, Dakota and Minnesota, the air was filled with grasshoppers. There were billions of them in the great clouds which darkened the sun. Noise made by their wings filled the ear with a roaring sound like a rushing storm."[10] Assisting the hundreds of Nebraskans whose entire field crops and food for the animals and themselves were wiped out in a matter of hours took a serious relief effort. While Anna's mother assisted the communities,

Dake continued to teach.

It was not his teaching at the University that would become controversial, but his first book. However, Dake would not live long enough after the publication to discuss the intentions of his work. Anna wrote: "Having always risen in his endeavors and written a book of poems, my father at forty-three years of age, died of a cerebral hemorrhage."[4] The death was notably remembered by young Anna as she started school in September 1875, and her father died in October. Mrs. Dake took the children back to Illinois to live with her parents for a while. It was a shock to lose Orsamus. His own father had died when he was sixteen months old when a blood vessel broke while trying to lift a heavy log. The family had seen Nebraska and the growing United States through changing times: 1863-1875.

It is generally agreed that the Welshman, Orsamus C. Dake, was the first and only serious poet in Nebraska for nearly a generation. His first publication was the first on many levels: the first publication of poetry, the first known Nebraska book, the first publication by a member of the University faculty, and according to Cox and McDaniels, "It was also the first substantial attempt to interpret Nebraska life through literature."[2]

What is the controversy that surrounds Nebraska's first book? Notes from the NSHS website and *Nebraska History* magazine, Cox and McDaniels' Guide to Nebraska Authors, The Weeping Water Legend, An anthology and Commentary, compiled by Iain C. G. Campbell, City Historian,[11] and numerous literature critics suggest that the most famous poem that Rev. Dake wrote was fiction and not a factual incident. It is the poem "Weeping Water" that brings on the most critical response. The fact or fiction issue is a stumbling block for many scholars.

First, there has been much research by scholars to see if the legend had a factual basis. Accounts of both the Otoe and Omaha Indians have been checked as well as sites examined and there is no known battle between the two tribes at Weeping Water, Nebraska. The scholars today are still concerned about it being fact or fiction rather than, as the author wrote, providing a comparison between the humans of European battles of 'glory years' and the 'glory years' of the human battles of the Plains. At the time this poem was written the battles of the Iliad and the Odyssey were still considered myth. Heinrich Schliemann's archeological digs were just making news that, in fact, Troy was being excavated as a real city for the first time since the fabled Trojan War. It would have been with the first news of the possibility of the 'dig' being Troy that coincided with Dake's book.

Looking at the preface of the first book, pages seven and eight, a reader sees the author yearning for the old days of intellectual stimulation; bemoaning his remoteness, but considering he may be in a better place than the condition of the Eastern cities; confronting the Indian fears carried by his Illinois family to their new home on the Plains, and understanding his own weaknesses in writing a book without peer review on style. In part he wrote: *"These poems are tentative, both of my own strength and of the public taste. They have been produced at a point remote from literary fellowship where I have been thrown solely on my own judgment. My surroundings and the incidents of life have suggested them all. Possibly I have hereafter touch them into fairer proportion after hearing the views of competent critics."*[12]

He continued: *"In the development of the two* Nebraska Legends *I have treated my Indian characters as noble and possessed of a true sentiment. A brutal savage is not a poetical object, and except under rare conditions, has no business in poetry. If the Indian, like his human brethren of more favorable opportunities has his worse side, he also has his better. Until corrupted by intercourse with the whites, his nature was simple, affectionate, childlike. Certainly he is no worse than the old pagan Greeks of Homer and the Dramatists, who were separated into little tribes forever at war, and whose common occupation was the sacking of towns and the carrying off of defenseless women for concubines. Every inducement, therefore, that could urge an ancient poet to portray prehistoric peoples as chivalrous and of a sustained dignity, should impel the writer of today to do likewise. Elemental poetic conditions do not change."*

He concluded: *"Should time and space be granted me, I hope at no distant day, to again make trial for the public favor. Certain ideas, originated by social aspects have long lain in my mind and I should be glad to work them into a poem. This, however, must depend upon the time and strength snatched from duties of a more practical kind."* Fremont, Nebraska, September 20, 1870. [O.C.Dake][12]

Second, biting criticism can be easily found by readers of other works on Plains history from authors who quote Dake using one-liners regarding his use of 'savages'. Iowa professor Dr. Dorothy Anne Dondore is one such critic, saying that his use of the terms 'brutal savage' and the fact he was a professor, showed just what the early teachers of that state expounded as theory about the natives.[13] Yet, Professor Dake's own full context produces a more complementary view showing how these natives are likely no different than their counterparts in ancient days during the wars back then. In his writings, Dake made the Nebraska natives equal to the natives of Greece and Rome.

Third, the <u>Nebraska History</u> "The Beginning of Nebraska Literature" article, like other reviews, criticizes Dake's work saying, *"It is perfectly clear to anyone familiar with literature who reads this poem, that the writer brought to his theme a mind filled with Greek and Latin poetry and that he never freed himself from their overwhelming influence in the attempt to portray the life of the wild west. Moreover, the figures of speech employed in the poem "Weeping Water" are derived from the <u>Iliad</u>. The setting of the dialogues, the tone of the conversation between the characters, is of the same kind. Consciously or unconsciously the writer is transcribing his own memory of college day instruction in the literature of southern Europe. Such equipment could not produce the real spirit of the western life."* [14]

The Nebraska Authors Project® will leave the commentary up to you, the reader, regarding point three and other criticism issues that have been printed for and against the Dake poem(s). As you read his work(s), be sure to read the preface and introduction just as you would any other book. It tells you the author's thoughts toward his or her own writing; and in this case, shows that the author wasn't writing a western life poem, but showing that western life was likely no different than that of the noble Romans or Greeks. Put yourself in the shoes of this author. Could you write a poem reflecting your neighborhood in the terms and understanding of the Greek and Latin style of olden days? Dake did.

In an email from Cathy Tibbels at Brownell-Talbot, she noted that the school has established a 'house' system in the Upper School with six houses for boys and six for girls. Each of the houses are named for historical figures at the school. Dake House is one of them.

Rev. O.C. Dake wrote his two books, not for Pulitzer Prizes, but for scholarly expression of what he saw in the Nebraska landscape and world around him. As you read his work, take time to visualize what he saw in his mind's eye and expressed in his words during his short life.

Endnotes, Footnotes & Sources:

Some of O.C. Dake's papers are found at the Nebraska State Historical Society in Lincoln and some of his papers are found at the Illinois State Historical Library.

[1] www.Nebraska State Historical Society. Orsamus C. Dake, and collections at the NSHS offices. Reviewed July-August 2012.

[2] Cox, Gerry and Carol MacDaniels. Guide to Nebraska Authors. Dageforde Publishing, Inc., Lincoln, Nebraska, 1998, 271 pp.

[3] Morton, J. Sterling, Albert Watkins, editor in chief; Dr. George L. Miller, associate editor. Illustrated History of Nebraska : A History of Nebraska from the Earliest Explorations of the Trans-Mississippi Region. Volume II. Lincoln: Jacob North and Co. 1906. p 393, 400, 509 and Volume III 294, 300, 304.

[4] *My Pioneer Mother*, written by Mrs. Anna Dake Love for Mothers' Celebration 1947 in Illinois copy in NSHS collections. Reviewed July-August 2012.

[5] Hansen, Nancy Sue and Dush, Barbara Ann. Nebraska Authors Volume One. "O.A. Abbott". Fullerton: D & H Adventures Publishing, 2013.

[6] "The school was founded by the Rev. Joseph C. Talbot who was the Episcopal Bishop of the Northwest. The funding to establish the school came primarily from the Connecticut parish of the Right Rev. Thomas C. Brownell, who was presiding Bishop of the United States. Thus the school got its name Brownell Hall. Omaha joined other cities in the establishment schools for girls. It became co-educational in 1963 ending a hundred years of boarding girls. In 1968, the school became independent, breaking official ties with the Episcopal Church. Today it is the oldest school in continuous operation in Nebraska," wrote Cathy Tibbels, 2012.

[7] Morton, J. Sterling, Albert Watkins, editor in chief; Dr. George L. Miller, associate editor. Illustrated History of Nebraska : A History of Nebraska from the Earliest Explorations of the Trans-Mississippi Region. Volume II. Lincoln: Jacob North and Co. 1906. "Templar Masons" pp. 399-400 – "On June 16, 1865, M.'.E.'. Benjamin B. French Grand Master of the Grand Encampment, U.S.A. issued a dispensation to Robert C. Jordon of Chillicothe Commandery No. 8 of Chilliothe, Ohio, Herman Kountze of Massillion, Commandery, Massillion, Ohio, George B. Graff and Robert W. Furnas of Columbia Commandery U.'.D.'., Washington District of Columbia being the only known Knights Templar in (at the time), authorizing any three of the above Sir Knights, hailing from three different Commanderes to open a Commandery of Knights Templar and the appendant Orders at Omaha, and

then to create a sufficient number to regularly petition to open and form a Commandery of Knights Templar. On July 14, 1865, under dispensation, a Commandery was formed…Orders of Knighthood:…Orsamus C. Dake…"

[8] Morton, J. Sterling, Albert Watkins, editor in chief; Dr. George L. Miller, associate editor. Illustrated History of Nebraska : A History of Nebraska from the Earliest Explorations of the Trans-Mississippi Region. Volume II. Lincoln: Jacob North and Co. 1906. "Royal Arch Masonry" p 393 "On Nov. 21, 1859, upon a duly prepared petition recommended by a Royal Arch Chapter of Aurora, Illinois Ira A.W. Buck General Grand King of the General Grand Chapter of the U.S.A. issued a dispensation to form Omaha Chapter U.D. at Omaha, Nebraska appointing Robert C. Jordan to be the first high priest, appointing Charles W. Hamilton, the first king, and Robert W. Furnas, the first scribe. The first returns from this chapter show the following as having received the degrees of Royal Arch Masonry from the 29th day of Nov 1859 to the 25th day August 1865…Orsamus C. Dake…"

[9] Morton, J. Sterling and Albert Watkins. History of Nebraska from the Earliest Explorations of the Trans-Mississippi region. A Revised Edition. Edited and revised by Augustus O. Thomas, James A. Beattie, Arthur C. Wakeley. Lincoln, Western Publishing and Engraving Company. 1918. [History of Nebraska From the Earliest Explorations to the Present Time by Albert Watkins, Volume III First Edition. Lincoln: Western Publishing and Engraving Company, 1913.] Pages "UNL faculty" 294, 304 Note: faculty included Allen R. Benton, A.M . L.L.D, Chancellor and professor of intellectual and moral Science; S.H. Manley (Methodist) A.M. professor of ancient languages and literature; Henry E. Hitchcock (Presbyterian) A.M. Prof of Mathematics; O.C. Dake (Episcopal) professor of rhetoric and English literature; Samuel Aughey, A.M. professor chemistry and natural sciences; George E. Church A.M. principal of the Latin school; S.R. Thompson, professor in Agricultural Department.

[10] Sheldon, Addison Erwin. Nebraska Old and New, Lincoln: The University Publishing Company, 1937, 470 pp. "Drought, Grasshoppers, Panic," p 334.

[11] The Weeping Water Legend, An anthology and Commentary, complied by Iain C. G. Campbell, City Historian and other materials by Campbell as available at the Nebraska State Historical Society, Lincoln.

[12] Dake, O.C., Nebraska Legends and Poems. Cooper Union, New York. Pott and Amery, 1871, 165 pp.

[13] Dondore, Dorothy Anne. The Prairie and the Making of Middle America: Four Centuries of Description. Cedar Rapids, Iowa, The Torch Press, 1926 472 pp.

[14] Sheldon, Addison E, Editor. *Nebraska History.* "Beginnings of Nebraska Literature" page 47, and "Orsamus Charles Dake, Portrait and Sketch" p 42-44; volume VI April-June 1923, published by Nebraska State Historical Society.

[15] www.usgennet.org. *Historical Sketch of Brownell Hall 1863-64 to 1913-14* by Fanny Clark Potter. Cover of the book which can be read on-line, "that our daughters may be as the polished corners of the temple."

[16] Words on stain glass window to honor Dake at St. James Episcopal church in Fremont as of June 2013: "In memory of the Rev. O.C. Dake, 1865 Entered into Rest 1875, The first missionary and Rector." In the area around the entered into rest are the light impression words: "By those who knew him longest and loved him best."

www. wikipedia.com. *Brownell-Talbot School.* Reviewed August 2012.

Special thanks to: Cathy Tibbels, Director of Public Relations and Publications, Brownell-Talbot School, 400 N. Happy Hollow Blvd, Omaha, Nebraska 68132.

And thank you to St. James Church, Fremont, for allowing Nancy Sue Hansen to take a photograph of the stain glass window near the altar for publication.

Nebraska Authors Book & Travel Club
Visit or attend an event at Brownell-Talbot School. Have an official of the school sign and date this box or attach a photo of you at the event.

BARBARA ANN DUSH

Barbara Ann Dush

Date of Birth: August 25, 1949
Location of Birth: Genoa, NE
Education: District 34 country
school to eighth grade;
Fullerton High School, 1967;
Central Community College-Platte
Campus, Columbus, Nebraska,
1994
**What town called home in
Nebraska:** Clarks

Dush, Barbara Ann. <u>Listen With The Heart</u>, non-fiction. Old 101 Press, 2004. 153 pp.

After working for twenty years in the banking field, Barbara Dush-Micek stumbled upon the communications field accidentally. Her oldest daughter was going off to college, and to qualify for a Pell grant, two members of their family needed to be in college. Dush decided to return to school to help her daughter; however, she was completely lost about what to major in, or what classes to take. She took a test designed to determine what career she should pursue and scored highest in the written communications category. Her counselor strongly encouraged her to enter this field, and she considered this advice.

While attending Central Community College at the Platte Campus in Columbus, Nebraska, Dush studied every written communications class and journalism course she found available. She believes that a community college is a wise choice to begin a college education and start training for a career. Furthermore, she is a strong advocate of adults returning to school. The opportunity to go back to college changed her life.

Living in Fullerton, Dush worked for the *Nance County Journal*. When she first spoke to the publisher about a job, the only opening on staff was a proofreader. Being passionate and enthusiastic about her new-found field, Dush was "willing to start at anything."

Soon she was not only proofreading but writing feature stories, snapping photographs, editing and planning layouts. Having no previous experience in this field, she was trained by her publisher, as well as self-taught.

Dush stresses that having the perfect spot to write, the right frame of mind, and sometimes the stress of meeting a deadline are key requirements in her writing style.

When experiencing that lost feeling of having nothing to write about, she says that she feels a "strong hunger to write after experiencing a dry spell." Dush enjoys writing about human triumphs and trials, and often delves into a great deal of history to give the story "real meat" and to appeal and relate to her readers.

She tries to conduct each interview in person if possible. "The story means much more to see and hear personally," she said; and she believes that every story is important because every person is important. Knowing that this article could be a person's "only chance to be in the spotlight," and making the person feel special by being in the headlines are definitely the greatest rewards she receives from writing.

Dush's favorite author is Willa Cather, with Mari Sandoz being a strong second. Another Nebraska author whose books she finds hard to put down are those written by Marie Kramer of York; however, "I look forward to reading more books by all Nebraska authors," she commented.

In 2004, through the strong encouragement of the late Dr. Emily Jane Uzendoski, her former literature teacher at the Platte Campus, Dush put together her first book, Listen with the Heart. The book was published by Billie Thornburg of the Old 101 Press in North Platte, and features "everyday lives lived in the extraordinary."

One of the endorsers of the book, Norma Ann Molacek of Lincoln, wrote: "(Dush) hears the whispers before they are voices. She sees into souls, messages to be shared, then writes in a language we can all understand."

Dush has won numerous writing, photography and layout awards from the Nebraska Press Women, the National Federation of Press Women, the Nebraska Press Association, the Society of Professional Journalists, and has twice won the Jim Raglin award. In 2004, she was the first woman from Nebraska to win the first place Sweepstakes Award from the National Federation of Press Women, and was named the Nebraska Press Women Communicator of Achievement in 2008.

Stepping out of the newspaper office, Dush is now the co-author of the Nebraska Authors Project® and the Nebraska Military Project. She currently serves as secretary on the Nebraska Press Women Board, and is serving her fourth term as an appointed director on the National Federation of Press Women board.

Endnotes, Footnotes & Sources:

Written with major contributions by Angela Russell Gustafson of Fullerton, Nebraska.

Memorial photos by Barbara Ann Dush.

The Clarks Veterans Memorial, which sets on the east side of Clark's main street, was dedicated on November 11, 2006, "To honor the brave men and women who honorably served their country in war and in peace."

A close-up of just a few of the names on the Clarks Veterans Memorial. Included in the list are two of the author's cousins: Andrew Dush Jr. and Donald Dush.

DOUGLAS, ROBERT
DOUGLAS, THOMAS G.
DOUGLAS, TONY
DOUGLAS, WILLIAM
DUSH, ANDREW JR.
DUSH, DONALD
ELLER, GEORGE
ELLIOTT, GEORGE
ELLIOTT, HANSON S.
EVERS, RICHARD
FEEHAN, ELIZABETH
FEEHAN, JOHN J.
FERGUSON, CARL W.
FERGUSON, EARL
FERGUSON, LESTER
FERGUSON, MICHAEL

This trio of Nebraska Press Women were Sweepstakes winners in an annual NPW Communications Contest. From left are Lori Potter of the *Kearney Hub* in Kearney, Mary Pierce of the *Keith County News* in Ogallala, and Barbara Dush-Micek of the *Nance County Journal* in Fullerton.

Nebraska Authors Book & Travel Club
Signature or visit Clarks and the Veterans Memorial on main street. Attach a photo reflecting your visit, perhaps of a veteran you know personally.

DIXIE ECKHOFF

Date of Birth: April 17, 1948
Location of Birth: North Platte, NE
Education: elementary in North
Platte, Concord District 63 country
school in Hayes County;
Hayes County High School, 1966;
McCook Jr. College, 1968 with
Associate of Arts degree
What town called home in Nebraska:
Hayes Center

Dixie Eckhoff

Eckhoff, Dixie. <u>Just A Little Bull and A Few Cowtales</u>, Old 101 Press,
2005. 130 pp.

When Dixie Eckhoff was born, Nebraska was already snugly
encompassed around her heart.

"I love Nebraska," she said with enthusiasm. "I'm very uncomfort-
able any place else but Nebraska."

Eckhoff was born in North Platte, and lived at Dickens where her
parents owned and managed a grocery store. The family moved to a
ranch in Hayes County when she was eight years old. Eckhoff has continued to live in the same area all her life.

After graduating from Hayes Center High School and McCook Jr.
College, Eckhoff married and started a family. She helped make ends
meet by working full-time as a bookkeeper for a cattle ranch, and then
for the Union Pacific Railroad, for a sum total of thirty years. But it
wasn't until she suffered a heart attack in 2001 that she "got to writing
seriously."

"I think at that late age, I found what I really love to do. I did writings earlier but I never did anything with them. I just put them in a
drawer and that's where they stayed, or I would write something for a
family member for a birthday or anniversary or something like that."

However, Eckhoff's writings didn't stay tucked in a drawer long after she met North Platte publisher Billie Thornburg.

"I met Billie in a doctor's office and when I realized who she was, I struck up a conversation with her because I already planned to take the next day off work so I could go to her book signing at the library. When I told her I like to write poetry, she invited me to her home to her writing classes. The very first night that I was there, she started on me about putting a book together."

It took two more years for Eckhoff to put her material together for publication. The process would have taken even longer if not for Thornburg's consistent encouragement.

"I just thought it was beyond my reach," Eckhoff mused. "Billie encouraged me to put things together for a book, as did my husband. Whenever I would write something new, I would take it to Billie and share, and she pretty much wanted everything that I put together."

The result was Dixie's first book: <u>Just A Little Bull and A Few Cow-tales</u>. The book's rhythmic style of cowboy poetry entertains readers to tears of laughter that relaxes the soul. Each turn of the page takes a unique road into new adventures and a view of pure country.

Eckhoff's favorite style of writing has always been humor. In fact, she finds it hard not to write in humorous style.

"I have a few serious poems, but it's very difficult for me to write serious poems because I get part way through it, then I start getting silly and things just run through my mind and pretty soon it's a humorous poem."

Having grown up on a ranch, creating poems about funny things that happened on the rural scene are plentiful. "Believe me, there's a lot of good stories around," she laughed. "I have a lot of childhood memories in my Little Bull book. My sister and I milked cows, fed hogs and worked cattle, so I had a lot of experiences that I could draw on."

Putting funny stories in poetic verse is Eckhoff's specialty, and a requested favorite at speaking engagements is *The Hitchhiker*. "This poem kills them every time, and I love to do it," she said.

Eckhoff recites her poetry from memory in a mesmerizing form with her unique southern-style accent, which often leaves listeners asking if she is a native of the southern United States.

Her writing skills have been rewarded with first place awards for three consecutive years (2005-2007) in the Nebraska Mothers Association Contest with poetry written about her children titled *The Best Bouquet, Kindergarten* and *The Middle Child*. They went on to national competition where she won first place for *The Best Bouquet* and *Kindergarten,* while *The Middle Child* appropriately was garnered with a second place win.

The Nebraska author also gives presentations and readings at luncheons, for tour groups visiting the North Platte Museum, church and book club gatherings; conference events, and birthday and anniversary parties.

After she retired from her Union Pacific job, Eckhoff and her husband Kent moved from North Platte to rural Hayes Center in 2008, but retirement didn't last long.

She soon received a call from the local newspaper publisher, asking if she was interested in being the editor. Eckhoff immersed herself into the new adventure and brought new life to the small town paper, the *Times-Republican*, with her reporting, photography, columns and features.

"It was something I always wanted to do. I started doing interviews of people with interesting hobbies or interesting work. I started a recipe column and I have a column, Just a Little Bull, that's about anything. It was fun coming up with something new for next week's paper."

However, after working for the *Times-Republican* for two and a half years, Eckhoff retired in January 2013 due to health issues.

Eckhoff is now working on two books: a humorous mystery novel and a book about her father-in-law's journal written while he was in World War II. "That's different for me," she reflected. "My inspiration comes from Nebraska and the farming and ranching aspect of it. I write the best when I wake up in the middle of the night and things start going through my head. The next thing I'm downstairs writing and I keep going until I'm finished. It's hard for me to schedule writing. They say you should write every day, and I don't do that. If I get an idea, then I go with it."

When she's not putting words to paper, Eckhoff also enjoys gardening, embroidery and dancing; however, even then you can rest assured a new writing idea is never far from this author's mind. B

Endnotes, Footnotes & Sources:

Interview with Dixie Eckhoff/photo by Barbara Ann Dush.

Dixie Eckhoff displays her book, <u>Just A Little Bull and A Few Cowtails</u>.

The Best Bouquet

National Award Winner by
Dixie Eckhoff

The best ones that I ever got
were never in a flower pot
nor pinned upon the gown I wore
to high school prom in sixty-four.

I do recall the flowers, still,
That I received when I was ill ...
roses and carnations sweet,
white daisies are a favorite treat.

Those flowers have become a blur.
They never quite gave me the stir
like those that left me most beguiled
clutched in the hands of my own child.

Dandelions by the score,
growing wild by my back door.
My heart set sail when you-know-who
said, "Mom, I picked these just for you."

Visit A-Z Books, North Platte,
for Open-Mic night

GENEVIEVE EPPENS

Date of Birth: January 18, 1925
Location of Birth: Weeping Water, NE
Education: Weeping Water public schools
Moved: to Lincoln after World War II

Genevieve Eppens

Eppens, Genevieve. <u>Waiting for My Sailor</u>, Lincoln: Infusion Media Publishing, 2000. 66 pages.

Genevieve Eppens has written an incredibly touching memoir in her book, <u>Waiting for My Sailor</u>, that brings a fresh awareness of life on the home front during World War II, masterfully intertwined with a powerful love story.

What started out as a diary of her life events during the war, turned into a book for this masterful Nebraska author. "It was so emotional I tried to forget it, and it took a long time to bring the memories back," she reminisced. "I wrote it in the beginning as an account to give my children; but as I went on, my husband gave me the encouragement to write a book."

Published in 2000, the book is accompanied with forty photographs of the Eppens couple, their family and friends, and World War II memorabilia. The inspiration for the writing was derived from her dedicated life as a wife and mother of six, as well as her Nebraska roots.

Eppens attended country school through her elementary grades, and three years of high school in Weeping Water. She quit high school when she was a junior to marry her sweetheart, Glen Eppens.

<u>Waiting for My Sailor</u> brings to life the years 1942 through 1945 when as a tender teenage bride, Eppen's life was met with the fears and challenges of the Second World War mixed with the newlywed's deep desire to be together.

The author captures the difficulties of leaving her parent's rural Nebraska home and being thrust into a California military lifestyle, all so new and often frightening from the Midwest security she was familiar with. As readers walk softly through each chapter – written in a captivating conversational style – they discover the emotions and fears this generation experienced waiting for their soldiers to come home.

Genevieve Eppens displays her book in front of a painting done by her youngest daughter, Rachel, for her parent's 50th wedding anniversary.

It is an inspired work that focuses on the home front, and the sacrifices made by those left behind to keep the home front running smoothly – stories often neglected to be told.

"That was my life," Eppens said. "I didn't read the newspapers or keep up with the war. We were just living every day until hopefully he would be home.

"I was lucky though," she adds. "A lot of women didn't get to be with their husbands as often as I did." After her children were grown, Eppens attended writing classes at the University of Nebraska-Lincoln where she was told to write like she was having a conversation with her readers.

The advice worked.

And although her husband encouraged her to write and publish, she cleverly discloses: "I wrote it. I didn't let him write it. I knew that if I even told him what I was writing, he was kind of assertive and his idea of the war and what happened was different from mine. I didn't let him read it until it was printed, and I gave him the first copy."

Eppen's book has been recognized in <u>Our Mother's War: American Women At Home And At The Front During World War II</u> by Emily Yellin, and she has had several written works published in the *Lincoln Journal Star* newspaper.

Eppens continues to live in Lincoln and entertain her thoughts on paper. She wants to publish her files of anecdotes into another book about a mother and her children – an experienced life this mother is well versed in. B

Mrs. Eppens sifts through writings she has stored in a workroom in her Lincoln home.

Excerpt from the preface of <u>Waiting for My Sailor</u>

I often thought I'd like to write about our life during World War II, but as time went on it was more difficult to remember everything that happened and in order. Many years ago, when we were vacationing in Colorado, I attempted to begin, and each time I tried I would start to cry and had to give it up.

When I did try to write it later, I struggled to remember. It seemed after I spent more and more time recalling the events, it got easier. I believe it is correct now, and it really brought back a lot of the feelings we had. I hope and pray my children never have to experience the helplessness and loss of control in their lives.

We did return to civilian life, all we wanted to do was forget, and we made very little attempt to keep things as mementos. Years later, Glen wished he had kept some of the thing he had collected, but he had given most of it away.

We were some of the more fortunate ones. He survived, and our time during the war was unique in that he could be in the war zone one day and in a few days be back in the States, making it possible for us to see each other and pretend we were a normal family again.

I hope our story will give my children and others a better appreciation of what life was like for so many during that time in history and realize how fortunate they are today.

Endnotes, Footnotes & Sources:

Interview with Genevieve Eppens/photos by Barbara Ann Dush.

Eppens, Genevieve <u>Waiting for My Sailor</u>, Lincoln: Infusion Media Publishing, 2000, 66 pages.

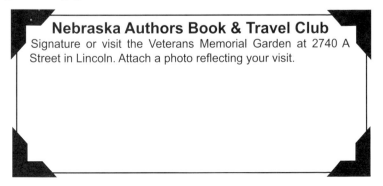

Nebraska Authors Book & Travel Club
Signature or visit the Veterans Memorial Garden at 2740 A Street in Lincoln. Attach a photo reflecting your visit.

FRED ROGERS FAIRCHILD

Date of birth: Aug. 5, 1877
Location of birth: Crete, NE
Education: Crete Public School, grad 1894
Doane College, 1898 A.B & L.L.D., 1929;
Yale, PhD, 1904.
Military: Doane College Light Guards
1894-1898
Date of Death: April 14, 1966
Home at death: Guilford, CT

Fred Rogers Fairchild
Crete High School
graduation 1894

Known Publications:

Fairchild, Fred Rogers <u>The financing of the South African War</u>.
Philadelphia : American Academy of Political and Social Science,
1902.

Fairchild, Fred Rogers. <u>The factory legislation of the State of New
York by Fred Rogers Fairchild.</u> New York : Macmillan Co., 1905.
(London, For the American economic Association by the Macmillan
Co.)

Fairchild, Fred Rogers. <u>Our currency reform problem : a paper</u>. New
Haven? : s.n., 1907?

Fairchild, Fred Rogers, B E Fernow, A.C. Shaw. <u>Forest taxation</u>;
Columbus, O., International tax association. 1908.

Fairchild, Fred Rogers <u>The economic problem of forest taxation, a
paper</u>. New Haven, 1909.

Fairchild, Fred Rogers. <u>Forest taxation.</u> Publisher: [N.p., 1912].

Fairchild, Fred Rogers The present state of forest tax legislation ... N.p., 1912.

Fairchild, Fred Rogers, National Tax Association. Committee on Forest Taxation. Report of the Committee of the National Tax Association on forest taxation, Madison, Wis., National Tax Association, 1914.

Fairchild, Fred Rogers, Henry Freeman Walradt; Connecticut. Chamber of Commerce, Harford. Joint Committee on Taxation and State Finance. Report of the Joint Committee on Taxation and State Finance to the Connecticut Chamber of Commerce, embracing the Report of a special study of the Connecticut tax system, New Haven, Conn., Printed for the Connecticut Chamber of Commerce, by the Tuttle, Morehouse & Taylor Co., 1917.

Fairchild, Fred Rogers The public finance of Santo Domingo... New York, 1918.

Fairchild, Fred Rogers Essentials of economics, New York, Cincinnati [etc.] American Book Company, 1923.

Fairchild, Fred Rogers, Norman Sydney Buck, Edgar Stevenson Furniss. Elementary Economics of Fairchild, Buck and Furniss. Macmillan Co.: New York, 1926. (Elementary Economics: Volume I, Elementary Economics: Volume II).

Fairchild, Fred Rogers, Ralph Theodore Compton. Opinions on economic problems; a book of selected readings, New Haven, Conn., Printed for the use of students in Yale University, 1927.

Fairchild, Fred Rogers, Herman Haupt Chapman. Forest taxation in a cutover region, New York, [1927?].

Fairchild, Fred Rogers Principles of forest taxation... [n.p., 1927].

Fairchild, Fred Rogers, National Tax Association. Preliminary report of the committee of the National Tax Association on tax delinquency.

Fairchild, Fred Rogers. Law enforcement; should the tax laws be enforced and enforceable? ... [New York, 1927].

Fairchild, Fred Rogers, George Dwight Haskell, R. Emmett Taylor. Questions and problems in economics to accompany Fairchild, Furniss, and Buck, Elementary economics, vols. I and II. New York, Macmillan Co., 1927.

Fairchild, Fred Rogers, Ralph Theodore Compton. Economic problems; New York, The Macmillan Company, 1928.

Fairchild, Fred Rogers, Ralph Theodore Compton. Economic problems; a book of selected readings, New York, Macmillan Co., 1928, 1930.

Fairchild, Fred Rogers, George Dwight Haskell, R Emmett Taylor. Questions and problems in economics, to accompany Fairchild, Furniss, and Buck, Elementary economics, vols. I and II, revised edition. New York, Macmillan, 1930.

Fairchild, Fred Rogers, Hawaii, Tax Board. Report of the Tax Board of the territory of Hawaii; submitted to the governor, territory of Hawaii, January 31, 1931 ... Honolulu. Hawaiian Prtg. Co. Ltd., 1931.

Fairchild, Fred Rogers. Essentials of Economics, American Book Co. 1931.

Fairchild, Fred Rogers, Edgar S. Furniss, Norman Sydney Buck, Chester Howard Wheldon. A description of the "New Deal", book and John Clifford Lecture. Macmillan Company, 1934.

Fairchild, Fred Rogers, The business cycle and the "New Deal": a supplementary chapter in economics. New York: American Book Co., 1934.

Fairchild, Fred Rogers Suggestions for the solution of the forest tax problem: [1934].

Fairchild, Fred Rogers. Connecticut. Commission to Study the State Tax Laws. <u>Report of the Connecticut temporary Commission to Study the Tax Laws of the state and to make recommendations concerning their revision as provided by Special act no. 474 of 1933 and submitted to the Governor of Connecticut, November 9, 1934.</u> Publisher: Hartford, The State, 1934.

Fairchild, Fred Rogers, Connecticut. Commission to Study the State Tax Laws. <u>Summary of the report of the Connecticut temporary commission to study the tax laws of the state and to make recommendations concerning their revision.</u> Hartford, Connecticut, The State, 1934.

Fairchild, Fred Rogers. <u>Forest taxation in the United States,</u> Washington : U.S. Department of Agriculture, 1935.

Fairchild, Fred Rogers. <u>Elementary economics,</u> (Vol 1 and Vol 2). New York, Macmillan [1936/1939].

Fairchild, Fred Rogers, Graeme O'Geran, Edgar S Furniss, Norman Sydney Buck. <u>Problems and questions to accompany Fairchild, Furniss, Buck "Economics,"</u> New York, Macmillan, 1937.

Fairchild, Fred Rogers, George Dwight Haskell. <u>Questions and problems in economics, to accompany Fairchild, Furniss, and Buck, Elementary economics, vols. I and II, third edition.</u> New York, Macmillan, 1937. Vols 1 and II, fourth edition, 1939.

Fairchild, Fred Rogers, Edgar S Furniss, Norman Sydney Buck. <u>Economics,</u> New York, The Macmillan Company, 1940. (Economics, MacMillan Company. 1948.)

Fairchild, Fred Rogers. <u>Government spending, now and later.</u> Washington [D.C.] : Chamber of Commerce of the United States, [1943].

Fairchild, Fred Rogers, Committee on Postwar Tax Policy; et al. <u>A tax program for a solvent America.</u> New York : Ronald Press, 1945.

74

Fairchild, Fred Rogers. Profits and the ability to pay wages. Irvington-on-Hudson, N.Y. Foundation for Economic Education, 1946.

Fairchild, Fred Rogers. Understanding our free economy; an introduction to economics, New York, Van Nostrand [1952].

Fairchild, Fred Rogers. Principles of economics. New York, Macmillan [1954].

Fairchild, Fred R., Henry P. Fairchild, Helen P. Curtis, Ralph D. Brown, Gertrude Brown, and Thomas D. Perry. History of Doane College: 1872 to 1912 Crete, Nebraska. Crete, Nebraska: Doane College, 1957. xi + 312 pp. History.

Fairchild, Fred Rogers. Understanding our Free Economy, with Thomas J. Shelley. D. Van Nostrand Company, Inc. 1962. (Princeton, N.J. Van Nostrand. 1965.)

Fairchild, Fred Rogers, Thomas J. Shelly. Teacher's guide to understanding our free economy : an introduction to economics. Toronto: D. Van Nostrand Co., [19--?].

Fred Rogers Fairchild was born to Arthur Babbitt Fairchild of Hartford, Ohio, and Isabel Amanda Pratt of Camp Creek, Nebraska, where her father was the minister. It was in 1874 when Arthur began teaching at the new college in Crete. Doane College had begun the first classes in 1872, and the first graduating class was honored the same year Fred was born.

Arthur taught at Doane College until he took leave in 1883 to finish a Bachelor of Divinity at Oberlin Theological Seminary. When he returned to Doane he taught mathematics and became college treasurer. He traveled considerably as part of his treasurer tasks and for a year, 1889-1890, he headquartered his family in Andover, Massachusetts, returning to Crete in the summer of 1890. As Fred entered high school at Crete Public School, the news of the year included US 7th Cavalry and the Sioux at Wounded Knee, South Dakota, Buffalo Bill Cody was on the road with his Wild West Show based about two hundred miles west of Crete, and Congress passed the Sherman Anti-Trust Act. Nebraska Governor Boyd had appointed Victor Vifquain as the Adjutant-General of the Nebraska State Militia in 1891.[2] And when Grover Cleveland was elected President of the United States, he asked J. Sterling Morton of Nebraska City, less than a hundred miles southeast of Crete, to be Secretary of Agriculture. Morton served from 1893-1897.[3] Morton had made his voice clear on the need for trees in the endless Nebraska territory of grass. Fred became interested in trees and legislation as he ventured back to the East Coast after college graduation.

The weather during Fred's high school and college years was momentous for devastating the crops with abnormally high temperatures and less than normal rain in Nebraska. Tree leaves were curled as if they had been in a fire. The National Forest Service was organized in June of 1891, but was of little help with the nation's tree dilemma. While it had been dry with hot winds where Fred and his family lived, hail killed six horses in Rapid City, South Dakota, and snow and hail had fallen in Maine in July in a previous year.

Odd weather was not the only thing Fred and his classmates faced. The general public was dissatisfied with both the Democrat and Republican parties and the Populist Party was on the rise. Luna Kellie of the Nebraska Farmers' Alliance and other farm workers made their voices known.[4] The commodity prices were already low and the property taxes and railroad freight prices were high. The farmers were not able to secure loans. Businesses and banks were failing nationwide and there were employee layoffs in the urban areas. In December 1893, the Omaha weekly *Figaro* declared there were over 2,000 homeless in Omaha with no means of support. The newspaper urged readers to give at least one person a place to sleep and some food. The 1894-96 years were known as the financial depression years. Fred's ideas of wealth and capitol, trees and commodities, military and freedom were born from these times.

In the fall of 1893, the Doane College Military Department met and *"decided to make military drill compulsory for all male students below the senior year, provided a regular army officer could be secured to instruct the cadets in military science and tactics….Due in part to the interest in preparedness on the part of the government and because of the Cuban situation, the United States sent First Lieutenant Charles B. Hardin, Eighteenth Infantry, U.S. Army to become Professor of Military*

Males in graduation class of 1894[6]

In Uniform, Standing: -
Roscoe King
Fred Fairchild
Frank Stephens
Seated -
Will Russell
Charles Bohac

Science and Tactics and take charge of the Military Department," wrote the authors of Doane College History.[1]

While not yet in college, the high school males opted to take part in the training. Camp mock battles, target practice, neatness and high standards prompted their pride in their high school yearbook photo. Fairchild continued with the military unit as he entered Doane College. When school opened in 1895, Fred R. Fairchild was listed as Captain in Company A.

Doane College history notes, "According to a bill that was passed by the Nebraska State Legislature in 1897, officer graduates of the Military Department of Doane College would be commissioned in the Nebraska State Militia with the same rank that they held at the time of graduation." Commander Hardin was recalled to active duty in April 1898 and replaced with Lt. James M. Arrasmith, but less than a month later he was recalled due to the declaration of the Spanish American War. Cadet Captain Fred R. Fairchild was appointed by the faculty as Commandant of the cadet battalion until he graduated in June. Nebraska Adjutant-General Vifquain joined the Third Nebraska Infantry under Col. William Jennings Bryan fighting the Spanish-American War and the Cuban aftermath. With all the officers recalled, the college military department ceased training until the outbreak of World War I.[1]

Fred was one of four boys born to the Arthur Fairchild household (Arthur born in 1875 died in infancy, Fred in 1877, Henry in 1880 and Frank 1884-1908). His mother became a semi-invalid after the last birth, which prevented her from taking part in many of the public activities at Doane. She moved to be with Fred in New Haven, Connecticut, after Arthur died in 1927 until her death in 1937. She had studied Greek, Latin and French and continued to share her interest in literature though her aging years. Fred, among his other obligations, was responsible for her elder care. Along with his brother, Henry Pratt Fairchild, they took a wide view of family and social issues.[5]

Fred's achievements seemed to follow the interests of his father. Arthur's teaching career included his Doane College teacher's position as Professor of Economics and Ethics. Arthur held this professorship and was treasurer of the college until he retired in 1918. He was given an honorary Doctor of Laws degree and the title Professor Emeritus of Economics and Sociology. The year before his father retired, Fred married Ruth L. Evans. Fred was well into his professorship at Yale before he began his own family. The couple raised two children.

The book, <u>History of Doane College 1872-1912</u>, noted: "Professor (Arthur) Fairchild was decidedly the 'watch dog of the Treasury'. He hated debt and deficit finance." [1-p225] As treasurer of the college it was up to Arthur to invest and maintain the security of the funds. Arthur came from an educational pioneering heritage and always remembered that "To all pioneers one dollar was big." [1-p 231] In 1936, it was Fred as a Yale professor who stood before the United States Senate Finance Committee trying to persuade those in leadership that revisions of the federal tax structure should be coupled with a definite plan to balance the budget. Speaking before the Senate in 1936 was only part of Fred's history.

In 1920, Fred had published an article proposing a restructuring of the post-war, World War I, tax system. The public was calling for the repeal of the excess profits tax which had been enacted during the war. Fred proposed that the government could expect reasonable revenue with justice to the differing classes of taxpayers by changing the tax codes to make corporations exempt from paying taxes on their income, and spreading the payment through the dividends to the stockholders to pay the taxes.

In 1908, Fred published articles on forest taxation and by 1924 had headed a movement to enact what would become the Clarke-McNary Act related to forest taxation. He was a tax advisor to countries such as the Republic of Santo Domingo from 1917-18, the Republic of Columbia in 1923, and the territory of Hawaii in 1930. He held positions as director in banks and trust companies and discussed how to make profits and still have the ability to pay wages (1946). He was an open critic of the New Deal.

Fred and his brother Henry joined other children of original families at Doane College [Helen P. Curtis, Ralph D. Brown, Gertrude Brown and Thomas D. Perry] to write the <u>History of Doane College: 1872 to 1912</u>. The book was presented to Doane in a ceremony in 1955 and published in 1957.

Headlines in an article in the *New York Times* at the time of Fred's death declared that "Fred R. Fairchild of Yale dies at 88; Economist Who Specialized in Taxes Wrote Textbook." He had become known as the man who wrote the tax textbook(s).

He retired as Knox Professor Emeritus of Economics at Yale University. Fairchild's writings were many, but the two blue volumes of <u>Principles of Economics</u> were textbooks widely used in the 1920s and early 1930s. He also was a trustee of the Foundation for Economic Education (FEE) and served as an honorary member of the National Tax Association which was an educational association of taxation experts.

Like his father Arthur, Fred's achievements included Emeritus of Economics and an honorary Doctor of Laws degree. He also had the reputation of 'watch dog' fighting to make Congress balance the budget of the nation, like his father had done as treasurer at Doane College. Becoming the man known for writing the textbooks on "taxes" after 1913 was his own economic legacy.

The Fred Rogers Fairchild writings are still discussed as to the pros and cons of what he said and how his works, both written and orally, have shaped portions of United States history. N

Endnotes, Footnotes & Sources:

[1]Fairchild, Fred R. Henry P. Fairchild, Helen P. Curtis, Ralph D. Brown, Gertrude Brown and Thomas D. Perry. <u>History of Doane College: 1872-1912</u> Crete, Nebraska. Crete, Nebraska: Doane College, 1957. Xi+312 pp. History.

[2] Hansen, Nancy Sue, Dush, Barbara Ann. <u>Nebraska Authors Volume One</u>. "Jean-Baptist Victor Vifquain." Fullerton: D & H Adventures Publishing, 2013.

[3] Hansen, Nancy Sue, Dush, Barbara Ann. <u>Nebraska Authors Volume One</u>. "Julius Sterling Morton." Fullerton: D & H Adventures Publishing, 2013.

[4] Hansen, Nancy Sue, Dush, Barbara Ann. <u>Nebraska Authors Volume One</u>. "Luna Kellie." Fullerton: D & H Adventures Publishing, 2013.

[5] Hansen,Nancy Sue, Dush, Barbara Ann. <u>Nebraska Authors Volume One</u>. "Henry Pratt Fairchild." Fullerton: D & H Adventures Publishing, 2013.

[6] 1894 Crete High School [Nebraska] Yearbook. Entire class photo not shown in this volume.

Fred R. Fairchild of Yale. http:selectnytimes.com April 15, 1966, Page 39, reviewed 10/8/11.

Urges Tax Changes Await Budget Plan: Fairchild of Yale Asserts Program of Balancing Should Come First. Business Men Protest O'Leary of Machinery Trade, Lists Eight Objections to Bill Before Senators., http: selectnytimes.com May 3, 1936, Page 32,: reviewed 1/8/12.

Fred R. Fairchild . www.wikepedia.org reviewed 10/8/11.

Fairchild, Fred R. <u>Who Was Who In America</u>, Volume IV 1961-1968, Marquis-Who's Who, Inc., Illinois, Chicago, p. 297.

Special thanks to Janet Jeffries, Doane College Archivist, for assistance with material to review for this author; and to Jo Wielage, Administrative Assistant Superintendent of Schools Crete High School, for assistance with the high school graduation photo(s).

Nebraska Authors Book & Travel Club
Visit a recreation area in Saline County and have your photo taken as you enjoy the trees that likely were not in the area when Fred was young.

HENRY PRATT FAIRCHILD

Date of birth: Aug. 18, 1880
Location of birth: Dundee, Illinois
NE town was called home: Crete, NE
Education: Doane College A.B., grad 1900
Yale, Ph.D 1909
Doane, honorary L.L.D. 1930
Military: WWI, War Camp Community Service Administration Office
Date of Death: Oct. 2, 1956
Location of Death: North Hollywood, CA.
Buried at Crete, NE

Henry Pratt Fairchild
graduation Doane College.[4]

Known Publications:

Fairchild, Henry Pratt, Herman L. Fairchild, Rudolf Ruedemann, Charles Henry Smyth. <u>Geology of the Thousand Islands region; Alexandria Bay, Cape Vincent, Clayton, Grindstone and Theresa quadrangles</u>, State or province government publication. Albany, University of the State of New York, 1910.

Fairchild, Henry Pratt. <u>Greek immigration to the United States</u>. New Haven: Yale University Press, 1911.

Fairchild, Henry Pratt. <u>Immigration : a world movement and its American significance</u>. New York : Macmillan, 1913.

Fairchild, Henry Pratt. <u>Outline of applied sociology</u>, New York, Macmillan, 1916.

Fairchild, Henry Pratt. <u>Outline of applied sociology, by Henry Pratt Fairchild,</u> New York, Macmillan, 1918.

Fairchild, Henry Pratt. American Educational Institute. <u>Social science</u>. Philadelphia, American Educational Institute, 1921.

Fairchild, Henry Prat. <u>Elements of social science; an introduction to the study of life in human society</u>, New York, The Macmillan Company, 1924.

Fairchild, Henry Pratt. <u>Immigration, a world movement and its American significance</u>, New York, Macmillan Co., 1925.

Fairchild, Henry Pratt. <u>The melting-pot mistake</u>, Boston, Little, Brown and Co., 1926.

Fairchild, Henry Pratt, et al. <u>Immigrant backgrounds</u>, New York, J. Wiley & Sons; London, Chapman & Hall, 1927.

Fairchild, Henry Pratt. <u>The foundations of social life</u>, New York, J. Wiley & Sons; London, Chapman & Hall, 1927.

Fairchild, Henry Pratt. <u>Immigrations: a world movement and its American significance</u>. New York, Macmillan, 1928.

Fairchild, Henry Pratt. <u>The facts about birth control</u>. New York, N.Y. : National Committee on Federal Legislation for Birth Control, [1929?]

Fairchild, Henry Pratt. Boys Scouts of America. <u>Conduct habits of Boy Scouts</u>, New York, Boy Scouts of America [1931].

Fairchild, Henry Pratt. <u>Profits or prosperity</u>? New York, London, Harper & Bros., 1932.

Fairchild, Henry Pratt, New York University Conference Publication. <u>The obligation of universities to the social order; addresses and discussion at a Conference of Universities under the auspices of New York University at the Waldorf-Astoria in New York, November 15-17, 1932</u>. New York, New York University Press; London, H. Milford, Oxford University Press, 1933.

Fairchild, Henry Pratt. <u>Survey of contemporary sociology</u>, New York, T. Nelson and Sons, 1934.

Fairchild, Henry Pratt. <u>General sociology</u>, New York, J. Wiley & Sons, inc., London, Chapman & Hall limited, 1934.

Fairchild, Henry Pratt. <u>This way out</u>, People's League for Economic Security, New York. New York, London, Harper & Bros., 1936.

Fairchild, Henry Pratt. <u>People; the quantity and quality of population</u>, New York, H. Holt and Co. 1939, 1940.

Fairchild, Henry Pratt. <u>Economics for the millions</u>. New York, Modern Age Books, 1940.

Fairchild, Henry Pratt. <u>Main Street : The American Town Past and Present</u> New York : The Greystone Press, 1941.

Fairchild, Henry Pratt. <u>Dictionary of sociology and related sciences</u> Totowa, N.J. : Rowman & Allanheld, 1944. (1970, 1984).

Fairchild, Henry Pratt <u>Dictionary of Sociology</u>. New York Philosophical Library 1944 (Totowa, N.J. : Littlefield, Adams, 1970).

Fairchild, Henry Pratt. <u>Population and peace. Address. annual meeting Friday, October 6, 1944 of the Virginia League for Planned Parenthood</u>, Richmond, 1944?

Fairchild, Henry Pratt, <u>World population movements and the United States</u>. New York University. Institute on Postwar Reconstruction. New York : Institute on Postwar Reconstruction, New York University, 1944.

Fairchild, Henry Pratt. <u>Race and nationality as factors in American life</u>. New York : Ronald Press Co., ©1947.

Fairchild, Henry Pratt. <u>Versus: reflections of a sociologist</u>. New York, Philosophical Library ©1950 (Port Washington, N.Y., Kennikat Press, 1969).

Fairchild, Henry Pratt. <u>The prodigal century</u>. New York: Philosophical Library. 1950.

Fairchild, Henry Pratt <u>The anatomy of freedom</u>. New York, Philosophical Library [1957].

Fairchild, Henry Pratt, Fred R. Fairchild, Helen P. Curtis, Ralph D. Brown, Gertrude Brown, and Thomas D. Perry. <u>History of Doane College: 1872 to 1912 Crete, Nebraska</u>. Crete, Nebraska.: Doane College, 1957. xi + 312 pp. History.

Known as "Hal" by his Doane College friends, Henry Pratt Fairchild followed in the education career footsteps of his father, uncles and grandfather. His focus became Sociology, not the college presidency of his elders. Henry was the third son born to Arthur Babbitt Fairchild and Isabel Amanda Pratt in 1880. Arthur was the son of Edward Henry Fairchild who was president of Berea College in Berea, Kentucky. Edward Henry was a descendant of Thomas Fairchild who settled in New England in 1639. Hal's mother, Isabel, was a descendant of the Pratt industrial family. Arthur and Isabel married on March 19, 1874, at Camp Creek, Nebraska, where her father was a minister of the church.

His father Arthur moved his new wife to Crete, Nebraska, where he taught from 1874 until 1883 when he took leave to finish a Bachelor of Divinity degree at Oberlin Theological Seminary in 1884. He returned to Doane to teach mathematics and became college treasurer. Arthur focused on raising funds for the college. As the financial agent, he traveled considerably. From 1889-90 he headquartered his family in Andover, Massachusetts, returning to Crete in the summer of 1890.

Henry was now ten years old. It was tough times in Nebraska: low farm prices, high freight charges, disruption in banking and business with layoffs and closures were evident throughout the state. The winds were hot and the drought would make history for several years. Ellis Island in New York City opened as a U.S. Immigration Depot and within a year the Treasury Department hosted the newly created Office of Superintendent of Immigration. The United Mine Workers of America was formed. Nebraska introduced an eight-hour work day the next year. Alice Sanger became the first female White House staffer and Wyoming became the 44th state and the first state with female suffrage. The Mormon Church renounced polygamy in May and the president of that church issued a manifesto in September advising members to abandon the practice.[1] The German Emperor Wilhelm II fired republican chancellor Otto Von Bismarck. Many of these historic events became a foundation point for Henry's adult life.

Nebraskans, like the Fairchilds, lived through the financial depression years of 1894-1896. Things began to turn around and the Trans-Mississippi and International Exposition and Nebraska State Fair of 1898 were planned for Omaha. By the time Henry graduated from Doane College in 1900, the Nebraska economy and social spirit was mending. Henry was noted as the youngest member of his Doane College graduation class and he had the highest marks in the class.[2]

In 1899, Professor Arthur Fairchild's chair was changed to Professor of Economics and Ethics. He held the teaching and treasurer positions with the college until he retired in 1918 as Professor Emeritus of Economics and Sociology. Henry and his brother, Fred Rogers Fairchild, became distinguished educators with Hal focusing on sociology and economics and Fred on economics and taxation.[3]

Following Henry's graduation in 1900, he began a teaching career at the International College at Smyrna (Izmir) Turkey. After three years in Turkey, he returned to Nebraska and worked at Doane College recruiting students and working as a financial agent with his father. According to the History of Doane,[4- p 225] *"[Arthur,] as Treasurer Professor Fairchild had the responsibility for investing all the College's funds, small in amount in those days, but none the less important. His financial policy was strongly on the conservative side. He avoided stocks and bonds, a field unfamiliar to him, and put all the funds of the College into Nebraska mortgages. He knew Nebraska real estate. However he did not rely solely on the security, but laid great stress on the character and habits of the borrower..."* Other trustees urged him to get into the stock market for a higher return, however, Arthur held fast. *"As a result of his shrewd and conservative policy, Professor Fairchild had the satisfaction of knowing that throughout his long term as Treasurer, the College had never lost a dollar through a bad investment, either of principal or of interest."* It was into that Doane environment that Henry returned to work for the next few years. He began to understand how the stability of the investments his father was making assisted in the recruiting of quality students. He took these lessons as a lens to see the future of the American public: sociology and economics in action.

In 1909, Henry P. Fairchild had received his Ph.D. from Yale. His writing career began with a joint authorship government publication for the state of New York on the <u>Geology of the Thousand Islands region</u>. Following that joint publication, he produced nearly one book a year working with various publishers.

Dr. Fairchild joined the faculty at Bowdoin College, Brunswick, Maine, for the fall semester of 1909. In 1894, Bowdoin College president William DeWitt Hyde joined A. Lawrence Lowell, the President of Harvard; James T. Young, the director of Wharton School; and David Starr Jordan, the president of Stanford University among the membership of the new Immigration Restriction League. The League lobbied for literacy tests for immigrants among other issues. Literacy test bills were vetoed by Presidents in 1897, 1913, and 1915; but Congress would override President Wilson's second veto in 1917. This league became known as the first American entity associated officially with eugenics. Eugenics became one of the focuses of Dr. Henry P. Fairchild for the rest of his life.

Dr. Fairchild remained at Bowdoin only one year. He returned to Yale where he taught economics and the science of society from 1910-1918. During these years he wrote on Greek immigration to the United States; immigration as a world movement and how America was affected; and began his outlines of applied sociology which he would revise and publish through the next decades. World War I took him to an administrative position, associate director of personnel, in the War Camp Community Service 1918-1919. Amid all the teaching, research, and writing, he married Mary Eleanor Townsend. They had one daughter. His wife preceded him in death.

He joined the faculty of New York University as a Professor of Social Economy and Director of the Bureau of Community Service and Research. Dr. Fairchild became executive secretary for the Connecticut State Commission on Child Welfare from 1919-1921, and served as an investigator for the National Research Council and Special Immigration agent in Europe for the U.S. Department of Labor in 1923.

In the years after World War I, several organizations had been formed to promote birth control in the world. Several authors suggest that these competing organizations were created out of fears of the American affluent educated elite: that they needed to have more time and money for themselves and they didn't want the poor, uneducated and less desirable people around with needs that their money and time would have to care for. These elite were having fewer children and saw the high birth rates among those with less than themselves as alarming. Feminist Margaret Sanger began calling the situation a peril for the civilization of the future. Sanger and others promoted careers for women and that they have less children. Sanger began suggesting sterilization for those unable to use birth control, but according to her writings she rejected euthanasia. The National Federation of Women's Clubs, the Woman's Christian Temperance Union and the National League of Women Voters were among the groups who often lobbied for various issues of eugenic reform.

Of all the movements there were two basic camps: eugenics and birth control. Those in the eugenics camp warned that less children among the Northern European people would mean 'race suicide'. President Theodore Roosevelt had made his voice known in March 1905 attacking women who used birth control as a crime against their race. The eugenics group wanted children to be 'fit'. The birth controllers believed they could plan race-building by forcing down the birth rate of the 'unfit' using birth control. Posters describing the need to remove genetic defects such as feeble-mindedness from the population were common across the country by the early 1920s.

The birth control and eugenics debates were nationwide as Dr. Fairchild taught his undergraduate classes. He lectured at the University of California summer school programs. These summer lectures continued for many years. His writings changed tone from applied sociology to social science and how elements of social science affected human life. Now he had field knowledge in immigrant backgrounds using his time in Turkey, growing up in the Nebraska Territory created by numerous immigrants, a year traveling with his parents headquartered in Massachusetts, as a child welfare and special immigration agent in Europe, his studies in New York and California, and WWI experiences.

In 1924, he began serving New York University (NYU) as Professor of Sociology at the Graduate School. Courses in sociology covered a vast array of topics, including race; nationalism; health, educational and mental developmental characteristics; immigration; economic and social consequences, eugenics, euthanasia, and ethnic conflict. According to U.S. academic history, eugenics was studied in 376 separate university courses around the country. More than 20,000 students came in contact with eugenics in their curriculum by 1928.

Dr. Fairchild was not alone is his consideration of the subject; however, may have become among the most vocal in declaring what he saw in the world around him. In 1926 he wrote one of his most controversial books, The Melting-Pot Mistake.

From 1929-1931 Dr. Fairchild was president of the American Eugenics Society. In 1931 he helped to organize the Population Association of America. The organization promoted and stimulated research on problems connected with the quantitative and qualitative aspects of human population. He was president of the organization from 1931-1935. He became part of the People's League for Economic Security, 1934-1938, and wrote his book The Way Out.

As the 26th president of the American Sociological Society in 1936, his presidential address was titled "Business as an Institution." He combined his two favorite issues: the relationship of sociology and economics. He presented his concepts: that business was an organization of social elements for production of goods and services and the role of those in sociology was to analyze and integrate social elements in the process of business and the economists were to review the productive aspects. He taught and wrote on these principles and how the various governmental and social, business, and economic groups should be working together.

By the mid 1930s, the Rockefeller and Harriman American elitists were funding studies in Europe on eugenics and birth control. When Germany began to euthanize people considered 'unfit' many of the organizations in the United States from both eugenics and birth control groups voiced their support. By the late 1930s, the United States public became hostile to what they saw happening in Germany, and eugenics and birth control groups could no longer compete for donations from the wealthy due to the Nazi label. This created the need for the two movements to unite in 1938, forming the Birth Control Federation of America (BCFA). While this merger was going on Dr. Fairchild became president of the Film Audiences for Democracy, 1938-1940.

New York University elevated Dr. Fairchild to Chairman of the Department from 1938 to 1945 when he retired as Professor Emeritus. His teaching and department chairman duties did not change Dr. Fairchild's off-campus activities.

In January 1940, the BCFA had their annual meeting in New York City. The title for the year was "Race Building in a Democracy." Dr. Henry Fairchild gave the luncheon speech with the same title. He noted that the conference showed how close the two great movements of eugenics and birth control had come in working together and they were "almost indistinguishable." At the meeting, the group acknowledged their work was now seen as Nazi-like. They decided that the name of the group needed to change, yet their ideologies could remain the same. Dr. Fairchild began a fund drive for "The Citizens Committee for Planned Parenthood" and the organizations honorary chairman, Margaret Sanger, hired D. Kenneth Rose as public relations consultant. While she did not like the new name, the organization changed its title to the Planned Parenthood Federation of America (PPFA) in 1942. Sanger was firm: she said it was an individual woman and not the state who should determine whether she should have a child or not. Dr. Fairchild was vice-president of the organization until 1948.

A year before he retired from NYU, he edited the Dictionary of Sociology and worked with the Institute on Postwar Reconstruction writing: World Population Movements and the United States. His retirement in 1945 opened a new door to more international work and reflections on his sociologist life. He wrote Versus: Reflections of a Sociologist and The Prodigal Century in 1950. He wrote The Anatomy of Freedom which was not published until after his death.

In 1952, he served in a United Nations special service engagement at the Solvay Institute in Brussels Belgium and served as secretary of the American-Soviet Friendship Club. He and his brother Fred joined other children of original families at Doane College [Helen P. Curtis, Ralph D. Brown, Gertrude Brown and Thomas D. Perry] to write the History of Doane College: 1872 to 1912. The book was presented to Doane in a ceremony in 1955 and published in 1957 after Dr. Henry Fairchild's death.

Dr. Henry Fairchild became skillful in research, oratory, teaching, writing and managing organizations. His focus on race relations, economics and social issues, abortion and contraception, immigration, nationalism, and ethnic conflict created over sixty articles and books. He was taught that one of the elements of a career sociologist is to help the public to understand sociological findings. He presented those elements in the actions of his life.

At his death, Emory S. Bogardus wrote about Henry P. Fairchild in The American Sociological Review, 21(6): 783: "Always an independent thinker, he did not hesitate to speak forthrightly on leading social and economic problems."[5] N

Endnotes, Footnotes & Sources:

[1] Hansen, Nancy Sue, Dush, Barbara Ann, <u>Nebraska Authors Volume One</u>. "Albert Watkins." Fullerton: D and H Adventures Publishing, 2013.

[2] <u>The Crete News</u>. *Dr. Henry Fairchild, Doane College Leader Dies Oct 2 in California*. Oct. 11, 1956, page 1.

[3] Hansen, Nancy Sue, Dush, Barbara Ann, <u>Nebraska Authors Volume One</u>. "Fred Rogers Fairchild." Fullerton: D and H Adventures Publishing, 2013.

[4] Fairchild, Henry P., Fred R. Fairchild, Helen P Curtis, Ralph D. Brown, Gertrude Brown and Thomas D. Perry. <u>History of Doane College 1872 to 1912</u>. Crete, Nebraska. 1955. Chapter 34.

[5] Bogardus, Emory S. <u>The American Sociological Review</u>, *Henry P. Fairchild* 21(6) 783. www.asanet.org reviewed 10/8/2011.

<u>Doane College Newsletter</u>. *Henry P. Fairchild Class of 1900, Dies*. Oct. 1956.

Eugenics in the United States. www.wikipedia. 12/27/2012 reviewed.

<u>Fairchild, Henry Pratt</u> www.Wikipedia. Reviewed 10/8/2011.

Perry, Mike. *The History of Planned Parenthood*. www.metrovoice.net. Reviewed 1/27/2012.

<u>Who Was Who in America</u>, *Henry Pratt Fairchild*. Vol 3 Chicago, 1960, page 270.

Nebraska Authors Book & Travel Club

Ticket to a Doane College event or a photo of time spent visiting the Doane College campus.

REX LeROY GERMAN

Date of Birth: Oct. 28, 1934
Location of Birth: Cozad, NE
Education: Cozad Public Schools
High School grad, 1952
Currently lives in Cozad

Rex German[1]
Cozad High School
Senior[2]

German, Rex LeRoy, Czaplewski, Russ. <u>Battle of the Bridges</u>, Lexington: Dawson County Historical Society, 1988, first edition, 171 pp.

The Nebraska territory was called the Great American Desert by the first explorers.[3] The major river through the state is the Platte River which crosses the state west to east. The Platte River is a meandering guide through the landscape adjacent to what became two of the trails west: Oregon and Mormon. The river is also a problem: it was, and is today, a mile wide and about an inch deep in many parts with the water being too dirty to drink and the ground too thin to plow.[3] It becomes a raging, bank overflowing terror with Rocky Mountain snowmelt, and completely dry in the summer with thin ice throughout the winter. Pioneers, homesteaders, and the railroad needed to ford this river for trade and commerce, just as farmers, ranchers, and Nebraska travelers do today.

One area along the Platte River became known as Dawson County. Dawson County has four towns built along the railroad: Overton; Plum Creek, now Lexington; Cozad and Gothenburg.[3] Every town on one side of the Platte River needed a bridge to connect it to the commerce on the other side of the River and the trails west. Bridges cost money. Dawson County was not a wealthy county. The county lines were created straddling a geological phenomenon known as the 100th Meridian: "where the humid east meets the arid west."[4] While the bridges were necessary for trade and travel, the river they crossed was of little use in farming and sustaining of family life for the households in the area.

In the windswept prairie, grain famers without a means to water their crops are at the mercy of the rain from the Pacific Coast over the Rocky Mountains, southern winds bringing rain clouds from the Gulf, or Northern Canadian winter snows moving from the far north regions. When rainfall is not timely during the growing season, there is a drought and crops are lost. Irrigation, which is common in all countries of the world, is a method to bring water to farms from rivers and lakes usually through man-made ditches, canals and aquaducts. Sometimes a farm has resources under their land to furnish a deep well which provides water for a family, livestock and irrigation. Farmers with access to water for their fields use irrigation methods in their farming operations Farms without the aid of irrigation are called dryland operations.

Nebraska homesteaders did not have access to irrigation in any part of the Kansas-Nebraska territory in the beginning. C.D. Wilber popularized a theory "rain followed the plow."[5] It was dozens of years before the theory was proven incorrect, but by then the railroads and the first agricultural department at the new University of Nebraska in Lincoln [Professors S.R. Thompson, Agriculture and Samuel Aughey, Chemistry and Natural Science] circulated the theory and sodbusters from all over the world flocked to the new territories. As settlers became more numerous and the cycles of drought and flooding became part of the history of the new state, enterprising men attempted to obtain and control the necessary water, and later electric power, using the waterways available in Nebraska.[6] Between the need for irrigation and the need for bridges to cross the seemingly useless waterways, Nebraska had developed an obsession with water.

When Plum Creek, the county seat of Dawson County, built their bridge in 1873, it was the first across the Platte west of Columbus. It was a boon to the economy of the entire mid-Nebraska region. A.E. Sheldon wrote a children's Nebraska history textbook in 1937 and explained the use of the various water projects for irrigation and power.

The effect on Nebraska was monumental.[7] Bridges and irrigation were a continuous need.

It is onto the Dawson County 100th Meridian landscape that Rex LeRoy German was born in 1934. The rivalry between the towns to build their bridge to prosperity and fame was part of history, the court battles with the farmers, cattleman and the Olive gang was a distant memory while the battle of the weather cycles continued: Dust Bowl and Depression. German was born about four miles south of Cozad, across the river.

A quarter page advertisement with inch-high letters in the *Cozad Local* newspaper of March 14, 1944, grabbed attention: *1000 Men Wanted.* While the advertisement was placed with stories of local military men and women home on leave, lost at war or headed away for their first campaign, the Ad was not about the war. It was about an *Important Irrigation Meeting, Cozad City Hall, Tuesday March 14th at 8 p.m. sharp. This meeting is one of great importance to both the farmer and the town man – so be there Tuesday night. This is urgent! Irrigation Committeee.*[8]

Headlines above the newspaper's banner on March 17, in half-inch letters read: "On to North Platte Saturday is Cozad's slogan. "No water diversion is the Motto." A map below the banner declared that the outcome of a meeting in North Platte on Saturday would affect every land owner and business in the Cozad valley.[8]

When the paper printed the results of the meeting from an Associated Press story in their March 24, 1944, edition the headlines read that five hundred farmers and businessmen from Dawson County attended the meeting in North Platte. Irrigations districts, canal rights, water tables, and numerous issues were discussed. This event, like meetings before it and meetings thereafter, affected the citizens of the area and defined how water needed to be utilized economically in finances as well as quality and quality of water as a product. Rex, now ten, knew that water was needed on his great-grandfather Jensen's hog farm as well as the crop farming operations his family relied on.[8]

Since the Platte River could not be relied upon, especially in July and August, canals had been dug to provide continuous flows of water. Use of syphons to take the water from the canals to the fields was common, using metal to manufacture the syphons; however with the war consuming the metal, it was difficult to obtain and the use of plastic was considered an alternative. Rex's father Milo German, proprietor of the Cozad Implement Company, placed a palm-sized advertisement in the April 11, 1944, *Cozad Local* giving notice that he would have "plastic syphon tubes for irrigation in five different sizes! Drop in and see us." [8]

A year later in the April 6, 1945, edition of the *Cozad Local,* education about plastics was front and center. A special box called "Our Democracy, by Mat" noted that the peanut had been brought from Africa in slave ships, became popular at circuses, ballgames, and as a staple in military ration kits. Now through the work of George Washington Carver, the peanut provided oil and the basics to make plastics.[8] Crude oil also became a source to make plastics after the war. Into this plastics world forged Rex German's family making the first plastic grated pipe and the first PVC fence at their manufacturing company in Cozad.[9]

German attended rural schools and graduated high school in Cozad in 1952. He completed normal training at Cozad High School at the age of seventeen. He went on to teach rural schools near Cozad and Gothenburg for five years, having as

Schoolhouse where German did his practice teaching. Photo taken 2013.[10]

many as thirty-five students one semester. When the pay would not support his growing family, he went to work for his father. He remains at the Nebraska Plastics Company today.[9]

The German manufacturing skills had advanced the quality of plastics, especially the siphons, by the time Rex graduated and they placed a page advertisement in the year book his senior year.[11] Rex, however, taught school and lived on a farm with his new wife, Lois, doing the chores and raising his three sons and a daughter. When he did join the family business, he remained on the multi-generational farm while he worked in town. Manufacturing, farming, family life and putting all four children through the University of Nebraska at Lincoln were not the only interests for German. He made time to volunteer with the Dawson County Historical Society.

During the summer of 1986, Steve Holen, Director of the Dawson County Museum, asked German, a member of the board at the time, to help him with an article about the historical conflict over Dawson County's bridges. The goal was for the three-page article to be published in the fall newsletter. Holden had research done by Russ Czaplewski, the Research Historian for the Museum, which he gave to German as a starter. As German began his task, he realized that the historical subject was more than a three-page article. There was a historical need for the information to be in book form.

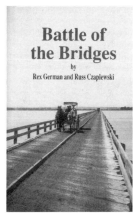

Battle of the Bridges
by
Rex German and Russ Czaplewski

Front cover of the Battle of the Bridges[3]

Three years later, after trips to Texas and Nebraska archives searching for facts and issues that were gleaned from research; the Dawson County Historical Society was presented a 169-page well-researched and documented account of "sweat, tears and an unnatural faith."[3] With assistance from his family in doing the farm chores, he researched and put together documents showing the issues in the words of the citizens of Dawson County as they had made their own history.

Czaplewski's research presented his unique research ability to find interesting material. German took the threads, and with the Holen's guidance and encouragement, the long trips to Texas, hours of checking documents from courthouses to libraries, walking cemeteries and talking to locals, energized the book: The Battle of the Bridges-Community Rivalry in Dawson County, Nebraska. The impact of seeing words from diaries, court cases, commissioners' minutes, newspapers, letters, biographies, and autobiographies were harder to believe for some than the half-remembered gossip and face-saving dialogue that had been considered history among some resident families for generations.[3] Some of the rivalry and misconceptions of facts were still just under the surface in the late 1980s as they had been a hundred years previous. The book had some minor side effects, but "through their words you will hear the 'voice' of the hard-working sincere pioneers who, in relative obscurity, became the backbone of Central Nebraska."[3-p-iv]

Every town needed its bridge across the Platte, and the book tells the beginning of the settlers coping with problems of the day and how they laid the foundations for the prosperous land of mid-Nebraska today, including a chapter on the notorious Olive gang.

German's book describes one of Custer County's most memorable cattle kings: Ison Prentice Olive, also known as Print. Print and his brother Bob left Texas in 1876 with three huge herds of cattle estimated between 15,000 and 20,000 head. He had moved cattle to Fort Kearny as early as 1869 and had seen the grasslands of the area; however, as they moved north to live their brand of business was as cattlemen without a country. The ruthless pair came to Nebraska after becoming known as cattle rustlers with murder and self-defense as part of their history.

Print resided in Plum Creek (now Lexington), but his ranch was on the South Loup River, about four miles east of Callaway, in Custer County. Print's herd became so large he began pushing people off other land so his cattle could graze everywhere. They became known as the rowdy Olive Gang.

According to reports, Print's only concession to civilized life was marrying Louisa Reno. They had seven children; however, he didn't spend much time with this family. After each child was born, Print would wait until Louisa was back on her feet and leave again to enlarge his cattle herd.

As the gang monitored the cattle sales for other cowman who had rustled their cattle, they found Luther Mitchell and Ami Ketchum selling some of the Olive cattle at Kearney, so they captured them, hung them, burned them, and buried them. When they had the trial for Print Olive, the Dawson County part of the country wasn't settled enough so they moved the trial to Hastings. At one point, so many ranchers came into Hastings they had to declare martial law. The Olive gang thrived and was on trial in late 1878-1879. Print was found guilty, but judges decided to let him go free [the details are in the book]. He died in a gun fight in 1886. Brother Ira remained living near Cozad. The only thing left from the actual Olive Ranch is a post full of old square nails that are still visible.

The Federal Government's *Homestead Law* and the Nebraska *Herd Law* were as much of the Olive trial as the later trials involving the *Kinkaid Act of 1904,* showing errors in the law(s) as cattleman Bartlett Richards Sr. and the Old Spade Ranch of Ellsworth (Alliance) went on trial in Hastings in 1909.[12] Both trials were major events in the history of Nebraska and gave the cities of eastern Nebraska the notion that western Nebraska was lawless and unsafe.

As the sodbuster farmers and the cattlemen, the government and the lawmen duked it out, the need for bridges across the Platte River [and other rivers] continued. Towns lived and died due to natural issues such as lack of rain, flooding, range fires and grasshoppers.[7] The new settlers had produce and cattle they needed to take to market at the closest railroad. They couldn't manipulate the weather with accuracy, but the lack of bridges was something they could change.

German, with Czaplewski's notes, researched newspapers and documents for the creation of all the bridges of Dawson County. Using the old sources of the day, he provides a snapshot in time of who, what, where, when and how the bridges were conceived, managed and the history of the economy and public relations between communities. Accidents, fights-murders in self-defense and otherwise, and old fashioned mob law were part of his finds. Even John J. Cozad [the man who had been on a train traveling through the area and had seen the first 100th Meridian sign and decided to bring a colony from Ohio to the area] would leave town with his family due to a fight which ended with a gunshot, a trial and death. History is never outdated nor is a book presented in the voice of the history maker.[3]

Just as bridges changed the history of the county, so did irrigation. Plastic irrigation syphon products are part of the history and changes in irrigation. The syphon assisted farmers in giving life-saving water to their crops for over fifty years. The light-weight post World War II syphon was a 'bridge' of its own, carrying water from one irrigation ditch at a time to the dusty dry fields of one farmer at a time. Each farmer's toils built the state and the nation one season at a time conducting business over one bridge at a time.

German looks ahead more than he looks back at his family business, but noted that it is believed that Nebraska Plastics is the oldest family-owned plastics extrusion company in the United States.[1] The family, including three children spread around the country who participate in the business from their homes, and youngest son Paul, who moved his family from Iowa, continue the history as a leading manufacturer of vinyl fence, deck, and railing products.

Dawson County continues providing bridges across the Platte for travelers and locals alike. A sequel based on the conversations of the people involved in providing the information for the first book was a goal for German; but as other writers lament, they get too busy with life and the writing doesn't get done. It is a fragment of history that is lost to time.

There was one parting reflection on the history of his county and the book: "Our heritage is rich. Our roots are deep. There is no river we cannot bridge."[3] BN

Endnotes, Footnotes and Sources:

[1] German is pronounced Grrr-man.
Interview with Rex German, transcription of audio recording and notes of tour of area given by German in Barbara Ann Dush file.

[2] Cozad Haymaker Yearbook 1952. Thank you to the Wilson Library staff in Cozad for their assistance with locating the yearbook.

[3] German, Rex LeRoy, Czaplewski, Russ. Battle of the Bridges, Lexington: Dawson County Historical Society, 1988, first edition, 171 pp.

[4] D.A.R. Stone with plaque. Nebraska has a historic geological line running through the state called the 100th Meridian. It is a natural demarcation line between the humid east and the arid west. In 1879, Major John Wesley Powell made this determination in his report for the United States Geological Survey. The 100th Meridian runs north and south near what is now the town of Cozad, Nebraska. Powell declared that west of this line the precipitation, which comes largely from the Pacific, is insufficient for agricultural needs without irrigation. His observations have held to this date. A stone with a plaque was placed at the site of his survey declaring the location of the 100th Meridian. The Global Positioning System (GPS) located the 100th Meridian about 4,000 feet west of the previously declared site. Another marker was placed at that location.

[5] Wilber, C.D. The Great Valleys and Prairies of Nebraska and the Northwest. Omaha, 1881.

[6] Hansen, Nancy Sue and Dush, Barbara Ann. Nebraska Authors Volume One. "Frederic Babcock." Fullerton: D & H Adventures Publishing. 2013.

[7] Sheldon, A.E. Nebraska Old and New. Lincoln: University Publishing Company. 1937, 470 pp. Irrigation 392, 393, 438-440. A.E. Sheldon wrote a children's Nebraska history textbook in 1937 and explained it this way: *"The Sutherland Project, near North Platte, takes water from the North Platte River for power and also supplies water for smaller irrigation districts east of North Platte. The Tri-County Project in central Nebraska will take water from*

the North Platte River, bringing it down to power plants south of Lexington to make electricity. Several hundred thousand acres on the south side of the Platte in Phelps, Kearney, and Adams counties may also be irrigated. The Columbus Project, near Columbus, uses water from the Loup River to make electricity. Farther west on two of the forks of the Loup are the North Loup and the Middle Loup Projects which are using the water of those rivers to irrigate the counties just southeast of the Sandhills. They will also distribute electircity."
7-p440

[8] Thank you to the Wilson Library Staff at Cozad for assistance with the microfilm of the *Cozad Local* and copies of research for this story.

[9] Nebraska Plastics website: Country Estates. Nebraskaplastics.com.

[10] Schoolhouse photo by Barbara Ann Dush, 2013, in her files.

[11] See appendix for Nebraska Plastic's advertisement, 1952 Cozad Haymaker School Yearbook.

[12] Hansen, Nancy Sue and Dush, Barbara Ann. <u>Nebraska Authors Volume One</u>. "Ruth Van Ackeren," "Robert Howard." Fullerton: D & H Adventures Publishing. 2013.

Hansen, Nancy Sue and Dush, Barbara Ann. <u>Nebraska Authors Volume One</u>. "O.C. Dake," "Fred R. Fairchild," "Henry P. Fairchild." Fullerton: D & H Adventures Publishing. 2013.

"Farming in the 1940s." www.livinghistoryfarm.org. Reviewed August 8, 2013.

The One Hundredth
Meridian, 1933

Nebraska Authors Book & Travel Club

Plan a road trip on the Lincoln Highway Scenic and Historic Byway (Nebraska Highway 30) in honor of its 100 year anniversary 1913-2013. As you arrive in Cozad visit the 100th Meridian Nebraska State Historical Society and D.A.R. marker at the train depot museum. Reaching this spot was a major goal of the transcontinental railroad and was completed to the 100th Meridian on October 5, 1866. Land for the town was purchased in December 1873 by John J. Cozad.

JAMES R. GRIESS

Date of Birth: April 12, 1941
Location of Birth: Lushton, NE
Education: Sutton High School, 1959;
attended UN-L and University of
Wyoming 1960;
Kearney State College BA and MA in
Education 1963

James Griess

Griess, James R. <u>The German Russians, Those Who Came to Sutton</u>, Service Press, Henderson, Nebraska, first edition published 1970; second edition published 2008. 335 pp.

Numerous articles written for quarterlies and journals.

James R. Griess attended school near the farm in York County, Nebraska, where he was born. It was during this time his interest in history was being formed. "My mom, being a history teacher, got me interested in history because she would have history fairs and the children would have to bring something about their family and their family background," he said.

Griess's own personal history was also intriguing: "Grandfather Ehly, who was born in Russia, was an interesting man and he still corresponded with the German relatives left behind in Russia. In about 1950, one of the sisters got out of Russia. Another relative, a niece and her son who had been living at a slave labor camp in Russia, got into Canada and they came to visit my grandfather. I was old enough to sit in on that meeting and hear the stories."

While Griess may have had a love of history, his Regents' Scholars advisors at the University of Nebraska at Lincoln thought he should study to be a bacteriologist, so he began his studies under Dr. Nightingale who taught chemistry. However, through a series of events, Griess decided to drop out of the university science program and transfer to Kearney State College where he graduated mid-term and became a history and biology teacher.

As part of completing his master's degree he had to write a thesis. His advisor was Dr. Philip Holmgren from Naper, Nebraska – a Swede from a German-Russian settlement. Dr. Holmgren's interest in that part of history peaked Griess's curiosity, so he decided to research German-Russian history as his master's thesis.

"The German Russian people were just in the process of getting organized and trying to preserve their history, so there was not an organization like the American History Society of Germans from Russia (AHSGR) as there is now," Griess explained. There was no Internet at the time, so his research started with interviewing his grandfather and other people in the community who had come from Russia.

Griess studied Nebraska immigrants who settled south of Henderson on the Blue River and through York County toward Sutton. It was serious research. "When I got the thesis done it was one hundred fifty pages – the longest graduate master's thesis that had ever been produced at Kearney State College. They used to get it out and show the graduate students the thesis and it would scare them because it was so long," Griess commented with a bit of humor. "It was typed on a Corona electric typewriter, and you had to make the corrections and go back and retype them. It was fun. It was a labor of love because I wanted to know."

The thesis became Griess's first publication in 1970: <u>The German Russians: Those Who Came to Sutton</u>. While the book was slowly going out of print, he started his teaching profession in Overton as a science teacher and later moved to social studies. Three years later he joined the staff of Hastings High School teaching American history.

After teaching, he went to Kansas to work for the Kansas National Education Association. Within six months he had been asked to join the Nebraska Association and returned to Nebraska. He held various positions while working for the Nebraska State Education Association in Lincoln for thirty-five years, including sixteen as the executive director. During this time he also married and raised a family.

Through the years people would ask to buy one of Griess's books which were long out of print. With his January 1, 2007, retirement he set to work, updating the original book. It had been thirty-nine years since he had written the original. "Starting January 2007, I spent eight months, almost every day like I was going to the office. I added four chapters and used lots of illustrations. Basically the book covers two thousand years of history from the coming of Christianity to Europe through the fall of the Soviet Union."

The book tells about the Burlington and Missouri River Railroad, the years after the civil war, and the colonizing and settling of Nebraska. Over three hundred pages are illustrated with photographs, charts and maps, many in color. Economic, political, social, and religious institutions begun in Russian by the immigrants are included with the motives behind the migration(s). Not all the German-Russians left Russia in 1872 and the years that followed. Some of their fate was extermination at the hands of Stalin at the time of World War II when he killed over twenty million of his own people.[1]

Griess has one regret about the new book: "I wish I would have given it a different name after I updated it and added all the illustrations and chapters that weren't in the first book. It isn't just about the settling of Sutton, Nebraska. It is more of the whole global history of the German-Russian people."

New title or not, "people write me letters thanking me for the work I did with this book," Griess said. It can be purchased on his website www.jimgriess.net or through the American Historical Society of Germans from Russia. He continues to chair the Editorial and Publication Committee for the AHSGR. "The last article that I did was the migration of the German-Russians to Latin America," he noted. "There were a lot of German Russians that went there."

Through the years Griess has not forgotten what brought him to this place in his life. He dedicated the book to his mother, Erna M. Ehly, "Who created in me a desire to learn, an appreciation for America's history; but most of all, a strong faith in our Lord and Savior Jesus Christ." B

Endnotes, Footnotes & Sources:

[1] http://www.ibtimes.com.

Griess, James R., The German Russians, Those Who Came to Sutton, Henderson: Service Press, 1970, 2008, 335 pp.

Interview with Jim Griess/photo by Barbara Ann Dush.

Jim Griess displays the second edition of his book <u>The German Russians, Those Who Came to Sutton</u>. Behind him are just some of the pieces in his Native American collection – another hobby in the life of this Nebraska author.

LAUREL "CHIEF" HAYMART

Date of birth: June 24, 1899 (twin)
Location of birth: Phillips, NE
Education: Douglas and Beaver
Country School
What NE town called home: Giltner
Date of Death: Jan. 25, 1985
Author's nickname "Chief"

Chief. A Collection of Early Giltner Stories

Haymart, Laurel "Chief". <u>Chief. A Collection of Early Giltner Stories.</u>
Hastings: The Cornhusker Press, 1984. 52 pp.

It was a couple of ex-confederate soldiers who had been taken prisoner in Georgia and sent to the prisoner of war camp near Chicago who were among the first to live near Giltner, Nebraska. In order to make a living and profit from their efforts, they dug a deep well to provide water to travelers on the Oregon Trail. That stop in the road became known as Deepwell Ranch. Later, a couple miles away, the town of Giltner took over the trading post duties and the growing community activities. Laurel Haymarts' father died and his mother moved the family from Phillips to Giltner.

Haymart lived most of his life in Hamilton County, Nebraska. The exception was between 1917 and 1932 when he worked on the railroad.

While he held various jobs in the Giltner community, he is best known as being 'the painter'. According to family friend, Peggy Hinricks, when a model of the old buildings of Giltner was being built for a local celebration, Haymart was consulted as to where the buildings were located and how they were built since he had repaired and painted so many of them over the years. He was married April 20, 1940. "Chief" and his wife Edna Dickey, originally of Central City, Nebraska, moved to Aurora, Nebraska, in 1970.

Haymart often told his friends stories of the old days in Giltner. Over the years Peggy and other friends tried to encourage him to allow his stories to be taped or written down as he talked. At age 84, "Chief" looked back over his life and decided to tell his grandchildren the stories. He told about his life during World War I, the Flu Epidemic, and the Blizzard of 1919. He told of pranks, how he met his wife, bank robberies, horse thieves, and the people and animals in his neighborhood. He described events such as dances during prohibition, hangings, deaths, and the railroad from a teenager's point of view. He left his memories in a small book with two printings. Several friends assisted the production of the book, writing the memories and creating the cover and illustrations: Donna Marie Tobler, with Peggy Hawthorne Hinricks and Beatrice Kingston Rhodes.

In the memories transcribed by his friends, Haymart described completing country school grades which was a fine education back in his day. He described issues with school culture including building conditions, teachers and the older students, and the heating stove. Each issue was described as a memory and will either open the reader's eyes to how things were back in the day or bring a grin or even an outright laugh.

One school memory was how he received the nickname "Chief." It was during a school play. He related that the Old Opera House hosted the school play where the cast of characters included soldiers and Indians. Laurel was cast as an Indian and his best friend was cast as one of the soldiers. The Indians had arrows with padded tips as part of their attire. Laurel says there was "quite a ruckus" after he shot one of those padded arrows which actually hit the back of the head of the soldier. Said soldier fell hard and remained dead as the play continued. Fortunately, the unconscious soldier awoke shortly after the play ended. For Laurel and his near deadly aim, the name "Chief" stuck. Laurel thought it was a funny nickname since he was a Frenchman.

As almost an afterthought, "Chief" tried to remember stories he'd been told about his grandparents. He told of how the immigrants came through New Orleans and went to various French towns around the United States. His story led to Yuma County, Colorado, then on to Nebraska. It has an all too often element of a mother who died in childbirth and a grief stricken father who is unable to care for a newborn, then hands the newborn to strangers to bring up as their own. That newborn, like so many others, grows up. In this case the newborn became Laurel's grandfather.

For the reader interested in Nebraska history in the early 1900's, this publishing endeavor is a snapshot of geography, law and order or lack thereof, culture of the day, politics and life issues from birth to death. It is the great frontier of Hamilton County, Nebraska, through a new grandpa's memories. N

Endnotes, Footnotes, & Sources:

Thank you to Higby-McQuiston Mortuary, Aurora, Nebraska, and Peggy Hinricks, Giltner, Nebraska.

Nebraska Authors Book & Travel Club

Haymart, it is said, loved the outdoors. Take a picnic and enjoy the Giltner, Nebraska, village park in Hamilton County, Nebraska. Take a photo to remember your time at the park.

Robert M. Howard

Date of birth: April 21, 1917
Location of birth: sod house near Flats, NE
Education: country school McPherson County
High School: McPherson Public at Tryon
University of Nebraska, Lincoln BA in Journalism 1941
NE town called home: Hyannis
Military: WWII-NE National Guard, Staff Sargent
Date of Death: Feb. 8, 2013
Location of Death: Alliance, NE

Robert M. Howard, 1996[1]

Known Publications:

Press-Dakotan newspaper in Yankton, SD, Advertising Department.

Grant County Tribune, Hyannis, Publisher, March 13, 1946 to June 2, 1949.

Nebraska Cattleman Magazine, Managing Editor, wrote "Hello There" columns from 1952-1984, and other articles for the magazine until 1988 (retired in 1982).

Howard, Robert M., Earl H. Monahan. Sandhills Horizons A story of the Monahan Ranch and history of the area. History for the Circle-Dot Ranch. Self-publish. 1987.

Van Ackeren, Ruth, Robert M. Howard. Lawrence Bixby: Preserver of The Old Spade Ranch. Idaho: Caxton Printers, distributed by the Nebraska State Historical Society, 1995.

Thornburg, Billie Lee Snyder. Forward by Robert M. Howard. Billie and Me: Kids on a Ranch. Publisher: 2002.

Robert M. Howard, "Bob", was born on April 21, 1917, in a sod house near Flats, Nebraska. He was born in the middle of World War I: the Great War.[2] When asked if he remembered growing up in the aftermath of the war he said 'no', everything was the same: "drought, transportation and cattle prices effect people regardless of war." He did remember going to country school four miles from his sod home in a sod built schoolhouse, and several of the neighbor children who had stayed friends all their lives.[3]

In a January 2013 Authors Project interview, Howard was still promoting the dry land cattle country where he lived most of his life: Flats in McPherson County to Hyannis then Alliance, Nebraska. It was obvious that the rough and tumble environment was in the blood of this gentle-spirited man.

Howard graduated from the University of Nebraska-Lincoln College of Journalism in 1941. "I took a job right after college in Yankton, South Dakota, doing advertising for a newspaper: *Press-Dakotan.* I knew right away that wasn't my favorite part of the journalism business," Howard began. "It didn't last long. I got drafted six weeks after I started the job." It was World War II.[3]

Howard had been drafted from McPherson County and sent to Fort Leavenworth, Kansas, then to Camp Joseph T. Robinson in North Little Rock, Arkansas.[5] His National Guard Unit, Company F out of Gering/Little Rock, was sent to California to patrol the entire west coast of the United States. Bob shook his head and said, "That was a huge area to patrol." [3]

In August 1942, he was on patrol in the Aleutian Islands of Alaska: "about 20 months of water and ships" for the land-locked Nebraskan. His main job was a company clerk. For three and a half years he made sure everyone got paid and the leave and points records were up to date. "I had to record everything that happened to a man so they got paid right."[3]

Robert Howard, 1945[4]

In the summer of 1945, he was sent to Fort Cook and then became one of four men picked to go to the Pacific. He served the rest of the war with a camera and a pen in Hawaii, Guam and other islands, following men around and writing about their activities to send home to their local papers. He chronicled the building of a mess hall and activity hall, the road dirt work and the welding before the same men were sent to Okinawa, Japan, for the final days of the war. Unknown to him, his future co-author Ruth was doing the same type of writing describing men at work and sending articles to the local newspaper from the Air Force Base in Alliance, Nebraska. He was discharged November 11, 1945, and came back to the States directly to Fort Leavenworth and then home.[3.6]

Wife Bernice at Klinotype machine[7]

Upon his arrival in Nebraska, he promptly went to the *Grant County Tribune* in Hyannis and became the publisher. He wrote from March 13, 1946, to June 2, 1949, for the *Tribune*. He smiled when he noted that he could write, but setting up the type for the stories was not his strongest suite. He held out his large hands and fingers, noting that it was hard to set type. The smile continued when he described the local woman, Bernice Miller, who had learned to "master the Model Klinotype." The two married and had four children.

From the *Grant County Tribune*, Howard took a job as secretary and then director of the Nebraska Stock Growers Association and manger of *The Nebraska Cattleman* magazine. "One of the biggest things I learned when I first started writing the cattlemen stories was about the depression that happened while I was at war. I learned more about it from each family I wrote about. I didn't know it myself 'cause I was in the war. Some people here had it really bad."[3]

Debbie Erickson, former employee of the Stock Growers, smiled in remembrance when asked about her former boss. "He was always typing on that old typewriter. He had books and papers and was always writing something. I can still see him typing away at his desk down the hall. He was such a nice man," she said.[8] It wasn't all typing and Stock Grower Association business meetings. Howard served as president of the Nebraska Writer's Guild, 1979-1980. He also had time to take his sons traveling to bull sales with him. "It was work and family," Sue said.[10]

Howard Children[9]
Harold, Harvey, twins Horace & Hester

Howard handed the interviewer bound copies of the famous "Hello There" columns that he and Ruth Van Ackeren had written. In his thirty-five years working for the Stock Growers Association and *The Cattleman Magazine,* he had written over two hundred twenty-five stories about Nebraska producer families. The "Hello There" columns featured cattlemen, usually producers, and their families. Most, but not all, were Sandhills operations and considered the who, what, where, why, and how of the family's move to the Sandhills, how their cattle operation was run, with the ups and downs and the learning curves of the process. "We wanted the generations to know not only their own family history, but how things were for Nebraska cattlemen and non-cattlemen in our state." [3,6]

When asked about various cattlemen issues, Bob was quick to say he rarely wrote about "crimes or that lot." He wanted to inspire his readers with the positive side of the industry and there were other outlets for the rest of "that." His one exception was the shadowy issue(s) of the Old Spade Ranch. Ruth Van Ackeren had written the story with Bartlett Richards Jr.[6] Howard's work with the Lawrence Bixby book was true to his form: he wrote about the preservation of the land and the positive memory of the Old Spade.[11]

Howard was author of a book with rancher Earl H. Monahan.[12] Bob leaned forward in his chair as he said, "It took five years to write. I'd go out to the house and we'd sit down and Earl would talk. I'd write it down and go back again another day. We would get more details and

talk again. Finally, we had enough for a book." The book is more of an as-told-to story about the Monahan Ranch and other ranches in the area rather than a true co-authorship. Bob said, "There were more ranches discussed in the book than just one and it made the history of the area much more real to a lot of people. Earl remembered a lot of things we could use."[3]

Howard photo from <u>Lawrence Bixby: Preserver of Old Spade Ranch</u>[11]

Did Howard have any hobbies or what did he read when he wasn't writing, the interviewer asked? Bob frowned slightly and said, "No, not really any hobbies. I collected a lot of material to read about the people I interviewed. I had to keep up with the cattle and ranching industry so there was always a lot of reading." Did he have any favorite of his own work? "Not an article or story as a favorite, but the changes in the world and how they changed the cattle industry," were the most interesting. He gave the example of one of the biggest things he noticed was the reduction of man-labor in putting up hay and taking care of the cattle. "One man now can operate a machine themselves," he said. It was the telling about the changes through the stories that was a favorite accomplishment for him.[3]

When asked how he wanted people to remember him, he said without hesitation that he felt like he accomplished something when he "helped someone by telling them something that was unknown to them." That is what his stories were all about. Introducing ranchers to each other, chronicling the cattle and ranching industry, and providing the information to non-cattlemen so they would better understand 'what goes on out here'. Then he added, "the off-spring of these pioneers that we interviewed have a history of what it was like then."[3]

Howard provided an article written about him by James Ducey from December 2010 to the interviewer.[13] "It has a little background," he said. He had arranged for the article to be brought to him by his son Horace and daughter-in-law Sue to share when the interview was arranged. He would rather talk about the Sandhills, the cattle, the land and not about himself. The *Grant County News*, "Beef Section Inside," by Sharon M. Wheelock, wrote a tribute to his work and that of Ruth

Van Ackeren for the Sandhills communities. The communities had not forgotten their contributions.[14] Another of his contributions was the creation of the Winkler Memorial Livestock Judging Scholarship at the agricultural college of the University of Nebraska-Lincoln to recognize Cyril W. Winkler and his career promoting livestock in the state. [13]

And, it did not go unnoticed throughout the years that Bob was quick with a thank you note, congratulations card, or condolence to anyone he knew in the community. Even in the later years, his daughter-in-law Sue said that people were coming up to her on the street and commenting that he was still sending cards with notes of things he remembered from long ago. These notes meant the world to the families. Sue said he still read the newspapers and, while he wasn't out in the community much anymore, he got as much information as he could and did what he did best: provide a positive note toward retaining a thriving community.[10]

"I never left the field of journalism-to the very last…here," Bob said as he pondered a new interview question and pointed to his new surroundings in a care home in Alliance, Nebraska. He put his arm on a stack of papers on his bedside stand. "I am still writing," he said "It is like an eight to ten page letter about occurrences that happened while I was interviewing for the "Hello There" stories. He said he vividly remembered conducting an interview in one home at the time when the children came home from school. One of the parents asked their little boy about school that day as the children came into the home. The little boy said that his elementary class was asked by their teacher what they wanted to do when they were twenty-one years old. The child said he told his class that he wanted to have a thousand head of cattle. No one laughed as the child told his story. As Bob looked back at the family and thought about that little boy becoming twenty-one, "he had those thousand head!" Bob said. "It can happen out here."[3]

Robert "Bob" Howard was not the only author to leave an unfinished manuscript on his desk at the time of his passing. Should his final letter be published, he will be among good company.[15] When asked if he was interested in having the "Hello There" columns republished in book form, he said he'd looked into it; but it was very expensive and he didn't think there would be enough response to cover the cost. However, he wasn't in opposition to the idea. Both authors, Bob and Ruth, have passed now so that project is left for someone else to consider.

Many of the historic materials and papers of the Stock Growers and *The Cattleman Magazine* can be found at the Sandoz Museum, on the lower floor of the Cattlemen's Museum at Chadron State College in Chadron, Nebraska. The Knight Museum and Sandhills Center in Alliance is the depository for some of Howard's own memoirs. He left them for future generations to "better understand where they came from."[3] For Bob Howard, his spirit seemed to hold true to and pass on the old song *Home on the Range:* "and seldom is heard a discouraging word and the skies are not cloudy all day." N

Endnotes, Footnotes & Sources:

[1] Photo of Bob Howard at book signing after publication of <u>Lawrence Bixby: Preserver of The Old Spade Ranch</u> in 1995. Photo provided for publication by Stephanie Bixby Graham, January, 2013. "Bob always wore his hat," Graham said. Interview with Stephanie Bixby Graham. Notes in Nancy Sue Hansen's files. January 2013.

[2] Kennedy, David M. <u>Over Here. The First World War and American Society</u>. New York: Oxford Univeristy Press. 1980, 2004; 428 pp.

[3] Interviews with Robert "Bob" Howard, January 8, 2013 to February 8, 2013. Notes in Nancy Sue Hansen's file.

[4] Military photo, Robert 1945. Provided for publication by Horace and Sue on behalf of the family.

[5] www.encyclopediaofarkansas.net. Camp Joseph T. Robinson, North Little Rock, Arkansas.

[6] Hansen, Nancy Sue, and Dush, Barbara Ann. <u>Nebraska Authors Volume One</u>. "Ruth Van Ackeren" Fullerton: D & H Adventures Publishing, 2013.

[7] Photo of Bernice Miller working at the Model Klinotype. Received for publication from son Harvey on behalf of the family.

[8] Interview with Debbie Erickson, January 2013. Notes in Nancy Sue Hansen's files.

[9] Photo: "The Robert Howard '4' 'H' club – Harold, Harvey and twins Hester and Horace provided for publication by Harold and Sue on behalf of the family.

[10] Letter and conversation with Sue Howard. January 2013, April 2013.

[11]Van Ackeren Ruth and Robert M. Howard. <u>Lawrence Bixby: Preserver of The Old Spade Ranch</u>. Idaho: Caxton Printers, distributed by the Nebraska State Historical Society, 1995.

[12] Howard, Robert, and Earl H. Monahan <u>Sandhills Horizons A story of the Monahan Ranch</u> and history of the area. History for the Circle-Dot Ranch. Self-publish. 1987.

[13] Ducey, James E. "Sandhills Historian, Bob Howard." *The Legal Newspaper of Grant County.* (Nebraska) December 16, 2010. Vol 126, Number 19.

[14]*<u>Grant County News,</u> Beef Section Inside..* Vol 116, No 38 May 20, 1999, by Sharon M. Wheelock.

[15] Hansen, Nancy Sue, and Dush, Barbara Ann. <u>Nebraska Authors Volume One</u>. "James Rawley," "Victor Vifquain," "J. Sterling Morton," "William Lawrence," and "David P. Abbott." Fullerton: D & H Adventures Publishing, 2013.

Thanks to Stephanie Bixby Graham for her interview time and enthusiasm to provide information for people interested in the area through the Ellsworth Old School Museum near the Original Old Spade ranch at Ellsworth, Nebraska.

Special thanks to Becci Thomas, Knight Museum and Sandhills Center in Alliance for providing name and location of Bob Howard during research visit to the Center, her work room for research, and her enthusiasm regarding the people and environment of the Sandhills.

Nebraska Authors Book & Travel Club

Visit the Knight Museum and Sandhills Center in Alliance. Attach a ticket or photo reflecting your visit or have this box signed and dated by Becci Thomas or other staff member.

VIRGINIA HELEN (HAHLBECK) INNESS

1943 Yearbook photo
Virginia Hahlbeck

Date of birth: July 28, 1925
Location of birth: Lincoln, NE
Education: District 20 Brunswick, NE: elementary school
Neligh High School, 1943 graduation

Inness, Virginia Helen Hahlbeck. <u>Alta's Visit to Nebraska</u>, Lincoln: Weber Printing Company, 1995, 51 pp.

Inness, Virginia Helen Hahlbeck. <u>Gertruda</u>, Lincoln: Dageforde Publishing, 2000, 76 pp.

From a sunny summer morning in Thedford, Nebraska, in 1921 where Alta's vacation started to her untimely death in March 1930, Alta Baldwin made the most of her life in Nebraska. She was the granddaughter of a Confederate military officer: Captain Jacob Baldwin. She was accustomed to the Appalachian Mountains of Virginia and coal dust. As she started her visit to Nebraska, she described sights and smells and differences in customs and lifestyles. Some were similar to how she grew up and some were rather strange to her, like sod houses and stories of the 1888 blizzard.

Alta had been a secretary in Washington D.C. during World War I. Her travel to Nebraska to meet with a secretary friend she had worked with in D.C. at the Department of Defense turned into whirlwind friendship with a local school teacher, Harry Hahlbeck, a WWI veteran who had been stationed at Camp Funston. Both were around thirty-years-old when they married on September 10, 1921. Harry took a teaching position in Creighton, Nebraska.

In 1924 the couple moved to Bristow, Nebraska, where he became superintendent. Moving was not one of Alta's enjoyments, but their work in the local Methodist churches and other organizations such as the Masonic Lodges gave them a sense of order wherever they went. Virginia came along in the summer of 1925 amidst her parents' concern for the coal miners' safety and possible unions being created in the mountains Alta's family called home. Politics and the issues of prohibition were also conversation topics.

Alta was a prohibitionist, but several in her husband families were Nebraska bootleggers. As the tenth year of prohibition (1930) was celebrated, the Metropolitan Life Insurance Company report showed they had six times as many deaths from alcoholism among their policyholders then they had before prohibition. Community discussion was both emotional and aware of these facts.

Alta's life with Harry became a sense of wonderment for the little girl named Virginia. The untimely death of her mother in March 1930, after the birth and death of infant Geraldine, left holes in the hearts of the five-year-old and her father. Virginia was left with family stories.

On the back cover of her first book, Virginia noted that the majority of her growing up years was in Antelope County, Nebraska. According to records at the Neligh Oakdale Schools in Neligh, Virginia went to country school at Brunswick, a small town near Neligh. In the Neligh Warrior yearbook it notes she was nicknamed "Ginny." A classmate, Merlin Hansen, said that the classes were arranged so the students sat in alphabetical order, and he remembered Virginia because they usually had just one person sitting between them. He thoughtfully remembered that he considered her a friend, but they didn't do a lot of things together because he lived in the country and she lived in town. He provided the Nebraska Authors Project® with her last known address from class reunions. When the authors tried to reach her through that address, the letter was returned as undeliverable. The printer of her book was also out of business, and a letter to the publisher was returned.

A file was located at the Nebraska State Historical Society with a

Virginia with father Harry.
Winter 1949

letter she had written to an Aunt Flora in Toledo, Ohio, in 1949. The twelve-page letter was complete with narrative and photographs of the historic blizzards of the year. She included photos of her father and of Joyce Jensen who stayed with Virginia while going to school. At the end of the letter Virginia wrote, "Well this concludes the story. I hope you liked it." Perhaps the letter was practice sharpening skills she would use later to write her two books.

Merlin said Virginia had married into an Inness family of Oakdale. According to the county clerk's office in Neligh, William C. Inness and Virginia Hahlbech were married June 11, 1950. According to the dedication in her book they had two children: Bruce and Carol. It was when one of her grandchildren asked her about her father that she realized that both of her parents had passed away before her own children knew them. Her father died suddenly in 1956 while Superintendent of Schools in Antelope County. Her mother Alta, the Captain's granddaughter, died in 1930. Alta became the focus of her first book.

According to the forward, Virginia did some research, including information given to her on trips to see her mother's relatives in 1943 and 1959. Armed with letters from her parents, which the relatives had saved, and speeches given by her father, some of them from WWI, she started on her quest to provide a foundational story for her generations.

Virginia may have intended the story to simply reflect her mother's military heritage, and how her parents met and began life in the 1920s; but by her descriptions, she provided a history of thought and lifestyle common to the citizen of the state of that day. Virginia's two books may be hard to find, but they are about real life with joy and pain. Reading them is a snapshot of the history in Nebraska. N

Cover of first book

119

1943 Class Reunion in 2003, Neligh High School.
Front row L-R: Iris (Reinke) Flenniken, Virginia (Hahlback) Inness, Nadeen (Good) Eymann, Audrey (Peterson) Adams, Meldon (Bertwell) Nelson, Norma (Miller) Hutchinson, Melva (Huston) Gadeken, Betty (Reutzel) Petersen.
Back row L-R: Merlin Hansen, Lloyd Forsell, Melvin Allen, Bud Furstenau, John Gadeken, Roy Schmidt.

Endnotes, Footnotes & Sources:

Virginia Inness. Nebraska State Historical Society Collections. Reviewed December 2012.

The Neligh News. Hahlbeck Succumbs, November 1, 1956. Reviewed September 2012.

Special thanks to Linda Wilkinson, Administrative Secretary Neligh-Oakdale Schools, for her valuable assistance; and to Merlin Hansen, class of 1943, for his time to interview and providing the class photo.

Thanks to Ronald Marshall, Antelope County Veteran Services; Eleanor Brady, Lisa Payne and Teresa Moore of the Clerk's office; and Jennifer Norton of the Neligh Public Library.

Nebraska Authors Book & Travel Club
Attend an event at Neligh High School (Neligh-Oakdale) and attach a ticket or photo.

MAXINE BRIDGMAN ISACKSON

Date of Birth: Nov. 7, 1933
Location of Birth: Near Ardmore, OK
Education: elementary at rural schools;
Ericson High School, Ericson, NE;
North Platte School of Commerce,
North Platte, NE
Currently lives in Brady, NE

Maxine Isackson

Known Publications:

Isackson, Maxine Bridgman. <u>The Sandhills Beckon</u>, Nebraska Print Works, Ogallala, Nebraska; First Printing 1977, Second Printing 2004, Third Printing 2007, Fourth Printing 2011. 156 pp.

Isackson, Maxine Bridgman. <u>Leather Hinges</u>. Spectrum, North Platte, Nebraska, and Nebraska Print Works, Ogallala, Nebraska; First Printing 2005, Second Printing 2009, Third Printing 2011. 236 pp.

Isackson, Maxine Bridgman. <u>Daughter of the Half Moon</u>, Nebraska Print Works, Ogallala, Nebraska; First Printing 2005, Second Printing 2009, Third Printing 2011. 297 pp.

TRIOLOGY:

Isackson, Maxine Bridgman. <u>Come Green Grass</u>, Spectrum, North Platte, Nebraska, and Nebraska Print Works, Ogallala, Nebraska; First Printing 2005, Second Printing 2009, Third Printing 2011. 308 pp.

Isackson, Maxine Bridgman. <u>Prairie Wind</u>, Nebraska Print Works, Ogallala, Nebraska; First Printing 2009, Second Printing 2011. 167 pp.

Isackson, Maxine Bridgman. <u>Shifting Sand</u>, Nebraska Print Works, Ogallala, Nebraska; First Printing 2009, Second Printing 2011. 240 pp.

Isackson, Maxine Bridgman. <u>Rustling Cottonwoods</u>, Nebraska Print Works LLC, Ogallala, Nebraska, 2011. 227 pp.

Maxine Bridgman Isackson was born in a rustic one-room log cabin near Ardmore, Oklahoma. Her parents, Howard and Thelma Bridgman, met while Howard and a friend were running the McCoy-Bridgman Wild West Show. The show traveled through several states for a few years. They were at Ardmore, Oklahoma, when the tight economy caused them to close the show. Howard took a job on the Double Dot Ranch where the young couple lived for the next three years.

While Thelma was pregnant with Maxine, "her pregnancy did little to curtail her activities," Maxine stated in her first book, <u>The Sandhills Beckon</u>. "She did give up riding the green colts but still accompanied Howard on a gentle horse up until a few weeks before her confinement. I have teasingly asked my mother if perhaps a few bumps against the saddle horn by my unborn skull might explain some of my peculiarities."

Maxine was born in November of 1933 – the same year cattle prices hit bottom, pastures were bare and feed practically non-existent. Her parents decided to move further west, where a cowboy could make a living. They would need the extra income, as three more children would be added to the Bridgman family as time ticked by.

The Bridgman's picked up stakes, moved to Wyoming, and found work on a farm. But "cowboys have a natural aversion to plows, bib overalls and milk cows," Maxine noted. Two years later, they traveled to Vashon Island, Washington, to visit relatives. After a hearty family reunion, the family settled in the Idaho mountains; however, the harsh winter months quickly dissipated their eagerness to settle there. It was about this time a letter arrived from an uncle in Nebraska, stating that a cousin was looking for a cattle hand. The opportunity sparked Howard's memories of his childhood in Nebraska. "At last it was settled," Maxine wrote. "We would move to this strange place called the Sandhills."

"My parents were people who moved a lot," Maxine explained. "They didn't let grass grow under their feet. Our people lived in Nebraska and Wyoming."

Maxine attended several rural schools, and sometimes had to find to board and room near the school since it was located too many miles from her home.

"Because I moved constantly, I was always the new girl and the library was where I turned first. That was where I found my companionship until I made friends," she said of her early years. "As soon as I learned to read, I began to read books of all kinds. I always said my favorite Christmas present was a large fat book containing wonderful stories like Heidi, The Silver Skates and Black Beauty. That was in the early grades. Then I discovered Pearl Buck and I've been reading ever since."

Books also became Maxine's close companions because "they were something you could carry from one place to another," she reflected of the family's many moves. "And I had younger siblings I told stories to."

By this time the Sandhills had a stronghold on Maxine's heart. She joined in the branding days and cattle drives. The memories recorded in her first book reflect that growing appreciation of her surroundings: "Dad and I would leave early, when the sun was just beginning to warm up, making a circle of the home pastures where the cows and calves were still being held. What a joy it was to ride through the awakening herd. Most of the cows were standing, giving the final touches to their babies' baths. These were administered with rough wet tongues while their offspring unconcernedly nursed, little white tipped tails wagging...

"The calves, tummies full, would lift sassy faces with chins still drooling bubbles of milk froth. They would scamper, tail in air, in and out among the cows until they'd gathered several playmates to join in a game of tag or just plain showing off for their elders.

"Wild flowers grew in haphazard profusion, adding touches of gold, purple and pink to our early morning world, lidded by the clear blue sky. You'd have to be half dead and on your way to one place or the other, not to feel a tug at the old heartstrings when you found yourself in the middle of all that surging, bounding new life.

"Pausing on a knoll, Dad gazed out over the scene we'd just left. He licked a cigarette paper, absent mindedly shaping it around the tobacco and said, 'Well Max, in your day you'll see bigger hills, taller trees, some high buildings and things folks call sights, but you'll never see anything to top this.' At the time I wondered, but he was right."

As a youngster, writing hadn't been one of Maxine's dreams; however, it may have been unconsciously pulling at her heartstrings through a childhood experience she shares in her book:

"On one of our stops at the old place, I noticed a wreck of a type-writer that had been tossed in the junk pile. That abandoned machine fascinated me and I began to plan how I might get it home. I mentioned it to Dad but he didn't seem to think we needed any more junk carted back to the ranch. Not to be discouraged, I decided to get it home, one way or another. Once it was there, everyone would surely see what a really wonderful gadget it was.

"I tried to lift the machine once, and I knew it was too heavy to heft up on my saddle horse, so that was out. There was no use asking Mom to take the little ones in the car on such a wild goose chase. The only thing left, was for me to manage on foot. Of course it was too heavy for me to carry, so I took a big gunny sack along. I tumbled the ancient typewriter, which had a goodly amount of sand imbedded among its keys, into the sack and began the long trek home. And long it was, for though only a mile had to be covered, it took me two hours. I'd drag the sack for a ways, until I was all pooped out, then set and rest, regaining enough energy to make another hitch at it. In this fashion, I at last gained the backyard, where I installed the old backbreaker in all its glory on an orange crate.

"Finding out what I'd done, Mom prophesied that I would have back trouble the rest of my life, but they let me keep the rusty eyesore and I played office to my heart's content."

With the grim news of World War II and the Sandhills suffering from the dry years, another move was made to Wyoming where Maxine's father found work in the iron mines.

It was during this time her love for reading continued to evolve – a trait she attributes to her father who also loved to read. "I made the trips to the library, hiking the mile into town and back," she said of her new surroundings. "Our evenings were usually spent reading and listening to the radio."

In her book, Maxine notes: "One of my favorite stops was the tiny town library. I'd never gotten over my addiction to reading. Books were nearly as important to me as food. I would always be able to nose out a library in a strange town as quick as an alcoholic could a liquor store. I would curl up with a good story and forget my homesickness or anything else that was troubling me."

Eventually life took the Bridgman family back to the Sandhills. Maxine attended Ericson High School and later married; then went back to school and graduated from the School of Commerce in North Platte. She settled into Sandhill country with her farmer/rancher husband, Richard Isackson. "There's a special culture connected to the Sandhills, and the ranch life there is different from other places. It isn't one I particularly would have chosen, probably because so much of that is in isolation, but I admire it tremendously."

It was during the time her first son left for college that Maxine's father died of multiple sclerosis. "My sons and their cousins had never known him except in a wheel chair, more or less, as it got worse. So I wrote his story so they would know him as he was, because he was quite a cowboy ... a genuine cowboy."

The research and writing of the book, which is a biography of her father, took two years. The result, The Sandhills Beckon, covers a lot of territory and people. Maxine found after she had finished it, "I couldn't stop writing. I was hooked. So I went to fiction, which I loved, and tried to portray life in the Sandhills as it truly existed, and I've been writing ever since."

Maxine's next writing project was a triology – Come Green Grass, Prairie Wind and Shifting Sand – bringing her characters up from the 1890s to the first world war and after the war.

"There's a lot of modern books that are written about the Sandhills that I can find flaws in. I grew up knowing so many of the old timers, and a lot of my relatives were the old timers. I had listened to their stories and was always fascinated by the things that happened, the way they happened, and the way of life. I wanted to get that across to the young people – how it really was to live in the dugouts for instance. Everything wasn't romantic, everything wasn't fun. In fact, most of it was just the opposite. So I have tried to portray life as it really was in the late 1800s."

Another book is about a young couple's first year of homestead life, and "what a shock that was to their constitution to come out here, and start out in a dugout. Life was so much harder on the women than the men because they were the ones stuck in the little dugout with the baby, and trying to get laundry dry and work in the little confined areas. The story is fictionalized, but it's based on the way that life truly was."

Maxine's latest and seventh book, <u>Rustling Cottonwoods</u>, is again written of the Sandhills of Nebraska that she knows so well, and garnered from stories passed down by those who pioneered those very hills. She is currently working on her eighth publication.

Maxine has garnered a first place in the Nebraska Mother's Short Story Contest, and won third place in the Bess Streeter Aldrich contest. She also freelances and has had stories published in The *Fencepost, Nebraska Farmer, Good Ol' Boys, Farm Journal,* <u>The Pelican in the Desert</u> and <u>Leaning into the Wind : Women Write from the Heart of the West</u>.

What this Nebraska author would like her readers to discover and understand is "how people truly lived, what it was really like in the homestead days and the ranching days," she said. "I try to make my books as authentic as possible. It wasn't all gun fights and that type of thing. There was a lot of violence, but it was mostly a day-to-day struggle simply to live and aim at success. Some made it and some didn't."

Retired from active farm/ranch life, Maxine and her husband still live in the Wild Horse Valley north of Brady surrounded by cattle, corn fields, and the hills and canyons they love. B

Endnotes, Footnotes & Sources:

Interview with Maxine Bridgman Isackson/photos by Barbara Ann Dush.

www.maxineisackson.com.

Thank you to Paula Hannon, clerk at the Brady Dairy Queen, for answering Nancy's question if she had ever heard of author Isackson. Hannon responded that Maxine was still living and was one of her favorite authors.

Maxine Bridgman Isackson displays two of her books: The Sandhills Beckon and Leather Hinges.

Nebraska Authors Book & Travel Club

Signature or visit "Brady Days" or one of Brady's eating places. Check the Brady website at www.villageofbrady.com for details. Attach a copy of a receipt or photo reflecting your visit.

GEORGE LOUIS JACKSON

Date of birth: Jan. 3, 1893
Location of birth: on a farm in Custer County near Mason City, NE
Education: entered Round Grove country school 1899
University of Nebraska School of Agriculture 1915
UNL, BS and MA in Education, 1927
Military: US Navy, World War I, 1917
Barracks No. NE 2528, T.P.A.*
Date of Death: Oct. 6, 1978
Home at time of death: Kearney, NE

George L. Jackson
University of Nebraska 1927
yearbook photo[1]

Known Publications:

Jackson, George L. The Honky-Tonk Piano in Deadwood Gulch, The Saga of John O. Jackson, non fiction. Article found in the files of the Custer County Historical Society, Broken Bow, no date on the article, reviewed June 27, 2012.

Faulkner, Virginia complier and editor. Round-Up Nebraska Reader. Lincoln: University of Nebraska Press. 1957. 493 pp. "Cyclone Yarns" by George L. Jackson; page 269, first published by Prairie Schooner, Lincoln, Nebraska. April 27, 1929.

Jackson, George L. Daddy-Tell Me a Story. Drawings by Mildred Palmgren and Walter Thomas, Kearney, Nebraska: Pioneer Publishing Co, 1962. 111 pp. Juvenile fiction. Book for ages 4-8.

Jackson, George L. The Wonderful World Outdoors, poem, by George L. Jackson dedicated to the Fish, Game and Park Commissions in the various states of the United States. Copyrighted 1962. Copy received from daughter Georgia Van Ornam, July 20, 2012.

Jackson, George L., <u>Sod House Memories</u>, published by the Sod House Society. Copyright Francis Jacobs Albert. Vol I-II-III. First printing June 1972, 285 pp. *The Bob-Tailed Coyote* p 131, and *The Snow-water Bath* p 226. [Copy of *Bob-Tail* also found in files of the Custer County Historical Society, Broken Bow, no date on the article, reviewed June 27, 2012].

He submitted stories to the newspaper in Custer County, the *Kearney Daily Hub,* and *Omaha World Herald* as he and his wife traveled around the world over several years.

According to a typewritten article that found its way into the files of the Custer County Historical Society written by George L. Jackson, it was a honky-tonk piano headed to a gold miner's 'entertainment establishment' in the Black Hills that brought George's Swedish uncle, John O. Jackson [Johann Oskar Jakobsson], to the Great Plains from working the mines in Pennsylvania. It was a back injury in the transport of that piano which took John to Grand Island, Nebraska. The funds he had made in the transportation of the piano made it possible to settle in Custer County. [2,3]

Like many immigrant families, John's brother Ludwig Matthew joined him working on the land. Ludwig soon met the hired girl, Sadie Bray, and they married. George Louis Jackson was the oldest of seven children born to Ludwig Matthew and Sadie. All of the children were born and raised in a sod house. Later it was this sod house experience that gave George insight and understanding to become an active member in the Nebraska Sod House Society and to write about his experiences.

George's daughter, Georgia, remembers her father telling that their Uncle John hired workers to work his farm, but their father didn't because he had five boys to help him. The boys would sometimes become irritated in this arrangement. But George learned the lessons of the stewardship of the land well, and it stayed with him throughout his life. By example it was taught to his daughter.

A newspaper article about a Round Grove country school reunion indicated George entered the school in 1899. [4] The school history showed that at one time there were ten grades at the school. There were only eight grades available at Round Grove when George attended. He

130

completed school and continued to farm before attending the University of Nebraska, School of Agriculture, in Lincoln. He graduated in 1915.

George and his brother Edward went to Wyoming for 'free land' that was available for homesteading. They were awarded plots side-by-side. The requirement for this 'free land' was that it had to be improved and that the homesteader had to live there. The brothers didn't have a lot of funds for improvement so they made a unique arrangement. They built a temporary building over their property lines giving Edward a place for a bed on his land where he slept and George a place for a bed on his land where he slept. Their plan met the requirement.[3]

George Jackson
World War I veteran.[5]

It was now World War I. George and his brother knew that they would be given time for homesteading for serving in the military. George went into the Navy. According to his daughter Georgia's recollections, her father told her he soon learned not to volunteer for anything. He watched the men be lined up and officials would ask things like: "All lawyers step forward." These men would be sent to some dirty, laborious job. He was sent to Harvard for the signal school.[3]

Georgia recalls that her father would not eat pumpkin pie, telling how the Navy cooks would prepare a crust, dump in a can of pumpkin without seasoning and "bake the mess." George was among thousands worldwide that became ill with what would become known in history as the Spanish flu. He was among the few who survived. Georgia remembers her father saying the "medical people did not treat him as his mother would have."

When he finished signal school, the war had basically ended. He joined the signal crew of a ship bound for Great Britain using his signal skills before returning to the United States and making his way back to his Wyoming homestead.

Georgia also recalled her father talking about the lack of water. While they had a small well at the homestead during those years, the brothers would move the animals downstream, give the water some time to settle and then the water in the creek would be clean enough to drink.

Needing income, George was hired to teach school at a little country school near Lost Spring. He taught there for a year and met his wife to be, Mildred Hungerford. George and Mildred drove to Douglas, Wyoming, on June 21, 1922, and were married.[6] After a brief honeymoon they drove to Nebraska and George taught a year at a newly consolidated school in southern Custer County: Hoosier Valley School.[4]

It was during this time that George's hard working parents retired and moved from their farm home to Mason City. George and Mildred moved onto the Jackson farm. According to Georgia, her father knew how to farm, but there were things about it he didn't like. One cold, windy winter day when George came into the house after picking and shucking corn he said, "Millie, let's go to school." Georgia said her mother told about suggesting this option for them for a while. According to Georgia, "the remaining corn was sold in the field," and both Mildred and George returned to school at the University of Nebraska in 1924.[3]

George received both a BS and MA degree by 1927. Lowry Wimberly of the University English Department was in the process of creating a literary magazine called the *Prairie Schooner* in 1927 which, in time, became known as a quality publication throughout the country. In the April 27, 1927, issue a story by Jackson, *Cyclone Yarns*, was published. [7]

Professor Jackson and Grafton Team Trophy, 1929[8]

After graduation he was hired as the Superintendent of Schools at Grafton, Nebraska. This meant doing just about everything including coaching the basketball team. Georgia said her "father didn't know anything about basketball when he started, but he was a quick learner." If you were to walk the hall of the Grafton Village offices today, you will find a basketball trophy in a trophy case announcing the victory of the Grafton team of 1929 at the York Classic Basketball Tournament. Photographs in a hanging glass display case show that the superintendent that year was "Professor Jackson." He was in Grafton for two years. It was during this time that Georgia was born.

At this point, George and his family had moved to Lincoln and he had joined a janitorial company as a salesman going to schools. It was the beginning of the Great Depression and the company closed. "My parents, being the thrifty kind, had saved money. They found a very reasonably priced farm in Custer County that they could buy," Georgia explained. The little family moved out of the city.

She continued, "They had no farm equipment so they had to rent out the land to be farmed, but for the next five years they had security with a home, garden, orchard, and farm animals to sustain them with income."

Georgia remembers the farming area as a kind, friendly community. "We had lots of family in the area. I am still in touch with the girl, Bonnie Leonhardt Stephens, who lived at a nearby farm. Mildred Palmgren, who did the drawings for Daddy Tell Me A Story was our teacher at our little country school."

While still on the farm, George diversified again and in the mid 1930s began a school supply and publishing business: the Pioneer Publishing Company. He and Mildred began by selling school supplies and later library books for schools. Georgia remembers her father would leave on Monday morning and return on Friday evening. It was Mildred who kept the farm operating with chores, including milking the seven cows twice a day, and the parenting of their elementary school daughter. Saturday and Sunday were the days the packing, shipping of supplies and the book work was done. "It was long hours during the school year, but the company was very good to us," Georgia said. When a house became available in Mason City with running water, indoor plumbing and electricity they moved. Georgia remembers, "It was no longer a mile and half walk to country school."

George and Mildred decided they would like to live in a larger town. They moved to Kearney with a population of 10,000 in 1940, two blocks from Kearney State Teachers College [now the University of Nebraska at Kearney]. Georgia remembers being able to walk to college classes. They owned and operated the publishing business at that location until George sold it to a long time employee and he retired in 1970.

If you were reading old newspapers from *Custer County*, the *Kearney Hub* or the *Omaha World Herald,* you might find travel stories complete with history of the area from all over the world written by George Jackson. Georgia recalled those times: "My parents enjoyed traveling. We were the only family I know from central Nebraska who went to the 1939 World's Fair in New York City, which was wonderful! Along the way we stayed with friends and relatives and went into Canada and to Niagara Falls. We were gone for weeks. In 1953 my parents came to Germany to visit my husband and me. At that time they visited many parts of Europe and completed a dream to meet their wonderful Swedish relatives."

Later there were trips to Mexico, Bermuda, and a cruise to Central America. "They came to visit my husband, two children and me in Puerto Rico. But their highlight was several weeks in a tour of Africa." During his travels within the continental United States, George saw the efforts and issues the Park Commissions had in maintaining the recreation areas for the general public. He wrote a poem dedicated to the Fish, Game and Park Commissions in the various states of the United States of America to thank them for their tireless work, and remind those who used the facilities that they should be more thoughtful and revere nature, keeping the future generations in mind.

As the years progressed George found time for a membership in the First United Presbyterian Church, American Legion, World War I Barracks and T.P.A.* In the early 1960s, George wrote his thoughts about what he saw happening in the education system in the United States. He was concerned with one issue that plagued the day labeled "Why Johnny Can't Read." Many experts discussed the subject. George presented his thoughts in his children's book, <u>Daddy, Tell Me a Story</u>. He wrote that his "book was for readers, not just picture-lookers. Children learn to read by reading-not by looking at pictures. We want them to learn to read. Here are stories with action, plot and climax. They stimulate imagination. Children catch on that exciting things can be found on a printed page. This discovery is the key that opens the door into a literate world."

He dedicated the book 'To my daughter Georgia Lois, who enjoyed these stories when she was a very little girl a long time ago." While the book is out of print, the Nebraska Authors Project® has been given permission to reprint the essay, "Why Johnny Can't Read," which precedes several stories for young readers. The essay is presented in this publication and is just as relevant today as it was when it was published in 1962.

It was just after World War II when the farming roots surfaced for George and Mildred and they purchased a farm near Gibbon. George was remembered as a progressive landlord who tried new farming methods. In a *Kearney Hub* newspaper article entitled, "Woman gives land in parents' memory," by Lori Potter: ninety-seven acres of the Jackson land was donated to the National Audubon Society's Rowe Sanctuary as a tribute to George and Mildred by Georgia.[9]

The Nebraska Authors Project® was introduced to George by his book and later in memories of Georgia who corresponded from her home in Florida. *"When my parents and I visited our Swedish family in 1953, I asked why my grandfather had immigrated to the United States. The lady who translated for us, very vehemently told us that in Sweden a penny would always be a penny, but in the United States a penny had the chance to be a dollar! Ludwig Matthew came to this country a number of years after his brother John O. Jackson had settled in Custer County. He is on the census as being a brother to John O. Jackson and a laborer on his farm. My grandfather was an extraordinary man! He had just two years of formal schooling in Sweden. He learned English during the two-week journey on the ship using a Swedish-English dictionary. From what my mother told me, his English was very good. A minister was to say Ludwig Matthew was 'the most well-read man he ever met.' Four of his children became teachers."*

Thus, George had a heritage of learning with books and discovery, a work ethic and the understanding of how to use his talents to his best ability in whatever situation the world and the economy gave him. He had learned to see an opportunity and take advantage of it. His thrifty behavior from the beginning had maintained his family through the Depression years, several different wars and world conditions. His daughter followed her parents example and left Nebraska with a legacy of land and options for nature education.

Georgia wrote, "My father was a multi-talented, kind, decent, generous man and a progressive farmer. Writing was an important part of my father's life. I'm sure he would be so pleased to have this article included in the Nebraska Author's Project®." N

Endnotes, Footnotes & Sources:

*T.P.A. means Travelers Protective Association. Assistance with Liberty Loan campaigns, Red Cross campaigns and other war efforts.

[1] The Cornhusker, 1927. Yearbook verification of George Louis Jackson graduation. Thank you to UNL archives for assistance in locating the photo.

[2] Custer County Historical Society, Broken Bow. Jackson, George L., *The Honky-Tonk Piano in Deadwood Gulch, The Saga of John O. Jackson,* no date on the article. Reviewed June 27, 2012.

[3] Correspondence with Georgia (Jackson) Van Ornam, Florida, in files of Nancy Sue Hansen.

[4] Custer County Historical Society, Broken Bow, Round Rock School, Hoosier Valley, from archives. Reviewed June 27, 2012.

[5] *Kearney (Nebr) Daily Hub.* October 9, 1978. Local, Area Deaths. *George L. Jackson*, Microfilm,@ Kearney Public Library. Reviewed 6/21/2012.

[6] Internet obituaries. *The Lusk Herald.* November 2, 1978. "Former Rural Teacher Dies" reviewed 6/20/2012.

[7] Round-Up Nebraska Reader. *"Cyclone Yarns"* by George L. Jackson; originally published by Prairie Schooner, Lincoln, Nebraska. April 27, 1927.

[8] Photo by Nancy Sue Hansen during research at Grafton. Interview and photos in Hansen files.

[9] Potter, Lori. "Woman gives land in parents memory." *Kearney Hub.*

Custer County Chief, October 19, 1978, Broken Bow, Nebraska page 5. "George L. Jackson"

Thanks to the Custer County Historical Society: Carol Christen, curator; Rosalie McKnight and Tammy Hendrikson for their help at the beginning of the search when all we knew was that an author named George L. Jackson was originally from Custer County.

Thank you to Roxann Baumann, Clerk of the Village of Grafton, for the time spent looking for photos of "Professor Jackson" and opening the trophy case to verify a surprise fact for the story.

And thanks to Robert J. Routh who took time to respond to the Nebraska Authors Project® research inquiry addressed to the old Publishing Company and for providing information for Georgia and the Project authors to contact each other. (Robert is the son of Truxton W. Routh who worked for George Jackson and Pioneer Publishing Company from 1948-1969. In 1969, Truxton purchased the Company from Jackson.)

Special Thanks to Georgia (Jackson) Van Ornam, Florida, for permission to reprint her father's essay and for providing the photographs and notes about her parents. Her letters and phone calls increased the accuracy of this story and are much appreciated.

George Jackson
and
Mildred Hungerford
Begin a
Great Adventure,
Douglas, Wyoming
June 21, 1922

Mr. and Mrs. George L. Jackson
Kearney, Nebraska
After
Fifty Years of Happy Living
June 21, 1972

50th wedding anniversary.

CARL DEAN JENNINGS

Carl D. Jennings, 2004

Date of birth: July 14, 1955
Location of birth: Omaha
Education: Omaha Westside High School, 1974
Attended University of Nebraska-Lincoln; University of Nebraska at Omaha; University of State of New York, Albany, bachelor's 1987.
Military: U.S. Navy 1974-1991
Currently lives in Omaha.

Known Publications:

Jennings, Carl D. Omaha's Peony Park : an American Legend. Arcadia Publishing, 2001.

Wrote numerous publications for military tasks throughout career.

"**I** got letters from all over the country and even overseas when the Peony Park book was published," smiled Carl Jennings over a cup of coffee. "The Park meant so many good times to so many generations of people." As the Cass Street operations closed down Jennings had piles of photos, mountains of equipment and a near lifetime of memories. With encouragement from friends he sorted the photos, added captions and presented the basic history of one of the premier Great Plains entertainment oasis based in Omaha, Nebraska, from 1919-1995. The thirty-five acres were a refuge during economic depressions and years of plenty for many families. Carl Jennings found a personal stability through his job at the Park through the ups and downs of life, too.[2,3,4]

During the 1950s symptoms of continued stress after wartime wasn't called PTSD (Post Traumatic Stress Disorder), but many a post-war military member had injuries and memories that didn't heal. Some military members, from any theatre of war, gradually worked themselves back into society and no one was the wiser about the snap-shots of terror that occasionally sparked the senses. Some, however, took a bottle or other means to dull the continual reign of terror that accompanied them home. Sometimes a member's spouse joined the unhealthy activities to drown the family sorrows in one way or the other. Carl Dean Jennings was the son of such a circumstance. It was within his first eighteen months of life that his parents asked the maternal grandmother to care for him. It was the home of [John N.] Hilma Anderson that shaped his life both in her loving guidance and location of the home.

"I grew up around older people with my grandmother and her friends," Jennings explained during an interview. "So, when I got a job just down the street from our home, at age fourteen, I got along with the older men in charge. They'd tell me to go do something and I'd do it, just like I did with my grandmother." It would be the diligence to the task at hand, dependability, and not asking questions that he had been taught by his grandmother that became his trademark.

"I had been swimming at the Park and had made friends with the lifeguard and others that worked there," Jennings reminisced. "John Green [now a teacher at UN-O] and Bill Cathright [now a dentist] interviewed me and I started working at the pool in the summer and the ballroom in the winter. It was maintenance, painting, and clean-up work."[4]

"We had been a Navy family for generations," Jennings continued. "It was just assumed I'd go to the Navy right out of high school, so I didn't take college prep classes. I figured I might get some classes later on the G.I. Bill, but it would be the Navy right away." He signed a delayed entry program while still in high school at Omaha Westside.

While the Vietnam War loomed and high school graduation and draft cards were in the conversations, Jennings had his job with all the long hours. "I worked for Joe Malec, Sr. in the beginning. Later when his son Joe Malec, Jr. came back from the Navy [Academy graduate class of 1955], he and I would work together to keep Peony Park in top operation. When the Park at the Cass Street location closed in 1995, it was my Westside classmate Joe Malec, III and I who made the arrangements for me to purchase it," Jennings explained.

"There was always a job for me when I came back from wherever my military unit was sent: Vietnam, South America, Desert Storm or Afghanistan, and anywhere else in those years," Jennings continued. "I learned early that although there was a job for me with increasing responsibilities, I would never be able to advance to the core group of management. At first I didn't understand, but after a while I figured out they were near the same age and they had been together a long time both at work and in the community.

Partial wall and fence of old
Peony Park at 78th & Cass[5]

"Peony Park really didn't have the Peony plants, the gardens outside the park did. Carl Rosenfield owned the gardens. In fact, if you drive around the 78th and Cass area some of the yards have some of the original peonies from the gardens," Jennings said, leaning forward in his chair, comfortable in the telling of part of Omaha history. "See, back around 1919 it was considered a 'trip to the country' for the Omaha city families to drive 'out' of town on Lincoln Highway (Highway 30) to Peony Gardens, stay at the Peony Inn, get automobile fuel at the little gas station or eat at the restaurant across from the Gardens." There was an outside stage called the Royal Grove. After a time a beer garden was added and then a ballroom: the Royal Terrace. The famed swimming pool with the beach was added in 1926. Joe Malec, Sr. and his two brothers started the amusements in 1958, when Jennings was three. More amusements were added in 1970. "I helped build the roller coaster in 1972," Jennings noted. At the end of its seventy-five year operation the Peony Park Corporation owned a number of small businesses including the Warehouse Ballroom near Carter Lake, a portion of the New Tower Inn, office buildings and rental properties.

Peony Park's golden age was during the 1930s and 1940s when it became a big band magnet. Mr. Malec is credited with coining the term "Champaign Music" as a trademark of the Lawrence Welk Band. The Welk band used the Park as its official headquarters in the 1930s. They weren't the only headliners. Jennings thought back to history. He had heard about, "the Tommy Dorsey band, the Glenn Miller Band, Duke Ellington, Guy Lombardo and the Royal Canadians, Mel Dun, the Bobby Mills Band, then Bobby Vee, Ricky Nelson, the Beach Boys, Pearl Jam and so many more. The Carter Lake booking agents, like Shorty Vess, could get some real popular ones. The ballroom was built so it was acoustic for the big band sound before sound systems. Bands liked to play there."[4]

It wasn't just the music that created headlines, so did the political events and other public activities. Jennings remembered working his Peony Park job during political events at the ballroom involving Vice President Agnew, Presidents Ford, Reagan and Bush Sr. He shook his head, saying there were many memories of secret service actions and meeting various family members and their friends at each event. He related his favorite story: "I had just come home from a military tour in Desert Storm and I was in uniform with my young son in the crowd at the Ballroom. Bob Kerrey was announcing he was going to run for President. Kerrey came off the stage and said, 'How are you doing Carl?' and then patted my son on the head, got down eye level with him and said, 'Aren't you glad to have your dad home from war?' I won't ever forget that."[4]

Remembering the day-to-day operations of the park and some of the highlights are interspersed with memories of military activities for Jennings. He flew out on his first amphibious training mission in 1975. His training would eventually place him in Saigon as the country fell and the evacuations were taking place. He returned to Nebraska in the summer of 1977 and to his job at Peony Park. Fighting for freedom for others in faraway places would soon take a turn for Jennings and he would be experiencing the fight for justice for his mother in his hometown.

"I was to be at a Navy Reserve class one morning [August 1979], but I forgot my books so I went home to get them. It was Saturday and I usually had coffee with my mother, but since the class was that morning I had not gone to see her at my usual time. I picked up my books and drove by her house on the way back to class. I was surprised to see the morning paper still on the porch. I stopped in. She was an early riser, but when I got into the house she wasn't up and the coffee wasn't on. I kept calling out to her to let her know I was there. I started the coffee then went down the hall to her room. The door was closed, and that was unusual, too. I opened the door and found that she had been murdered." Jennings said that she had been killed by a serial killer. Circumstances had played an interesting part of that Saturday morning's events. The killer had called for a cab from his mother's living room and the first cab had gone to the wrong house. He called again and the second cabbie remembered a disheveled, agitated man when he arrived for the fare. The cab had made his pick-up only a short time before Jennings arrived. It was the description given by that Middle Eastern student cab driver that helped to capture the killer. It wasn't until a year and a week later that he was caught, and he had killed at least three other women. Jennings spent the next few years experiencing the judicial system and the conviction of her killer. "There were several murders that the authorities thought this guy did, but they could only get him on my mother's. Even when he was about to die they went with photos to his bedside to try to get him to clear up old cases, but he wouldn't say yes or no. That is hard."

Dividing his time between Navy call-ups and his job at Peony Park with ever increasing responsibilities, Jennings married Vicki on May 24, 1980. "My son came a year and a day later. I have a daughter and two grandchildren," Jennings smiled.

About the same time he also started a business providing coin operated vending machines to businesses and for parties: C J Palace Vending. "Like the pin-ball machines, anything that used a coin," he explained. "The only other business like it in Omaha was the Zorinski business [H N Z Vending]; and while we competed for business, we also worked together sometimes. If he needed a machine for an order that I had, we'd arrange for his customer to rent my machine(s). It worked well. When he was in Washington as Nebraska Senator, I'd talk with him about these machines sometimes." Jennings went on to explain it was through working with Zorinski that his military career took a turn into working in "Intelligence." "Remember the Achille Laruo? That is about the time things really changed for me. Both my wife and I are retired military." [6]

Jennings continued with the story saying he went looking for new property to start a new set of memories for continued generations and a new Peony Park. "The real estate agent was excited to tell me about a historic ballroom that burned down years ago and is now surrounded by weeds. She was sure it, Wanohoo Amusement Park, would fit my needs." While Jennings was skeptical at first, the more he heard about the history of the property the more he was interested in pursuing the purchase. "The owner also owned the Surf Ballroom in Iowa which is still in business. Remember Buddy Holly's last concert? It was there. She had been holding on to the Wahoo property as a bird sanctuary and wildlife park, but when she heard that it was the old Peony Park being started anew she was willing to sell," Jennings explained.[7]

"I loved the whole original Peony Park in Omaha," said Jennings, now CEO of Peony Park, Inc. "I didn't know then that one day I'd maintain the tradition that the park began with: ballroom and rustic accommodations for families outside of Omaha. We call it: The Legend Returns." Groundbreaking was May 19, 2001.[8]

The old-fashioned business or family getaway for a day or special event has re-materialized east of the town of Wahoo, Nebraska, on the grounds of the old Dance Island ballroom and park. It's a short drive 'out-of-town', just like in 'the good old days', but this time it is west of Omaha on Highway 92.

Carl Jennings opening Old Peony Park Royal Grove Gate at new location in Wahoo, 2004.[4]

Jennings explained that he still travels some as he is an EMT (emergency medical technician) and takes classes around the state. "The new Peony Park had to have an EMT for licensing so I took the training and keep it updated. There are still a lot of little things that I have to do now that remind me of what I did when I first started." He explained that when he opened the new park, the road to the area was not regularly used and he picked up enough aluminum cans and sold them to donate money to the Wahoo library.

"Picking up aluminum cans, and painting over graffiti and pranks are a couple of the down sides to owning the property. The upside is providing jobs for the community, doing tasks that I did when I was younger, and seeing the fun people can have as they relax away from

Jennings with blue pickup, 2013[5]

the work at home for a while," Jennings laughed. "I'm my own booking agent for those activities. I have to keep up the website, too." Bookings come from all over the state, Jennings said.

"You never know how the friends you make working will carry on later in life. [Congressman] Lee Terry was a bus boy at Peony Park when I was there. Some friends have asked if I would be interested in running for Congress when Terry retires. I usually answer I'm not saying 'no', but I don't like running against friends.

"My English teacher from Westside High School called me when she read my Peony Park book," Jennings laughed. "Back in those days I was more interested in my blue 1968 Camaro with the rag top and 396 engine cruising down Dodge Street. She didn't think I'd ever publish a book." Jennings didn't think she ever thought he might run for a political office someday either.

Times have changed and yet stayed the same. When the original Peony Park opened its doors, World War I had just ended. The economy and the citizenry needed cheering up and a get-a-way to change an attitude for a night or afternoon. Music, amusements in the outdoors, food, good friends and family were the ingredients for generations of memories. As the revitalized historic location east of Wahoo continues through another season of wild flowers and an occasional Peony bush, the memories made by those taking part in the growing number of activities available at the site becomes snapshots of the 'Legend' of the future.

How does Carl D. Jennings want to be remembered? "As a firm believer in service to country and community." He has decades of actions to show he lives what he believes. N

Endnotes, Footnotes & Sources:

[1] Thank you to Sherisa Lumpkin at Omaha Westside High School for information that the yearbooks were packed as the library was being remodeled, and it would be several months before they would be available.

[2] www.Wikipedia.org <u>Peony Park</u> Reviewed March 5, 2013.

[3] Palmer, J. (2004) "Cass Street area blooms," *Omaha World Herald.* June 24, 2004. Reviewed 3/27/2013.

[4] Photos and interview with Carl D. Jennings March 26, 2013. in Omaha. Notes in Nancy Sue Hansen's file.

[5] Photos by Nancy Sue Hansen. Located in Hansen's files.

[6] MS Achille Lauro was Hijacked by Palestinian Terrorists on the Mediterranean Sea in October 1985. It was an Italian Cruise Ship. One American was murdered. www.specialoperationscom reviewed June 7, 2013.

[7] Buddy Holly, Ritchie Valens, J.P. "The Big Bopper" Richardson left Clear Lake Iowa by plane in route to Moorhead, Minnesota on February 2, 1959. The plane crashed. The last concert was at the Surf Ballroom, Iowa.

[8]Todd, Jenni. "Wahoo to have Peony Park ground breaking." *Fremont Tribune*, May 12, 2001.

Peony Park booking office: 402-391-6253, www.peonyparkomaha.com.

Nebraska Authors Book & Travel Club

Signature of author, attend event at "The Legend Returns" Peony Park site *or* visit cafe area of the HyVee grocery store at the corner of 78th and Cass and see the photos of the original Peony Park that was located on that spot. Take a photo of yourself viewing the photos.

J. (JOHANNES) "JOE" MARTIN KLOTSCHE

Date of birth: Nov. 28, 1907
Location of birth: Scribner, NE
Education: Education through age 13 unverified
Midland College, Fremont, NE B.S.,1925
University of NE, Lincoln, MA, 1928
University of Wisconsin Ph.D. in history, 1931.
Date of Death: Feb. 4, 1995
Location of Death: Wisconsin

Dr. J. Martin Klotsche[1]
From the Archives Department,
University of Wisconsin,
Milwaukee Libraries.

Known Publications:

Klotsche J. Martin. The Role of the United States in World Affairs. Publisher: 1940.

Klotsche J. Martin. The United States and Latin America. Publisher: 1940.

Klotsche J. Martin. The Role of the University in an Urban Society. University of Wisconsin. 1961. 5 pp.

Klotsche J. Martin. The Urban University and the Future of Our Cities, Harper & Row Publishers, 1966. 140 pp.

Klotsche J. Martin. The University of Wisconsin-Milwaukee: An Urban University, University of Wisconsin-Milwaukee Publisher. 1972.

Klotsche J. Martin. <u>Confessions of an Educator: my personal and professional memoirs</u>, Milwaukee: UW-Milwaukee, 1985.

Klotsche J. Martin. <u>Together We Travelled</u>, Self Published, 1986. 301 pp.

Klotsche J. Martin. <u>Then and Now : Views of an Educator</u>. Self Published, 1987. 128 pp.

Klotsche J. Martin, Roberta Roberts Klotsche. <u>A Woman of Courage: The Life and Times of Annette Roberts</u>. Self Published, 1988.

Klotsche J. Martin, Dr. Adolph Suppan. <u>Life Begins At 80</u>. Kenwood Press, 1991. 81 pp.

Klotsche J. Martin, Frank A. Cassell, and Frederick I. Olson, with the assistance of Donald R. Shea and Bea Bourgeois <u>The University of Wisconsin–Milwaukee : A Historical Profile, 1885-1992</u>, UWM Foundation, 1992.

It was only his mother that called him by his first name, he was quoted as saying.[2] His friends called him Joe. Born Johannes Martin Klotsche, " J. Martin" came into the Dr. Ernst Heinrich "E. H." Klotsche family in November 1907. Dr. Ernest Klotsche (1875-1937) was pastor of St. John's Ridgely Lutheran Church in Scribner, Nebraska from 1910-1925 and again, as needed, 1929-1930. Dr. Ernst Klotsche was also on the faculty of Midland Lutheran College[3] and Western Theological Seminary in Fremont, Nebraska. While Joe's father enjoyed reading satirical writings of ancient authors, he also wrote and published several books, such as <u>Christian Symbolics</u>, in 1929 and <u>The History of Christian Doctrine</u>. As the son of an active pastor, author, college and seminary professor, Joe learned early about the concept of using the multi-talents that were given to him in a positive fashion. According to several accounts he had a constructive attitude and was a 'good mixer', like his father.[4]

Joe was thirteen when he entered Midland Lutheran College, 1920-21. According to the digital library at the University of Wisconsin, Milwaukee website, he graduated from Midland four years later, at age seventeen, with the highest scholastic average in his class. He earned his M.A. at the University of Nebraska in 1928, and received his PhD in history from the University of Wisconsin in 1931.

"A dimpled cherubim, with an iridescent ever present smile that plays over his features like ripples moved by zephyrs on the bosom of a frog pond."[4] 1924 yearbook notation with Johannes Jr. year photo.

J. Martin Klotsche, Junior 1924 yearbook, Midland College.

Besides his high level of achievement at Midland College academics, Joe was active in the Wynn Literary Society holding offices such as treasurer his junior year [4-p124] and the History-English Club where he served as 1924 president. [4-p 126,5] He took interest in the role of the United States in Latin America and world affairs.

Milwaukee State Teachers College hired Dr. Joe Klotsche to teach history immediately after his 1931 graduation. There were about 1,700 students enrolled as the new professor entered his first classroom as a teacher. He was later quoted as saying this was the time that finding parking was not an issue.[2]

The world scene was turmoil from the aftermath of World War I as Klotsche graduated from high school, through the thirty years of plotting peace and the outbreak of World War II. In the following years he served in education administration through the Korean Conflict, the Cold War, the mid-sixty's assassinations, including that of President John F. Kennedy and into the next conflict of Vietnam. His first two books, published in 1940, reflected his experiences in travel to Europe and Latin America: The Role of the United States in World Affairs and The United States and Latin America. In 1942, the thirty-five year old was appointed dean of instruction. Four years later Dr. J. Martin Klotsche was named president of the College and would see the institution through the changes that accompanied it being renamed Wisconsin State College in 1951.

Dr. Klotsche was asked to speak at the Annual Honors Assembly at La Crosse [Wisconsin] State Teachers College. *The Racquet*, La Crosse school paper April 20, 1950, announced his visit saying: *An address entitled "The Risk of Being Intelligent" will be delivered by President J. Martin Klotsche of Milwaukee State Teachers College…President Klotsche is an outstanding educator, an eminent radio personality, and a brilliant lecturer. Prior to World War II Dr. Klotsche made annual visits to Europe and Latin America, a practice which he resumed during the summer of 1948. At the invitation of the Office of Military government, Dr. Klotsche traveled in the American zone of Germany, visiting educational institutions. He also was director of a summer institute for students held in Paris under the auspices of the Student International Union. For many years Dr. Klotsche has been identified with projects in the field of international education. He served as director of the Institute of World Affairs at Salisbury, Conn. for several years. He also has served as resident leader of the Institute for Social Progress held at Wellesley, Mass. and in the summer of 1947 was faculty chairman of that group. Dr. Klotsche's "Background of the News" radio broadcasts over station WTMJ in Milwaukee are well received for their timeliness and impartiality. For the last few years he has served as moderator of "Milwaukee Speaks" a popular forum-of-the-air discussion dealing with controversial national and international issues. His work in developing a better understanding of world affairs and in improving international relations has made Dr. Klotsche a distinguished member of 'Who's Who in America.'* [6]

Five years later, in 1956, Wisconsin State College became the University of Wisconsin-Milwaukee. Dr. Klotsche was appointed provost of the new university and his title was changed in 1965 to Chancellor. The Milwaukee campus owed its new existence to the forward thinking president of the University of Wisconsin, Fred Harvey Harrington. Edwin Young was chancellor of the Madison campus.

Dr. Klotsche's third book in 1966 followed his new job title, The Urban University and the Future of our Cities. *The Scribner Rustler* [Scribner, Nebraska] newspaper published a front page story by Al Harper about their native son on March 10, 1966. Harper quoted Dr. Joe Klotsche, *"Dr. Klotsche believes that the urban university is on the threshold of an unparalleled growth. More students will be knocking at its doors. Increasing demands will be made on it in the areas of teaching, research and serve...A phenomenon of this century, the growth of the urban university will be far more dramatic than that of any other instruction of higher learning. For this new kind of institution located in the city is at the very center of the most dynamic and volatile force in America today- the emerging metropolis."* [8]

True to his own prophetic words, the new University of Wisconsin-Milwaukee (UW-M) grew to almost 25,000 students and through his guidance more than twenty major on-campus buildings were constructed or purchased and ten schools or colleges were established. While the building was underway, Dr. Klotsche began writing on his next book. By the time he finished the book in 1972 about UW-M as a new type of university, the world itself had become a vastly different place than when he had begun teaching at the small teachers college. The University system had problems and they all weren't based on the flagship campus at Madison. His skill in conflict management honed by the Institute of World Affairs in Virginia was meant to be used between nations; however, Dr. Klotsche found himself, his University, his State, and his nation needing conflict analysis.[9]

President Richard Nixon announced that the U.S. and South Vietnamese forces were going to target Cambodia. The announcement set off student protests from April 30 to May 4, 1970, including the May 4 attack on Kent State University by the Ohio National Guardsmen. UWM students and some faculty and staff joined the groups with campus walkouts. By May 6, hundreds of protesters occupied the library and power plant leading to their closure and cancellation of numerous classes and programs. On May 7 Chancellor Klotsche declared a state of emergency on the UWM campus. The declaration made it illegal for individuals not affiliated with the university to be on campus.[10]

On May 11 the strike continued and protesters destroyed a computer in Mitchell Hall and the library again closed. Professors and the School of Education and the College of Letters and Science did not denounce the strikers and in some cases indicated that students would not be punished. By May 12, Chancellor Klotsche called for a "Day of Assessment." The day was to discuss the issues that were dividing the nation with the protesters and interested individuals. Five hundred strikers met in the Union ballroom and were removed with the assistance of the Milwaukee Police tactical squads. According to the University website on the riots, Klotsche later wrote: 'The effect of this Day of Assessment is hard to determine, but it certainly assisted in defusing the tension that had embroiled the campus for almost a week." The state of emergency was lifted on May 18. Campus investigation brought four faculty members before the UW System Counsel. The hearing was set for October 15, 1970. Between May and October the Milwaukee campus seemed subdued.[10]

The Milwaukee campus wasn't alone in campus unrest. The Madison campus was host to part of the United States Military research and education system. One of the major aspects of the military programs on the Madison campus was the Army Mathematics Research Center (AMRC). The Madison campus contracted with the Department of Defense, amid competition with forty-four other universities, for the Center and held the contract for many years. It was housed in Sterling Hall in the center of campus. Leading researchers such as Heinz Barschall, a Manhattan Project veteran with Nuclear physics, had his life's work housed in the building as did a graduate student named Bob Fassnacht who was close to finalizing practicality with superconductivity. [11]

Tom Bates[11] described one of the informal debates of the History Department at Madison, the response of some of the students, and some of the riots and violence that followed as part of the response against the Vietnam war. Both campuses seemed to have agitators who were not students. The Madison campus summer seemed to be simmering when suddenly on Sunday night, August 23, 1970, an anti-Vietnam war bomb exploded in the AMRC. The death and destruction changed many lives that night.

Dr. J. Martin Klotsche[12]
From the archives department,
University of Wisconsin-Milwaukee Libraries

Barschall was among those who lost their life's work and Fassnacht lost his life. Focus of the FBI and other agencies located the bombers in a nationwide man-hunt within a few weeks. A high profile trial followed.[11]

The entire University of Wisconsin System recoiled with the events, but the Milwaukee campus seemed to stay the course until the announcement of the findings of the UW System Counsel on October 15. Four faculty members who had been involved with the May strike were dismissed for disruptive behavior. This decision provoked students into rallies and walkouts to support the faculty members.[10] Both campuses had unions, other outsiders and faculty encouraging the students responses, and now had national media watching every move of the administration(s).

In the beginning of Bates book, he quotes the 1894 University of Wisconsin Board of Regents: *"We cannot believe that knowledge has reached its final goal, or that the present condition of society is perfect. In all lines of academic investigation it is of the utmost importance that the investigator should be absolutely free to follow the indications of truth where they may lead. We believe the great state University of Wisconsin should ever encourage that continual and fearless sifting and winnowing by which alone the truth can be found."* [11]

Dr. Klotsche had addressed such a time while he was President of the State Teachers College in 1951 in an article for *Educational Leadership*, March edition. "Preparing Teachers for Controversial Issues" was directed at understanding the new Communist threat of ideology and the American mistaken zeal to defend. In his opening paragraph he wrote, *"One fact seems to have emerged clearly out of the present world confusion. It is that we are engaged in a decisive struggle between those who want to remain free and those who are determined regardless of cost to enslave the human spirit."* Whether Klotsche knew it or not, he had given an outline to the Board of Regents words: *"Our free institutions depend upon an informed and an intelligent opinion. An opinion can be neither informed nor intelligent if, during the process of its formulation it has been deprived of the knowledge of the nonconformist and of the dissenter. Obviously we can not have the freedom that we cherish if we limit this freedom only to those who agree with us."* [13] But as the Board of Regents and Dr. Klotsche knew, violence does not make truth or conversation.

On February 11, 1971, UW-Milwaukee protesters clashed with campus police and office personnel in attempts to present demands to Chancellor Klotsche regarding President Nixon's invasion of Laos. In May, at the year anniversary, protests began on campus and proceeded downtown Milwaukee. The violence remained downtown with the campus rather subdued. In October a crowd met for a march to the Milwaukee War Memorial and the subdued group declared they do not plan for more rallies in the immediate future. In November 1972, the *UWM Post* described the latest student protest as one that "fizzled out for absence of quorum." The media turned back to Madison and the on-going bombing trial.[10]

The University of Wisconsin-Milwaukee, An Urban University, written by Dr. Klotsche was published in 1972. Dr. Klotsche retired as Chancellor in 1973; however, he remained with the faculty of the History Department until 1978.

The building projects he started at the beginning of his Chancellorship were winding down. One of the new buildings was the Physical Education building which was named the J. Martin Klotsche Center in 1977. The name was changed to The Klotsche Center. It is a 3,500 seat multi-purpose on-campus arena in Milwaukee.

After his retirement, he and his wife, Roberta Roberts Klotsche, lived in Arizona until her death. He returned to Wisconsin living in Oostburg in Sheboygan County until his own death in 1995.

Retirement was prime time for Joe to write. He published a book each year from 1985 to 1988 and in 1991 he and Adolph A Suppan wrote Life Begins at Eighty. His final publication, at age 85, was a co-authorship of the History of UW-M from 1885-1992.

Dr. J. "Joe" Martin Klotsche had earned a reputation as a supporter of student and faculty rights by taking stands to defend them. His stable guidance for education of students passed the test of time through multiple national conflicts and declared wars, ideology conflicts from the assassination of Presidents, Nazis and Communism, through home grown violence and confusion. He was a man for his time. N

Endnotes, Footnotes & Sources:

The Nebraska Authors Project® is unable to verify the early education of J. Martin. Many authors have Scribner, however, Scribner and Fremont have no records of attendance. Midland College is unable to locate records providing admission information.

[1] Photo from the Archives Department, University of Wisconsin, Milwaukee Libraries, date unknown.

[2] www.wikipedia.com *J Martin Klotsche*. Reviewed 5/4/2013.

[3] Midland Lutheran College, *Warrior Yearbook*, 1924 p. 20. Dr. E.H. Klotsche.

[4] Midland Lutheran College, Warrior Yearbook, 1924 p 48, Johannes Klotsche.

[5] Christensen, William E and Ann L. Wilhite. 125th Anniversary Publication with Fevrent Prayers and Buoyant Hopes. The Story of Midland Lutheran College. 2012. *Midland was a post-secondary institution which became a combination of Fremont College 1884-1919; Luther College 1883-1962; and Midland College 1887-2008.* In 1949 the Seminary moved to California, and in 2009 Midland became a University.

[6] *The Racquet*. Published by and for the Students of La Crosse State Teachers College, Vol. L, No 13, La Crosse, Wisconsin, April 20, 1950. "Klotsche to Speak at Annual Honors Assembly April 29."

[7] St. Johns Ridgely Lutheran Church Cemetery, June 2013 photo, rural Scribner, Nancy Sue Hansen's file.

[8] *The Scribner Rustler* [Scribner, Nebraska] newspaper published a front page story by Al Harper about their native son on March 10, 1966.

[9] Institute of World Affairs (IWA)was founded in 1924 by Alexander Meetier Hadden (1857-1942) and Maude Miner Hadden (1880-1967), wealthy social reformers. The IWA "is a not-for-profit, non-governmental organization working across cultural and political boundaries to advance creative approaches to conflict analysis, conflict management, and post-conflict peace-building." It began in Geneva, Switzerland, as the Student's International Union with the objective of providing a forum to enhance the further understanding of international problems as well promote a service ethic among the youth of various nationalities. In 1941, the SIU relocated its offices to New York City with summer seminars in Salisbury, Connecticut. September of 1977 saw the SIU merge with the American Universities Field Staff (AUFS) in an effort to expand services and to stabilize agency funding. In 1994, the organization merged with another non-profit organization, the Institute of Current World Affairs (ICWA), and offered overseas fellowships to American students.

[10] http://guides.library.uwm.edu/content.php?pid=85020, Vietnam War Protests at the University of Wisconsin-Milwaukee - Archives Dept. *The Student Strike and Later Protests, 1970-1972.* Reviewed 5/9/2013.

[11] Bates, Tom. RADS, The 1970 Bombing of the Army Math Research Center at the University of Wisconsin and Its Aftermath. New York: Harper Collins. 1992. 465 pp.

[12] Photo purchased from the Archives Department, University of Wisconsin-Milwaukee Libraries. Date of photo unknown.

[13]Klotsche, J. Martin. *Educational Leadership.* "Preparing Teachers for Controversial Issues." P 352- 355. Copyright 1951 by the Association for Supervision and Curriculum Development.

[14] UW-Milwaukee Office of the Chancellor Records, 1933-2011, Digital library site. http://digital.library.wisc.edu/1711.dl/wiarchives.uw-mil-uw-mac0046. Reviewed 5/4/2013.

[15] Hansen, Nancy Sue and Dush, Barbara Ann. Nebraska Authors Volume One. "Orville Zabel." Fullerton: D & H Publishing, 2013.

Thank you to the University of Wisconsin Charles Wilborn, UW-M Archives, and Ellen Engseth, Archivist for permission to publish photos.

Thank you to Sharon Meyer and Deb Wegner at Scribner High School for looking through numerous records to try to find verification that J. Martin went to school in the Scribner School system. No verification was found.

Thank you to Fremont High School for attempts to verify that J. Martin attended school at Fremont. No verification was found.

Nebraska Authors Book & Travel Club

Visit the Musbach Museum to enjoy their collection(s). It is found on main street, Scribner. It is open by appointment only so call ahead 402-664-2459. Have the guide date and sign your box.

DORTHY KNOUSE KOEPKE

Dorthy Koepke

Date of Birth: Jan. 24, 1922
Location of Birth: Kingsbury County near Iroquois, SD
Education: Cavour High School, Cavour SD, 1942;
attended journalism classes for one year at Huron College, Huron, SD
Moved to Nebraska: 1943
Date of death: Jan. 10, 2013
Location of death: Norfolk, NE

Known Publications:

Koepke, Dorthy. <u>Close To My Heart</u>. lulu.com, published 2011. 91 pp.

Koepke, Dorthy. <u>When I Was Young</u>, lulu.com, published 2011. 95 pp.

Koepke, Dorthy. <u>Magnificent White Oak</u>, lulu.com, published 2011. 95 pp.

Koepke, Dorthy. <u>Love Made Me Do It</u>, Walworth Publishing Co., published 1984.

Koepke, Dorthy. <u>Always Room for One More</u>, lulu.com, published 2012. 123 pp.

Dorthy Ione Knouse Koepke had a devoted love affair with her husband and always kept a watchful eye on their ten children. But all the while this farm wife was deep in "diapers and doughnuts, chickens and cows, cooking and weeding, and slopping the sows," she found time to have a second love affair with writing.

Claiming that her free time to write (after the gardening, canning, live-stock chores and cleaning were done) was "between midnight and four a.m." was a testimony that Koepke's first priority was always her family. However, this creative mother still managed to produce massive amounts of writing, and became in demand as a poet, author and speaker.

"I remember her dropping whatever she was doing and running back and typing stuff out. I think it was going through her head at all times," Koepke's daughter, Lana Koepke Johnson of Lincoln noted. "I have a big box of paper scraps, short paragraphs, and lists that she wrote her ideas down on. Some were on napkins, backs of envelopes, and some were on blank check blanks. She loved paper. She had all kinds of notebooks and pads of paper."

The third of nine children born in Iroquois County, South Dakota, Koepke knew she wanted to be a writer after she composed her first poem at the young age of twelve. But when she graduated from eighth grade and found out she couldn't go on to high school, "I thought I would die," she wrote in a memoir. "Can you imagine anybody crying on their knees every night to God for the chance to go to high school? Three times in the next year I started out to run away.

"The first two times I don't think my folks realized it, but the third time I was gone overnight. Out on the Dakota prairie I had to run at least eighteen miles on foot before I got anywhere. I spent the night in a straw pile and I did a lot of thinking lying there looking up at the stars. That was one of the turning points of my life. I learned an invaluable lesson: You can't run away from your troubles. Stick it out and fight your way through. With the Lord's help, that's what I did."

Koepke had her first poem published when she was only sixteen. It was titled *My Big Feet* and won first prize in a local competition. As a teenager, she was often accused of her poetry being copied from maga-zines. One summer she went to work for a doctor and his wife, and the wife was eventually convinced that the poems were not copied. The wife wanted her young worker to live with them and to place her in high school to further her writing talent. However, to Koepke's deep disap-pointment, she was told she had to go back home to work on the family farm and still could not attend high school.

Eventually she was able to fulfill her dream of attending high school while working for a couple for room and board. In the summer she worked on a farm doing housework and caring for an invalid woman,

Dorthy at age 18 or 19

with half of her wages going to help clothe her younger brothers and sisters for school.

She graduated from Cavour High School in Cavour, South Dakota, as valedictorian at age twenty, having had to delay her studies for three years to help care for her younger siblings.

That same year, she traveled to Hoskins, Nebraska, to visit relatives and while delivering lunch to farmers working in a hayfield, met the love of her life and future husband: Herman Koepke.

After completing her freshman year of college at Cavour, South Dakota, where she majored in journalism and also worked as a feature writer at a newspaper, she moved to Hoskins to become a farm wife.

Koepke stated that raising a family on the farm was an ideal place for them to grow up, and she always managed to glean humor from her lifestyle through poetry:

Country Calamity
I envy my friend in the city,
Where the lawns and walks are clean,
And there when her guests are greeted,
The hostess is calm and serene.
But woe is me in the country,
My guests are prepared for the worst;
It makes no difference where they walk –
My chickens have been there first.

Despite Koepke's decision to drop out of college, "It didn't stop her from learning new things or pursuing her need to be a writer," her daughter said of her mother's determination.

Koepke's first inspiration had been her grandmother from York, England, who was a storyteller with a keen sense of humor. Then came her mother, a talented singer. Koepke's life experiences were another source of inspiration.

"Her mind was always working on a poem or story. She used something my brother Jeff said on his first airplane ride at age five in a short story," her daughter added. "She would be working away cooking or canning corn or whatever and suddenly drop whatever she was doing and go back to her typewriter and type something out. When she was done she would come back and resume whatever she was doing.

"One time she was in the hospital and while there she had a lung embolism. Before she allowed them to treat her, she made the nurse write the poem that she had created in her mind onto paper because she knew she would forget it by the time they were done treating her."

Koepke attended workshops and conferences across the country, including the Billy Graham School of Writing, the Society of Children's Book Writers, and the Nebraska Chaparral Poets. She was an active member and officer of the Spindrift Poets Club. Her numerous honors and awards have been from local and national venues for her poems and short stories, and include first place in the Nebraska and National Mother's Association short story contest. She also earned a long list of awards from the Nebraska Chapparel poets contest, with the most recent being first place for her poem, "Utopia for Growing Old" in August 2012.

Her writing has been featured in the *New York Times, The Christian Science Monitor, Guideposts, Magazine of the Midlands*, *Nebraska State Medical Journal*, *Grit and Country People*, *This Day* magazine and other publications.

A popular speaker, Koepke was invited to many organizations to talk about her life as a farm wife, mother and writer. Her favorite presentation was "Love Made Me Do It," in which she spoke about why she married a farmer, raised ten children, and wrote when she could.

Koepke's favorite readings were books like The Shell Seekers, a novel by Rosamunde Pilcher. "She was always a voracious reader and loved all kinds of books," Johnson said. "I remember as a kid she always bought a lot of books for us kids. When we had to do projects for school we had our own mini library to do research. This made a lot of sense since we were eleven miles from the nearest tiny library."

Koepke died on January 10, 2103, at the age of ninety. Yet, her mind was "going a thousand miles per hour thinking of projects" she wanted to do or stories and poems she needed to finish or work on to make them right, her daughter said of the year before her mother died. "Her health, however, limited her greatly in doing so. She had all her writing in her head though. We would be working and she would tell me in the poem such and such, on line eight, change that word to a new word she wanted in there. She could remember every one of them and even though she couldn't get to her computer anymore, she was reworking them over in her mind."

Along with her daughter, Koepke also started assembling a cookbook of all the recipes created in their family kitchen throughout the years. Pictures of family, friends, and neighbors eating in their farm kitchen will be featured with the recipes.

As for all the dedication, passion and love Koepke had invested into her world of words, she always had one basic goal in mind for her readers: "I hope that the writings encourage people to be better and more loving." B

Love Made Me Do It

Why did I marry and live on the farm,
Awakened at dawn by a clanging alarm?
Why did I milk in a cold draft stall,
When farming was not my lifestyle at all?
Before we were married, really, I knew it,
Then why did I wed? Love made me do it!

My darling, who promised I'd be his queen,
Sent me to wash with his mother's machine,
He upped his production down on the farm,
Including ten babies crooked in my arm,
Work and more work, he kept adding to it?
Why did I stay? Love made me do it!

With diapers and doughnuts, chickens and cows,
Cooking and weeding, and slopping the sows,
Gardens and haying, and lunches for men,
Over and over, and over again,
All the while knowing that I really blew it,
Why did I stay? Love made me do it!

By Dorthy Knouse Koepke
Taken from her book Close To My Heart[1]

Endnotes, Footnotes & Sources:

Interview via e-mail with Lana Koepke Johnson of Lincoln, Nebraska. Notes in Barbara Ann Dush's files.

[1] Knouse Koepke, Dorthy. Close to My Heart.

Special thanks to Mary Pat Finn-Hoag of the *Norfolk Daily News* who graciously introduced us to Dorthy Knouse Koepke's publications.

Dorthy with her husband
and children.

Dorthy at the typewriter.

Nebraska Authors Book & Travel Club
Visit one of the activities at Hoskins, "The Small Town with a Big Heart," and attach a picture or receipt of your visit to Hoskins. For a schedule of activities, check their website at www.ptcnet.net/hoskins

FRANCIS "FRANK" LaFLESCHE

Date of birth: Dec. 25, 1857
Location of birth: Omaha
Reservation
Education: elementary school:
Presbyterian mission school
reservation-1869
Bachelor of Law degree, National
University in Washington, DC, 1892
Masters of Law, National University
in Washington, D.C., 1893
honorary Doctor of Letters degree
from the University of Nebraska in
1926.
Date of Death: Sept. 5, 1932
Home at death: Macy, NE

Francis Laflesche[1]

Known Publications:

Forty-third Annual Report of the Bureau of America Ethnology
to the Secretary of the Smithsonian Instiution 1925-1926,1928
Washington: Government Printing Office, 828 pps – *The Osage Tribe:
Two versions of the Child-naming Rite* by Frank La Flesche, 164 pp.

La Flesche, Francis. The Middle Five" Indian Schoolboys of the
Omaha Tribe, 1900, forward by David A. Daerreis, Lincoln:
University of Nebraska Press 152 pp. "Reprint of the ed. Published by
the University of Wisconsin Press. Madison, 1963. Nebraska Bison
book edition, 1978 edition.

La Flesche, Francis. A Dictionary of the Osage Language.
Washington, D.C., U.S. Govt print off, 1932.

La Flesche, Francis. The Osage and the invisible world from the works
of Francis La Flesche. Norman: University of Oklahoma Press, 1995.

La Flesche, Francis. A Study of Omaha Indian Music. Cambridge, Massachussetts Peabody museum of American archaeology and ethnology, 1893.

La Flesche, Francis. *War Ceremony and Peace Ceremony of the Osage Indians* 1939, Washington: Government Printing office, Smithsonian Institution, Bureau of America Ethnology Bulletin 101 p 20 *Language and signs.*

Thirty-Sixth Annual Report of the Bureau of American Ethnology to the Secretary of the Smithsonian Institution, 1921, 1914-1915, Washington: Government Printing Office. *The Osage Tribe: Rite of the Chiefs; saying of the ancient men,* by Frank La Flesche, 604 pp and The Osage tribe: rite of the chiefs; sayings of the ancient men New York : Johnson Reprint Corporation, 1970.

It was during the last of the days of roaming free on the Great Plains that Francis "Frank" LaFlesche began his life. President James Buchanan appointed J. Sterling Morton of Nebraska City as Secretary of the Nebraska Territory, the new territory charter banks failed and the first white child of Saline County was born to Victor and Caroline Vifquain about one hundred fifty miles south of the Omaha Reservation before Frank was one year old. [2,3]

Frank's father, Joseph "Iron Eye" LaFlesche, and mother, Elizabeth "Lissie" Esau, taught their children to see the past and future and make the present count. Frank became part of American history in several aspects. Along the way he wrote books and articles, leaving a trail for those that came later.

In 1935, after Francis' death, the Federal Writers' Project [4] began surveying and locating historical records of the past. The Project collected information about an area, its human history and natural resources so the people involved would understand more about their own community. It was touted as a new idea. However, the Omaha Native American Frank LaFlesche had already spent his life working in the fields of anthropology and ethnology. He had observed people, learned about their lifestyle and environment, and seen how their actions and environment interacted. The Nebraska and Federal Writers' Project picked up some pieces of Nebraska Native American history that Frank had started many years before.

It was Frank's belief that the Native American culture should be preserved for historic understanding as part of the country's history; and of course, for the benefit of the heritage and traditions of individual Native American families. He was introduced to linguistics and ethnology when James Owen Dorsey, in 1878, collected stories among the Omaha. Frank had been the translator when Dorsey interviewed his father, who was part French and Native American, for his memories of what the elders passed down to him.

One of the historic issues that Frank became involved in began in 1878 when the neighboring tribe of Ponca, who were friendly to the Omaha tribe, was forcibly removed to Indian Territory in Oklahoma. The distress was felt by Frank's family. When Ponca Chief Standing Bear led several hundred of his tribe back to Nebraska they were accepted by the Omaha tribe providing shelter and food. Standing Bear was arrested and the famous trial followed: were Indians really people with rights under American law? Franks half-sister, Susette "Bright Eyes" (LaFlesche) Tibbles, *Omaha World-Herald* newspaper reporter Thomas Henry Tibbles, and later Alice Fletcher became part of the Ponca/Omaha story. [5]

Senator Samuel J. Kirkwood of Iowa appointed Frank to the national Bureau of Indian Affairs in Washington, D.C. in 1881 after they met during the Ponca/Omaha speaking trips to D.C. Frank worked there until 1910. He transferred to the Bureau of American Ethnology. He interviewed the aging of his tribe to try to provide information for the public about the Omaha heritage. He preserved ancient songs and ceremonies of the Plains Indians.

When Frank earned his law degree he was able to help the tribes work with the federal agencies. Between assisting tribes with legal issues and doing research, he was writing.

His first book, The Middle Five: Indian Schoolboys of the Omaha Tribe, was finished in 1900, but did poorly in sales since it didn't meet with the stereotype of Indians of the day. It was republished in 1963. This autobiographical sketch of his school days at the Omaha Indian mission school is still recommended to the general reader. It is a resource to correct the distorted picture of Indian life as seen in the movies, comics, and television. The young Indian boys are caught between two cultures. Should they become make-believe white men and abandon the ways of their fathers? Teachers struggled to acquaint these young students with the new world of learning while everything around the school was changing: Civil War and Nebraska Statehood just for starters. Problems arose for both parents and teachers, included directing the schoolboy exuberance for life. It is how the boys handled their internal and external conflicts which contribute to Frank's portrait of the "universal boy" to whom La Flesche dedicated his book.

Frank was not detoured by the lack of sales of his first book. He continued to write and collect history. There was an opera, as well as plays and other books, articles, and a dictionary describing the Osage language that became Franks published legacy.

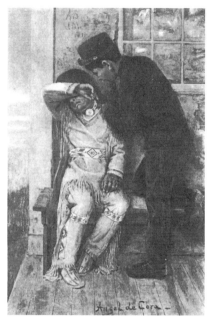

Winnebago Painter Angel DeCora depiction of Frank's first day at school.[6]

La Flesche was asked for advice when Hartley Burr Alexander was hired to work with the proposed Nebraska State Capitol building. He became an advisor to several museums and collectors regarding their Native American artifacts.

Several sources noted that Frank wanted his people to appreciate and understand their heritage, and remember their culture before they assimilated into the world around them. At his death he was honored with three services: Latter Day Saints, Masonic, and a traditional ritual from the Omaha Tribe. Had he become that 'universal boy' of his first book? N

Endnotes, Footnotes & Sources:

[1] Nebraska State Historical Society (NSHS), Lincoln, Nebraska. Collections: LaFleshe. Permission to publish photos. Thank you.

[2] Hansen, Nancy Sue and Dush, Barbara Ann. Nebraska Authors Volume One. "J. Sterling Morton," Fullerton: D & H Adventures Publishing, 2013.

[3] Hansen, Nancy Sue and Dush, Barbara Ann. <u>Nebraska Authors Volume One</u>. "Victor Vifquain," Fullerton: D & H Adventures Publishing, 2013.

[4] Hansen, Nancy Sue and Dush, Barbara Ann. <u>Nebraska Authors Volume One</u>. "Rudy Umland," Fullerton: D & H Adventures Publishing, 2013.

[5] Starita, Joe. <u>I am a Man</u>, St Martin Press, 2009, 272 pp.

[6] Photo from NSHS collection. The back of the photo states it was a depiction of the first day of school for Frank. The boy in the school uniform became a friend named Brush in Frank's first book: <u>The Middle Five: Indian Schoolboys of the Omaha Tribe</u>. Angel DeCora, Winnebago painter and illustrator, was the best known Native American artist before WWI. www.enwikipedia.org.

<u>Founders and Patriots of Nebraska.</u> Edited and published by the Nebraska Chapter of the National Society of the Daughters of Founders and Patriots of America.1935. Frank La Flesche, 30–32 pp.

Native American Authors. www.ipl.org. reviewed August 17, 2011.

Nebraska State Journal. Recognized Indian author "Honorary degree will be conferred on son of a chief by the University of Nebraska." June 4, 1926, 7.

Omaha World Herald. "Intermarriage doom of American Indian Frank LaFlesche says white women doing what white rifles couldn't. Does not regret Indians impending disappearance as a distinct race." December 7, 1919. 25."

Sanders, Jean. <u>Notable Nebraskans</u>, Lincoln: Media Productions and Marketing, Inc. 1998, 35-40. pps.

WILLIAM "BILL" H. LAWRENCE

Date of birth: Jan. 29, 1916
Location of birth: Lincoln, NE
Education: Lincoln High School grad 1932
Attended UN-L one semester
Date of Death: March 2, 1972
Location at Death: Manchester, NH while
covering the presidential primary for NBC

Bill Lawrence
Lincoln High School
yearbook, 1932[1]

Known Publications:

Lawrence, William H.: reporter *Lincoln Star*, Lincoln, Nebraska; joined Associated Press (AP), worked for the *Omaha World-Herald*; joined United Press International (UPI) serving in Chicago and then Washington D.C.; twenty years with the *New York Times* with several years as the White House correspondent, joined ABC News in 1961.

Lawrence, William "Bill" H. <u>Six Presidents, Too Many Wars</u>. New York: Saturday Review Press, 1972. 307 pp. Memoir.

William "Bill" H. Lawrence joined the newspaper staff at the *Lincoln Star* at age sixteen. Like Frederic Babcock[2] before him, Lawrence attended the University of Nebraska in Lincoln while working at the paper. Lawrence, however, attended the University for only one semester before moving on with his journalist career.[3]

Eight months before his sudden death, Lawrence was the speaker for the 1971 Lincoln High School graduation class. A news article recounted his speech. He remembered his own 1932 graduation, saying his graduation came when Nebraska was more dependent on farming and the farm income was low "as it is now, and we had just experienced ten years of unbroken drought…there was widespread unemployment in the state," just as these graduates were facing. He told them that through his experiences he found that *"Looseness with the truth, or if you will allow me to be blunt, just plain dishonesty, threatens to undermine our very system of government and of commerce. It is not confined to just one part; indeed all three major parties practice deception on the voter. And it is time we called them to account."* Lawrence tried to emphasize to the audience that there was a simple way to handle someone who didn't tell the truth: "boycott." What he meant was, withhold your vote. The author wanted everyone to exercise their vote wisely and stay in the middle of the road: "I don't want to take my cues from either Rennie Davis on the left or Martha Mitchell on the right." [4,5]

Who was this William H. Lawrence and how did he get enough experience to say that the American political parties, government officials, and industry told lies to voters?

Lawrence was the son of Mr. and Mrs. E.H. Lawrence of Lincoln, Nebraska. He graduated from Lincoln High School and took his first newspaper job with the *Lincoln Star*. He worked under James Lawrence who worked with the paper for fifty years including his forty-three years on the editorial staff. James and William were not related. William saw James Lawrence as a mentor and returned to Nebraska as a testimonial speaker to honor him after James' 1957 death. [3,6,7]

William Lawrence left the university after one semester. On page six of his memoir, published shortly after his death, he had written "*My journalist career began on the Lincoln, Nebraska Star back in 1932, and I hit the big time during the General Motors strike of 1936-37. On this first big front-page assignment, I found myself involved deeply and personally in the efforts to settle the G.M. strike in early 1937. Because of a question I asked the UAW suddenly canceled its agreement to leave the Fisher body plants in Flint, MI…*" The G.M. strike would not be the only time a question asked by reporter Lawrence created a spark. [3]

He was known for the question he asked Russia's Premier Nikita S. Khrushchev. In an AP story of September 17, 1959, the event was reviewed. In front of a nationwide television audience Lawrence asked if he, Khrushchev, once admitted doing nothing to prevent Stalin's crimes against the Russian people. Khrushchev, stunned and flushed with anger, said the question was part of rumors and lies that were not true. As this first press conference and speech the Premier had on U.S. soil concluded, Khrushchev conversed with Lawrence and said he hoped he hadn't offended him or his audience with his blunt reply. Lawrence tried to smooth over the incident saying he had not been offended. Quoting the AP story Lawrence is reported to have said, "We ask the questions. You give the answers. Straight talk is never offensive." The story continued. "Wagging his head in agreement, Khrushchev smiled and replied: "I agree. That is the way to peace." As to whether it was just a coincidence that Russia shot the moon with a rocket on the eve of his visit to the United States, Khrushchev grinned and pronounced it "a simple, but a pleasant coincidence." Perhaps these events are two examples of what Lawrence was thinking about when he spoke to those Lincoln High School graduates in 1971.

Lawrence moved quickly into a United Press reporter position and talked his way into being assigned to the nation's capital covering Franklin D. Roosevelt's second term. From there he became the White House correspondent for the *New York Times* in 1941. He covered presidential campaigns in 1940, 1948, 1952, 1956, 1960, 1964 and 1968 for various news outlets. He had just begun covering the 1972 campaign in New Hampshire when he was found slumped in his chair by an ABC News assistant. He had a heart attack and had been suffering from pulmonary edema for several years. Nothing could have kept him from asking questions and trying to get at the truth as he saw it.[8,9]

It wasn't just presidential campaigns that he wrote about. He had many years as a foreign correspondent: Moscow, Guam, Okinawa and Japan in World II; the Balkans, Poland and South America, then the Korean Conflict 1950-51. The stay in Moscow was twenty-one months of following the Russian armies in the field. Then he was assigned to the Pacific area where he was one of the first of a group of American newspaper men to visit Nagasaki after the atom bomb fell. After the war, it was on to Central and South America.[3]

In May 1958, he returned to Nebraska to take part in the University of Nebraska Journalism Week activities and visited the *Lincoln Star* newsroom. He had been in Algeria hunting (military) guerilla with French parachute General Jacques Massu by helicopter. The fighting had been going on in the area for four years and engaging the entire French army (France had occupied the area since 1830 and needed the resources of the area). Lawrence wrote about the guerillas coming into the area from Egypt, Syria and the Communist bloc nations, the Moslems lack of education or representation under the French, the anti-American thoughts of the area and peace negotiations. He was concerned about American prestige all over the world and many times wrote the fact that the attitude "America is imperialistic" takes a long time to repair, so presidential actions need to be mindful of their words and actions. He believed that Nixon had caused imperialistic confusion in South America and Lawrence wasn't impressed.[10,11,12,13]

Later in 1958 Lawrence wrote to the world that it was nationalism, not communism, which was behind the Arabs and their revolution in Lebanon. He had accompanied the U.S. Marines to Lebanon and stayed until August when the U.S. withdrew. Leaving countries he was covering as a foreign correspondent wasn't always easy. About ten years prior to his Lebanon and Algeria coverage he had been in Bulgaria. He had been taken into custody by the Communists at Belgrade, fined the equivalent of $22.50 and kicked out of the country for failure to register with the police, as was required by every visitor. Lawrence had rented an apartment for his time in the country and thus had not stopped at the hotel to register as was the custom. Kicking him out of the Russian satellite capital was not a hardship since it was the day he was already scheduled to leave on a flight to London.

In 1958 he became the newly elected president of the National Press Club in Washington. He considered Nebraska's Fred Seaton as a contender for the GOP vice-presidential nomination in the forthcoming election cycle. Seaton, the editor of the *Hastings Tribune,* had been the publicity manager of the Minnesota Governor Harold Stassen presidential campaign which Lawrence had covered devotedly. Once when asked if Lawrence thought that a film personality, such as Reagan, should seek a governorship Lawrence responded saying that it would be like an agriculturalist running in Nebraska. Motion pictures are a major industry in California, he reminded his audience. As usual it wasn't just national politics and foreign wars that had Lawrence's attention, it was Nebraska's politics, too, and how it affected the nation as a whole. [14,15,16]

In the 1968 election, Senator Roman Hruska and the 'favorite son' primary was to have kept the Nebraska GOP national convention delegates with Hruska until he released them at the convention. Lawrence said that move might have been a mistake considering the election he sensed was ahead. Lawrence had been accused of making a mistake back in June of 1966 when he stood alone on the national stage saying he didn't think President Lyndon Johnson would run again and that Governor Ronald Reagan and Governor George Romney would 'kill each other in the primaries'. If President Johnson didn't run, *"the President would probably attempt to 'rig' the Democratic convention for Vice President Hubert Humphrey and against Senator Robert Kennedy,… Vietnam and internal division ("there's a terrible hatred in the land") will damage Democratic chances in 1968, Lawrence said."*[7] President Johnson didn't declare he wasn't running until March 31, 1968. Lawrence hadn't waivered. Nor did Lawrence waiver from his 1966 statement when his friend Senator Robert Kennedy was murdered prior to the Democratic convention. [14,15,16]

He had joined the American Broadcasting Co. (ABC) News in 1961 at the urging of his personal friend, President John F. Kennedy. James C. Hagerty, vice president of ABC news, welcomed Lawrence noting he was an old friend. Hagerty was press secretary to former President Dwight D. Eisenhower and had formerly been a *Times* political reporter. According to a 1966 *Lincoln Star* interview with Gary Hill, Lawrence "established a reputation as 'the most knowledgeable reporter' covering the Presidents, serving more terms at the White House than any chief executive." But as far as predictions go: "I covered the presidential election in 1948," Lawrence said, "In May of that year I decided that Dewey was going to win. I just cover elections now, I don't predict them".[16]

What could be predicted, however, was Lawrence's broadcast style. It was distinguished by his gruff voice and frank reporting of events as he saw them. In death, he was considered the textbook model of straight reporting. In the *Journal-Star* 1972 article announcing Lawrence's book, they wrote that Lawrence's style was *"not simply the kind of clod-like regurgitation of statements put out by self-serving politicians and vested interests and pomp-*

Lawrence at ABC TV Studio[19]

173

ously called news by vastly too many print and electronic communication media….Lawrence worked the doctrine of telling as much of the story as he knew, including filling in parts which public figures often seek to obscure. That requires hard digging, cultivation of sources so that they trust your judgment and constant homework to understand complex situations." He worked for ABC News for eleven years. He was political affairs editor by 1965 and national affairs editor at the time of his death. [17,18]

As the 1971 *Lincoln Star* reporters covered the Lawrence speech to the high school graduation class, they noted he said he was not naïve "enough to think we can reform the whole human race," but he considered himself still naïve enough to "think we can take some short steps in those directions." He gave the example that the government officials in both the Nixon and Johnson administrations had not kept their promises in Southeast Asia. This concerned him. "The polite word for official falsehoods in Washington is credibility gap," he said, "and credibility gap remains the most enduring, early recognizable bipartisan landmark in the whole capital city." The article went on to quote Lawrence's speech regarding credibility saying "credibility gaps are not confined to government," suggesting the "doubletalk of George Orwell's <u>1984</u> may already be here….Dishonesty threatens to undermine our very system of government and of commerce… it is not just confined to one (political) party."[4,5]

He made numerous trips back to Nebraska to see his parents over the years. His last trip had been in October of 1971 to attend his father's funeral which was just a month after his mother's death. Between his foreign and domestic work flights, his responsibilities with his wife, children and parents and his occasional overindulgence in strong drink, he had made time to write about his life. His book was updated and ready to publish. Reviews of his book published on the inside flap include Harrison Salisbury, Walter Cronkite, Abraham Ribicoff, Barry Goldwater, Lawrence F. O'Brien and Bill Moyer. They were reviews that Lawrence would never know about his work. The compliments and respect were evident.[3]

Lawrence wrote about his career on page 293 of his book: "From the General Motors strike onward, through six Presidents and too many wars, I could not have hoped for a better epitaph to cap my journalistic career."[3] N

Endnotes, Footnotes & Sources:

[1] Photo from Lincoln Public High School yearbook, 1932. Thank you to Larry Dawson of LHS and the library staff for their assistance.

[2] Hansen, Nancy Sue and Dush, Barbara Ann. Nebraska Authors Volume One. "Frederic Babcock" Fullerton: D & H Adventures Publishing, 2013.

[3] Lawrence, William "Bill" H. Six Presidents, Too Many Wars. New York : Saturday Review Press, 1972. 307 pp. Memoir.

[4] "Lawrence Says: Return to 'Truth Standard" *Lincoln Star*, Lincoln, Nebraska, June 5, 1971.

[5] "'Exercise Vote Right Wisely' Lawrence is LHS Speaker." *Lincoln Journal*, Lincoln Nebraska, June 5, 1971.

[6] "New York Times Writer is Testimonial Speaker…to Honor Late James Lawrence." *Lincoln Star*. Lincoln, Nebraska, April 12, 1958.

[7] Hansen, Nancy Sue and Dush, Barbara Ann. Nebraska Authors Volume One. " Rudolph Umland" Fullerton: D & H Adventures Publishing, 2013.

[8] "Bill Lawrence Becomes ABC's Political Editor," United Press International (UPI), *Lincoln Star*, Lincoln, Nebraska, May 30, 1961.

[9] "William H. Lawrence, Veteran Reporter, Dies" UPI, *Lincoln Star*, Lincoln, Nebraska, March 3, 1972.

[10] Walton, Don. "N.Y. Times Writer Lawrence Ready to Return to Algeria." *Lincoln Star*. Lincoln, Nebraska, May 15, 1958.

[11] Anderson, Bill. "Non-recognition is 'not helping U.S.': Lawrence" *Lincoln Star,* Lincoln, Nebraska, May 17, 1958.

[12] "Nationalism, Unrest, Lawrence." *Lincoln Journal*. Lincoln, Nebraska, December 18, 1958.

[13] Rothenberger, B.R. "Bill Lawrence Says: Accept, Learn to Live With 'Arab Problem." *Lincoln Star*. Lincoln, Nebraska, December 18, 1958.

[14] Lawrence J.E. "Stassen Makes Stop in Lincoln: Landon Sees Deadlock," *Lincoln Star*, Lincoln, Nebraska, May 1948.

[15] Walton, Don. "Lawrence Believes Hruska Drive 'Screwed Up' Primary." *Lincoln Star*. Lincoln, Nebraska, October 31, 1967.

[16] Hill, Gary. "ABC's William H. Lawrence… California's Brown in Election Trouble," *Lincoln Evening Journal & Nebraska State Journal.* Lincoln, Nebraska, June 15, 1966.

[17] McIntosh, Alan. "It Seems to Me." *Lincoln Journal.* Lincoln, Nebraska. June 13, 1972.

[18] "Bill Lawrence: Always Candor," *Lincoln Journal Star.* Lincoln, Nebraska, August 13, 1972.

[19] Photo of Bill Lawrence provided by Department of Journalism, UN-L. Thank you Larry Walklin and staff for assistance with the photo of Lawrence.

"Pioneer of rural electrification is Nebraska." *Lincoln Journal Star.* Lincoln, Nebraska, February 6, 1956.

"Political Scandal Brewing. Goldfine, Friend May "tell all," United Press International (UPI), *Lincoln Star.* Lincoln, Nebraska, December 2, 1961.

Thank you to Tammi Peterson of the *Lincoln Journal Star* for her assistance in retrieving old envelopes of newspapers clippings to review.

Nebraska Authors Book & Travel Club
Attend an event at Lincoln High School and attach a photo or ticket.

GEORGE LORIN MILLER

Date of birth: 1830
Location of birth: Boonville, NY
Education: early education
unknown
College of Physicians and Surgeons, New York City, grad 1852
Moved to Omaha: 1854
Military: Civilian Clerk/sutler[1] at
Fort Kearny, NE until 1864
Date of Death: Aug. 28, 1920
Location of Death: Omaha

Nebraska State Historical Society Collection
George Lorin Miller

Known Publications:

Omaha Daily Herald, created, co-owned, managed, and edited by George Lorin Miller, 1865-1887.

Morton, J. Sterling, Albert Watkins editor in chief; Dr. George L. Miller associate editor. Illustrated History of Nebraska: A History of Nebraska from the Earliest Exploration of the Trans-Mississippi Region. Volume I. Lincoln: Jacob North and Co. 1906, 1907, third edition 1911. And Volume II, 1906.

It is 1854. Dr. George L. Miller is contemplating a move from the East Coast to the new frontier. News of the day includes the new invention of street lights being lit with coal for the first time, Charles Miller patents the first U.S. sewing machine to stitch buttonholes and Allen Wilson patents a sewing machine to sew curving seams, and Aaron Allen of Boston patents folding theater chairs. George F.B. Reiman proposed that space is curved. Charles Dickens begins to serialize his work "Hard Times" in the *Household Words* magazine. And despite numerous steamboat and ferry boat accidents killing many riders on both the East and West Coast during the year, a "Grand Excursion" took prominent Easterners from Chicago to Rock Island, Illinois, by railroad and then up the Mississippi to St. Paul, Minnesota, by steamboat in June.

Local News: While the Marine Telegraph was being completed from Fort Point to San Francisco and first telegraph lines between Texas and New Orleans were constructed, the Territories of Kansas and Nebraska were created. The Kansas-Nebraska Act repealed the Missouri Compromise (of 1820).

In World News: An April earthquake destroyed San Salvador; the Dutch army stops a Chinese uprising in Borneo; Australian miners are killed by state troopers over mining licenses; Commodore Matthew Perry of the United States Navy signs the Treaty/Convention of Kanagawa with the Japanese government, opening the ports of Shimoda and Hakadate to American Trade; United States diplomatic minister Robert McLane arrives at the Heavenly Capital aboard the American warship USS Susquehanna during the Taiping Rebellion; the Crimean War begins; and on October 21, Florence Nightingale and a staff of thirty-eight nurses were sent into the war. On October 25 the Charge of the Light Brigade/Battle of Balaklava was conducted showing the world, once again, that military officers will knowingly send their men to their death and the men will go without a whimper. A famous poem by Alfred Lord Tennyson followed the slaughter.

Back in the States: The first meetings of the newly named Republican Party are held in Ripon, Wisconsin. Abraham Lincoln makes his first political speech at the Illinois State Fair. And in December, Roman Catholics find out that Pope Pius IX proclaimed Immaculate Conception and made Mary free from original sin.

It would still be nearly twenty years before Mr. Arthur Fairchild[2] ventures West to teach at the new Doane College and four years before General Vifquain[3] brings his new bride to the Saline County. Othman Abbott,[4] age twelve, wouldn't move to the Grand Island area for another thirteen years. O.C. Dake[5] is a newspaperman traveling his state with a new speaker named Abraham Lincoln, and it would be nearly ten years before he and his family moved to the state.

In the meantime, before the end of 1854, Dr. George Lorin Miller resigned his position as city physician of Syracuse, New York. He moved to Omaha with his wife, Harriet Elizabeth. In October 1954,

J. Sterling Morton[6] and his new bride moved south of Omaha. The Miller's and the Morton's meet within the next year and begin an interesting history together tied to their new land.

Dr. Miller wasn't the only family member in the new territory village of Omaha. His father, Lorin Miller, had moved to Omaha in 1852 when there were about twenty people in the river town area. The streets were mud, and law and order was in the imagination. Lorin later became mayor. When Dr. Miller moved to Nebraska he set up the first medical practice in the city. He was elected as a representative to the first Nebraska Territorial Legislature the same year. He served four years on the territorial council, serving as president in his second term.

By 1855, Dr. Miller asked the Congregationalist religious denomination to have a minister sent to Omaha. The church assigned Reuben Gaylord to the area. Gaylord became a well-known Christian missionary in the state's early years.[5,7]

Dr. Miller built the Herndon Hotel, the first in town, at 9th and Farnam. Later it became the Union Pacific headquarters. In 1860, giving up his medical practice in Omaha, Dr. Miller moved to St. Joseph, Missouri, where he began putting his thoughts on paper and submitting them to local newspapers. According to Wallace Brown who wrote his thesis in 1959 on <u>George L. Miller and the Omaha Herald 1854-1869</u>,[8] his research found Miller had written: "It was some writing that I did in St. Joseph on the Gazette in the absence of its editor in 1860, and the rankling recollection of this campaign against the South Platte mobs that led me to start the Omaha Daily Herald in 1865." Miller conceded that there was a dislike of Democrats in the area but it didn't dissuade him from starting the paper. According to Brown, Miller wrote, "It took years for me to trim down my fluffy style to cleanness of expression. Scholars and men of experience were arrayed in opposition on every hand and I lacked self-confidence."

Miller returned to the Nebraska territory from his experiences in St. Joe to help recruit for the First Nebraska Regiment which formed before the Civil War. He served as a civilian clerk/sutler[1] at Fort Kearny until 1864.

According to D. Ray Wilson's research on Fort Kearny, a territorial militia was organized to protect settlers south of the Platte. "Acting Territorial Governor T.B. Cuming had authorized the formation of two regiments of Volunteers in an order issued December 23, 1854…M.H. Clark was the regimental surgeon and he was assisted by George L.

Miller." Miller had joined the volunteers in 1861 when John Heth resigned the post of sutler. Heth, like many of the volunteers of the Nebraska territory militia, was sympathetic to the cause of the Southern states. Many left their post in Nebraska and joined active civil war regiments. Heth, however, returned to Nebraska City as a businessman and Dr. Miller took his position.[9] According to the "Least We Forget" column, Miller was appointed to that position by President Lincoln.[10]

Dr. Miller returned to Omaha in the summer of 1864 and was nominated as a Democratic candidate to run for the territorial delegate to Congress, but was defeated. Within the next year, he and Dan W. Carpenter started the Democratic *Omaha Daily Herald* as an evening paper. Lyman Richardson soon bought out Carpenter's interest in the paper. Miller remained editor until March 1, 1887. He had a vigorous writing style and soon became a power in journalism and politics. With his editorship, he was also the president of the Western Associated Press - a forerunner of the Associated Press - adds the "Least We Forget" column writer.[10]

The already-established Republican *Omaha Bee* newspaper editor was Edward Rosewater and he did not like the competition. According to an article on September 6, 1876, Rosewater called Dr. Miller, "jack-of-all trades and master of none" listing many of Dr. Millers previous jobs: "a medicine man, a hotel builder, an army sutler, a cotton speculator, a railroad jobber, an eating-house keeper, journalist, and a politician." He added some adjectives which would set up a rivalry between the two papers, and others like the *Bee*, for years to come: 'a dishonest, unscrupulous, and unprincipled money-grabber'.

J. Sterling Morton, a Democratic newspaper editor in Nebraska City, did not always see eye-to-eye with Dr. Miller's points of view. History records a bitter personal feud between them that arose from time to time. However, Morton recognized Miller's ability and said of him: "No other man, either by the power of money, or by the power of brawn, or by the strength of brain, did as much to make Omaha a city," noted the Nebraska State Historical Society (NSHS) website.[11] According to Brown, J. Sterling Morton added, "Every morning there was something new in the way of hope, suggestion or fact for the benefit of Omaha and its resources."[8-p93]

While Dr. Miller served as editor of his paper and saw the new State as a whole, he was a promoter of tree-planting. Dr. Miller also focused on Nebraska Agriculture. He and George Holdrege, the manager of the

Burlington Railroad lines west of the Missouri, were "instrumental in successfully introducing winter wheat into Nebraska, and advocated a new method of sowing wheat," summarized an NSHS article.[11,12]

Dr. Miller worked to have the transcontinental railroad and the Union Pacific Missouri River Bridge located at Omaha. According to the "Least We Forget" column: "At a time when the issue seemed doubtful he went to New York to see Dr. Durant, one of the builders and Vice President, and through his friendship secured the prize. Associated in this task with Dr. Miller were Ezra Millard and Augustus Kountze." [10]

The *Omaha Daily Herald* was sold by Miller in 1887. It, like the *Bee*, eventually became part of the *Omaha World Herald*. While Rosewater may not have been impressed by Dr. Miller's opinions, writing, and editing skills, James C. Olson wrote that "Dr. George L. Miller began the quarter-century of editorial service which transformed the *Omaha Herald* from a struggling frontier paper to a journal of national importance" [13-p354.]

According to an *Omaha World Herald* story of July 2, 1987, writer Rosse wrote that Dr. George Miller moved his sights to a hill outside of Omaha and built "a castle on a hill." He had stones for the castle shipped from Scotland for the seventeen-room home. "Miller, a friend of Arbor Day founder J. Sterling Morton, planted thousands of trees, stocked the area with deer…" and called the estate Deerfield. Perhaps a memorial article about his wife Harriett found in the files of the Omaha Library describing her November 2, 1899, death gives the reason for the luxury: Mrs. Miller *"came to Omaha with her husband in 1854 sharing the privations of earliest settlers who had brought education and refinement to the prairie camp. Her health never was robust and for forty years previous to her death she was an invalid. On this account she was prevented from taking part in the social life of the city for which her culture and tastes fitted her. But through her long years of invalids her kind heart and generous impulses have been manifest from time to time."[14]*

Rosse's article continues; "In 1888 Miller began turning the rest of his 460 acres into a small suburb named Seymour, named after another friend Congressman Horatio Seymour [the area of Seymour part has become Lakewood Country Club]. Miller's castle burned around the turn of the century, and Miller left the area soon after. The Scottish stones were recovered and used in building St. Martin Episcopal Church in South Omaha."

Dr. Miller, having lost his wife and his home, continued to promote Omaha and Nebraska. He served on the committee to promote the Trans-Mississippi and International Exposition in Omaha of 1899, offering a portion of his own land for the event. An area near what is now Kountze Park was chosen, but Dr. Miller was chosen president of the event committee.

During the planning stages of the Exposition, somewhere around 1887, C.S. Paine[15] and other men asked J. Sterling Morton[6] to be supervising editor of a <u>History of Nebraska</u>. Morton agreed and asked Albert Watkins[16] to assist him. Through the course of the compiling, prioritizing and editing, Dr. George Miller became the associate editor to Watkins, especially following the untimely death of Morton. [6,15,16,17]

Rosse's article continues: "Although Miller is considered the founder of Ralston, the city takes its name from Edgar Ralston a Chicago financier who, in 1908, helped completed Millers plan of building houses and laying out streets for the newly incorporated town."

Dr. Miller served as the president of the Nebraska State Historical Society from 1907 to 1909, and continued in politics. He did not support Nebraska Democrat William Jennings Bryan for President stating openly that he did not consider Bryan a real democrat as his politics were radical.

Once again death took its toll at the Miller home. On May 19, 1910, the *Omaha World Herald* ran a story about the passing of Francis Briggs, Dr. Miller's new wife of four years. She died of acute Bright's disease following an attack of erysipelas which followed an operation. Dr. Miller was recovering from a sudden illness of his own at the sanitarium at the time of her death. When he recovered, he continued with his civic interests until his own death ten years later. He never wavered from the unashamed promotion of Omaha, and in exposing issues that he considered jeopardizing the stability of the Omaha area and the State of Nebraska.[18]

George L. Miller.
Morton Illustrated History of Nebraska. Photo, inside cover, circa 1906

Dr. Miller became the first president of the Board of Park Commissioners in Omaha and it is during his administration that the present system of parks and boulevards was initiated. He served as a member of the fire and police commissioners. He was one of the founders of the Omaha Club. There are several schools, and Miller Park, named after this historic editor and promoter of Nebraska. A portion of Miller Park is located near Sorenson Parkway and 30th Street in North Omaha.

According to the column "Least We Forget," *Dr. George Miller, one of the founders of the Omaha Herald and known in later years as the "Father of Omaha" was one of the earliest of pioneer residents here and was identified from the first with the city's growth and progress. He died at age 90 and lies at rest in Forest Lawn Cemetery.*[10] N

Endnotes, Footnotes & Sources:

President's Annual Address by Robert B. Windham, Nebraska State Historical Society. www.usgenet.org. Reviewed November 28, 2012.

www.wikipedia. George L. Miller. Reviewed November 28, 2012.

[1] www.wikipedia. Sutler. Reviewed January 13, 2013. *"A sutler or victualer is a civilian merchant who sells provisions to an army in the field, in camp or in quarters. The sulter sold wares from the back of a wagon or temporary tent, allowing them to travel along with an army or to remote military outposts. Sulters wagons were associated with the military while chuck wagons served a similar purpose for civilian wagon trains and outposts."* The operation had to have the approval of the local commanding officer.

[2] Hansen, Nancy Sue and Dush, Barbara Ann. Nebraska Authors Volume One. "Fred Rogers Fairchild," "Henry Pratt Fairchild." Fullerton: D & H Adventures Publishing. 2013.

[3] Hansen, Nancy Sue and Dush, Barbara Ann. Nebraska Authors Volume One. "Jean-Baptist Victor Vifquain." Fullerton: D & H Adventures Publishing. 2013.

[4] Hansen, Nancy Sue and Dush, Barbara Ann. Nebraska Authors Volume One. "Othman A. Abbott." Fullerton: D & H Adventures Publishing. 2013.

[5] Hansen, Nancy Sue and Dush, Barbara Ann. Nebraska Authors Volume One. "O.C. Dake." Fullerton: D & H Adventures Publishing. 2013.

[6] Hansen, Nancy Sue and Dush, Barbara Ann. <u>Nebraska Authors Volume One</u>. "J. Sterling Morton". Fullerton: D & H Adventures Publishing. 2013.

[7] Editor's note: Reading about Omaha history from various authors will give you an idea why Miller called for assistance in the area. One author is: Bristow, David L. <u>A Dirty, Wicked Town: tales of 19th Century Omaha</u>. Caxton Press, 2000.

[8] Brown, Wallace. <u>George L. Miller and the Omaha Herald 1854-1869</u>. A thesis presented to University of Nebraska, Lincoln, July 1959.

[9] Wilson, D. Ray. <u>Fort Kearny on the Platte</u>. Ill: Crossroads Communications.1980, p 231.

[10] " Least We Forget Dr. George L. Miller 1830-1920". *Omaha World Herald*, Omaha, Nebraska, date unknown.

[11] *Miller. George L.* Nebraska State Historical Society. NSHAS Website. Reviewed September 2012.

[12] Miller corresponded with C.S. Paine in 1903 discussing a newspaper article about Miller and his role in Nebraska Agriculture. Both the article and the letter can be found in the Miller papers at NSHS.

[13] Olson, James C. <u>History of Nebraska</u>. Lincoln: University of Nebraska Press, 1955, 370 pp.

[14] Rosse, Sharon. "Birthday Candles Join Roman Candles in Ralston." *Omaha World Herald*, Omaha, Nebraska, July 2, 1987.

[15] Hansen, Nancy Sue and Dush, Barbara Ann. <u>Nebraska Authors Volume One</u>. "C. S. Paine." Fullerton: D & H Adventures Publishing. 2013.

[16] Hansen, Nancy Sue and Dush, Barbara Ann. <u>Nebraska Authors Volume One</u>. "Albert Watkins." Fullerton: D & H Adventures Publishing. 2013.

[17] Hansen, Nancy Sue and Dush, Barbara Ann. <u>Nebraska Authors Volume One</u>. "Grant L. Shumway." Fullerton: D & H Adventures Publishing. 2013.

[18] As the final editing of the Morton <u>Illustrated History of Nebraska</u> was concluding a letter dated February 17, 1912, from J.W. Hallam, lawyer, from Sioux City, Iowa, was addressed to Miller's co-editor Albert Watkins. There is no known notation that Miller saw the letter, but the content was apparently visible to him at the time of the previous election

as he stood against fellow Nebraskan for President on similar subjects. *"My dear Mr. Watkins: I have just received your letter of yesterday and in reply say that you are right in saying that our city government has usually been controlled very largely by the corporations. I think, however, I can say that under the new plan thus far, this has not been so apparent. We were fortunate in getting one or two very good men elected under the new plan. With bad men, in corporation control would be just as easy or possibly easier, than under the old system. You see we have had only one election since adopting this plank and how it will be in the future, only time can tell. I think it is undoubtedly true that there should, as you suggest, be a separate and real executive with greater responsibilities. The Mayor under our plan is a good deal of a figure head. In fact, I am inclined to think that we could get better results if we could get one good capable man to manage and be responsible for the entire city government. One who would be about the same as a manager of a private corporation. It would be perhaps as well if he were not a resident of the city at all, prior to his appointment. The great trouble in our city government is that on account of frequent elections and changes in office, no man can formulate and carry out any very definite policy of his own. There has been some friction among our commissioners, but nothing very serious thus far. They have worked together fairly well as yet. I am free to say, however, that I can see very little difference in the methods or the results. It is probably a step in the right direction away from the old plan, but only a step in my judgment. By the way, have you a curfew ordinance in Lincoln? If so, how does it work? If you have not any, you need not take the trouble of answering this question, but the matter is being agitated here...."*

JULIUS "J" STERLING MORTON

Date of birth: April 22, 1832
Location of birth: Adams, NY
Education: Monroe, MI until
age 14 apprenticed as a printer
with Uncle Edward G. Morton
Wesleyan Seminary prep school,
Albion MI, 1847
attended University of Michigan,
Ann Arbor 1850-1854 (reinstat-
ed with diploma 1858)
Honorary B.A. Union College
Schenectady, NY, 1856
Moved to Bellevue, NE, Oct 30,
1854
**What town called home in Ne-
braska:** Nebraska City
Date of Death: April 27, 1902
Location of Death: Lake Forest,
IL, at home of his son Mark

Known Publications:

J. Sterling Morton contributed articles to the *Detroit Free Press* while
he was in college. His grandfather was the editor. At the University of
Michigan, as a junior, he published *The Peninsular Quarterly and University Magazine.* When he moved to the Nebraska territory he wrote
for the territory's first newspaper: *The Nebraska Palladium,* Bellevue.
When he moved his family to Nebraska City he became the editor of
the *Nebraska City News.* He founded *The Conservative* weekly magazine in 1898.

Morton, J. Sterling. Reminiscences of the Lower St. Joseph River Valley. St. Joseph, Michigan : A. B. Morse Co., n.d. 106 pp. Memoir.

Morton, J. Sterling. <u>Report of the Secretary of Agriculture, 1893</u>. United States Department of Agriculture, 1894.

Beattie, James A, editor; Morton, J Sterling, Watkins, Albert. <u>School History of Nebraska</u>. Lincoln: Western, 1920.

Morton, J. Sterling, succeeded by Albert Watkins, editor in chief; Dr. George L. Miller, associate editor. <u>Illustrated History of Nebraska : A History of Nebraska from the Earliest Explorations of the Trans-Mississippi Region</u>. Volume I. Lincoln: Jacob North and Co. 1906, 1907, third edition 1911.

Morton, J. Sterling, succeeded by Albert Watkins, editor in chief; Dr. George L. Miller, associate editor. <u>Illustrated History of Nebraska : A History of Nebraska from the Earliest Explorations of the Trans-Mississippi Region</u>. Volume II. Lincoln: Jacob North and Co. 1906,

Morton, J. Sterling, Albert Watkins, Grant L. Shumway. <u>History of Nebraska from the earliest explorations of the trans-Mississippi region</u>. Revised edition. Lincoln: Western Publishing. 1918.

Morton, J. Sterling and Albert Watkins. <u>History of Nebraska from the Earliest Explorations of the Trans-Mississippi region</u>. A Revised Edition. Edited and revised by Augustus O. Thomas, James A. Beattie, Arthur C. Wakeley. Lincoln, Western Publishing and Engraving Company. 1918. [History of Nebraska From the Earliest Explorations to the Present Time by Albert Watkins, Volume III First Edition. Lincoln: Western Publishing and Engraving Company, 1913].

Morton, J. Sterling [Conservative]. <u>White Cow : and other tales : being some anecdotes about Indian orators of the territorial period of Nebraska</u>. Publisher: Paul Morton. 1908.

The printed word was expression for J. Sterling Morton. He wrote numerous articles, editorials and letters expressing his points of view. While most people use a journal or a diary to preserve their private thoughts, Morton wrote many emotional memories inside a prize possession: his own collection of books. While anyone can research the Morton letters and documents at the Nebraska State Historical Society, few have seen inside his library collection at Arbor Lodge.

In 2008, Special Events Coordinator/Curator Laura Steinman was hired for the J. Sterling Morton family legacy: Arbor Lodge State Historical Park. She made a surprising discovery about J. Sterling Morton and his book collection. She wrote for a grant to compile what she found and has given the Nebraska Authors Project® a copy of the grant proposal which is reproduced here, in part, as a glimpse into the private life of the man and his books.

"J. Sterling Morton was an avid collector of books. Topics range from classical literature, poetry, science, religion, agriculture, home health remedies, and politics. As a lover of both books and history, I was thrilled and amazed with what I discovered as I arranged Morton's books within his office. Not only did nearly every book contain a personalized bookplate, but many included personal inscriptions. These included observations of the day, where he was traveling to/from, where he purchased the book/ how much he paid for it, and sometimes even his political thoughts of the time. Morton used the books as diaries, recording some of his innermost thoughts. …Morton signed many books on page thirty-two (he was born in 1832). He was a deep thinking man, who was politically ahead of his time. He was an avid reader, compiling his profound thoughts into the margins of books, apparently for later use in speeches and for personal reflection.

Other inscriptions seem to recall his travels. Within his book <u>Victor Hugo: His Life and Works</u>, Morton wrote, "Left Arbor Lodge November 5, 1885 for Chicago, because of telegram from Paul announcing the death in Paris, France on Saturday last, October 31ˢᵗ, 1885 of E.I. Wheeler Esqr, Joy's partner. On CB&2 Train."

Sometimes Morton's inscriptions provide information regarding how he obtained the book (gift) or why it was meaningful to him. One such example is <u>OO-MAH-HA TA-WA-THA (Omaha City)</u> by Fannie Reed Giffen. On the back cover of the book, Morton wrote in black ink. "J. Sterling Morton of Arbor Lodge near Nebraska City Otoe County Nebraska USA." Published in 1898, it includes biographical sketches and history of the Omaha Indians. Morton wrote, "J. Sterling Morton became acquainted with the Omaha Indians at their village near Bellevue Nebraska in November 1854 and personally knew many of the signers of the treaty herein biographed as participators and signators of the treaty *of March 16, 1854."*

While Morton recorded his observations within the margins of his books, his books also reveal him to be a man who could also grasp true depth of emotions, from joy to sorrow. These personal touches reveal another side to the seemingly austere politician. Upon the death of his wife, Caroline J. Sterling, he had a book stamp made. The purple-ink stamp is in several of J. Sterling's books, as well as J. Sterling and Caroline's family Bible. The inscription on the stamp reads, Caroline Morton…wife of J. STERLING MORTON and Mother of JOY, PAUL, MARK, and CARL MORTON. Embroidered, and painted on china, and on canvas, with skill, and played upon the piano with vivacity and expression. She died on June 29, 1881. This is a memento to her industry, fidelity, cheerfulness and courage. Her competent and efficient administration of the household was incomparable.

A few years later, Morton was still expressing grief over the loss of his beloved Caroline. In 1884, friend George H. Pendleton gave him a book on Tariff Laws. Within the book, Morton wrote, Arbor Lodge Founded June 1855. Since that date has been the home of J. Sterling Morton and his family. But 'the light went out on June 29th, 1881.'

In the foreword pages of a book titled <u>The Essays or Counsels Civil and Moral of Francis Bacon</u>*, J. Sterling recorded the death of his youngest son, Carl. Carl Morton died January 7th, 1901 at Waukegan, Illinois, where he was General Manager and President of the United States Sugar Refining Company. Carl was born February 18th, 1865 at Arbor Lodge. He was a good son, an able man, a faithful husband and an affectionate father. JSM*

When people write diaries, especially notables like Morton, they have to know there is a chance that someday their private thoughts may be publicized. However, when he recorded his thoughts within the margins and covers of his books, I believe these were meant for his eyes and his comfort. Little did he know, that approximately one hundred thirty years later an Arbor Lodge employee and history enthusiast would be inspired to reveal the man she found within the pages.

W ho was this book lover and author J. Sterling Morton? True to the constraints of the Nebraska Authors Project,® a full biography of an author is not written in this volume; but instead, an overview of what made the author qualified or otherwise driven to pursue the writing and publication of a book(s) about the history of Nebraska.

James C. Olson described the writings from the new western frontier in his 1955 book <u>History of Nebraska</u> [1-p 354] "…*The first, and for many years only, outlet for literary expression was that provided by the press. A number of the early editors were conscious of the literary aspects of their calling, and some of their work may properly be considered as a contribution to the literature of the region. Their primary interests were progress and politics. They were a vigorous breed of men, never a loss for words, and never without an opinion. They described political opponents in terms that would bring libel suits today. They had an inexhaustible store of adjectives with which to describe the present condition and future prospects of their state and community.*"

J. Sterling Morton was one of those men. Morton, known as a mischievous, stubborn youth, found that due to neglecting his recitations at the University of Michigan he would not be graduating with his class in May 1854. He had achieved many things while at the University, however, not enough attention had been paid to specific requirements. The day before he was to be expelled, six weeks before graduation, a favorite professor from the medical department was expelled. This was immediately unpopular with the students and faculty. In a public protest Morton spoke out against what he saw as an injustice to a friendly professor.

When Morton's removal occurred the next day, there was another protest and even the newspapers in the state took notice of the trouble at the University. Morton's work was praised. The University wanted him to make a concession of some kind to be restored to school. Morton did not characteristically offer retractions for anything, but finally did sign a statement. He was admitted into school only to have the school authorities change his statement to fit their agenda. Morton found out and wrote a "blistering letter to the *Free Press*, reviewing the whole affair, and in a style that is precursory of the brilliant invective he was to use against opponents in later years."[2-p. 28] Morton was re-expelled. He was granted an honorary Bachelor of Arts degree by Union College in Schenectady, New York, in 1856. Later, according to Olson, "the University of Michigan in September 1858, the faculty adopted a remission of expulsion and granted the usual diploma."[2-p. 29]

While J. Sterling Morton's higher education diploma was being debated, he and Caroline Joy French, a Wesleyan Seminary prep school sweetheart, were married and moved to the newly opened Nebraska Territory the same day: October 30, 1854.

Morton began writing for the Territory's first newspaper: *The Nebraska Palladium*. The conversation of the day was the location of the new capitol. Once again Morton's opinions would cost him something of value: a seat in the first Nebraska legislature. Acting Governor Thomas B. Cuming wanted Omaha as the state capitol and Morton printed his favor of Bellevue. Later it would be Cuming who made sure Morton did not get seated in the first Legislature for Morton's attack against Cuming's capitol stance.

In that first 1855 legislature, the name of Pierce County was changed to Otoe County making Nebraska City the county seat. Morton was appointed clerk of the territory's Supreme Court. About this time Caroline and J. Sterling decided to move to Nebraska City where he would be the editor of the *Nebraska City News*. The news of the area included: There were no bridges across the Missouri River yet, but many plans were proposed and there was a need for lumber which was difficult to find in the treeless prairie. [9]

The Morton's began building a new home. As soon as it was finished they planted trees around it and called it Arbor Lodge. As the years progressed Morton became a respected agriculturalist and was teaching people the modern techniques of farming and forestry. By

2012 view of Morton Home at Arbor Lodge.[14]

January 4, 1872, Morton was successful in moving the state board of agriculture to adopt a resolution to appoint a day to be known as Arbor Day. It was celebrated on April 10 of the same year and has continued to spread across the country as a celebration today. He and Caroline raised four boys at Arbor Lodge: Joy, Paul, Mark and Carl.

While building his new home, working in agriculture and writing, Morton was elected and seated in the second territorial legislature meeting in Omaha in December 1855. He did not shy away from the controversial subjects. His opinion was heard when he wrote that the natural boundary between Nebraska and Kansas was the Platte River and of his position charter banks, which he called fraudulent. The bank issues passed and J. Sterling was defeated in a re-election bid in 1856. He was proven correct when the banks failed the next year and the year following he was re-elected to the legislature. Morton also lobbied various interests of the railroads during these early years.

Morton was known as a Bourbon Democrat[3] which meant he took the conservative position on political, economic, and social issues and opposed political agrarianism. Morton's views, according to biographer James C. Olson, were more like his uncle Edward's than his father J.D. Morton. J.D. was interested in Republican movement "and often deplored his son's Democratic views." [2-p.15]

Nebraska Capitol photo of Morton hanging on wall honoring territorial government officials.

When United States President James Buchanan was elected to office, he appointed J. Sterling Morton to Secretary of the Territory in July 1858. Morton had also served as Acting Governor from December 5, 1858, to May 2, 1859. When Abraham Lincoln became President in 1861, Morton was replaced as Secretary of the Territory with a Republican.[3] While Morton preferred a States Rights attitude on slavery, his family publication history in Michigan of anti-mason, anti-monopoly, and slavery issues and J. Sterling's own association with these ideas in his own writings were known. His Michigan publisher Uncle Edward was against President Lincoln and the Republicans. J Sterling Morton ran for several offices in his lifetime and was often defeated only to have the winner become controversial, or in the case of Governor David Butler, impeached.

Nebraska Statehood was March 1, 1867. From his Nebraska City home Morton continued to write and teach modern farming and forestry to the new immigrants. Future governor Robert Furnas and Morton founded the Nebraska State Horticultural Society in 1869. The concept was to give fruit growers a place to obtain ideas and information. As president of the State Board of Agriculture, Morton issued an appeal in 1874 for agricultural exhibits at a Nebraska State Fair to be held in Omaha. Newspapers, such as the Plattsmouth *Nebraska Herald,* ran the request for exhibitors in May; and on September 29 of that year, the State Fair opened.[4] In 1891, Morton became president of the Nebraska State Historical Society and served until his death. [5]

When the United States elected President Grover Cleveland, Morton was asked to be United States Secretary of Agriculture [the third for the nation, the first for a Nebraskan]. He served from March 7, 1893, to March 5, 1897. His priority was tightening the agricultural budget: he closed some experimental stations, but increased other research and weather stations. He established the Farmers' Bulletins which provided farmers with information about increasing production. History credits Morton with helping to change the department into a coordinated service to farmers and assisting Cleveland to set up national forest reservations.[6]

Morton returned to Nebraska to promote conservative causes. In 1898 he started a weekly magazine, *The Conservative,* which he continued to publish until his death. The Spanish American War was 1898 headline news with the Third Nebraska Infantry led by Lieutenant-Colonel Victor Vifquain[7] and Colonel William Jennings Bryan. While it was in progress Americans, including Morton, debated merits of the venture. In a typewritten letter written to Mr. Albert Watkins[8] December 19, 1900, Morton reflected back on this time:*" My dear Watkins: …I am glad that you are pleased with the Conservative's reminiscent side and hope to be able to publish at least one article of that character each week. Politically I have no predictions to make, but I am glad to see that the two ex-presidents-Cleveland and Harrison-perfectly agree as to insular possessions and the policies which threaten the government because of them. Personally, I was against the Spanish war. It never should have been commenced. It could have been avoided. It was avoided by Grover Cleveland and he was importuned by as many jingoists as ever swarmed around the White House since McKinley came in. All of our sentimental gush in behalf of Cubans has resulted in bloodshed, disaster, taxes, dishonor, disgrace. And the end is not yet in sight. When one recalls the peurile disputes in the house of representatives between Bailey on one side and Grosvenor on the other, as to whether this was a Republican or a Democratic war, it nauseates the memory. Yours truly,"* In a handwritten note at the bottom of the letter Morton wrote: *"Had the Treaty of Paris never been ratified there would be less complication, Bryan, McKinley &Co did the ratification."*

When William Jennings Bryan retired from the military, he became a writer and started *The Commoner* in Lincoln modeled after Morton's *The Conservative*, according to Olson.[1] Morton was against the ideals of Bryan and wrote openly about their differences. Morton had differences of opinions with other newspaper editors including George L. Miller[9] in Omaha. Miller later assisted with the editorship of the <u>History of Nebraska</u> volumes started by J. Sterling Morton.

The Trans-Mississippi and International Exposition was held in Omaha from June 8 to October 31, 1898. Morton had been the Nebraska representative at the Paris Exposition and was one of the commissioners at the Philadelphia Exposition. While several versions of the story are recalled by other authors, it was sometime during the planning of the 1898 Exposition that J. Sterling Morton was asked by a group of men, including C.S. Paine,[10] to be the editor of a book on Nebraska history. He agreed. Morton also persuaded Albert Watkins to assist him in the editorship of the project. As a faithful friend, Watkins work would last from 1898 to 1911 and the completion of the three volumes at his death.[8] Gathering the information and planning the project began as Morton's responsibility.

In a letter dated April 28, 1898, from J. Sterling Morton to Mrs. N.M. Richardson of Lincoln, Nebraska, he wrote: *"Having, at the suggestion of good friends, assumed the duties of editor-in-chief of a comprehensive History of the State of Nebraska and the Trans-Mississippi Exposition together with biographies and portraits of the progressive men and representative women of the state, I realize the vital importance of securing verified historical data and facts from all parts of the Commonwealth. Consequently I presume sufficiently upon your connection with this work to ask that you will carefully search out in the different localities where you may sojourn everything worthy of record in the past and in the present, and having perfectly proved the same to be accurate, you will do me the favor of forwarding it to me at Arbor Lodge, Nebraska City, Otoe County. Your attention is especially directed to the value of such data and the facts as will best illustrate the growth and success of agriculture and horticulture together with commercial and manufacturing enterprises in each locality."* Many such letters were written to leaders of each county, church, and organization of the day. Each highlighted the need for detailed accuracy in the information so the proposed book would be as correct to date as possible.

In a second letter on April 28, Morton wrote to Mr. C.S. Paine[10] the Superintendent of Agents at Omaha, Nebraska *"...And now having taken this responsibility, I am impressed that it is my serious duty to ask you to gather for me and verify such historical data as you may meet with during your travels in behalf of the circulation of the work. It is exceedingly important that this work be made absolutely accurate and perfectly truthful. Consequently in securing subscriptions you are at liberty to assure all patrons that nothing shall appear in these volumes that can not be verified, provided vigilance in behalf of the unvarnished truth can be made efficient and fictitious. There can be no compensation great enough to pay me or any other person having self-respect, for telling lies about the Pioneer generation of a great commonwealth. By sending to me at Arbor Lodge, Nebraska City, Otoe County, any data from any city, county or precinct which you deem worth of historical record and preservation, either from an agricultural, horticultural, commercial or manufacturing standpoint, you will confer a great personal favor."* Mr. Clarence S. "C.S." Paine became the managing editor for the Morton-Watkins historical volumes which were sold prior to publication using the system known as "subscriptions."[8,9,10,11]

It wasn't just the many Nebraskans that received requests for information letters. Letters were sent to persons outside the State of Nebraska to ask them about their connections with the state and to provide documentation for those activities. Massive amounts of material were received, sorted and prioritized before writing began.

On April 30, 1898, Morton received a letter from Thomas Benacum Bishop of Lincoln: *"I have just been informed that at the repeated and urgent solicitation of many of our foremost citizens, you have at length consented to write a History of the State of Nebraska. The news gratifies me beyond expression. Someone has said that only a Livy could have written the history of Rome, and that only a Thucydides could have told us of the fortunes and vicissitudes of Greece. If this is true-and I see no reason to question the statement – it follows that only a Nebraskan can and should write the History of Nebraska. And if only a Nebraskan who is more eminently qualified for the task than the Sage of Arbor Lodge? You have made the name of our Commonwealth known and respected where the English language is spoken. From the beginning of our Territorial Government down to the present day you have been a witness*

Morton reading a letter Cira 1900[5]

of the growth of our State and of the events which transpired during that time. There has not been within our borders a social or political movement of any consequence of which you can not truthfully say in the words of Aneus: _Quoreni magna pars fui_. Add to this your great and acknowledged literary ability, your varied, extensive and profound knowledge and unbounded love of the subject – in a word, the possession of all these qualities of the mind which go to make up the historian, and who will deny that Nebraska has been singularity fortunate in the selection of the chronicler who is to tell her story to posterity? Wishing you a full measure of success in your undertaking, I have the better to be, dear sir, Your faithful servant."

By May 1898, a letter written by J. Sterling Morton as a response to the Honorable Thomas P. Kinnard noted: "_My dear Sir: I thank you very sincerely for your complimentary and kindly sympathetic note of May 9 relative to the coming History of the State of Nebraska. It will be my endeavor as supervising editor of the work to see that every character which is prominent in the history of the state is treated justly. The great difficulty of such a work is in keeping out irrelevant rather that in putting in valuable data and statistic. The opulence of the last forty years in instance of wonder advancement and development is much that the historian must be rather bewildered in making choice of the best examples._"[12]

As part of the project planning Morton had requested various citizens to help verify and prioritize material that came to him for the project. Simply reading the material and sending it to the designated person was one of the tasks for Morton. One note he sent while forwarding material was to Mr. H. L. Rucker at the Jacob, North & Co. publishing office on May 9, 1898: "_Dear Sir: I enclose you a letter written to me by C.J. Ernst on May 7 with memorandum for his biography. Turn this over to the person who is doing the biographical work_ *for Lincoln and Lancaster County. Mr. Ernst came under my personal observation when a mere boy and I take a great interest in him and if I remember correctly, I was the one who recommended him for a position in the B.&M. R.R. Co. and was instrumental in getting him started with that corporation. The biographer who is going to do this work had better inquire of Mr. Ernst as to his relations with the undersigned. Let me see this sketch as soon as it is finished."*

Back in 1891 when Morton had taken on the position of president of the Nebraska State Historical Society, he not only presided over meetings, but attempted to encourage others to become interested in the history of the state. On January 17, 1898, before the Exposition in Omaha and the proposal of the history of Nebraska book gained popularity, Morton wrote a letter to Albert Watkins who was then working as a Receiver for failed banks. *"My dear Watkins: I received your letter of September 24, 1897, in due time and postponed answering the same because I thought I should see you at Lincoln during the annual meeting of the State Historical Society of Nebraska, which transpired on the 11th and 12th of this month. But I neither saw nor heard anything of you, except that someone suggested that you were absent from the city. However, it is not too late for me to thank you for the kindly manner in which you received and acknowledged the newspaper notice of the "Overland" Opening. To me the word 'overland' means a great deal more than it possibly can to those who came into the trans-Missouri country by Pullman cars or by any sort of railroad conveyance. Sometime when you have leisure and are so included I shall be glad to have you come down to Nebraska City and make a visit at Arbor Lodge.*

"You say, in closing "I am inclined to feel that we are overworking 'intellectual culture'." Possibly it would be better to say that we are overworking intellectual irritation. The universities of this day are filled with students working almost exclusively for degrees and many of those degrees are for specialties. Formerly the student was inspired to intellectual effort because of his love of knowledge and because of an insatiable thirst for knowledge. The universities and colleges of this day seem willing to sacrifice everything for numbers. Each one desires to boast of an attendance of from one thousand to three thousand students. Quantity rather than quality seems sought for in all the educational institutions of the country. There is only a small percentage of the studentship of the United States at the present time taking the regular, old-fashioned classical and mathematical course. It may be that the supply of that class of learned

men and women which the old curriculum provided outran the demand; but if that be true, when and where will the supply of specialties-half-educated men and women, whose intellects are only freckled here and there with little splotches of learning – find a corresponding demand? But I did not intend to bore you with the disquisition, and sending my regards to Mrs. Watkins and the children, I remain, Very sincerely your friend."

On January 24, 1902, with Watkins and Morton now working closely on the first volume of the Nebraska history book, Morton took *The Conservative* letterhead paper and typed Watkins his thoughts on the work at hand. *"My dear Sir: I reply to yours of the 22d and wish that you would ask the M.P. and Rock-Island folks for very brief statements of their entrance into the state and the extension of their lines since their entrance.*

"The chapter on geology, fossils, etc. together with archaeology, might be written very briefly by Blackman. The chapters should be very short.

"The University men in the several departments have never taken any interest in the Historical Society, and apparently none in the history of the territory and state, and I am not prepared to enter into any contract by which I shall be obligated for $1.50 a page for what they might prepare for us. You had better write directly to Mr. Lindsey and tell what they propose to charge, and ask him directly whether he will authorize the contract or make the contract in accordance with their terms.

"Your own compilation of the physical geography, from Barrett's data, will be sufficient along that line.

"My sympathies with the University men are not very strong, as you may by this time understand, because they never have shown the slightest sympathy in the historical work of our society. I think the Kennedy and Harwood sketches could be profitably used in the work. However, I expect you to use your own judgment in getting the railroad and other data together, but under no circumstances to involve me in a liability for paying the University men or anyone else for their work. You are aware of the fact that I am not the proprietor of the History, nor anxious to incur financial liabilities on its behalf.

"If Mr. Lindsey does not provide a typewriter, please inform me what it will cost to get one and I will write you immediately.

"Sayre's territorial maps should go in, by all means. They will be a valuable feature of the work. The nomenclature of all territorial officers and of the members of the several legislatures ought to be included in the work.

"I am delighted to know that you hope to furnish some available editorial for the Conservative *next week, because it is quite possible that I must go down south for a little while, as I am not recovered from my cold and cough.*

"Rev. Mr. Bross should make his history of the Congregational Church in Nebraska pretty short. The ecclesiastical part of the volumes can not be too brief to suit the general public. None of the church histories should exceed a chapter each. Let me hear from you at your earliest convenience. Yours truly."

In February, he accompanied his son Paul on a trip to Mexico; however, on his return March 2, Olson[2] notes that Morton wrote a note in his diary that his physical and intellectual state was 'dilapidated'. By April 5 "he was removed to the home of his son Mark, in Lake Forest, Illinois, so that he might have the care of specialists." [1-p429] He seemed to have a couple of days of strength and was unconscious by his seventieth birthday with a clot in an artery of the brain. He passed on April 27, having never regained consciousness. A "special train draped in mourning, brought the body from Chicago to Nebraska City." There were several days of public mourning.

According to Olson[1-p 427] *"An important reason for Morton's position as patriarch of the community was that his name was associated with virtually all of its improvements. For many of them he or his sons were wholly responsible. Morton Park had been a gift to Nebraska City by J. Sterling Morton. The public library had been built by Joy Morton. Capital of the sons had been invested in a starch works, a packing plant, a cereal mill, a creamery, stockyards, an elevator, and the printing company. The family had built the "Overland" theatre, 'as fine as any in the Middle West outside of Chicago', which for a time brought the best in road shows to Nebraska City. Morton found great pleasure in the theatre and frequently was seen in his box. Occasionally the actors were entertained at Arbor Lodge."*

The Morton sons also left a lasting historical imprint. Son Joy is best known as the founder of the Joy Morton [Salt] Company in Chicago, Illinois, and for the Morton Arboretum in Lisle, Illinois, which opened in 1922. Paul became known as a Progressive Republican and served as Secretary of the Navy from 1904-1905 under Democratic President Theodore Roosevelt, and president of the Equitable Life Assurance Society in New York City, taking over after the scandals and later served as vice president of the Atchison, Topeka and Santa Fe

Railroad. Mark was a principle with the Joy Morton Co. and the son most strongly turned toward agriculture with farms and practical farming experience. Carl started as manager of the Argo Starch Works in Nebraska City then moved to Waukegan, Illinois, to take over the management of a factory he acquired from Joy and became General Manager and President of the United States Sugar Refining Company.

The tasks which J. Sterling Morton had diligently focused his attention-with the volumes of the History of Nebraska-now fell to Albert Watkins[8], George L. Miller,[9] and C.S. Paine.[10] Others[11] were persuaded to assist with work to complete what had been promised in the name of J. Sterling Morton. Several books, including the three volume history in the name of J. Sterling Morton, were completed after his death.

J. Sterling Morton's historical computations were not the first about Nebraska. The first extended history was Harrison <u>Johnson's History of Nebraska of 1880</u>. Two years later Alfred T. Andreas published his monumental <u>History of the State of Nebraska</u>. Morton, Watkins, and Paine carried forward these previous efforts. Addison E. Sheldon's <u>Nebraska: The Land and the People</u> followed the Morton, Watkins, Paine work as subscription history in three volumes.

J. Sterling Morton's public life revealed an intelligent, confident man with opinions he was able to share in speeches, his personal actions and the printed word.[13] He had skills of organization for large assignments such as the Department of Agriculture in Washington, D.C., the various functions in the new territory government before the ink was dry on Nebraska statehood, and one-to-one teaching farmers and the general public about planting trees and how to help themselves with better crops. Most of all, he knew the power of the printed word and produced the actions that went with the rhetoric.

In 1923, eldest son Joy Morton gave Arbor Lodge and the surrounding grounds to the State of Nebraska

The last known photo of J. Sterling Morton. He is sitting in a chair used by President Cleveland when he visited Arbor Lodge.

to become a state park. It is a lasting memory to the father of Arbor Day: J. Sterling Morton. It is open to the public year round. N

Endnotes, Footnotes & Sources:

[1] Olson, James C. <u>History of Nebraska</u>. University of Nebraska Press, 1955. 370 pp,p 354-356.

[2] Olson, James C. <u>J. Sterling Morton, Pioneer Statesman Founder of Arbor Day</u> Lincoln, Nebraska: University of Nebraska Press, 1942. pp 451.

[3] Definitions of terms used in Morton's Day: According to the <u>American Dictionary of the English Language</u> by Noah Webster, 1828.

Bourbon Democrats, like President S. Grover Cleveland were pro-business, opposed high tariffs, free silver, inflation and imperialism. They fought for fiscal conservatism and against political corruption in all political parties, among many other public issues.

Conservative is an adjective meaning "Preservative; having power to preserve in a safe or entire state, or from loss, waste or injury."

Democrat was a noun meaning "One who adheres to a government by the people, or favors the extension of the right of suffrage to all classes of men."

Republican was an adjective referring to the noun "Republic. A commonwealth; a state in which the exercise of the sovereign power is lodged in representatives elected by the people. In modern usage, it differs from a democracy or democratic state, in which the people exercise the powers of sovereignty in person. Yet the democracies of Greece are often called republics. 2) Common interest; the public."

Progressive is also an adjective meaning "Moving forward; proceeding onward; advancing; as progressive motion or course; opposed to retrograde."

Agrarianism. It has two meanings. The *first* is a social or philosophical meaning, which briefly means that someone values rural society as superior to urban society. Thomas Jefferson represented this type of thought. The *second* is the political meaning which proposes political land redistribution from the rich to the poor, often called "agrarian reform."

[4] The Nebraska State Fair would be moved to various locations through the

years until the legislature gave funds to locate it in a permanent home at the Lincoln Lancaster fairgrounds in Lincoln in1901. It moved to Grand Island in 2010.

[5] J. Sterling Morton Papers 1849-1902. Nebraska State Historical Society. Lincoln, Nebraska, reviewed summer and fall 2012.

[6] Hansen, Nancy Sue and Dush, Barbara Ann. Nebraska Authors Volume One. "Fred Rogers Fairchild." Fullerton: D & H Adventures Publishing, 2013.

[7] Hansen, Nancy Sue and Dush, Barbara Ann. Nebraska Authors Volume One. "Jean-Baptist Victor Vifquain." Fullerton: D & H Adventures Publishing, 2013.

[8] Hansen, Nancy Sue and Dush, Barbara Ann. Nebraska Authors Volume One. "Albert Watkins." Fullerton: D & H Adventures Publishing, 2013.

[9] Hansen, Nancy Sue and Dush, Barbara Ann. Nebraska Authors Volume One. "George L. Miller." Fullerton: D & H Adventures Publishing, 2013.

[10] Hansen, Nancy Sue and Dush, Barbara Ann. Nebraska Authors Volume One. "C.S. Paine." Fullerton: D & H Adventures Publishing, 2013.

[11] Hansen, Nancy Sue and Dush, Barbara Ann. Nebraska Authors Volume One. "Grant L. Shumway." Fullerton: D & H Adventures Publishing, 2013.

[12] Kinnard was the first elected Secretary of State for the State of Nebraska.

[13] Hansen, Nancy Sue and Dush, Barbara Ann. Nebraska Authors Volume One. "A.O. Abbott." Fullerton: D & H Adventures Publishing, 2013. Abbott wrote about J. Sterling Morton's writing of Nebraska History in his book.

[14] 2012 View of Morton Home at Arbor Lodge. Photo by Nancy Sue Hansen.

Hon J. Sterling Morton. History of the State of Nebraska, Excerps 14 - 2012 view of Morton home at Arbor Lodge. Photo by Nancy Hansen from Nebraska, a Guide to the Cornhusker State. Originally published by the Western Historical Co. Chicago, Illinois 1882. Compiled and was written by the Federal Writers' Project of the Works Progress Administration for the State of Nebraska, American Guide Series. The Viking Press: New York, 1939. Page 1225-6.

Sanders, Jean. Notable Nebraskans. Lincoln: Media Productions and Marketing, Inc. 1998, pp 141-147.

www.wikipedia.org <u>Julius Sterling Morton</u>. reviewed June 4, 2012.

Thanks to: Laura Steinman, Special Events Coordinator/Curator at Arbor Lodge State Historical Park, for response to our inquiry about information on the books J. Sterling Morton wrote with a couple of e-mails and visiting with the Nebraska Authors Project® at the Lodge on September 26, 2012. A *special thanks* for sharing the grant request document and permission to publish with this article about J. Sterling Morton.

Nebraska Authors Book & Travel Club

Attach a ticket and/or photo of visit to Arbor Lodge, Nebraska City.

DALE WILLIAM NICHOLS

Date of birth: July 13, 1904
Location of birth: David City,
NE
Education: East Olive township
rural school
David City High School, 1924
Chicago Academy of Fine Arts
for two months
Date of Death: Oct. 19, 1995
Home at death: Sedona, AZ

Dale William Nichols in favorite
hat, November 1979[1]

Known Publications:

Nichols, Dale W. <u>A Philosophy of Esthetics</u>. Expanded edition.
Chicago: Black Cat Press, 1938. xi+ 82 p. (first edition 1935).

Nichols, Dale W. <u>Pilgrimage to Paradise</u>. Fictional story of young
man's journey to Alaska written after 1938.

Nichols, Dale W. <u>Encyclopedia Britannica Junior</u>, 1943-1948. Art
Editor and contributor.

Nichols, Dale. *Omaha World Herald*, "Travel series" in 1950's about
his driving adventures in his 1927 Model A he named Ophelia
Bumps.

Nichols, Dale W. <u>The Animal Stalks</u>. Booklet, as discussed in *Lincoln
Star*, February 5, 1953.

Nichols, Dale W. <u>Figure drawing: a system of drawing and design</u>.
Watson-Guptill, 1957.

Nichols, Dale W. The Pyramid Text of the Ancient Maya and the Magnificent Mystery Tikal and other titles published by Mazdan Press, a Guatemalan printing house.

Nichols, Dale W. Numerous essays written from Guatemala 1960-1975, self-published and distributed in three-ring binders.

Two older brothers welcomed Dale William Nichols to the homestead in 1904. A sister followed a few years later. Dale's parents Edith Pollman and John Dale Nickles, married and moved to Butler County, Nebraska, in 1889 from Pennsylvania by way of Iowa. During the process of applying for homestead rights to property south of David City, a spelling error on the paperwork changed the Nickles name to Nichols.

The misspelling of the name did not affect the daily farm chores so the family chose to ignore the error. While Dale learned the routine of farming, his thoughts were not so much on how much grain to feed the cattle, but how the light from the sun fell on the pasture in each season. Dale was an artist, not a farmer.

Nichols was fascinated with various arts, music, and fashion. According to the research of author Amanda Mobley Guenther for her book, Dale Nichols: Transcending Regionalism, Dale's classmates "labeled him an artsy dandy of sorts."[2 p40] He felt out of place. He sensed his younger sister was getting more attention than he was, his oldest brother died in an automobile accident just after returning home from his military service in World War I, and he felt the majority of his home community did not provide a place of belonging and acceptance for him and his sense of artistry.[2] While Nichols was building internal strength and the will to make a name for himself and find a place to belong, his grandfather Pollman played an important role in his life. Nichols wrote an unpublished story in his memory after his death under the name William Pollman.[2]

In later years, Nichols also credited the local public library for giving him inspiration as an artist. In a letter to Marilyn McDowell, executive director of the David City Public Library, Nichols wrote that when he was at the East Olive School he would go to the library, then at the courthouse, and was excited to see so many books. He favored those that featured a "hero type of young man who was with Lewis and Clark on their great explorations of the Northwest areas that were still Indian." Nichols continued, "I wasn't of the state of mind to be a farmer. I was too chicken hearted. To see hogs shipped off to market made me cry. This state of mind, helped by several of my grade school teachers of which Otto Hasik is the most outstanding (he gave me one hour a day to do nothing but draw), and then several more in high school…well I am deeply grateful to them all." [3] Nichols would make explorations of his own, perhaps to replicate his storybook heroes.

The regionalism movement was sweeping the nation in the 20's and 30's. This movement promoted nationalism and tried to encourage communities and individuals to learn about one's ethnic and religious background. The theory of the Progressives was that if Americans would get to know more about their local history, they would have more of a sense of community. The hard times and years of desperation in the 1920's and 30's had given rise to the need of people to help each other. Spiritualism had preceded the regionalism movement into Nebraska and was in full swing among the art and literary minded citizens of Lincoln about an hour's travel southeast of the Nichols home. For Nichols, it was the regionalism movement that shaped the foundation in his art, but didn't hold him into one era of time.

The curves of the snow and sunlight on a windswept hill or roof of a barn burned themselves into Nichols memory as he worked on

the farm for those first twenty years of his life. While young men like Rudy Umland[4] were finding their experiences in the world of hobos and traveling the nation by train, in 1924 Dale Nichols went to Chicago. The social environment of the day became part of Nichols need to travel to experience more of the world and to become successful in the process. In a 1979 story by Gerald Wade in the *Omaha World Herald*; Nichols said he thought the wandering was in his blood.[5]

Nichols at piano - Courtesy of Banner Press, David City[1] Sept. 27, 1979

While his memory was in visual art forms, he applied the piano lessons of his youth to earn his first wages. He became a jazz pianist with the Lunsford Brothers' Band. He occasionally played in various venues throughout his life.

Nichols was accepted as a student to the Chicago Academy of Fine Arts, but only attended two months saying he realized he needed to sharpen his skills through experience. He joined the numerous other artists in the Chicago area at the time. Here he had a place to find his own style and what his ideals of a finished product(s) would be.

After a year in Chicago Nichols married his high school sweetheart, Minnie "Lucile" McIntosh, on July 13, 1925, in a small Chicago wedding. Since Lucile was a concert violinist she got a job preforming with an orchestra. According to friends and family, she was always a supporter of her husband's work. Nichols concentrated on designing publications and advertising. After ten years he began to paint. He declared that humans had lost their day-to-day contact with their natural environment through their artificial living conditions, and as a result their "deeper spiritual instincts became dormant."[2-p49] The couple had a baby girl, Joan Lucile, in 1931.

While Dale's brother Floyd was working the Nebraska farm and making military combat knives for the soldiers of World War II (which are now collectors' items), Dale was painting, including his successful: *End of the Hunt*. His first book, <u>A Philosophy of Esthetics</u>, a monograph, was published in 1935 outlining his personal philosophies and principles of design art. Three years later the book was expanded and published by Black Cat press under the same title.

Nichols considered the need to experience more of the world to enhance his convictions that man, especially those with artistic talents, should get inspiration from natural environment. He decided to live what he believed and took off to Alaska. He traveled around and settled in Wasilla for a summer.[6]

In 1939, Nichols was awarded a Carnegie Visiting Professorship at the University of Illinois Urbana for one year. His work was on exhibition across the country and he was recognized as one of the top names in American Art. His painting *Big City News* was selected to represent Nebraska at the New York World's Fair. This notoriety so early in his artistic life was not the norm for so many struggling artists. Nichols' work was taking top honors from juried competitions, and he and his wife were part of prestigious social circles. In September 1939, Nichols was featured in *Time Magazine*. They acknowledged his preference for prairie landscapes which he remembered from his youth. One of the most notable features was his use of snow effects in his paintings, the article stated. Indeed these were two trademarks of his artistry.

Nichols had been in Illinois fifteen years with one summer in Alaska. His daughter, now eight, suffered from asthma and the family moved to Tucson for her health. While World War II became the center of attention of the world news, Nichols continued to work in various forms of art, including concentrating on drawings of current fashion. Lucile continued her violinist concert work with a new audience in Arizona. She was known for her high society style with her evening attire often making the local papers with notations about how her silver jewelry was 'worn well'.

In 1942, a winter scene Nichols had painted was selected by the United States Post Office for a stamp. They selected his work again in 1995 when his art was published on postcards sold by the USPS.

He began illustrating for the Encyclopedia Britannica in 1943 and by 1945 was named art editor. The position included overseeing format styling, commissioning illustrations, and contributing his own material. He worked for the Encyclopedia Britannica Junior 1943-1948.

According to research by Guenther, Nichols could not just sit still: "In 1945 while Nichols and his wife were vacationing in Mexico for two months, Nichols produced one hundred twelve paintings, gave four lectures and wrote one article."[2-p61]

During these years there was a feud over the title of "Nebraska Painter." Some believed it should be Polk County Nebraskan Terence Duren (1907-1968). Duren emphasized dramatic presentations of small-town life. Nichols work used the "power of nature to transform human experience in rural areas."[2-p68] In 1945 both had exhibitions in Nebraska. Duren was exhibiting in Shelby township and Nichols had a showing in David City, Butler County. They saw each other's work as misrepresenting Nebraska life. In an article by Gil Savery *Artists Without Honor…* he published a portion of a letter he had received from Nichols regarding an article about Duren's work. In part Nichols wrote: "*Yet he made a mistake common to many in our profession: he had expected honor in his own country, especially, Nebraska. Not even the name of He, honored now at Christmas, was so received in his own part of the Near East. We, in our trade, seldom think of ourselves as prophets. Nor can we expect unusual recognition from communities where culture is mostly agriculture. I say this with no intent of the derogatory. Out of agriculture came all culture…"* Nichols, in the article, went on: *"But I don't paint Nebraska. I never have painted Nebraska. Probably, that is where I differ from Terence Duren…I paint those several things which generate all the life of Nebraska: light, color, air, time, space, opposing forces, growth, death, contrasts, radiances, symmetry, cold, warm, soul and spirit. It is because I know the Nebraska scene best that I utilize all the forms, both natural and synthetic, to reflect the hidden messages…"[7]*

Daughter Joan graduated from high school and the twenty year marriage of her parents dissolved. The court allowed her to choose which parent she wanted to stay with and she chose her father. While they had a good relationship, it was impossible for him to maintain good parenting while working and recovering from the divorce. She eventually lived in David City with his parents. Nichols had always looked for belonging and support of others in his work and he would look for other women in his life that would fill his need. His personal life was a roller coast ride, including a short marriage to a family friend Fehr and having a daughter Carla who stayed with her mother when the marriage ended.

His changing interests kept him evolving as an artist. In 1948, he started the Dale Nichols School of Art, also known as Tubac Art School in Tubac, Arizona. His teaching methods were consistent with this own work style. Concentration was on the principles of natural law and presenting an image that was both visually and psychologically correct. The *Lincoln Journal* wrote a feature story about the school on July 25, 1948. They quoted Nichols, "Explaining that the school of art reflects American ideals and ideas," he said, "America is a precision minded nation. We Americans want things to work and we want to see how they work and know why they work. At our school of art in Tubac we teach precision art directed by a sound knowledge of psychology. We call it 'psycho-precisionism.'"[8] The restless spirit soon invaded and the school lasted a little over a year.

Nichols loved to drive and had a car he loved to use during his travel adventures. Readers of the *Omaha World Herald* in the 1950s would have had the opportunity to read a long series of articles about his driving adventures with his 1927 Model A which he called Ophelia Bumps. Nichols traveled to Mexico in 1949 and 1951, and lived briefly with the Navajo Indians using watercolor to record their culture.

Nichols had been retained on long term art contracts over the years and now found these expiring, so in 1954 he decided to revive the old or create something new. What he found was several short-term options. He was a guest lecturer at the Arts League of Brownsville, Texas, where he had presented workshops four years previous and returned in 1969. He tried to start his art school again, but was unsuccessful.

He tried to reunite with his daughter Joan and moved to Biloxi, Mississippi, where he lived until 1960 working in commercial advertising and painting murals. In 1960 he made a surprise move to Guatemala where he stayed for the next sixteen years.

Nichols and his Mayan hieroglyphics, 1988[9]

He was fascinated with Mayan culture. A local printing business published several books written by Nichols describing discoveries he made about the Mayan people while studying stone rubbings. He wrote considerably about his claim that the key to the symbolism of the Mayan hieroglyphics was based on the numbering system of nine. "The Dictionary of International Biography credited Nichols in 1975 with founding Psycho Symbolic Investigation Archeology based on his discoveries."[2p71] His work, once again, became popular and his paintings began to sell.

Nichols became ill and a native woman helped him back to health during this time. They married and lived in Antigua. The February 4, 1976, earthquake that devastated the area did not level their house as it did those around them. Nichols had constructed his home with materials other than the local adobe brick and he credited his farm-boy construction with saving his home. Concern from family and friends mounted, however, when they couldn't be located for several days. Nichols wrote about his experiences in the earthquake and the *Lincoln Journal Star* printed the story in their March 7, 1976, issue.[10]

The couple found it difficult to recover from this event in their life. While Nichols stayed in Guatemala for a few more years, the earthquake had started the restless spirit once again. His wife did not want to be too far away from her family in Guatemala so they parted, although did briefly reunite in Nichols' hometown of David City to celebrate a solo exhibition of his work in 1988 sponsored by the local arts councils.

Nichols went back to his old stomping grounds in Alaska and his wife made plans to join him. In 1989, as he awaited her arrival word came instead that she had died of a brain aneurism. Suddenly the man

Dale Nichols and Norman Rockwell[3]

with tremendous energy and keen senses began to deteriorate steadily. For the next six years there were signs of Alzheimers and his inability to forgive himself for leaving his wife to go to Alaska. Dale W. Nichols died in Sedona, Arizona, in 1995 of previously undetected prostate cancer.

The popular Dale Nichols did not want a biography to be written and kept putting off an autobiography. He noted to friends that he would rather not discuss all the issues with his family life if he wrote about himself. He didn't shy away from the press and had written articles that reflected contemporary thought about science and psychology. In a visit to a classroom in David City he told the youngsters that they should be proud to be from Nebraska no matter where they went in life.

Besides the books on his Mayan discoveries, Nichols wrote fifteen essays while he was in Guatemala in 1960-1975. These discussed the basic purpose of his art. He had to self-publish and did not have wide circulation for these works. He bound them in three-ring folders and mailed them to people he knew back in the States. These writings came after most of his awarded paintings but what he wrote about was the earliest part of his career. While it showed consistency in thought of his earliest work, it also showed there was a complex development that had evolved through time.

Works he painted remain hanging in the Smithsonian American Art Museum, the Metropolitan Museum of Art, the Museum of Nebraska Art, and are memorialized in Guenther's book and at Bone Creek Museum of Agrarian Art in David City, Nebraska.

He was a master of drawing, calligraphy and design for printing with awards in these fields, in addition to the title of Fellow in the Society of Typographic Arts of Chicago. His mastery of subjects including history, psychology, geology, archeology, art and music were evident in the activity of his life in each of the fields.

Dale W. Nichols lived his life through art. According to friends and family, he was known for the twinkle in his eye and his quickness to laugh. This man, who as a farmer's son, saw the light and the snowfall differently than his neighbors, and found a way to bring his awareness of what he saw and share it with all who take time to look. He will be remembered as a great Nebraska painter and thoughtful prolific writer. N

Endnotes, Footnotes & Sources:

[1] Photo of Dale Nichols with Panama hat by Gail Fulda staff photo for story by Linda Ulrich "Nichols stands up for self and for art at county fairs." *The Banner-Press,* David City, Nebraska, November 1979.

[2] Guenther, Amanda Mobley, <u>Dale Nichols: Transcending Regionalism</u>. Lincoln: Great Plains Art Museum University of Nebraska, 2011, pp 197.

[3] *The Banner-Press*, David City, Nebraska. "Library gets credit for inspiring Dale Nichols", April 2, 1987. "Nichols said he first found Rockwell on the cover of *The Saturday Evening Post* at the David City Library in the 1920s." Later they became personal friends.

[4] Hansen, Nancy Sue and Dush, Barbara Ann. <u>Nebraska Authors Volume One</u>. "Rudolph Umland," Fullerton: D & H Adventures Publishing, 2013.

[5] Wade, Gerald. *Omaha World Herald. Sunday World-Herald Magazine of the Midlands.* "Wanderlust Feeds His Artistic Soul." November 18, 1979, pp 28.

[6] In 2006 Wasilla would become nationally known as the hometown of the youngest female governor of Alaska. Sarah Palin, born1964, Sandpoint, Idaho. She entered politics in 1992, just after Nichols last known visit to the area.

[7]Savery, Gil. *Lincoln Journal.* "Artists without Honor…" February 5, 1969.

[8]*Lincoln Star.* "Dale Nichols Has Own Art School." July 25, 1948.

[9] Krepel, Terry, *Columbus Telegram*. "Artist returns home; plans area art shows." August 30, 1988.

[10] Nichols, Dale W. *Lincoln Journal Star*. "Nebraskan Experienced Guatemala's Earthquake." March 7, 1976. 10F

Boys Town Times. "Nichols Starts Art Collection for Boys Town". Volume XXCI, Issue No. 19, October 10, 1941.

Lincoln Star. "Dale Nichols Speaks of Modern Art in His Booklet "The Animal Stalks," February 5, 1953.

Nichols, Dale W. *Lincoln Star*. "Modern Art," column, June 2, 1953.

Nichols, Dale . *Lincoln Journal*. "Nebraska Artists" column, February 5, 1954.

www.wikipedia.com. Dale Nichols. Reviewed December 30, 2012.

www.monetunk.edu. Dale Nichols. Reviewed December 30, 2012.

Thank you to the Boston Studio Project and the Butler County Gallery, Bonnie Luckey, and the Roman L. and Victoria E Hruska Memorial Public Library of David City: Cheryl Hein, Gina Clymer and Kenneth Pohl.

Thank you to the *Columbus Telegram* and the *David City Banner* for permission to publish the photos.

Nebraska Authors Book & Travel Club

Photo of your visit to the Bone Creek Museum of Agrarian Art, 575 E Street, David City (402-367-4488). Attach a photo reflecting your visit or have this box signed and dated by a staff member.

FERN NILSON

Date of Birth: June 29, 1924
Location of Birth: Stratton, NE
Education: High School in Stratton;
B.S. University of Nebraska
Currently lives in: Aurora, NE

Fern Nilson

Nilson, Fern. <u>History of Prayer in America</u>. McBeth Corporation, published January 2, 2008. 64 pp.

Nilson, Fern. CDs: The Gift of Christmas and The Gift of Easter. Lincoln: Master Track Production, 2012.

Nilson, Fern. <u>My Life on the Prairie</u>. Grand Island; Copycat Printing, 2013. 116 pp.

Fern Nilson had a definite goal in mind when she wrote her book: <u>The History of Prayer in America</u>. That goal was to teach how prayer was an important part in our nation's beginning.

With 15,000 copies in schools and libraries across the United States, "This book is going to be my legacy," Nilson stated. "I hope that someday there will be presidents, congressmen, and governors who will say, 'I'm here because I read your book.'"

A teacher at heart, Nilson graduated from the University of Nebraska, and taught in the Nebraska Public Schools. Her love for sharing what was important in her life led her to become a writer and speaker. Nilson and her husband, Erick, also sponsored Campus Crusade for

Christ for twenty-five years at Kansas State University. It was during that time that she began presenting "The Gift of Christmas" to students, faculty, and audiences in several large cities.

Nilson has worked with Shirley Dobson, chairman of the National Day of Prayer Task Force, for over twenty years – ever since she attended a President's Prayer Breakfast in Washington, D.C. On the flight back to her home in Aurora, Nebraska, an associate of Dobson asked if he could sit next to her. During the conversation, Nilson was asked if she would head up a National Day of Prayer in Nebraska. She agreed.

"For the past sixty-five years I have been in one organization or another," she noted.

After working as a regional coordinator for six states, Dobson's office asked her to join the national staff. As a retired teacher, it was soon evident to her that there was a large void in the school system.

"In setting up prayer events, I soon began to realize there was one segment we were not reaching. That was our schools. We had been made to believe by the courts that we couldn't talk about God or prayer in the schools.

"I decided to find out if that was true, so I called the State Attorney General's office," Nilson said. "Since National Day of Prayer is a national day just like the Fourth of July and Thanksgiving Day – days that the schools are observing – I asked if the schools could also observe National Day of Prayer and talk about our history. I was given one word for an answer: Absolutely."

Nilson called the American Center for Law and Justice and received eight pages of legal rights. It was then she decided she wanted to teach about the history of prayer in the United States.

"I went to the teachers and said they could talk about what our founding fathers did and said, to make us a great nation, and how prayer had been a major influence in the nation's founding. They said it's not in our history books today, so I called the National Day of Prayer office and asked if they could put together a pamphlet to give to the teachers to use in the schools. They said, 'You're the one with the vision, you write it up.' And so I did." That was the beginning of nearly five years of research and study it took to put together Nilson's book.

In 2005, Nilson traveled to Colorado Springs, Colorado, where she was awarded the National Coordinator of the Year Award by Shirley Dobson and the National Day of Prayer Task Force for her service and leadership in the cause of prayer. She asked her publisher to bring two hundred fifty copies to the event: "I wanted the state coordinators to know what I had done. I did not know how I was going to get the books out across the United States, but for hours it seemed they were picking up books and asking me to sign them. The next day I went to the airport to come home and as I went by the gates, many were sitting there reading my book," she said with delight.

It didn't take long for other state coordinators to want the The History of Prayer in America in their schools and libraries.

The book contains quotes from our founding fathers and what they did. "George Washington said it's the duty of all nations to acknowledge God," Nilson said.

"Thomas Jefferson said, 'Can the liberties of a nation be thought secure when we have removed their only firm basis, a conviction in the minds of the people that these liberties are the gift of God? Jefferson went on to say, 'Indeed, I tremble for my country when I reflect that God is just: that His justice cannot sleep forever.'"

Benjamin Franklin once addressed George Washington, requesting that "prayers imploring the assistance of Heaven and its blessing on our deliberations, be held in this assembly every morning."

Later presidents, such as Ronald Reagan, are quoted as saying: "Let us, young and old, join together, as did the First Continental Congress in their first step–humble, heartfelt prayer."

Our forty-third president, George W. Bush, said: "The greatest gift you can give anybody is to pray on his behalf. The prayers of the people in this country sustain me. I can ask for no greater gift from my countrymen."

The publication not only contains sixty-four pages of educational material about our nation's history and Constitution, it also covers details about the National Seal, Pledge of Allegiance, National Anthem, and Motto, as well as the National Monuments. Additional study challenge questions are included at the end of the book.

"It's a small book," Nilson said. "I did that on purpose. I wanted students to be willing to open that book and read it all the way through and not be a lot of heavy reading and a lot of wordy paragraphs. It tells how down through the years other presidents have said how important prayer is in our nation." Nebraska's Attorney General Jon Bruning was the first to endorse the book, followed by the American Center for Law and Justice, and scores of teachers and leaders from across the United States.

Nilson has also worked with Christian Women's Club in Kansas and served as area representative for the eastern third of the state.

"My life has been so full," Nilson commented. "People say to me, why did you write the book? Well, tomorrow's leaders are going to come from every one of our states. We simply must impact their lives, and if they don't know where they came from, how will they know what to return to. That summarizes the whole thing." B

Endnotes, Footnotes & Sources:

Interview withe Fern Nilson/photos by Barbara Ann Dush.

History of Prayer in America by Fern Nilson.

Nebraska Authors Book & Travel Club
Signature or Participate in a Nebraska World Day of Prayer or spiritual retreat of your choice and share a spiritual insight in this box.

TOM OSBORNE

Dr. Tom Osborne

Date of Birth: Feb. 23, 1937
Location of Birth: Hastings, NE
Education: Hastings High School;
Hastings College-BA, 1959;
University of Nebraska, MA, PhD
Currently lives in Lincoln.

Known Publications:

Osborne, Tom with John E. Roberts. <u>More Than Winning: The Story of Nebraska's Tom Osborne</u>, Thomas Nelson Inc., 1985. 162 pp.

Osborne, Tom. <u>On Solid Ground</u>, Nebraska Book Publishing Co., 1996. 266 pp.

Osborne, Tom. <u>Faith in the Game; Lessons on Football, Work and Life</u>, Broadway Books, co-published with Waterbrook Press, 1999. 156 pp.

Osborne, Tom. <u>Beyond the Final Score: There's More to Life Than the Game</u>, Regal Books, 2009. 256 pp.

Osborne, Tom. <u>Secrets to Becoming a Leader: Discover a Lifetime of Lessons</u>.

The mention of Dr. Tom Osborne is instantly associated with the world of football, having taken the Nebraska Cornhuskers to three national championships and numerous conference titles as the University of Nebraska's head coach. However, that is just one segment of a career marked with success.

As a U.S. Congressman, Osborne left his mark of leadership when he introduced a program to train Iraqi women in leadership skills. The TeamMates Mentoring Program, co-founded by Osborne and his wife Nancy in 1991 which provides support to school-aged youth, now has one hundred chapters in one hundred twenty communities. The list of accomplishments is as long as it is varied.

The line-up isn't complete, however, without the mention of another noted accomplishment – that of author. Osborne has written five books, his favorite works being, <u>Faith in the Game: Lessons on Football, Work and Life</u>, a memoir and motivational guide; and <u>Beyond the Final Score: There's More to Life Than the Game</u>.

Those lessons were learned early in Osborne's personal life. Born and raised in Hastings, he was a star athlete at Hastings High School in football, basketball and the discus throw; and a star football quarterback and outstanding basketball player in college. When Osborne joined the Cornhusker coaching staff in 1964, his thirty-seven year career – twenty-five years as head coach – boasted of an almost unheard of eighty-four percent winning record.

It's through his books, such as <u>Faith in the Game</u>, that Osborne is able to share "the philosophy he used to create not only a champion football team but also a meaningful life." The book reveals "both a memoir of Osborne's career with the Cornhuskers and an inspirational guide to making the most out of life by cultivating core values like honesty, courage, and loyalty."

As an author, Osborne wants his readers to learn more about athletics, leadership, and spiritual growth. His book, <u>Beyond the Final Score</u>, chronicles his years as a congressman, educator, family man, mentor and athletic director, while revealing the character, values and faith that have always grounded him. It shows the true heart of Osborne and shares his wisdom, dignity, views, leadership skills, and common sense approach to life.

His intentions in the book were made clear when Osborne wrote: "This book is a collection of my observations about life, character and spiritual significance, and of reflections on the lessons I have learned in the many roles I have played. It is my hope that, as I tell these stories, you will be inspired to think about the roles you play and how you measure success in each one."

Osborne cited John Wooden, former Head Basketball Coach at UCLA, as his hero. Wooden returned the compliment with these words: "Tom Osborne has always gone beyond the final score, achieving competitive greatness with integrity, hard work, selfless service to others, and a strong faith."

The Osborne's still reside in Lincoln where Tom, as Warren Buffet noted, continues to "improve the lives of everyone he encounters."

In his humble spirit, Osborne sums up his varied roles as a gift: "I have been blessed to take on a wide variety of roles in my lifetime. I have been a professional athlete, a coach, a congressman, a teacher, and an administrator. I have been a leader in various capacities, a public figure, a father and a husband – and a fisherman. It is my hope that, through it all, I have been God's servant."

Which, when simply put, is summed up on the last line on the cover of one of Osborne's books: <u>There's More to Life than the Game</u>. ʙ

Endnotes, Footnotes & Sources:

Interview via e-mail, notes in Barbara Ann Dush's file, 2012.

Nebraska Authors Book & Travel Club
Signature or attend a TeamMates event or log onto www.teammates.org & share an inspiration in this box.

JIM OVERTURF

Date of Birth: Jan. 16, 1940
Location of Birth: Lincoln, NE
Education: country schools and
Hawthorne elementary in Lincoln, NE;
California High School in Whittier, CA;
college degrees: BA in Applied
Engineering Mathematics, LLB in law,
MBA in Project Management, and
Ph.D. in Financial Management
Town in Nebraska called home:
Lincoln

Jim Overturf

Overturf, Jim. <u>Masonville: A Mystery</u>, fiction, IUniverse, fiction, 2007. 260 pp.

Overturf, Jim. <u>King Rapids: A Kurt Maxxon Mystery</u>, fiction, IUniverse, 2009. 312 pp.

Overturf, Jim. <u>Carpentier Falls: A Kurt Maxxon Mystery</u>, fiction, IUniverse, 2010. 336 pp.

Overturf, Jim. <u>Gunning for the Finish: A Kurt Maxxon Mystery</u>, fiction, Three Cords Publishing, 2011. 330 pp.

Jim Overturf grew up in Eastern Nebraska, mainly in Lincoln, and the Hastings/Kearney areas until he was fifteen. It was then his family pulled up stakes and moved to Southern California in the mid-1950s where he completed his education.

That education earned him a position with an engineering company traveling the world building power plants as an engineer/project manager. "I guess I've been around the world a couple of times," Jim grinned as he recollected his many travel miles.

He attributes some of his success to his rural Nebraska roots: "Most of the time I went to country school," Jim explained. "I am amazed at how well people do from one-room schools. I went to high school at Bladen, just before we left for California. This was in 1955, and high schools in those days just wanted to graduate somebody who could take over the farm. I was fortunate. I paid attention."

While he was a senior at California High School, Jim worked after school and weekends at a publication house that produced Assembly Manuals and Maintenance Manuals for military equipment and weapons. He pursued a college degree while working days and going to school nights. "I love math," he stated. "I started working toward a bachelor of science degree in engineering. By 1964 I'd been going to school for eight years and I was still quite a ways from a bachelor of science degree so I backed off and took a bachelor of arts degree."

In 1967, Jim went to work on construction of the Quad City Nuclear Power Plant in the Quad Cities as a site engineer. While living in Bettendorf, Iowa, he hooked up with the *Bettendorf News*. "The first thing I did for them was cartoons. My cartooning abilities go all the way back to grade school. I did political cartoons and feature articles, and also picked up photography along the way for the *News*."

Because of medical problems, Jim moved to the Colorado climate, working for the *Golden Transcript* in Golden doing the same type of stringer work. "I did a series of photographic journalism on the jeep passes over the mountains for the newspaper and later ran it in *Four-Corners Wonderland* magazine," he said. "I belonged to the Shriners. They had a jeep patrol — a group of four-wheelers who did weekend outings all year. I'd take pictures along the way and dictate into my trusty mini-recorder."

Jim later became the editor of the *Four-Corners Wonderland* travel magazine. That magazine folded a few years later due to the owner's health problems.

After a rather circuitous route, Jim and his wife, Carol, moved back to Iowa in the late 1980s and he managed construction projects around the country using his farm in southern Iowa as a home base.

"I've always attributed my writing as being the reason for my success in engineering. My first inkling that I had good writing skills came in college. You had to take humanities courses and the final grades for those courses are typically based upon a term paper or essay. Just about every term paper I turned in I got an A+, and a great compliment from the instructor, so that tipped me off," he smiled.

The engineering companies were steadily moving Jim up the ladder, "and I guess it was because of my writing," he noted. "Later in my career when I was recruiting and hiring, I knew if I found an engineering student who could string five words into a comprehensive sentence, you had someone worth training."

At one time Jim managed projects in Hawaii and Utah simultaneously, which put a strain on travel schedules and free time. Still, in between the work load he managed to work on a novel he had been pondering. "When I first developed Kurt Maxxon, my first image of him was an Indy race car driver. Then I went through a whole evolution of how I developed that character. I went to my first NASCAR race at Talladega in 1987 while I was working in Athens, Alabama. It was the race where Bobby Allison plowed through the fence into the crowd in the grandstands. Carol and I were only about fifty feet away from the main impact area.

"The biggest memory of NASCAR was not Bobby; but Bobby's son, Davey. He had a megawatt smile, four times as much charisma as JFK, and a lot of racing credential to boots. Unfortunately, he was killed in a helicopter crash. Carol and I went to the funeral. We had gone to several victory parties when the Allison boys were in Birmingham – that's how I got into NASCAR. So I developed a NASCAR character about the same time. I didn't have quality time to pound out two or three pages so I made a lot of notes. I was on the go all the time with work, so for fifteen to twenty years I wrote one novel and never attempted to publish it"

In 2003, Jim's wife of forty years, Carol, was diagnosed with lung cancer and he came home to take care of her. It was during this time he began seriously writing his first Kurt Maxxon mystery novel. "I had typed some of the scenes in the computer so when I came home to take care of Carol, I had three ring-binders full of notes. When I sat down to write the book I probably had the first half of the first book written. I worked on it just to keep from going insane with the stress. When my wife passed away (July 2004), I decided to keep writing and kept working on it and got it to where I thought it was ready to publish."

To help him in his quest to become a published author, Jim attended several writer's workshops at the University of Iowa. The first one was on beginning a novel. He submitted his first two chapters. Nearly all the critiques told him to delete the first twenty pages and start with the action on page twenty-one. That left "me a little confounded."

Jim continued to attend writer's conferences to hone his writing skills. He attended conferences in Albuquerque, St. Louis, Kansas City, Chicago, the Iowa summer writing festival, and the writers institute in Madison, Wisconsin.

When Jim retired in 2004, he said, "I never want to get on another plane. I donated several hundred thousand frequent flyer miles to charity. I drove everywhere, even to a conference to Tucson, and when I got home I said that's too far to drive."

"Then I discovered Amtrak," he said with delight. "When I discovered Amtrak I went to Miami two years in a row to the writing conference, and went to conferences in New York, Boston, and Philadelphia. You learn something, pick up some little trick or some new thing at every writer's conference.

In 2006, with the first book "so discombobulated I didn't know if the first page was the last, I felt lost." That's when a long-time acquaintance, Karen Davis, who lived in Lincoln, Nebraska, came to my rescue." In discussing the book with her, she offered to beta read and edit it. Jim began e-mailing her the copy of his novel as he finished chapters. "She salvaged the book," Jim said of her excellent editing and proofreading skills. "Eventually we published my first book."

In early 2007, Jim started writing his second novel, King Rapids: A Kurt Maxxon Mystery.

In June 2008, Jim proposed to Karen and she accepted. They married in June and he moved back to Lincoln, where the couple currently live.

With Karen and her sharp editing skills at his side, Jim pursued his writing with a new vigor. Having raced sports cars while in high school and college, he wanted to continue his love of the sport through his Kurt Maxxon series.

Of the four books he has written, Jim's favorite remains Carpentier Falls in which race car driver Kurt Maxxon catches two little underprivileged boys running around at the tracks. It turns out their mother is missing and they've been living under a bridge, so Kurt takes them under his wings. The boys stumble upon the body of a restaurant owner while foraging for food. The deceased is Kurt's friend and he is determined to find the killer.

A new mystery series is in the works as Jim develops his next set of characters. He likes to add history into his writing, so he also invests many hours into research. Jim's greatest satisfaction, however, is in the reward for the reader: "I just want people to enjoy the books and be entertained," he said. B

Endnotes, Footnotes & Sources:

[1] beta - www.en.wikipedia.org. a person who reads a written work, generally fiction, with a critical eye.

Interview with Jim and Karen Overturf, 2013. Notes in Barbara Ann Dush's files.

www.kurtmaxxonracing.com

amazon.com

Sample provided by Jim Overturf.

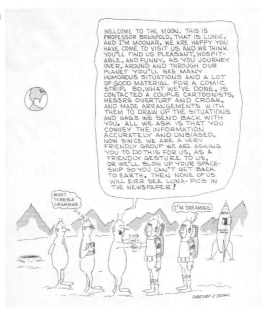

Nebraska Authors Book & Travel Club
Signature or visit a Nebraska automobile race track and attach a photo or ticket from your experience.

CLARENCE SUMNER "C. S." PAINE

Nebraska State Historical Society Collection.
Clarence Sumner "C.S." Paine

Date of birth: June 11, 1867
Location of birth: Eden Prairie Township, MN
Education: MN district school a few years
Minneapolis school at age 16 and took some business college courses
moved to NE from Iowa: 1897
Date of Death: June 14, 1916

Known Publications As Managing Editor:

Morton, J. Sterling, succeeded by Albert Watkins, editor in chief; Dr. George L. Miller, associate editor. <u>Illustrated History of Nebraska: A History of Nebraska from the Earliest Explorations fo the Trans-Mississippi Region</u>. Volume I. Lincoln: Jacob North and Co. 1906, 1907, third edition 1911.

Morton, J. Sterling, succeeded by Albert Watkins, editor in chief; Dr. George L. Miller, associate editor. <u>Illustrated History of Nebraska: A History of Nebraska from the Earliest Exploration of the Trans-Mississippi Region</u>. Volume II. Lincoln: Jacob North and Co. 1906.

Morton, J. Sterling and Albert Watkins. <u>History of Nebraska from the Earliest Exploration of the Trans-Mississippi region</u>. A revised Edition. Edited and revised by Augustus O. Thomas, James A. Beattie, Arthur C. Wakeley. Lincoln: Western Publishing and Engraving Company. 1918. (History of Nebraska from the Earliest Explorations of the Present Time by Albert Watkins, Volume III First Edition. Lincoln: Western Publishing and Engraving Company, 1913.)

W hile C.S. Paine does not seem to have a published book or series of historic articles written by him, his contribution to the Illustrated History of Nebraska volumes edited by J. Sterling Morton[1], Albert Watkins,[2] Dr. George Miller[3] and others[4] should not go unnoticed. According to historic accounts, the inspiration for the project came from Paine and other men prior to the Omaha Expo of 1898. It was Paine, from his home in Iowa, who began the concept of researching the history of Nebraska and assisted in the proposition to J. Sterling Morton that he become the editor-in-chief. Morton accepted and began the project. Paine moved to Nebraska, became the managing editor, and later served on several boards of organizations memorializing Nebraska history.

In the History of Nebraska by James C. Olson,[5-p 354-56] he wrote of other books of history that had been written previous to the Morton volumes. He continued with, "The well-known Morton-Watkins Illustrated History was a subscription history originally project by J. Sterling Morton and completed by Albert Watkins with assistance of Clarence S. Paine."

On April 28, 1898, J. Sterling Morton[1] wrote a letter to Mr. C.S. Paine in Omaha while he was Superintendent of Agents and Morton responded to correspondence from Paine in another letter of May 2, 1898: *"My dear Sir: I am very much pleased to acknowledge the receipt of your encouraging letter of the 20th ult., recounting your interview with Bishop Bonacum of Lincoln, in the interests of the forthcoming "History of Nebraska." The assurance of that distinguished prelate that he will cooperate with us in ascertaining the truth, for historical purposes, wherever his Church is organized, is equivalent of the promise of most efficient and satisfactory aid in every county of the state. Convey to Bishop Bonacum my very profound and sincere gratitude. He has placed us all under very great obligations and I shall not hesitate to avail myself of the first opportunity to call upon him personally and thank him for his public spirited and exceedingly valuable offer. He is a particular friend of the*

Hon. A.J. Sawyer, whom I class among my choicest and nearest friends, and therefore when I visit Lincoln again I shall make the endeavor to meet the Bishop by the kind offices of our mutual friend Sawyer. I am delighted by your promise that you will honestly endeavor at all times to gather data and facts so carefully and with such discrimination to the false and the true, that the History of Nebraska may be made creditable to the state and to all connected with its publication..."

From the beginning, Paine's background was in business and organization and not in day-to-day editorials or authorship. He was born in Eden Prairie township in Minnesota to Ezra Kempton Paine and Alice C. Brown Paine. His New England roots included his great-great-grandfather William Paine and his great-great-great-grandfather John Paine who both served in major battles of the American Revolution.

Born and raised on his father's homestead, Paine was educated at the local district school. Historic accounts show he left school at an early age working in lumber camps in northern Minnesota. He decided he didn't want to work at that trade all of his life, so at age sixteen he became a foreman on one of the largest stock farms in the state at that time. Soon after he went to Minneapolis to attend school, finishing his academic work and taking a business college course. It was that business course that connected with his spirit and he moved to Boone, Iowa, where he established a business college and later, according to Mrs. Knotts *In Memoriam*, "controlled a number of commercial schools at various points in that state."[6]

While managing his schools, Paine became interested in the work of Charles Aldrich who was devoting his life to the preservation of Iowa history. Paine became a collector of Iowa memorabilia. Soon the subject of history preservation took over his interests and with the Trans-Mississippi Expo being planned for Omaha, Paine became interested in the history of Nebraska. The meeting of the Expo committee president Dr. George Miller and C.S. Paine is unknown, but they became friends working together years later on the Nebraska State Historical Society board of directors: Miller as president and in 1907 Paine as secretary.[7,8]

Paine and other prominent Nebraska men approached J. Sterling Morton to become editor-in-chief of their proposed history project. Paine moved to Nebraska in 1897 to take charge of the commercial phase of the Morton History of Nebraska project. He and his wife and four children made Omaha their home. He immediately set out to participate in the society of Nebraska. He joined the Christian Church and became a member of the Elks, the Rotary and the Knights of Pythias serving as a chancellor of his lodge. Paine juggled his time between the business of the Morton-Watkins volumes and his own historic interests.

Paine used his enthusiasm and ability to get active co-operation of large numbers of groups and individuals to persuade Nebraskans to mark the Oregon Trail. He is remembered as the man "keen" on preserving this portion of history of Nebraska.

Paine became the secretary-registrar and historian for the Nebraska Society Sons of the American Revolution and served as secretary-treasurer of the Nebraska Memorial association until his death. His *Memoriam*[6] also notes that "His keen human sympa-

The Oregon Trail Nebraska Historical Marker located: US 6 - six miles west of Hastings[9]

thies and interest in his fellow men led him to take an official interest in the Nebraska Children's home society, local and national humane societies and other kindred organizations."

He saw the need for a coordinated effort of historical societies like those in the Mississippi valley and assisted to create a seven-state Mississippi Valley Historical Association. Paine held the secretary-treasurer position of this association throughout his life.

By June 1903, he was elected as a board of trustees of Cotner University in Lincoln. He was known to be an active board member. Paine also saw the need for the Nebraska State Historical Society to occupy a building of their own and worked toward that end throughout the rest of his life.

While business with his own family and historic interests were prominent in his life, his work with the <u>Morton Illustrated History of</u>

Nebraska also continued until his death. As managing editor of the History of Nebraska he and Albert Watkins signed contracts with the publisher Jacob North and Co. to publish the volumes on a subscription basis.[1,2,3,4] Subscriptions were sold as early as 1898; however, the first volume was not printed until 1906. While Albert Watkins painstakingly edited the volumes after the untimely death of J. Sterling Morton in April 1902, Paine took on the issues that occurred along the way.

The transition and continuity of the project began immediately. On June 28, 1902, a letter to Albert Watkins from C.S. Paine on stationary of the General Committee of Arrangements, headquarters at Millard Hotel, advertising the International Convention of the Disciples of Christ of 1902 listing Paine as Chairman read: *"Dear Mr. Watkins: I did not know that you were expecting me in Lincoln yesterday, and it is simply impossible for me to get there today, owing to a previous engagement. I do not see the necessity of my presence there; as I told Mr. North that I was perfectly satisfied with the agreement as amended by you and regardless of that agreement, I was perfectly willing to go ahead and pay you and take our chances on getting it out of the Morton estate, in case they refuse to come to terms. I have, this morning telephoned Mr. North again, stating my position in the matter, but somehow or other, he hesitates to do anything until matters are entirely adjusted. I will, however, be in Lincoln Monday, if nothing prevents. Yours very truly,"*

Like Watkins, Paine addressed issues of sales agent fraud, subscribers that decided they wanted their money back before and after the publication(s) were completed, errors or omissions in the text, and the delivery of the finished editions. Many letters in the collections of the Nebraska State Historical Society (NSHS) refer to people who were asked to provide information and did not do so, then were angry when information about them or their area was not included. One such trail with letters from and to both Watkins and Paine was with Peter Ebbeson from St. Paul, Nebraska. Signed contracts prior to 1901 and numerous 1907 letters regarding a Mr. Anderson whose portrait and information did not get in the volume that was expected, as well as his own, resulted in letters several pages long. Both Ebbeson and Anderson were assured to be in the third volume; however, like many others, the length of time from the original request for information and financial exchange prior to the book(s) publication had been over a decade and many people were impatient with receipt of the product.

Ebbeson wasn't alone. The Buffalo Public Library of New York had dated a letter January 2, 1906, to Jacob North and Co. which was answered by Paine a few days later regarding the Library being surprised to receive information about the previously ordered <u>Illustrated History of Nebraska</u>. Paine's previous letter noted that they ordered the book August 22, 1901, and the library said, *"It was so long ago that we feel that we can take advantage of the law of limitation, and refuse to accept it. It is a book that we do not feel like purchasing at the present time, and are certain that we never gave an order to be filled at an indefinite time. We are holding this book subject to your order. Kindly advise us as to how we shall return it."* Paine immediately replied that the law of limitation did not apply in this case. The library replied on January 8 that they would keep the book, but to cancel any other orders if they had made any. The librarian writing the letter said that the assistant librarian who wrote the first note was only using the law of limitation as a figure of speech. This exchange seemed to smooth things over between the Library and the business side of the <u>Morton Illustrated History of Nebraska</u>.

By 1907, Louis R. Smith was the business manager while C.S. Paine was the managing editor of the Western Publishing & Engraving Co. The letterhead of the stationary noted the names of Miller, Paine, Smith, and Albert Watkins editor-in-chief, successor to J. Sterling Morton. The letterhead noted that Western Publishers was the publishers of <u>Illustrated History of Nebraska</u> and Jacob North & Co, Printers. (A letter from Smith about the issues of the project is reproduced in the Watkins section.)

On April 23, 1907, a contract was made between *"C.S. Paine, owner and publisher of the Illustrated History of Nebraska, party of the first part and Albert Watkins, editor of said History, party of the second part, ...said party of the first part agrees to publish said matter so to be furnished in said third volume of said History in the same form and style as that of volumes one and two thereof and print and place on the back of all copies of volumes three and on all copies of volumes one and two to accompany same, the following, "Morton-Watkins" or else bind and published the same with no name or names whatever thereon except that of Jacob North & Company, or Western Publishing & Engraving Company. In order to harmonize the contents of volume three, and for the purpose of insuring accuracy and the best literary form, the party the second part, shall at all times have free access to all the matter to be contained in said their volume, provided, however, that no changes may be made in said matter after same is in type ex-cept with the consent of party of the first part. The party of the first part reserves the right to add to the details of said History whenever, in his opinion such additions, will add to the value of said History. It is understood and agreed that the mutual promises herein contained are the sole consideration for such promises and such party waives all claim for compensation from the other and it is further agreed that the party of the second part shall not be held responsible in damages for any alleged defect or deficiency in the matter so to be furnished by him for said third volume...*"

They had learned to cover their bases even among themselves. The work went on until the last known edition in 1918; however, Paine passed away in 1916 before the final deliveries were made.

In a November 5, 1907, letter to Mr. N.C. Abbott of Houston, Texas, Watkins [for Paine and all] responded: "*Dear Mr. Abbott: I have your letter of the 2d inst., in re the Morton History of Nebraska. You seem not to have understood the conditions under which this His-tory was published. I am anxious that you should know, for we do not want your $15, neither are we in any position to pay it back, and you cannot afford to miss the opportunity to get these volumes, even if you had to pay $25 more instead of $10. Mr. Morton, myself [Watkins] and some others went into this enterprise upon the plan devised by Mr. Morton, whereby the people themselves were to furnish the money to carry on this work, by making an advance payment of $15 on their orders. This money was to be used in the work of research and in pre-paring the manuscript to be used in this History. The printers were to publish it, and get their pay cut of the $10 remaining due on the contracts. Now as a matter of fact, we have put nearly $100,000 into the work of this history. The mechanical work alone, has cost $6.00 on each volume. This has been due to the fact that the work grew upon us as it progressed, and in the meantime the cost of labor, paper, and everything else has been going up. In our work of research we dug up so much valuable history that ought to be published that it seemed a pity to omit it. We have therefore spared neither time nor expense to make this work all that it ought to be and it is the judgment of the best au-thorities that there is not published a history of any state in the union to compare with it. Now the first $15 that you paid has been used just as we proposed to use it, and expended just as wisely as we knew how. We have published the two volumes and have them on hand, and if any* *considerable number of subscribers repudiate their contracts, it is going to go hard with us, and while we have been willing to sacrifice our time for eleven years, we do not feel that we should be required to do more. However, I have gone into this matter thus fully, not because I am especially anxious to send you then two volumes on the payment of $10, and especially to prepay the charges, but because I want you to get the idea out of your head that we are morally or legally bound to refund to you the $15. That you aid. We are ready to send you the books on the payment of $10, this is the best we can do. Your contract is in our possession, and bears date of July 12, 1898, one of the first contracts taken. It provided for a payment of $15 on demand, "the balance, $10, on delivery of the work complete." On May 18, 1898 you paid the $15. on demand. Yours very truly."*

Other responses were shorter, but similar. On November 15, 1907, a letter from Paine on the Western Publishing stationary was written to A.E. Bartee of Arcadia, Nebraska: "*Dear Sir; Fearing that our representative, who delivered to you the two volumes of the Morton History, did not explain fully about the third volume, I hasten to write you. When we have assembled all our material for the second volume, we found that we had enough for two. We were therefore compelled to divide it and make a third volume, and this threw into the third volume all the later history of the state, including all the biographies and portraits of the younger men, among them your own. In order to publish the third volume at all, it has been necessary to deliver these two volumes, and collect the balance due on our contracts. I wanted you to understand this matter, and this your biographical sketch would appear later. "*

With two volumes now delivered and the third edition well underway, Paine could focus some time on the needs of his special project: finding a permanent building to house the first fifty years of Nebraska history materials, be accessible to the public, and have room to grow as the state grew.

"Minutes of a meeting of the joint committee of the Lincoln Commercial Club, the Nebraska State Historical Society, the Nebraska Territorial Pioneers' Association and the Lincoln City Council, held at the Commercial Club Rooms, January 21, 1908...Present, Thomas P. Kennard, Will O. Jones, Charles W. Bryan, Dr. J.S. Leonhardt, B.A. George, Charles Wake, C.S. Paine, H.W. Caldwell, C.F. Harpham, H.F. Bishop and City Attorney, John M. Stewart. *The meeting was called to order by Thomas P. Kennard, who was elected chairman. On motion of H.F. Bishop, C.S. Paine was elected secretary. After some informal discussion, the secretary was requested to make a statement of the position of the executive Board of the State Historical Society with reference to the building site. Dr. J.S. Leonhardt made a motion that "it is the sense of the committee that the proposed Historical Society building site be located on the University campus." This motion was seconded by the secretary, but after discussion the motion was withdrawn by Dr. Leonhardt, with the consent of the second. Motion by Dr. Leonhardt that "we tender to the Nebraska State Historical Society, in accordance with the act of the legislature known as H.R. No 431, the north half of Block 29, known as Market Square, for a site for the proposed Historical Society building." This motion was not seconded. Motion by B.A. George, seconded by C.F. Harpham, that the chairman appoint a committee of five, to consider all available sites and report at a meeting of the general committee, to be called by the secretary. The chairman named as four members of this committee, Mr. W. O. Jones, H.F. Bishop, C.S. Paine and B.A. George….."*

A typed and hand-written draft of 'a bill' to be enacted by the Nebraska legislature shows that Paine attempted to provide an avenue of a levy of tax, *"and the appropriation of the proceeds for the construction of a fireproof building for the permanent home of and to be known as 'the Nebraska State Historical Society Building,' and for the accommodation therein of the Supreme Court, The State Library, the Attorney General, Nebraska Public Library Commission, State Board of Agriculture, State Horticultural Society and the Grant Army of the Republic."* The bill and revenue stream to accommodate the Nebraska State Historical Society and its building on the campus of the University of Nebraska would undergo several changes.

While Paine was writing bills for the legislature, he also directed the new treasurer of the Western Publishing and Engraving Co, Mr. W. H. Roach, to enter into a contract with Albert Watkins on September 1909, as to the ownership of the copyright and the assignment or heirs related to the selling of the History books. Their working relationship maintained over the years was continually updated legally thanks to Paine's business organization.

Mrs. Knotts wrote, in the *Memoriam*[6] for Mr. Paine, "His breadth of view regarding the possibilities of the society [NSHS], combined with his enthusiasm, made a very marked increase in the growth of the society and in the scope of its work. His keen appreciation of the hardships endured and overcome during the development of this state, together with the realization of its importance in national history, inspired him to strenuous effort in the preservation of the story. His enthusiasm aroused others….The same energy and enthusiasm with which he pushed forward his historical work also characterized his attitude toward the movements for a better community and state, optimism, human sympathy, and generosity, combined with energy and enthusiasm of purpose, were the dominant features of his active life [June 1987 to June 1916]." N

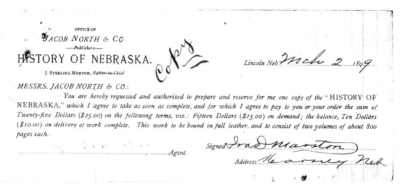

Copy of order blank for Morton book signed 1899.

Endnotes, Footnotes & Sources:

[1]Hansen, Nancy Sue and Dush, Barbara Ann. Nebraska Author Volume One. "J. Sterling Morton," Fullerton: D & H Adventures Publishing, 2013.

[2]Hansen, Nancy Sue and Dush, Barbara Ann. Nebraska Author Volume One. "Albert Watkins." Fullerton: D & H Adventures Publishing, 2013.

[3]Hansen, Nancy Sue and Dush, Barbara Ann. Nebraska Author Volume One. "Dr. George Miller." Fullerton: D & H Adventures Publishing, 2013.

[4]Hansen, Nancy Sue and Dush, Barbara Ann. Nebraska Author Volume One. "Grant L.Shumway." Fullerton: D & H Adventures Publishing, 2013.

[5]Olson, James C. History of Nebraska. 1955, University of Nebraska Press, 370 pp, 354-356.

[6]Knotts, Minnie Prey, *Clarence S. Paine, In Memoriam*. Nebraska State Historical Society. www.usgenet.org. reviewed November 28, 2012.

[7]*Paine, Clarence S.* Nebraska Historical Society Collections, Lincoln. Reviewed prior to December 15, 2012.

[8]Windham, Robert B. *President's Annual Address. Nebraska State Historical Society.* www.usgenet.org. Reviewed November 28, 2012.

[9] Oregon Trail marker photo by Nancy Sue Hansen, June 2013.

Nebraska Authors Book & Travel Club

Photo from a visit to a spot marked as part of the Oregon Trail in Nebraska or visit an exhibit about it through Nebraska. Remember it was Paine who pushed to have Nebraska history memorialized for you to visit.

CAROLINE SANDOZ PIFER

Date of Birth: May 21, 1910
Location of Birth: "River Place,"
Sheridan County, NE
Education: rural elementary
school;
Gordon High School; 1927;
Chadron Normal School;
Chadron State College, 1928-1929;
CSC, earning degree in English in
1981.
Date of Death: March 12, 2012, at
age 101
Location of Death: Gordon, NE

Caroline Pifer

Known Publications:

Pifer, Mrs. Robert. "This is your church : a pageant presented in the sanctuary May 10, 1959." Publisher: Gordon, Nebraska : First Methodist Church - 1959?; five leaves.

Pifer, Caroline Sandoz. "Sands of time, 1960: Pageant of seventy-five years of progress," Gordon, Nebraska; typewritten. 41 pp.

Pifer, Caroline Sandoz. Sandoz, Jules. Son of Old Jules: memoirs of Jules Sandoz, Jr., University of Nebraska Press, 1989. 125 pp.

Sandoz, Caroline. A kinkaider's child / Caroline Sandoz Pifer. Publisher: Gordon, Nebraska, 1995. 78 pp.

Pifer, Caroline Sandoz. Making of an Author: Mari Sandoz, Book I, Cottonwood Press, 1972. 61 pp.

Pifer, Caroline Sandoz. <u>Making of an Author: Mari Sandoz, Book II</u>, Cottonwood Press, 1982. 160 pp.

Pifer, Caroline Sandoz. <u>Making of an Author: Mari Sandoz. Book III</u>, Cottonwood Press, 1984. 152 pp.

Pifer, Caroline Sandoz. <u>Making of an Author: Mari Sandoz, Book IV</u>, The Ad Pad, 1997. 220 pp.

The famous Sandoz legacy is as vast and ageless as the Nebraska Sandhills where it was brought to life. That family legacy is shared by author Caroline Sandoz Pifer.

Caroline was the youngest of six children born to Jules Ami and Mary Fehr Sandoz at the "River Place" in Sheridan County. She was fourteen years younger than her author sister, Mari Sandoz, who first carried the family name into literary fame with the publication of her first book, <u>Old Jules</u>.

Caroline clearly recalled her childhood years in a 2004 interview with Barbara Dush, and did so with a vibrancy evident of the Sandoz pioneer spirit.

"I was born south of Hay Springs and was only six months old when we moved to the Sandhills. I was carried into the Sandhills you could say," Caroline smiled. "The family moved in the fall of the year. It was warm enough they could go around without coats. They told me about it so many times I could visualize it."

But when Caroline came into the world, no one welcomed her.

<u>The Story Catcher</u>, a publication of the Mari Sandoz Heritage Society, revealed: *To oldest sister, Mari, it meant another baby to care for. To her mother Mary, who was back working outside within 10 days of the baby's birth, it meant more work and another mouth to feed.*

When she was young, Caroline felt like an only child because Mari was already teaching school and Flora was four years older. Flora, she remembered, helped her by braiding her blonde hair and tying it in blue ribbons that were peeled off Blue Ribbon beer bottle labels.

"I was an intruder you might say, because nobody wanted me," Caroline added. "Mother said she would give ten years of her life if she hadn't become pregnant with me at the time. I think she was around forty-two when she had me. But I was a blessing to her later in life because I was her only transportation."

Caroline was also a blessing as a young child, helping to run the family store. Once again, from The Story Catcher: *There was no store between Ellsworth and Gordon back then except the Sandoz store; and as a young girl, Caroline was put in charge of it. She would wait on customers, count the change out loud and climb up and down on a little stool so she could reach the cash register.*

By this time, Jules had lost most of his sting and her relationship with him was different from that of her siblings. Riding beside him on the spring seat of the wagon, she would listen for hours to his orations ...

The barn on the Sandoz place wasn't just for livestock. "We had school in the barn. We were a self-contained outfit," Caroline laughed. Oldest sister Mari was her school teacher, and she never forgot the "daily spankings" she got from her older sister. When she asked why she received the constant paddling and not the other students, she was told, "Because the other kids didn't matter. You do – you're a Sandoz."

When she started school at 4, Caroline didn't have far to go as it was held upstairs in the Sandoz barn," The Story Catcher *details. "Mari was the teacher for her first two years and pressed her very hard because she didn't want anyone to think she showed favoritism. Siblings, James, Fritz and Flora as well as several neighbor children attended school in the barn as well.*

And it was a spectacular barn. With its 600-foot roof spreading out from its 20-foot gable top in long, gradual wings down almost to the ground. It was similar to a barn Jules had seen near Neuchatel. In the center of the loft was the schoolroom, but the barn was also used as a community center and dances were held there once a month.

Soon after Jules died, a tornado-like wind lifted the east roof off the majestic barn and laid it on a hillside across the valley.

Caroline attended country school every year until she finished ninth grade at the age of fifteen and graduated from Gordon High School.

She was a popular young lady, but education was always a priority, and Mari seen to it that it remained that way. It was said that Mari's advice, "Get your education," rang in Caroline and sister Flora's ears any time they were around boys.

When Caroline's father died in 1928, she was just out of high school and expected to "fill in" at the ranch, including the responsibility of taking care of her mother, who could not write English. Despite these heavy responsibilities, she was able to attend Chadron State College from 1928 to 1929. Her first teaching job was at the Hebbert School earning sixty dollars a month. From 1929 to 1933, she taught in Sheridan and Cherry Counties.

On May 4, 1935, despite her mother's criticism of her choice of boyfriends, Caroline married her cowboy sweetheart with the "cold blue eyes," Bob Pifer, and they rented part of her mother's place. "We became Dust Bowlers. We got married right at the worst time as far as the Dust Bowl was concerned, but it was the best time for us because we bought everything cheap."

The couple had two daughters, Eleanor and Mary Ann. Their hard work and savvy pulled them out of the struggles of the Dust Bowl and into a successful ranching operation. In addition to being a ranch wife and mother, Caroline served as a school district moderator for ten years and on the election board for fifteen years, and was a member of the Sunbeam Calyx Federated Garden Club from 1954 to 1992 and the Nebraska Historical Society from 1968 to 2001. Caroline also continued ranching after Bob's death.

Meantime, Caroline's sister Mari was experiencing writing success. In 1935, after fifteen years of rejection letters from publishers, Mari's book Old Jules won the Atlantic Press nonfiction contest, which lifted her to literary fame. As an eleven-year-old, Mari had been beaten by her father and locked in a cellar as reward for the first publication of one of her short stories written in school. "We could write," Caroline explained. "There was nothing wrong with writing, but we were supposed to write practical stuff, nothing made up."

After Mari's death in 1966, Caroline became her sister's biggest promoter. She was named Mari's executrix and carried out her literary sister's last distinctive wishes and the management of her literary estate. She gave presentations to scholars and school children, and one hundred fifty mile day long tours through Sandoz country.

In addition to her dedication to Mari's literary career, Caroline decided to complete her college education and enrolled in classes at Chadron State College. She graduated in 1981 at the age of seventy with a bachelor of science degree in literature. "I didn't like to write," she noted, "but when I went to college, writing turned out to be fun, and sometimes a whole paragraph would just come to me. A friend told me God sent me that talent." In 1987, Caroline was presented the

Distinguished Service Award by the college.

Between 1969 and 2001, Caroline wrote articles and four books in a series under the title, <u>Making of an Author</u>, gleaned from Mari's letters. Her neighbor, Sybil Malmberg Berndt, assisted in the last writing. Caroline has also written a publication titled <u>A Diary – My Sense and Sensibility</u>, and co-wrote a biography about her brother, Jules Jr. titled <u>Son of Old Jules: memoirs of Jules Sandoz, Jr.</u>

Pifer spent her last years at Countryside Care in Gordon. She was no longer able to write; however, her books continued to gain popularity. Caroline died March 12, 2012, at the age of 101, the last remaining child of the Jules Sandoz family.

"I just got a call that I need to get more of my books published," she said during the 2004 interview. "Mari was very professional and I think in a way, she had a sad life because she didn't accomplish what she wanted to. She wanted to not only be a good writer, she wanted to be a master writer. She wanted to be like Dickens, be read years and years later, and maybe she will. Who knows?"

Who knows.

Perhaps there was a bit of Dickens in Caroline Sandoz Pifer, too. B

Endnotes, Footnotes & Sources:

Barbara Ann Dush interview with Caroline Sandoz Pifer in February 2004.

www.meaningfulfunerals.net/fh/obituaries/obituary.cfm?o_id...fh.

www.marisandoz,org/.../2009-05-the-story-cathcer.pdf.

Many thanks to Theresa McGahan of North Platte, Nebraska, for all her help in obtaining information.

Thank you to Cindy Drake, Library Curator, Statewide Cemetery Registry Coordinator, at the Nebraska State Historical Society for her research aid.

Caroline Sandoz Pifer (right) and Barbara Dush in
a 2004 interview at Countryside Care in Gordon.

Nebraska Authors Book & Travel Club

Visit the Ad Pad at 158 N Sheridan Street in Gordon to view
Caroline Pifer memorabilia. Attach a photo or have a staff member sign and date this box.

AMIL QUAYLE

Date of Birth: March 31, 1938
Location of Birth: St. Anthony, ID
Education: South Fremont High
School grad, St. Anthony ID;
Ricks College, Reburg, ID, associates
degree, 1963;
Sociology University of Utah, BS
degree and teachers certificate, 1968;
University of Nebraska, MA and PhD
English, 1991
Military: served eight years in Idaho
National Guard and Utah National
Guard
What town called home in Nebraska:
Lincoln
Currently lives in Idaho

Amil Quayle

Known Publications:

Quayle, Amil. <u>Pebble Creek</u>. Slow Tempo Press, 1991.

Quayle, Amil. <u>Grand Canyon and Other Selected Poems</u>. Black Star Press, 2009, 34 illustrations, 112 pp.

Quayle, Amil. <u>Upset in Upset</u>. Henry's Fork Books, 2011, 30 pp.

Amil Quayle has returned to his native St. Anthony, Idaho, to stay; however, his passion for nature merged with his talents as poet, painter, and river guide and left its imprint on Nebraska soil where he resided for fifteen years.

Quayle worked as a guide during the early years of commercial river-running in the Grand Canyon. It was in 1961 that he ran his first river trip, and that initial trip has had him hooked ever since. He was a full-time guide, mostly in the Grand Canyon for thirteen years.

When Quayle decided to venture into new territory, he sold his river business and bought a cattle ranch in 1975 in Sargent, Nebraska. He raised cattle for seven years, then he earned an MA and PhD in English from the University of Nebraska. He taught English for Utah State University and Idaho State University.

In 1991, Quayle returned to his childhood home, a small house his father had built near the Henry's Fork of the Snake River in St. Anthony. As a boy, he spent many happy hours there playing on the banks and in the water, and developed a keen appreciation and love for the land.

Quayle's heart had never left the river. He is still running the river and sharing his vast knowledge. Two of his sons and two of his grandchildren are also river guides, with other grandchildren wanting to follow in the same footsteps.

He began writing in earnest in 1982, citing "encouragement from professors at the University of Nebraska" as his reassuring push into the writing world, "though I was always a wannabee," he added.

However, inspiration was always close at hand for this river guide. "My inspirations are rivers, wilderness, and a host of friends who are willing to defend them and their right to exist," Quayle said. "I love this earth beyond any possible measure. I believe the earth is our mother and I believe we should treat the earth like we would treat any wonderful mother that has given us all we have and more."

Quayle penned two award-winning books of poetry, <u>Pebble Creek</u> and <u>Grand Canyon and Other Selected Poems</u>, which draw on his family's long intimacy with the rugged landscapes and rural cultures of the American West.[1] In his favorite work, <u>Grand Canyon and Other Selected Poems</u>, there are two great rivers in the book: the river that runs through the Grand Canyon and the river that flows through Quayle's love for his family. His poetry also offers his readers a "finely detailed and sometimes sorrowful view of the changes that have overtaken the West's human and natural communities during the last century." His writing in graduate school garnered the Vreeland Award, the Mari Sandoz Award, and the American Poets Award.

Greg Kosmicki, editor/publisher of Backwater Press in Omaha, noted of Quayle: *This is a poet who grew up by water, was tested by water, found his spirt by water, lost his brother to water, located his life on the water, made lifelong friends on water, lost his wife and friends to water, and then, for reasons only an old boatman may know, changed course and abandoned water - but still he wrote his poems, poems that give one a heady sense of being on a river run with this skilled poet, the rush of the world safely navigated by his sure hand.*

As he enters his mid-seventies, Quayle reflects on his years in Nebraska, stating that he loved the prairie and the people. As for the future, "My plans are to make an attempt to die well without a lot of kicking and screaming, love my children and grandchildren more and to let them know it, and become even more grateful and reverent towards our great mother and to support the people who are working for that same end." B

Endnotes, Footnotes & Sources:

Rivers run through Quayle's 'Grand Canyon' Ground Zero - http://journalstar.com/entertainment/rivers-run-through-quayle-s-

Interview via e-mail with Amil Quayle in Barbara Ann Dush's files, 2013.

Hermit Rapids, Grand Canyon April 1967,
Amil Quayle - Boatman. (John Parks)

Nebraska Authors Book & Travel Club

Signature or visit the Niobrara River Canoe Trail. To access sites of points of interest go to www.outdoornebraska.org or call the Nebraska Games & Parks Commission at (402) 471-0641. Attach a photo of your experience.

DANIEL QUINN

Date of birth: Oct. 11, 1935
Location of birth: Omaha, NE,
Education: H. S. Creighton Prep,
Omaha, 1953,
studied at St. Louis University, St.
Louis, MO;
University of Vienna, Vienna,
Austria
Loyola University of Chicago,
Chicago, IL, Cum Laude,
Bachelors in English, 1957.
Current home: Houston, TX

Daniel Quinn

Known publications:

Quinn, Daniel. Ishmael. Bantam/Turner Publisher, 1992, 263 pp. fiction.

Quinn, Daniel. Providence: The Story of a Fifty-Year Vision Quest. Bantam Book Publishers, 1994.183 pp. autobiography.

Quinn, Daniel. The Story of B. Bantam Dell Publishers, 1996, 325 pp. fiction.

Quinn, Daniel. My Ishmael: A Sequel. Bantam Book Publishers, 1997, 92 pp. fiction.

Quinn, Daniel. Beyond Civilization: Humanity's Next Great Adventure. Three-Rivers Press, 1999, 202 pp. non-fiction.

Quinn, Daniel. After Dachau. Context Books, 2001, 192 pp. fiction. (Reissued in paperback 2006 by Zoland Books/Steerforth Press.)

Quinn, Daniel. <u>The Man Who Grew Young</u>. Context Books, 2001, 2002. 204 pp.graphic novel.

Quinn, Daniel. <u>The Holy</u>. Context Books, 2002, 416 p. fiction. (Reissued in paperback by Zoland Books/Steerforth Press.)

Quinn, Daniel. <u>Tales of Adam</u>. Steerforth Press first edition. 2005, 96 pp. fiction.

Quinn, Daniel. <u>Work, Work, Work</u>. Steerforth Press 2006, 32 pp. children's book for two years and up.

Quinn, Daniel. <u>If They Give You Lined Paper, Write Sideways</u>. Steerforth Press, 2007, 198 pp. non-fiction.

Quinn, Daniel. <u>At Woomeroo: Stories</u>. CreateSpace Publishing, 2012, 150 pp. fiction.

What book has sold more than a million copies in English, has been translated into more than thirty languages, and is used in high schools and colleges worldwide in history, philosophy, sociology, ecology, biology, political science, economics, and other courses? It is a novel by Daniel Quinn: <u>Ishmael</u>.

The native Omaha, Nebraska, author graduated from Creighton Prep in 1953. He and his family moved from the state when he was nearly twenty-two. In the interview for this introduction to Nebraska authors and their works, he said his only connection in Nebraska is the Creighton Prep alumni newsletter (and the Nebraskans that read his books and visit his website, www.Ishmael.org). <u>Ishmael</u> won the 1991 Turner Tomorrow Award, awarded to "a novel offering creative and positive solutions to global problems," chosen from among more than two thousand entries worldwide.

Between college graduation in 1957, the Turner Award, and the success of his first book, Daniel had careers in Chicago area educational and consumer publishing and raised a family. He also founded and ran the Stateville Penitentiary Writers workshop (1969-71). In addition, he served on the Board of Listeners of the 1992 World Uranium Hearing, Salzberg, Austria, convened to hear testimony of victims of uranium mining, nuclear waste disposal, and nuclear power disasters around the world.

Quinn describes the theme of his first five books as "an examination of our world-destroying culture, which was born about ten thousand years ago in the Near East and has been spreading across the planet ever since, reaching the New World at the end of the fifteenth century." He characterizes his later books as "more purely literary." His favorite Quinn book is <u>Ishmael</u>.

Are there more books in progress for Mr. Quinn? He answered, "A collection of my short stories will appear in a few weeks, but with the publication of <u>If They Give you Lined Paper, Write Sideways</u>, I've written all the books I have in mind to write for the time being."

He has addressed many organizations, student and faculty groups, and now conducts frequent teleconferences with high school and college classes. Daniel enjoys reading mysteries and painting as past times.

He and his wife, Rennie MacKay Quinn, have spent time creating and maintaining an enormous website: www.ishmael.org. In addition to information about his books, the site provides suggested readings, answers to more than five hundred questions about him and his work, and many key Quinn essays and speeches available nowhere else. Nebraskans and readers around the world are welcome to visit the guestbook and to add their comments to the thousands of comments already found there. N

Endnotes, Footnotes & Sources:

www.ishmael.org. Reviewed 1/2/2012.

www.cafepress.com/ishmaelsannex. Reviewed 1/2/2012.

www.rmqabstracts.com. Reviewed 1/2/2012.

Special thanks to Rennie and Daniel Quinn for the e-mail interview(s), 2012, notes in Nancy Sue Hansen's file.

Nebraska Authors Book & Travel Club
Signature or provide photo or ticket from visit to Creighton Prep School activity.

JAMES ALBERT RAWLEY

Date of Birth: Nov. 9, 1916
Location of Birth: Terre Haute, IN
Education: Univ. of Michigan B.S.,
M.S. History, 1939
Columbia University, Ph.D., 1949
Military: drafted Army, WWII
Date of Death: Nov. 29, 2005
Location at Death: Lincoln, NE

University of Nebraska Library
Archives Collection.
James A. Rawley

Known publications:

Rawley, James A. Edwin D. Morgan, 1811 – 1883: Merchant in Politics. New York: Columbia University Press, 1955. Columbia Studies in the Social Sciences, No. 582. 321 pp.

Rawley, James A., Ed. The American Civil War, an English View. Charlottesville: University Press of Virginia , 1964. xxxvii + 231 pp.

Rawley, James A. Turning Points of the Civil War. Lincoln: University of Nebraska Press, 1966. ix- 230 pp.

Rawley, James A. Ed. Lincoln and Civil War Politics. New York: Holt, Rinehart and Winston, Original edition 1969. Reprint 1977, In, Robert E. Krieger Pub American Problem Studies, 129 pp.

Rawley, James A. Race and Politics: "Bleeding Kansas" and the Coming of the Civil War. Philadelphia: J. B. Lippincott Co., 1969. xvi + 304 pp. Reprinted, 1979, Bison Books Publication.

Rawley, James A. The Politics of Union Northern Politics During the Civil War. Lincoln: University of Nebraska Press. 1974. 202 pp, 1980 Bison Printing. Reprinted of the ed. Published by Dryden Press, Hinsdale, Ill Series, Berkshire Studies in history.

Rawley, James A., Stephen D. Behrend. The Transatlantic Slave Trade. A History, Lincoln: University of Nebraska Press, 1981, 2005, p 441.

Rawley, James A. Secession The Disruption of the American Republic 1844-1861. Florida: Robert E. Krieger Pub, 1990. page 259.

Rawley, James A. London Metropolis of the Slave Trade. 2003. University of Missouri. 2003, 216 pp.

Many articles to historic quarterlys, annuals, and sketches to publications such as the Dictionary of American Biography. He spoke to many groups, societies and graduations.

A well-respected James A. Rawley was awarded the highest honor from the History Department at the University of Nebraska at Lincoln: the Carl Adolph Happold Professor of History (Emeritus). His fascination with history focused on the Civil War era, especially race relations and American History. He became a biographer of Abraham Lincoln.

At his death, an annual award is now given in his honor by the Organization of American Historians (OAH) to the best book concerning the history of race relations in the United States: the James A. Rawley Prize. Recipients and related information is found listed on their website.[1,2]

Born in Indiana in 1916, Rawley took his interest in studying history to the University of Michigan where he earned both a BA and MA by 1939. According to Lee W. Formwalt, who wrote *James Rawley: A Rich Career in American History*, OAH Newsletter May 2005, Rawley moved from Michigan to New York to begin his doctoral studies at Columbia University. *"Rawley had been drafted before the U.S. entered the war but was classified 4-F; after Pearl Harbor he was called up again and this time 'was declared to be 1-A.' All of his Army service was stateside from Texas, where he got his basic training to North Carolina where he was commissioned, to Cape Cod where he served in antiaircraft artillery and the transportation corps. He ended up at the New York Port of Embarkation, where, after the war ended, he was assigned to help write that installation's history."*[3,4]

When he returned from the war he attended Columbia University graduating in 1949 with his PhD. He married Ann and they raised two sons.

Rawley taught at Columbia University, Hunter College in New York, and at Sweet Briar College in Virginia before moving to the History Department at the University of Nebraska-Lincoln in 1964.

It was at Sweet Briar that he published his first book Edwin D. Morgan: Merchant in Politics, 1811-83 (1955). While another book wouldn't be published for a decade, Dr. Rawley wrote articles, including his most cited "The Nationalism of Abraham Lincoln" from Civil War History published in 1963.

In 1966, he published the first of four books on the Civil War era focusing on race, slavery and emancipation. The first of the four, Turning Points of the Civil War, is still in print and has been studied by countless undergraduates. In 1969, he published the book Race and Politics: "Bleeding Kansas" and the Coming of the Civil War, a detailed account of the Kansas Territory in the 1850s. Meanwhile he edited the book Lincoln and Civil War Politics which was also published in 1969. In 1974, the final of the four books was published The Politics of Union: Northern Politics during the Civil War.

For his article Formwalt asked Rawley how he ever got into his type of research. According to Formwalt, "he replied that in the 1960s J.B. Lippincott Company 'was doing a series of books, and I was asked to do a book on Bleeding Kansas, so I thought, well, this is going to be pretty much a political story, political parties, elections and so on.' Then as he got into the material it became very clear to him just how powerful a role race played in the events of the 1850s."[4]

Rawley wasn't satisfied to just read someone else's work and write it down with his name on it. According to biographical sources, he used what would be considered an innovative approach to historic research.[5] He took fragmentary sources and piece by piece tried to identify what happened to more than ten million Africans who had been involved in American slavery. The result of his quantitative style research was published in 1981 in The Transatlantic Slave Trade: A History. He returned to the topic again in his last book <u>London Metropolis of the Slave Trade</u> published in 2003. The book is a collection of three of his works of the past three decades and three new pieces, which includes research on the composer of "Amazing Grace."

Kathleen Rutledge of the *Lincoln Journal & Star* wrote: "Objectivity is not always appreciated" in October 25, 1981 about Rawley's Atlantic slave trade research.[6] The article described Rawley's writings had revealed myths in commonly held historic beliefs. Rawley had discovered that the slave trade was not quite as profitable on each voyage as history contends. Most trips were a profit of only ten percent, but once in a while that a very large profit was seen. That once-in-a-while large profit seemed to be the goal of the traders. In another myth, "slaves were kidnapped by whites or obtained through unequal bartering." Rawley found that most slaves were supplied to white traders by the Africans themselves.

He chaired the UN-L History Department in 1966-67 and from 1972 until 1982. In 1976, the Rockefeller Foundation awarded Dr. Rawley a residency for the Study and Conference Center in Bellagio, Italy. [7]

Continuing to research and teach, Rawley also served as Acting Dean of the University Libraries in 1984-1985. He retired from teaching in 1987. He received numerous awards in his career.

Retirement didn't stop the research and writing. In 1990, he published an undergraduate book with origins of the Civil War, <u>Secession: The Disruption of the American Republic 1844-1861,</u> and six years later in 1996 he wrote a biography, <u>Abraham Lincoln and a Nation Worth Fighting For</u>.

When his second transatlantic slave trade book was finished in 2003, he turned to two other books which were found in manuscript form at the time of his death: <u>A Lincoln Dialogue</u> and <u>New Turning Points of the Civil War</u>.

Research, teaching, writing, and family were only a part of his life. He served for eighteen years as a board member and for two years as president of the Board of Directors for the Nebraska State Historical Society, and served on the Board of Directors for the Nebraska Council for the Humanities Foundation. He also took time for duties at St. Matthews Episcopal Church.

For Dr. Rawley his focus of race, slavery, and emancipation were issues of history that were alive with the effects palpable today. N

Endnotes, Footnotes & Sources:

[1]*American Historical Association*. www.historians.org. reviewed June 4, 2012.

[2]Perspectives. *In Memoriam*, Column March 2006. Reviewed June 4, 2012.

[3] – www.usmilitaryabout.com Classifications and what they mean: 1-A – available immediately for military service; 4-F – not qualified for military service due to medical reason. Reviewed 6/2/2013.

[4] Formwalt, Lee W. *James Rawley: A Rich Career in American History*, OAH Newsletter May 2005. Reviewed in file of information from Rawley collection at the University of Nebraska archives. Reviewed December 11, 2012.

[5]*Lincoln Journal and Star.* "Dr. James A. Rawley, professor and chairman of the department of history at the University of Ne in Lincoln has done deep research into the origins and institutions of slavery in the United States and is the author of several books that deal with aspects of slavery." March 7, 1976, PG 9F:1 44" photo. Reviewed in card file of the State Historical Society June 4, 2012.

[6]*Lincoln Journal and Star.* By Kathleen Rutledge. *Objectivity is not always appreciated* October 25, 1981, reviewed in file of information from Rawley collection at the University of Nebraska archives. Reviewed December 11, 2012.

[7]*Lincoln Evening Journal.* "James Rawley, professor and chairman of the history department at UNL has been awarded a residency by the Rockefeller Foundation at the foundations Study and Conference Center in Bellagio, Italy." December 22, 1976 32:1 2." Reviewed in card file of the State Historical Society June 4, 2012.

James A. Rawley Prize. www.wikipedia.org. Reviewed June 4, 2012.

Several attempts were made to contact family members for this article; however, there has been no response to our inquires at this time.

Nebraska Authors Book & Travel Club

Photo of your visit to the Nebraska State Capitol grounds and President Lincoln's statue in Lincoln, Nebraska.

ARTHUR J. RIEDESEL

Date of Birth: Oct. 6, 1921
Location of Birth: Brule, NE
Education: Ogallala High School,
graduated 1938;
attended Nebraska Wesleyan (1939-
41), transferred to University of
Missouri-Columbia; Bachelor of
Journalism and Master of Art in
History, graduated 1947
Military: U. S. Army during World
War II
Date of Death: Feb. 23, 2010
Location of Death: Lincoln, NE
What town called home in Nebraska:
Ogallala

1979 photo of Arthur J.
Riedesel.

Known Publications:

Riedesel, Arthur J. The story of the Nebraska Press Association: 1873-
1973, Nebraska Press Assn (1973), 53 pp.

Riedesel, Arthur J. A new history of the 115th Station Hospital; publisher: A. J. Riedesel (1992), 23 pp.

T he story of a consummate small-town newspaperman ended
February 23, 2010, when Arthur J. Riedesel, publisher of *The Ashland
Gazette* died.

Arthur knew as a child he wanted to work in the newspaper business, according to his son, Paul Riedesel of Minneapolis.

"By the time he was in fourth grade, he knew he wanted to be a
newspaperman, which meant small-town Nebraska weeklies. History
was an extension of that interest in reporting what had happened ac-
curately and clearly" said Paul. "It goes that deep."

As early as 1934, Arthur started at *Keith County News* in Ogallala as an unpaid printer's devil, an apprentice who did the dirty work involved in running the presses, Paul explained. Arthur continued working there through high school and after graduation in 1938. He stayed in Ogallala one year after high school to take more shorthand and typing classes, according to his son, to hone his craft. "He was the fastest typist I know," Paul said.

In 1939, Arthur left Ogallala to attend Nebraska Wesleyan University, but his college years were interrupted by World War II. After attending Wesleyan for two years, he took a summer course at the University of Colorado in Boulder in 1942, then served forty months in the Army, including time in England, France, and Germany. "Dad served in the 115th Station Hospital in World War II," Paul said. "They processed casualties in England though his unit was later in the army of occupation in Augsburg and elsewhere. He was discharged with the rank of Technical Sergeant. Most of his work was administrative though I believe all personnel had some basic medical training. More of the soldiers from that war than not didn't talk much about what all they saw." After his discharge from the Army in 1946, Arthur continued his schooling at the University of Missouri in Columbia. He graduated in 1947 with a bachelor of journalism and a master of art in history.

Arthur was co-publisher of *The Sherman County Times* in Loup City from 1947 to 1953; publisher of *The York Republican* from 1954 to 1955 and became *The Ashland Gazette* publisher October 1, 1955, moving his young family to the community that would become his home for the next several decades.

When Arthur retired, he sold the paper to Zean and Marilyn Carney on January 1, 1986. In the last of over 1,500 editorials he wrote while publisher of the *Gazette*, Arthur paid tribute to the community. "When I came to Ashland in 1955 I bought a good property in a good town," he wrote.

"He was a professional in a field that had its share of hacks," Paul said. "He cared about this community – Ashland – even though he kept a certain dispassionate distance. One of his proudest achievements was his role in fighting a doofy idea by the Corps of Engineers to create a recreational lake on top of Ashland and the surrounding fertile farmland in the late '60s and '70s."

His editorial noted a highlight of his time as publisher – the decade long fight he led to keep the Corps of Engineers from damming the Platte River and drowning Ashland and the surrounding area in the 1960's, despite advice by fellow business owners to ignore or downplay the issue.

"I replied it was my responsibility to print the story right up to the last gurgle, if it came to that," he wrote. Fortunately, the idea was shelved in 1973. When it resurfaced in 2006, Arthur lent the *Gazette* a scrapbook he had meticulously created chronicling the previous fight.

These were just a few of the examples of how seriously Arthur took his responsibility as a newspaper editor in a small community. "It takes a certain kind of perseverance that most people would not pretend to have, to run a weekly newspaper," he wrote.

That perseverance included missing only six of 1,570 issues as the *Gazette* publisher. Paul remembers his father calling him up from Oklahoma where he was teaching in 1976 to run the newspaper while his parents took a trip to England. "I published the *Gazette* for three weeks," Paul proudly noted.

Nebraska Press Association Executive Director Allen Beermann said Riedesel was the "perfect example of the country editor/publisher." Arthur was known to have a lively, but precise writing style that he was very proud of, said his son. "He was always a stickler for writing."

But as many a newspaper publisher of a bygone era, Arthur did more than just write stories. He also sold ads, designed pages, covered sports and oversaw the production of the newspaper and other printing jobs. "He was forthright, his word was always true, and he loved the craft of journalism," said Beermann.

Arthur was also passionate about history, and lent his expertise to local projects. He wrote and published the Ashland centennial book, The First 100 Years: Ashland 1857 to 1957, and wrote the history portion of the Saline Ford Historical Preservation Society's book commemorating Ashland's 150th birthday in 2007. He also served as chairman and wrote the history of the Nebraska Press Association during its centennial celebration in 1973.

"He read extensively but as much in English history and WWII history as anything," Paul said. "He truly had the largest library of history in our small town of Ashland. He also knew as much about classical music as anyone in town (more than most of the choir directors)."

Arthur served on the board of Nebraska Press Association for ten years and was its president in 1979/1980, and also served on the

Nebraska Press Advertising Service for twelve years and was elected president. "He brought luster to the association," said Beermann. *The Ashland Gazette* also garnered numerous awards from the Nebraska Press Association for journalistic excellence. "That means as much to him as anything," Paul said.

Arthur's contributions to the community were also noteworthy. He served as president of the Ashland and Loup City Rotary Clubs, was a member of the Ashland American Legion Post 129, Veterans of Foreign Wars Post 9776 and Pomegranate Lodge 110 of Masons, and served as president of the Ashland Chamber of Commerce in 1968.

"For someone who spent most of his life in small-town Nebraska, he knew and was interested in the larger world. You could say he did many things his own way, a trait carried on in my generation and by my children," Paul reflected of his father's legacy. B

Endnotes, Footnotes & Sources:

Special thanks to Suzi Nelson, News Editor of *The Ashland Gazette,* for providing much of the copy for Arthur Riedesel's story; and to Paul Riedesel for personal comments which were added to the original copy.

Nebraska Authors Book & Travel Club
Obtain a copy of the Ashland Gazette at 1510 Silver Street in Ashland and make a comment here of an article you especially enjoyed.

GRANT LEE SHUMWAY

Date of birth: March 7, 1865
Location of birth: Oxford, Illinois
Education: prior to moving to Banner/Cheyenne County, NE in 1885 to homestead
Moved: to Scottsbluff in 1901 until death
Date of Death: Nov. 7, 1925

Nebraska State Historical
Society Collection
Grant Lee Shumway[5]

Known Publications:

Acquired country paper: Ashford, Nebraska.[1]

Shumway, Grant Lee. "The Sod Cabin," poem in five parts. Ashford: *Ashford Advocate,* 1889.[1]

Morton, J. Sterling, Albert Watkins, Grant L. Shumway. History of Nebraska from the earliest explorations of the trans-Mississippi Region. Lincoln: Western Publishing Co., 1918 revised edition.

Shumway, Grant Lee. History of Western Nebraska and Its People. Vol. 2 Lincoln: Western Publishing and Engraving Co., 1921.

Shumway, Grant Lee. History of Western Nebraska and Its People, General History [Vol. 2,3] by Shumway, Grant L; Morton, J. Sterling. Lincoln: Western Publishing and Engraving Co., 1921.

It would be a six-year recurring illness credited to gallstones that plagued Grant L. Shumway taking his life. He was known as a man with understanding of the history and workings of the Western Nebraska. Shumway was said to be a versatile writer of prose and poetry as well as being a lover of flowers, plants, animals and beautiful nature. He used the knowledge to become a 'man with a vision' for future generations.

G. L. Shumway homesteaded in 1885 in Cheyenne County near what became Ashford. Shumway purchased and published *The Ashford Advocate.*[1,2] According to the Sidney, Nebraska's, *The Telegraph* newspaper article describing his death, his focus at the newspaper was "farmer organizations and political activities."[3] Shumway married Gertrude Viola Ashford at Ashford, Nebraska, on September 10, 1890. They had one daughter, Floy.

Shumway was chief engrossing clerk in the state house of representatives in 1893. The Shumway's moved to Scottsbluff County where, according to *The Telegraph,* he "became identified with the building up of Scottsbluff and the North Platte Valley."[3]

According to *The Telegraph* it was during the times he was not holding public office that he did his 'literary work.' He wrote the <u>History of Western Nebraska and Its People</u> and added his expertise to the <u>Illustrated History of Nebraska</u> edited by J. Sterling Morton and Albert Watkins in their last volume, revised edition.[5,6,7,8,9] He continued to serve and worked as auditor of public accounts and as State Commissioner of Public Lands and Buildings from 1917-1918.

When William Jennings Bryan's brother, Charlie Bryan, was elected as Nebraska Governor for his first term, Shumway was named as deputy Secretary of Agriculture, 1923-1925. He passed away after only two years in office. "He was regarded as Bryan's chief advisor and friend," noted the Scottsbluff newspaper article. "One of the leading democrats in the state."[4]

It was during his years as Secretary of Agriculture that he promoted the idea to split Cheyenne County into two counties. Banner County

Nebraska State Historical
Society Collection
G.L. Shumway,
date unknown[5]

was created by legislative enactment November 6, 1888. According to Perky's, "It was named by enthusiastic citizens who wished to make it the 'banner county' of the state." Ashford was named the first county seat of Banner County on January 25, 1889, but lost its status in an election to Harrisburg in May 1889 where it remains today." [1,2]

According to the Scottsbluff newspaper article *Grant Lee Shumway, Pioneer of Western Nebraska and Active in History of this Valley, Passes On*, Grant was "gifted by nature, he was a talented writer, and his versatile and trenchant pen had given forth, not only poetry or beautiful cadences-but scientific, political and economic articles as well." According to the article, "For many years he had devoted much of his time to delving into ancient lore and traditions of this part of the country and was undoubtedly the best posted man in the valley on these matters."[4]

In his book <u>History of Western Nebraska</u>, Volume II, Chapter VII *General William H. Ashley's Trappers – Death of Hiram Scott* discusses the 1823 travels of General Ashley up the Missouri. One of his forty volunteers was a man named Hiram Scott. Scott is described as a man of education and romance. Shumway's research described their voyage and one version of the naming of "Scotts Bluff" after Hiram's death.

Shumway was a charter member of Robert W. Furnas Lodge No 265 A.F.-A.M. in 1908, a charter member of Hannibal Lodge No 40, Scottsbluff Knights of Pythias in 1904, and a member of the Methodist church. An undated postcard with a poem he wrote was found in the files at the Nebraska State Historical Society. N

Moonlight
on
Scottsbluff

Low in the West
    The silhouette of hills,
Then beetling crags
    Of Scottsbluff Mountain rise.
The atmosphere
    A vibrant silence fills
Presaging tempests;
    Hanging from the skies
Dark cumulus swings,
    And low upon the lands.

But through a rift
    Pierces a moonbeam bright
Revealing
    A shimmering expanse
Of water, all
    Aquivering with light.
And from the shade
    Ascending to the skies
The signal smokes
    Of Hiram Scott arise.

                    —*G. L. Shumway.*

Postcard: Moonlight on Scottsbluff[5]

Endnotes, Footnotes & Sources:

[1]According to <u>Perkey's Nebraska Place Names</u>, the Ashford post office was established October 1887 and was discontinued July, 1902. The town was named for William Ashford who located on Pumpkin Creek in 1885 on the stage road.

The *Ashford Advocate* has one edition at the Nebraska State Historical Society: August 23, 1889. In the edition "The Advocate office has just finished printing 'the sod cabin', a poem of five parts by Grant L. Shumway."

[2] Perky, Eldon A. <u>Perkey's Nebraska Place Names</u>. Lincoln: J.L. Lee Co. 1995. Revised edition 2003 (4th edition).

[3]*The Telegraph.* Sidney, Nebraska. "Grant L. Shumway is Dead at Scottsbluff." November 13, 1925. Page two.

[4] "Grant Lee Shumway, Pioneer of Western Nebraska and Active in History of this Valley, Passes on." Reprinted from Scottsbluff papers in NSHS collection.

[5]*Grant Lee Shumway*. Nebraska State Historical Society Collections. Reviewed prior to December 2012.

[6] Hansen, Nancy Sue and Dush, Barbara Ann. <u>Nebraska Authors Volume One</u>. "J. Sterling Morton." Fullerton: D & H Adventures Publishing, 2013.

[7] Hansen, Nancy Sue and Dush, Barbara Ann. <u>Nebraska Authors Volume One</u>. "Albert Watkins." Fullerton: D & H Adventures Publishing, 2013.

[8] Hansen, Nancy Sue and Dush, Barbara Ann. <u>Nebraska Authors Volume One</u>. "George L. Miller." Fullerton: D & H Adventures Publishing, 2013.

[9] Hansen, Nancy Sue and Dush, Barbara Ann. <u>Nebraska Authors Volume One</u>. "C.S.Paine." Fullerton: D & H Adventures Publishing, 2013.

Thanks to the Sidney Public Library, Director Doris Jensen and staff at Sidney, Nebraska. And thanks to the Nebraska State Historical Society, Mary Jo, for assisting in checking the Nebraska Blue Books to find Shumway's two years of service.

Nebraska Authors Book & Travel Club

Photo or ticket from a visit to the ScottsBluff National Monument Museum, State Highway 92 West-the old Oregon Trail and follow the signs or follow signs 3 miles west of Gering, Nebraska. www.nps.gov for information. The site was established in 1919 as a National Monument.

DON STRINZ

Don Strinz

Date of Birth: Dec. 15, 1944,
Location of Birth: Seward County,
Milford
Education: Milford High School,
1962;
Southeast Community College, Diesel Mechanic, 1963-1965,
Currently lives near Milford, NE

Strinz, Don. <u>A Boy in a Man's Saddle</u>, illustration by Vern Friesen, Nebraska: Henderson Service Press Printing, 2010. 175 pp.

Seward County, Nebraska, has been the home of generations of Don Strinz's extended family and where he calls home. Born in 1944, he grew up on the farm and always wanted to be a farmer. At the age of seventeen he went to work on a farm near his home, working ten hours a day, six days a week for one dollar per hour. As a high school student, Strinz, considered this "a good job for the time."

His love of the outdoors and working the land gave him the inspiration to visit his mother's cousin in Canada, the summer between high school and attending Southeast Community College. He was going there to be a cowboy on a ranch: "the job of his dreams." So Don bought a one-way ticket to Calgary.

Hesitation about his decision did set in, but only momentarily. Strinz realized that if he didn't go he might have always wished that he had, and he didn't want to live the future with any regrets. It would prove to be a learning experience from the very start. Just the bus ride through the border crossing heading to Canada and the train ride home were learning experiences.

The work was hard, the days long and many of the jobs as "foreign to me as any job could be," he said. "There was the time I went to rake the hay and it was a different type of machine than what we used and I was doing it all wrong. Then I learned that fixing fence in the mountains is different than fixing fence in the soil of Nebraska. There was the job of rolling-logs-off-the-pile at the saw mill. And always there were plenty of rocks that needed to be removed from fields, and tending to the horses, moving cattle and working with bulls." The barley in Nebraska was about twelve bushels to the acre and knee high. Don worked with barley put into shocks – called stucks - about six feet high and that made about sixty bushels to the acre.

"Going to town was a reprieve," Don said of the relief from field work. "The town had what one today would call a convenience store: a gas station which had a little grocery store in it, a little bit of hardware, a small amount of most everything that you might need, a tire shop and in one corner of the store there was a post office."

Rounding up horses and cattle proved to be a discomforting experience. Strinz would later take the readers of his book, <u>A Boy in a Man's Saddle</u>, through each saddle-sore experience. His inexperience in the cowboy ranch world eventually earned him the nickname "Nebraska Kid."

As the day came for Don to pack up and head back to Nebraska, a get-together was held inviting neighbors and relatives. He thought it was a good-bye party. It wasn't. Even through all the inexperience he had exhibited they wanted him to stay. The party was to try to get him to change his plans. This Nebraska cowboy did return to his native state, and why he made that decision is tucked away in the last chapters of his intriguing book.

When Don left Canada he had no idea he would ever write a book about his six months of experiences there. In fact, no one was more surprised than Don himself. It was a serious challenge because he is severely dyslexic and considered illiterate. Don had never let those issues handicap him. He went to Southeast Community College (SCC) in Milford when he returned from Canada and studied diesel mechanics.

After SCC, he worked at New Holland in Grand Island as a forklift operator, but within six months he was in the company's tool and die training class. He worked for New Holland for twenty years. It was during this time that he took a look at the Damascus shotgun his grandfather had left him at his passing. Don found out he couldn't use regular ammunition in the gun and began a quest to locate black powder and learn how to use it. He joined the Muzzle Loading Gun Club in Grand Island and "one thing led to another and I got black powder shooting in my veins," he grinned.

Don and his wife went to various events, sleeping in tents like others in the group. However, for his wife it was not a pleasant experience. She became ill after being outside for a couple of nights. During one adventure they stayed in a tepee and woke up feeling great. Later they found that the lack of humidity in a tepee helped her breathe and sleep. His wife liked the idea so well, she bought fabric from JC Penney and made a tepee from a pattern they found. It was labor intensive and she soon became discouraged with the process, but when it was finished it worked well.

One day Don didn't set that homemade tepee up correctly and part of it fell into the fire. She was in no mood to fix it so he had to find a way. There began the tepee business. He worked part-time at it while working at New Holland. When he no longer had his tool and die job he went into making tepees full time, but it became too much for the residential area of Grand Island where they lived. He bought a piece of land from his father, and he and his wife moved back to Seward County in 1995.

He'd been away for about thirty years. Farming had changed so much in that time he decided to hire the farming done and concentrate on manufacturing tepees.

A few years ago Don was diagnosed with Alzheimers and he wanted to write down his thoughts for his children and grandchildren: "Just to let my family know about my younger days, and then I decided to publish it."

He already had his tepee business in Seward County and his employees would come to work at 8 a.m. so he went to the office at 7 a.m. and typed a couple of pages. Don would take it to the house and his wife would look at it. She made spelling suggestions and he would change it the next morning. He would do that every day until he was done.

He began writing about a person named "Dan" because it was easier to write about someone else. He wrote the first draft in about three months, in the winter, and set it aside until the next winter. His children read it and said he had to write about himself, so he used the computer key to change all the Dan's to Don and added some thoughts to the second draft. Again, he put it away when spring came. Again, the children said he had to make it first person and that was more of a challenge, but he did it.

The childhood dyslexia was still there and he typed with just one finger. He knew he read only short stories so the stories in the book are in somewhat larger print and written as short story chapters. The writing flowed easily for Don because he'd always been a story and joke teller. He just didn't have all the English and spelling needed for a book. He had several people read the book and correct the spelling and grammar, but the rest represents how people talk. Again, Don turned the skills he had into a constructive endeavor. His book was published in December of 2010.

Don dedicated his book to all the boys who wanted to be a cowboy and never had the chance; or more so, to the ones that had the chance to do it and passed it by.

Technology changed and as Don thought of publishing, he found the best picture for the back cover of the book was the one someone took using a cell phone. A local illustrator, Vern Friesen, captured the title of the book and a summary of the inside stories in the book cover. A printing company was located across the street from the illustrator. He considered himself blessed. The book is available on Kindle, at tipi-guy@hotmail.com, www.strinztipi.com, or at his office.

Strinz talks to organizations and school groups about his tepees and sometimes is asked to do readings from his book. "I have to read over a section I am going to read many times so I don't stutter when I read it. Story telling is still easier."

If your cowboy dream never came to pass, you will find each paragraph of A Boy in a Man's Saddle a read that will take you through the life of a rancher cowboy as if you were riding in the saddle yourself. You'll want to pull up your cowboy boots and take a memorable reading ride of your life. B

Endnotes, Footnotes & Sources:

Interview/photos by Barbara A. Dush, 2011.

Strinz, Don. A Boy in a Man's Saddle.

ISABELLA TAVES
(Mrs. Daniel Mich)

Date of birth: Sept. 20, 1905
Location of birth: Lincoln, NE
Education: unknown
B.S. Northwestern University 1932
Date of Death: June 25, 2005
Location at Death: New York

Known Publications:

Taves, Isabella. <u>Successful Women and How They Attained Success</u>.
New York : E. P. Dutton and Co., 1943. vii + 320 pp. Biography.

Taves, Isabella and Harriet H. Ayer. <u>The Three Lives of Harriet Hubbard Ayer</u>. Philadelphia : J. P. Lippincott Co., 1957. 284 pp. Autobiography. (Ayer June 27, 1849-Chicago, IL; November 25, 1903-died in New York).

Taves, Isabella. <u>The Quick Rich Fox</u>. New York: Random House, 1959. 304 pp. Novel.

Taves, Isabella and Virgil G. Damon. Forward by Helen Hayes.
<u>I Learned about Women from Them</u>. New York : D. McKay Co., 1962. 300 pp.

Taves, Isabella. <u>Woman Alone</u>. A Practical Handbook for Widows and Divorcees. New York : Funk and Wagnalls, 1968. 316 pp.

Taves, Isabella, Katherine DeJersey. <u>Destiny Times Six-An Astrologer's Casebook</u>. 1970, 1971.

Taves, Isabella. <u>Not Bad for a Girl</u>. New York : M. Evans and Co., 1972. 95 pp. Juvenile.

Taves, Isabella. <u>Love Must Not Be Wasted: When Sorrow Comes Take It Gently by the Hand</u>. New York : Thomas Y. Crowell Co., 1974. 214 pp.

Taves, Isabella and Madame Wellington Koo. <u>No Feast Lasts Forever.</u> New York : Quadrangle, New York Times Book Co., 1975. 313 pp. Autobiography.

Taves, Isabella. <u>True Ghost Stories</u>. Publisher: Watts, 1978. Juvenile.

Taves, Isabella. <u>Widows Guide. Practical Advice on How to Deal with Grief, Stress, Health</u>. Publisher: 1988.

Taves, Isabella Katherine DeJersey and Eleanor Haspel-Portner. <u>Appointment With Destiny</u>. Publisher: 1995.

Isabella Taves was born September 20, 1905, in Lincoln, Nebraska.[1,2] The United States census of 1910 and 1920 lists Isabella in Cook County, Chicago, Illinois. The census notes that she arrived in Cook County in about 1906.[3]

According to the *New York Times,* she received her Bachelors of Science from Northwestern University, Summa Cum Laude and Phi Beta Kappa in 1926.[1] She took the position of entertainment editor of *Look Magazine;* and according to the information in the flap of her books,[4] worked as the entertainment editor until she married Minnesotan Daniel Danforth Mich. He was the Editorial Director of *Look* from 1942-1950 and 1954-1964. "He stressed the use of pictures to broaden the reader's perception of the news."[5,6]

After they were married she wrote short stories, novelettes, and articles for *Colliers, Cosmopolitan, McCall's, Today's Woman,* and *Look* magazines. With her husband she traveled the world meeting 'the great men and women of the mid-20th century'.[1] She wrote her first book, in 1943, <u>Successful Women and How They Attained Success</u>, about some of the women she met.

Not all the stories Taves heard as she traveled and wrote were happy endings. Harriet Hubbard Ayer, a Chicago socialite, had lived and died before Isabella was born. Ayers had become famous for beginning a cosmetic company and then learning to fight against the male dominated business culture. She had been the highest paid newspaper woman in the United States during the last seven years of her life; but prior to that, Ayer had been kidnapped, and endured numerous scandals and attempts to take over her business. Labeled with 'melancholia,' she was committed to the Bronxville Insane Asylum from which she finally was able to escape. Ayer's trials opened the way for other women to follow with their own careers in the beauty industry. Isabella Taves wrote <u>The Three Lives of Harriet Hubbard Ayer</u> which was published in 1957.[7,8]

Taves continued to write and publish books and magazine articles. She was also a dog lover and enjoyed breeding and showing Dalmatians. According to *New York Times* articles, she was a devoted wife and by all accounts found the death of her husband in 1965 and her new widowhood a challenging experience. Several of her remaining literary works dealt with love, sorrow, and women being alone. She wrote a syndicated weekly column called "Women Alone" for the *Des Moines Register & Tribune Syndicate*.[1,4]

In the flap of her book "Women Alone" was written: "She traveled throughout America and to resorts in the Far East, South America, and Europe questioning 'women alone:' how they react to their new life, how they travel, where they find men, what adjustments they have made in their moral code, how they cope with their children and those of prospective husbands where they find jobs, how they handle money." As a recent widow she had a book of insight and sympathy.[9]

In 1972, Taves wrote a children's book <u>Not Bad for a Girl</u>. The fiction portrayal of a pre-teen ball player with bat and glove struck a cord with many around the country and the book became a rally cry for many females who felt they had been left behind in the world of sports. Changes were being made in the high school and post-secondary athletic policies as Title IX[10] was signed into law in 1972. Taves related the position of the girl in the story, which was based on a real incident that made national news coverage, as the same as a woman in business walking into a field traditionally reserved for boys and men.[4]

Taves also was branching out into astrology working with the famous Katherine De Jersey to write a casebook of successes and a book of nonfiction ghost stories based on Taves' own "grandmothers precognition superpowers." A woman alone may be only as safe as her seasoned intuition.

In 1975, Taves wrote No Feast Lasts Forever. It was an autobiography of Madame Wellington Koo. V.K. Wellington Koo was a prominent Chinese diplomat and served as one of China's representatives at the Paris Peace Conference of 1919 after World War I. His credentials were many and his world experiences profound. Koo had four wives. Isabella wrote the autobiography with his third wife, Oei Hui-lan. They divorced after World War II. A note inside the book stated: "*This book is based on an incident which received national publicity. Names have been changed and imaginary situations and characters created which in no way are like the real participants. Any resemblance to actual persons other than the members of the Lee family are purely coincidental. However, the social issue the novel deals with is true to the actual event. This is what can happen when people of good will attempting to correct an unfair situation are thwarted by an inflexible standard of behavior.*"[11,12]

Isabella Taves passed away in New York on June 25, 2005. She was just three months short of her 100th birthday.[1] N

Endnotes, Footnotes & Sources:

[1]www.nytimes.com *Isabella Taves Mich*. Reviewed June 13, 2013.

[2]http://hackneys.com *Isabella Taves*. Reviewed June 13, 2013.

[3]US Census. 1910, 1920, on-line. *Isabella Taves*. Reviewed June 13, 2013.

[4]Taves, Isabella Not Bad for a Girl. New York : M. Evans and Co., 1972. 95 pp. Juvenile.

[5]Encyclopedia2.thefreedictionary.com. *Daniel Danforth Mich.* reviewed June 14, 2013.

[6]www.wikipedia.com *Look* (American Magazine). Reviewed June 13, 2013. *Look Magazine* was a bi-weekly general interest magazine published in Des Moines, Iowa 1937-1971. The emphasis was on photos. Their main competition was *Life Magazine*.

[7]www.wikipedia.com *Harriet Hubbard Ayer*. Reviewed June 13, 2013.

[8]Taves, Isabella and Harriet H. Ayer. The Three Lives of Harriet Hubbard Ayer. Philadelphia : J. P. Lippincott Co., 1957. 284 pp. Autobiography. (Ayer June 27, 1849-Chicago Ill; November 25, 1903-died in New York).

[9]Taves, Isabella. Woman Alone. A Practical Handbook for Widows and Divorcees. New York : Funk and Wagnalls, 1968. 316 pp. and Taves, Isabella. Widows Guide. Practical Advice on How to Deal with Grief, Stress, Health Publisher: 1988.

[10]www.titleixinfo. *Title IX*. Reviewed June 15, 2013. "requires gender equality for boys and girls in every educational program that receives Federal funding."

[11]www.wikipedia.com *V.K.Wellington Koo*. Reviewed June 13, 2013.

[12]Taves, Isabella and Madame Wellington Koo. No Feast Lasts Forever. New York : Quadrangle, New York Times Book Co., 1975. 313 pp. Autobiography.

Nebraska Authors Book & Travel Club

Isabella Taves was not alone when she was with her dog(s). Visit or participate in a formal dog show. From 4-H events to national breeders shows, Nebraska has a variety of events to choose from. Take a photograph of yourself at the dog show event.

BILLIE SNYDER THORNBURG

Date of Birth: April 12, 1912,
Location of Birth: Rural Cozad, NE
Education: country school near their ranch between Arthur and Tryon in the sandhills; graduated from high school in Salem, OR
Date of Death: Feb. 14, 2009
Location of Death: North Platte, NE

Billie Thornburg

Known Publications:

Thornburg, Billie Snyder. Bertie And Me: Kids on a Ranch, Old 101 Press Publishing Co., 2003. 144 pp.

Thornburg, Billie Snyder. Bertie And Me And Miles Too, Old 101 Press Publishing Co., 2003. 144 pp.

Thornburg, Billie Snyder. Sandhills Kid in the City: 1927-1938, Old 101 Press Publishing Co., 2004. 144 pp.

Thornburg, Billie Snyder, City and Prairie Bones, Old 101 Press Publishing Co., 2005. 144 pp.

"They say you can't take it with you, but you can. When you die, all the stories in your head go, too," Billie Lee Snyder Thornburg noted. She acted on her own advice and wrote four books before her death in 2009.

She was born in 1912 to Albert Benton Snyder, an early-day cowboy, and Grace Belle McCance Snyder, a world renowned quilt maker, in her maternal grandfather's sod house a few miles north of Cozad. Albert was more commonly known as 'Pinnacle Jake', or 'Jack Snyder', a name given by fellow cowboys on the old 101 Ranch when he was a horse breaker for Buffalo Bill.

Billie's early years were spent on the family ranch eleven miles west of Tryon, in a land immersed in the beauty of the Nebraska Sandhills. In the summer of 1927, when she was fifteen and her sister Bertie thirteen, the family moved to Salem, Oregon. For the next four years, her parents leased the ranch in Nebraska and sent the two girls to high school in Oregon.[1]

"It was thrilling, exciting and painful," Billie wrote of the move. "When I had finished grade school Dad had said, 'If you wait until Bertie graduates from eighth grade before you go to high school, I'll take you all out and show you there's something in this world besides the Sandhills.' Secretly, I think Dad was looking for better ranch country."

The family "toughed it out" and remained in Oregon until the girls finished high school and graduated. As soon as school was out, the family headed back to Nebraska and spent the rest of their lives in McPherson and Lincoln counties "where we belonged," Billie noted.

Billie started a dance studio in North Platte and was an instructor for seven years teaching acrobatics, ballet, tap, and ballroom dance. However, it was the 1930s and the Depression laid heavy on Nebraska. "Times were hard during the years I taught dancing in North Platte," she wrote in her book Sandhills Kid in the City. "People would come to me and ask if I would trade dancing lessons for whatever they had to offer. I traded lessons for milk, which worked out about right since the price of milk was ten cents a quart ... I drank a quart of milk a day because this little girl wanted to take dancing lessons."

She also exchanged lessons for permanents, facials, and manicures from a beauty operator who wanted private tap dancing lessons. Another lady asked if she could trade cleaning for ballroom dance lessons for her three boys in high school. "Would I trade cleaning for ballroom dancing lessons ... I had no idea if I could use up that much cleaning, but I had nothing to lose. We made a deal. I was the neatest dresser - or at least I wore the cleanest clothes in town for quite a while," she wrote.

Billie presented her last dance recital in June of 1938 at the Fox Theatre in North Platte. It is the same theatre that in 1988 Bob Hope gave a performance with his wife beside him: "In a sense, I shared the stage with Bob and Deloris Hope, only fifty years earlier. It was the closest I ever came to making the Big Time."

Billie later married Tiny Riley, who died from injuries sustained in a rodeo accident. In 1955, she married William Thornburg, a career Navy man. The couple lived in Japan for two years and later Norfolk, Virginia, where they were active in real estate. In 1977, they returned to North Platte to care for Billie's mother.

It wasn't until the age of ninety that Thornburg began writing. She formed The Old 101 Press Publishing Company and published for others as well, wanting to "publish history as told by those who lived it."

Her writing flourished, winning first place in the Nebraska Press Women's Contest for non-fiction Books with her memoir, Bertie And Me And Miles Too. The book detailed home remedies, clothing of the early 1900s, and the excitement of owning a "talking machine." Pictures highlighted early roundups (now rodeos) and Model T's. She told of how to get a tongue unstuck if you lick the "frosting" from a cold iron bolt in the middle of winter. The book also included an entertaining chapter on privies.

Also among her books is City and Prairie Bones, a story of North Platte's "Little Chicago" days. Sandhills Kid in the City continues the story of Thornburg and her sister, Bertie, that began in Bertie And Me: Kids on a Ranch and Bertie And Me And Miles Too. It covers the years from 1929 to 1937, when their father moved the family to Salem, Oregon, so his girls could to go high school.

Thornburg was working on her fifth book when her health and eyesight began to fail. She died at the age of 97.

The Sandhills lived inside of Thornburg's soul all her life. Her books display her passion for the land and for life, each page a magical and often humorous window into her life. B

Endnotes, Footnotes & Sources:

[1] Billie's Oldest Sister is Nellie Snyder Yost [author who will be featured in a future volume]; brother Miles and descendants own the family ranch; Billie and Bertie were the youngest.

buffalocommons.org

www.amazon.com

www.cowboypoetry11.htm

Many thanks to Theresa McGahan of North Platte, Nebraska, for answering so many e-mails and being so helpful.

Billie Thornburg at one of her book signings
in North Platte.

Nebraska Authors Book & Travel Club
Visit the old Fox Theatre at 301 E. Fifth Street in North Platte. Attach a photo or ticket reflecting your visit or have this box signed and dated.

RUDOLPH E. UMLAND

Date of birth: Dec. 26, 1907
Location of birth: Cass County, NE
Education: Eagle High School, NE, 1925
University of Nebraska, attended, 1929
Military: US Coast Guard, volunteer, New Orleans
drafted Army WWII: Infantry, Tech Sargent
Date of death: July 15, 1993

Rudi / Rudolph E. Umland

Known Publications:

Umland, Rudolph. <u>Scrapbooks</u> and other papers 1925-1988, Federal Writers Project/Nebraska (WPA); Prairie Schooner, Lincoln. Located at the Nebraska State Historical Society, Lincoln, Nebraska.

Umland, Rudolph. *Prairie Schooner,* "Sand Hill Interlude." V 6 n 4, Fall 1932, pp 271-282.

Umland, Rudolph. *Prairie Schooner.* "The Blessed Sweet Singer." V 8 n 4, Fall 1934, pp 201-212.

Umland, Rudolph. *Prairie Schooner.* "The Drouth of '34." V 9 n 2, Spring 1935, pp 101-107.

Umland, Rudolph. *Prairie Schooner.* "Spring of the Black Blizzards." V 9 n 4, Fall 1935, p 243-249.

Umland, Rudolph. *Prairie Schooner.* "The Rise and Fall of Woleben." V 10 n 1, Spring 1936, pp 25-35.

Umland, Rudolph, assistant State Supervisor for WPA published <u>Lincoln City Guide</u> in 1937 and <u>Nebraska: A Guide to the Cornhusker State</u> in 1939.

Umland, Rudolph. *Prairie Schooner.*" Early Press Humor." V 13 n 2, Summer 1939, 106-120 pp.

Umland, Rudolph. *Prairie Schooner.* "On Editing WPA Guide Books." V 13 no 3, Fall 1939, p 160-169.

Umland, Rudolph. *American Speech.* "To Scuttle," VIS n3, October 1940, pp. 327-328.

Umland, Rudolph. *Prairie Schooner.* "Short Essay on Bloomers." V 15, n 2, Summer 1941, p 114-117.

Umland, Rudolph. *American Speech.* "Words for South Omaha." V16 No 3, October 1941, pp. 235-236.

Umland, Rudolph. *Prairie Schooner.* "Henry C. Richmond: Politician of the Old School," V15 n 3, Fall 1941, pp. 176-185.

Umland, Rudolph. *American Speech.* "NE Cowboy Talk." V 17 n 1, February 1942, pp. 73-75.

Umland, Rudolph. *Prairie Schooner.* "Born in Nebraska." V 16 n 3, Fall 1942, pp. 172-183.

Umland, Rudolph. *Esquire Magazine.* "The Demise of the Little Moron." September 1943, p 32+.

Umland, Rudolph. *Prairie Schooner.* "A Thresher's Tale." V 17 n 4, Winter 1943, pp. 228-231.

Umland, Rudolph. *Prairie Schooner.* "Oui, Oui, The Little Guests". V 18 n 2, Summer 1944, pp. 107-110.

Umland, Rudolph, PVT. *Prairie Schooner.* "I Became A G I Joe." V 18 n 4, Winter 1944, pp. 284-295.

Umland, Rudolph. *Prairie Schooner*. "Fighting the War in Texas." V 19 n 4, Winter 1945, pp. 327-336.

Umland, Rudolph. *Prairie Schooner*. "The Enlisted Men verses the System." V 20 no 1, Spring 1946, pp. 7-13.

Umland, Rudolph. *Prairie Schooner*. "Little Shelves." V 20 n 3, Fall 1946, pp. 215-216.

Umland, Rudolph. *Prairie Schooner*. "A Whopper and What came of it." V 21 n 1, Spring 1947, pp. 102-107.

Umland, Rudolph. *Prairie Schooner*. "Dogs Have Little Hairy Faces." V 21 n 3, Fall 1947, pp. 298-308.

Umland, Rodolph. *Prairie Schooner*. "Apropos of Texans and Salty Dogs." V 22 n 1, Spring 1948, pp. 75-79.

Umland, Rudolph. *Prairie Schooner*. "What the Sixty Million Do." V 22 n 4, Winter 1948, pp. 406-409.

Umland, Rudolph. *Prairie Schooner*. "I like Doleful Music." V 23 n 2, Summer 1949, pp. 184-188.

Umland, Rudolph. *Prairie Schooner*. "They Broke the Sods," v 23 n 4, Winter 1949, pp. 378-384.

Umland, Rudolph. *Prairie Schooner*. "The Cries of the Little Children." V 25 n 2, Summer 1951, pp. 179-183.

Umland, Rudolph. *Prairie Schooner*. "How to Take a Bath." V 27 n 4, Winter 1953, pp. 361-365.

Umland, Rudolph. *Prairie Schooner*. "Family Trees." V 29 n 2, Summer 1955, pp. 161-170.

Umland, Rudolph. *Prairie Schooner*. "What makes an Imaginative Mind?" V 30 n 1, Spring 1956, pp. 15-24.

Umland, Rudolph. *Prairie Schooner*. "Nebraska Not in the Guidebook." V 31 n 1, Spring 1957, pp. 81-87.

Faulkner, Virginia complier and editor. <u>Roundup: A Nebraska Reader</u>. Lincoln: University of Nebraska Press. 1957. 493 pp by Rudolph Umland: "Politicians of the Old School" p 139, "Nebraska Cowboy Talk" p 344, "Nebraska Not in the Guidebook" p 412.

Umland, Rudolph. *Prairie Schooner*. "Phantom Airship of the Nineties." V 40 n 4, Winter 1966/67, pp 302-316.

Umland, Rudolph. *Prairie Schooner*. "L.C. Wimberly: A Book and a Memory." V 40 n 4, Winter 1966/67, pp 325-329.

Umland, Rudolph. *Prairie Schooner*. "A Ghost of Lowrey Wimberly." V 41 n 3, Fall 1967, pp 325-338.

Umland, Rudolph. *Prairie Schooner*. "Lowrey Wimberly and others: Recollections of a Beer Drinker." V 51 n 1, Spring 1977, pp 16-50.

It was the era of vagabonds (hobos) when Rudolph (Rudi/ Rudy) Umland was college age in the late 1920s[1]. Between working on the farm with his brothers when he was needed and attending the University of Nebraska in Lincoln in 1929, and other semesters when he could pay for it, he joined the freight train hopping - hitch hiking wanderers that crisscrossed the country. Odd jobs, cheap hotels, city parks, and jail stays provided him with a look at the world most people would rather not see. His travels took him through the United States and into Canada and Mexico. The experiences gave him a depth of history and people that would serve him well in later years. In 1932, he returned to his family farm in Nebraska.

By 1935, Rudy Umland had decided to leave the farm and not enroll in another semester but to become a 'traveler' on an extended trip again. According to his son, Eric, his dad went to the English Department office to say good-bye. Lowry Wimberly, a founding editor of the *Prairie Schooner,* remembered Umland. Wimberly suggested he consider a Nebraska Federal Writers' Project position. Umland joined seven others in the Nebraska office of the Federal Writers' Project (FWP).

It was partly the sense of humor and partly the ability to work with so many writers and situations that eventually gave Umland the distinction of 'saving' the Nebraska project. He was an Editor, Assistant State Director (1936-1940), and State Director (1940-1941). By 1941, there were fifty-seven employees in the Nebraska office. As he left his fellow project, employees made it clear in several written historical accounts that they respected his leadership and insights.

President Roosevelt's New Deal created the Federal Writers' Project (FWP) as part of the Works Progress Administration (WPA). It was primarily a work relief project designed to give unemployed teachers, librarians, writers and other white collar professionals work during the Depression years. The Civilian Conservation Corps (CCC), for those with labor skills, was also administered by the WPA. While history shows the FWP began in 1935, the Nebraska program actually began in the 1920s.[2] Bureaucratically there was to be an FWP office in each state with the WPA. (The WPA had previously been the Civil Works Administration-Federal Emergency Relief Agency, FERA). The project was to survey and inventory local historical records and there was room for creative and innovative projects within each state. It was also an avenue for interviews with Native Americans, Blacks, and other minority groups, slaves of all races, and women for 'their side of the story' on any and every subject. The idea was to let everyone have a voice and present their story, optimism, anger, and ideas in their own words.[3]

This communication avenue had been opened by the 'regionalism' movement that came from the issues of the 1920's and was depicted in the art and literature of the 1930's.[4] This movement promoted nationalism and learning about one's ethnic and religious background. The theory was that if Americans got to know more about their own local history they'd take more interest in the sense of community which was desperately needed in the hard times of the 1920's and 1930's. It was believed that this sense of community was necessary to continue the efforts of democracy. While all of the goals were not accomplished, the project did contribute to the survival of aspects of history as well as launch the literary success of many writers, including Mari Sandoz.[5,6]

The workers of the new Nebraska FWP worked with several hundred other employees of the state and district WPA in a railroad warehouse office space near the University. The train vibration, phones and about a hundred typewriters were distractions for the Project workers. Soon the group was looking for a quieter location for concentration sake.

The Federal Writers' Project (FWP) and the Nebraska branch were as full of controversy as the history of any of the public works agencies. The first Nebraska director was Miss Elizabeth Sheehan. Umland was hired as her assistant. Sheehan was hired on the recommendation of the editor of the *Lincoln Star*: James Lawrence[7] (their relationship would become part of the controversy). Her ex-schoolteacher experience was without publication, editorial, or administrative experience. Within the first week of the new job, according to reports, she was accusing other employees, including Rudy, of wanting her job. That was in October 1935.

By early 1936, the Federal Writers' Project (FWP) in Washington was aware of the disorganization in Nebraska. Letters from Lawrence to Congressman Norris[8] saved Sheehan's job from a Washington change proposed for the Nebraska office.

Sheehan saw Umland as her biggest threat and devised ways to discredit him. Once she accused him of being a communist. The FBI investigation concluded that the only thing 'red about him was in his mustache.' She said she had found out that Rudy and his brother had watched the five thousand farmers march on the State Capitol in 1933 and Communists were known to be at the event. She had so exaggerated the story that she accused Mother Bloor and Rudolph Umland as the antagonists. Her concerns about Umland were dismissed after the investigation.

In October of 1936, the Nebraska Federal Writers' Project (NFWP) published a single issue of a magazine called *Shucks*. The content - stories, sketches, and poetry - didn't seem to fit with other publications. Umland include a short sketch called "Arkansas Hoosier" describing his travels as a hobo.

In 1938, since Sheehan could not be fired, the Washington office came up with the plan that she could draw a salary and work from her apartment. She continued on the payroll without another day on the job until the project ended in 1942.

Although limited in funds for the rest of project due to her salary, the NFWP continued. Umland and others were asked who they thought should take the now vacant position and J. Harris (Jake) Gable was suggested. As an unemployed librarian, founding student editor of the *Prairie Schooner,* and author of an adventure book for boys, he was deemed qualified and appointed Assistant State Director. When scandal was discovered with the married Gable, Umland became State Director.

Rudolph had persevered in overseeing the Project's significant publications, including the 1939 Nebraska Guide to the Cornhusker State and the evolving Nebraska folklore collections. The "guide" contribution became part of the famed WPA American Guide Series covering the forty-eight contiguous states and Alaska using essays about natural settings, history, economic conditions, government, folk cultures, and the arts. Automobile tours of each state's landscape and unique history were part of the finished product. The sheer volume of material collected across the United States and quality of publication(s) is still evident today.

Omaha had collected materials for a guide of its own. It was never published. According to Umland, the sponsor for the manuscript was Omaha's Junior Chamber of Commerce and it was believed they deliberately prevented other organizations from assuming the sponsorship thus withholding the mixed history of Omaha: race riots, lynchings, labor conflicts, Saturday night brawls, gambling dens and the large number of prostitutes. The *New York World Telegram* printed a review of Omaha from the general information provided in the Nebraska Guide. It was likely as much as the Omaha sponsors wanted revealed. After August 31, 1939, The Nebraska Writers' Project became the Nebraska Writers Program and the University became the sponsor for all.

Rudy's deep interest in what words and context could mean to the world around him was evident when, as a ninth grader, he read George Eliot's novel Silas Marner. Rudy wrote to the district court Judge William Morning and asked if the events would have happened in Nebraska in 1921 how the court would have made its decision. After re-reading the novel the Judge responded. In later years (1942-1944), Rudy became a Training Chief of a U.S. Postal Censorship Station in New Orleans assigned censorship duties for wartime letters. This was a twist in the education and understanding how words were used, justice, and what was deemed national security.

Umland left his Nebraska Writers' position in February 1942 for the New Orleans position. His son Eric, in an interview with the Nebraska

Authors Project® said, "I was six-months-old when we moved and was three-years-old when we moved back to Nebraska." The government shifted all their resources to the war effort and the Federal Writers' Project was terminated March 1, 1942.

Jerre Mangione had been the FWP administrator in Washington D.C. As he looked back over the FWP he saw that there was a change in the country evident during the Great Depression and the stories that came from that time. Marx and Lenin were actually drawing converts in the United States with the Communist Party reconfiguring their slogans to seem interested in "Americanism." Mangione watched the national regionalism movement, including the FWP interviews, find out what real Americans said they believed and saw changes no one thought they would see. He was stunned. A historian, Jerrold Hirsch, wrote about the FWP and noted that the planners were "New Deal Progressives" who wanted to reshape the American identity to be more democratic and inclusive.

In reviewing the Nebraska Writers' Project/Program, Rudy Umland and the other Nebraska Writers' Project/Program writers had found a way to incorporate the spiritualism, mediums, and 'ghosts' that had infused Nebraska in the early 20's with the regionalism and progressivism of the 30's. David P. Abbott [4] had written his book attempting to expose the charlatans of Nebraska in 1907, but spiritualism in Nebraska had not dissipated. Nebraskans mixed spiritualism into ever increasing aspects of their lives. It would be a new country, a new state, vacillating between the whispers of the Constitutional Republic of the past and the evolving progressive democracy. It was the foundations of today.

While the historians were reflecting on the Writers' Project from the material from each state, Umland worked the civilian censorship job by day and volunteered with the Coast Guard at night as a Seaman First Class. This was his first military experience. For a year he served twelve hours of active duty a week guarding harbor installations and shipping in the area as part of the U.S. Coast Guard Reserve. But Uncle Sam wanted more. Rudy was drafted into the Army and sent to Fort Hood, Texas. When it was found he had office skills, he was kept at that location as office manager for the two and a half years of military service: Classification Specialist with Infantry Forces.

All the while Rudy kept writing. In one story for *Esquire* magazine in September 1943, the note at the preface of the story divulged a secret to his discovery of topics of many of his articles. He listened and observed what was going on around him. It was all history. The article was *The Demise of the Little Moron: "During the Winter of 1942-1943, little moron stories were current on every tongue in the U.S. … The stories made you laugh and forget for a moment the world at war. Then something happened. … Do you know what killed these stories? Just after the stories had started to lose their popularity, I chanced to be a passenger on a plane flying to California. Seated beside me in the plane was a big pompous man chewing the end of an unlit cigar. The tips of three other cigars stuck from the breast pocket of his coat. I immediately guessed the fellow to be a super-salesman of heavy machinery or something of the sort. Aggressiveness was written all over him. Following is the man's story of what actually happened to the little moron stories."* The long and the short of it all was that science stepped in and silenced the stories. Umland didn't let anything, including a pompous man, get in the way of a story that reflected the thinking in the entire country.

After service (1946), Rudy took a job as a Rehabilitation Training Officer with the Veterans Administration in Lincoln. He made supervisory visits to disabled veterans enrolled in courses of vocational rehabilitation all over Nebraska. In 1958, he moved to Kansas City to take a job as a Claims Authorizer for the Social Security Administration (SSA). All the while he continued to write articles; and in 1963 while still working for the SSA, he became a book reviewer for the *Kansas City Star* and *Kansas City Times*.

In the 40th anniversary issue of the *Prairie Schooner*, winter of 1966/67, Umland once again wrote about a shunned topic of history: "Phantom Airships of the Nineties." Stories from the earliest days of the United States, especially in the late 1800's, showed that not all the objects and lights in the skies had known origins. Nebraska was in the thick of what would be known the Unidentified Flying Objects (UFOs) phenomenon even though the Wright Brothers didn't have a successful flight until 1908. While people were being ridiculed by friends and the government for calling attention to these objects, Umland wrote about the long history of their existence. Like his other articles, he did his research and wrote about what he found. It was a continuation of the memorializing of the facts of history concept he had nurtured in the Nebraska Writers' Project/Program all those years ago. But, like a good historian, he paved the way for additional, well-researched, history to be added by someone else at a later date.

From 1972-1974, he added authorship to articles written about Kansas City history for *City Window*, a Kansas City magazine. While still writing for Kansas City outlets Umland moved back to Lincoln.

He kept scrapbooks throughout his life. His family left the scrapbooks and materials of his life available for the public to view. It is this trail of history that gives a unique view of the depression and other events during the war years, hobo and college life, and death. As an author he fused his life with those around him onto paper for all to read and ponder. Rudy's son, Eric, said he and his siblings had considered re-printing their father's works in an updated edition. As of this publication it is not yet available.

Craig, Yvonne and Eric, Rudi Umland children.

Umland and the other WPA employees looked around Nebraska to find out what people thought about what had happened to them in their lives: their folk remedies, immigration stories, ideas of democracy, and how their religions were part of their lives were only basic questions that started conversations. They took the information and complied it as part of Nebraska, United States, and world history. How does what you have done and seen in your life build your community? How did you feel about historic events in the world when you heard about them? Write it down. It is history. N

Endnotes, Footnotes & Sources:

[1] Hansen, Nancy Sue and Dush, Barbara Ann. Nebraska Authors Volume One. "Dale Nichols." Fullerton: D & H Adventures Publishers, 2013.

[2] It is worth taking the time as a reader to review the many sources on the Federal Emergency Relief Agency (FERA), WPA, CCC, and FWP, including those of the Nebraska State Historical Society and the Jane Pope Geske Heritage Room of Nebraska Authors at the Bennett Martin Library, Lincoln City Libraries and their websites, to understand what Rudolph Umland experienced during this time and why the Federal Writers' Project made a difference in the state.

[3]Hansen, Nancy Sue and Dush, Barbara Ann. Nebraska Authors Volume One. "Francis LeFleshe." Fullerton: D & H Adventures Publishers, 2013.

[4]Hansen, Nancy Sue and Dush, Barbara Ann. Nebraska Authors Volume One. "David P. Abbott." Fullerton: D & H Adventures Publishers, 2013.

[5]Hansen, Nancy Sue and Dush, Barbara Ann. Nebraska Authors Volume One. "Ruth Van Ackeren." Fullerton: D & H Adventures Publishers, 2013.

[6]Hansen, Nancy Sue and Dush, Barbara Ann. Nebraska Authors Volume One. "Caroline Sandoz Pifer." Fullerton: D & H Adventures Publishers, 2013.

[7]Hansen, Nancy Sue and Dush, Barbara Ann. Nebraska Authors Volume One. "William Lawrence." Fullerton: D & H Adventures Publishers, 2013.

[8]Hansen, Nancy Sue and Dush, Barbara Ann. Nebraska Authors Volume One. "Frederic Babcock." Fullerton: D & H Adventures Publishers, 2013.

Nebraska State Historical Society, website and reading room: manuscripts, notes, correspondence and other materials of his family life at Eagle.

Jane Pope Geske Heritage Room of Nebraska Authors at the Bennett Martin Library, Lincoln City Libraries, website and reading room.

Special Thank you to Eric Umland for the interview, photographs, and correspondence about his father.

Nebraska Authors Book & Travel Club

Attend a reading of a Nebraska author on their works at a library or other such location. Have the author sign this box and write the name of the book that they read, and the date and location of the reading event. Check listings at the Jane Pope Geske Heritage Room of Nebraska Authors at the Bennett Martin Library in Lincoln for options at that location.

DR. EMILY JANE UZENDOSKI

Date of Birth: Jan. 17, 1942
Location of Birth: Palmer, NE
Education: Fullerton Public Schools,
graduated 1959 as valedictorian;
College of St. Mary in Omaha, magna
cum laude graduate with bachelors
degree in English;
UN-L earned doctorate in American
literature, 1976.
Date of Death: Dec. 7, 2009
Location of Death: Columbus, NE

Dr. Emily Jane Uzendoski

Known Publications:

Bibliography, "A Handlist of Nebraska Authors," was published by the
Nebraska Department of Education in 1977.

Articles printed in:
 "Nebraskaland"
 "A River and Its People"
 "The Journal of American Culture"

Original speech on writing was published in "Writing it Down for
James: Writers on Life and Craft" by Beacon Press in 1995.

Poetry featured in The Nebraska English Journal: Poetry of Nebraska.

Edited "The Salt Creek Reader" with poet Ted Koozer.

$\mathbf{D}$r. Emily Jane Uzendoski is a third-generation American born into the culture of Nebraska. Her roots run deep in her Polish heritage and in the "valley" – the farm, ranch and wilderness land along the Loup River where she grew up on her parent's farm west of Fullerton in Nance County.

"I am a product of small-town culture," she wrote in her curriculum vitae as a senior at the College of Saint Mary in Omaha. "Perhaps I am one of those people whom Carol Kennicott was thinking of when she attempted to bring culture to Gopher Prairie, Mainstreet, U.S.A."

It was during her time at Saint Mary's that Uzendoski noted her *"chief sources of pleasure are derived from the imagination: Music – to express myself in playing my cornet or to experience the feeling of composers. Art – to feel the meaning of a painting or an unpainted scene. Nature – to imbibe the strength and pattern of its wholeness. People – to observe the confident 'being' in his element or the fleeting tell-tale characteristic. The challenge – to find the entrance into their minds. I am a searcher of new experience."*

Uzendoski was a magna cum laude graduate of the College of St. Mary, graduating with a bachelor's degree in English. In 1964-66 she was awarded a graduate teaching scholarship in the Department of English by Creighton University of Omaha, where she also earned her masters degree. She taught at North High School in Omaha while serving as a research associate and continuing her education at UN-L. There she earned a doctorate in American literature in 1976.

A year later her dissertation, *A Handlist of Nebraska Authors*, was published by the Nebraska Department of Education. She also had articles later printed in *Nebraskaland*, *A River and Its People* and *The Journal of American Culture.* An original speech on writing was published in <u>Writing it Down for James : Writers on Life and Craft</u> by Beacon Press.

Uzendoski joined the Central Community College-Columbus staff as an English instructor in 1978, the position she held until her death at the age of 67 on December 7, 2009, after a lengthy struggle with cancer.

She was a visionary for a grant proposal and wrote the proposal that was accepted for the National Endowment for Humanities for CCC-Columbus, "Legacy and Landmarks of Plains Native Americans."

Among her numerous accolades, she received the Platte Campus

APPLE Award. The award stands for "Accomplished Platte Professor and Leader for Excellence."

As a keynote speaker at the 1989 Nebraska Writing and Storytelling Festival in Lincoln, Uzendoski said, beginning with a quote from Eli Weisel, witness to the Holocaust and Nobel Peace Prize recipient: "Weisel said, 'Not to transmit an experience is to betray it. Nothing threatens and diminishes man more than silence.' Think about it – not to transmit an experience is to betray it. We have a duty to transmit our experiences.

"I would like to pause and say that a writer is an artist. Whether we write when we create, or sculpt, or paint, or make photographic images – we as artists give our interpretation of reality. Each one of us has our own individual experience of reality. Our writing is our interpretation of it. Weisel says we must 'Shatter the silence. Break the silence.' We have this duty to transmit our experiences."

Uzendoski goes on to say: "Even though Weisel is speaking out of the context of the Holocaust, I believe his following observation pertains to us, especially those of use who are writing autobiographical stories, memoirs, family stories, or reminiscences.

"We write and tell our stories as survivors. We are alive. The dead have died. As Weisel points out, the death of a single person is the death of an entire world. Weisel says that to write as a survivor is to write as a witness to what was, to speak as a witness for the dead.

"We tell the stories of our families, our family histories; we write autobiographies and memoirs; we write as survivors. We are the ones left alive to tell the story." B

Endnotes, Footnotes & Sources:

She was on the staff of "The Saltillo," which prints Nebraska poetry and critical articles about literature, served as co-chairman of the Nebraska Writing and Storytelling Festival, served on the committee for the Nebraska Literature Festival, and was a compiler and manager of a database of Nebraska authors and their published works.

Special thanks to Emily Jane's daughter, Michele Uzendoski for ideas and material from her mother's files and collections.

Also thank you to News Bureau Director Joni Ransom, Public Relations at CCC-Platte Campus, for all her help in obtaining information and photos.

This large rock was placed on the CCC-Platte Campus in Columbus to honor the late Dr. Emily Jane Uzendoski.

Nebraska Authors Book & Travel Club

Visit the Platte Campus of Central Community College in Columbus. Have a photo taken with the "Rock" placed at the campus in honor of Dr. Emily Jane Uzendoski.

RUTH POLLARD MORSE VAN ACKEREN

Date of Birth: May 13, 1905
Location of Birth: Kansas City, KS
Moved to NE before age one
Lived near Lakeside, NE
Education: Lakeside country school
to eighth grade
Alliance High School grad at age
sixteen
Normal School teaching certificate
from Kearney Teachers College
Date of Death: April 10, 2002
Location at Death: Omaha

Ruth Van Ackeren[10]

Known Publications:

Van Ackeren, (Pollard, Morse), Ruth, *Alliance Times-Herald* newspaper, including as the *Lakeside correspondent*; *The Big Walk* serial in the *Grant County News* and her articles, book reports, and short stories were printed in various additional publications.

Van Ackeren, (Morse), Ruth. "Hello There" monthly column in *The Nebraska Cattleman*. Official publication of The Nebraska Stock Growers Association of Alliance, Nebraska. Printed in Omaha. She wrote the column, 1941-1951, full-time and occasionally thereafter. She was a staff writer for forty-three years.

Van Ackeren, (Morse), Ruth. "Hello There" single columns published in pocket-sized paperback booklets. Number published and years unknown. Viewed at the Old Ellsworth School Museum, Stephanie Bixby Graham, curator.

Van Ackeren, Ruth, Harrison Ladies Community Club. <u>Sioux County: memoirs of its pioneers</u>. Publisher: Harrison, Nebraska, *Harrison Sun-News,* 1967.

Van Ackeren, Ruth and Bartlett Richards Jr. <u>Bartlett Richards: Nebraska Sandhills Cattleman</u>. *Introduction* by Nellie Snyder Yost, Lincoln: Nebraska State Historical Society, 1980. Original jacket painting: "Herd Bulls Stand" by Harry W. Brunk.

Van Ackeren, Ruth and Lyle (Van Ackeren) Bruere. *Heroine of Honey Creek* in <u>Women Who Made the West</u>. Doubleday, 1980, pp 252.

Van Ackeren, Ruth, Robert M. Howard<u>. Lawrence Bixby: preserver of The Old Spade Ranch</u>. Idaho: Caxton Printers and distributed by the Nebraska State Historical Society, 1995.

T he *Alliance Times-Herald* newspaper seems to have the first record of Ruth Pollard's writing. At age twelve she was the correspondent from her home town of Lakeside. Her mother had written the country news of the area as a correspondent and turned it over to Ruth for a few years. According to one memory, Ruth visited the paper one day and the staff was surprised to find out their correspondent was a young pre-teen.

Ruth Pollard teacher at Welch School, 1925.

Ruth's father died before she was one-year-old. Her mother remarried, moving to Nebraska and eventually giving her seven siblings. She graduated from high school in Alliance at age sixteen and completed the Normal School teaching Certificate at Kearney Teachers College before she was eighteen. Her first teaching position was at a Sandhills country school teaching children of ex-Spade Ranch workmen and their neighbors in the Redick Valley north of Bingham.

Warren DeBore and Ruth married on June 1, 1923. He was killed in an auto accident on October 1, 1926. She married Forrest Morse on October 23, 1927, in Hyannis. He worked on the railroad and became the railroad agent in Lakeview after Ruth's step-father retired. They had one daughter, Lyle.

Lakeside Station[5]

Ruth became a staff writer for *The Cattleman's Magazine* and by 1941 was writing the popular column "Hello There." Each column introduced readers to a cattle producer family from around the state. Ruth interviewed the families, saw their ranches and presented their accomplishments to readers. She wrote the column full time for ten years. According to former editor Robert Howard, "She wrote after that, too, whenever I called her to interview a family."[1,2]

During World War II Alliance was a bustling dot on the Nebraska map. A training air base was set up outside of town. The landscape was similar to the European areas where parachuting military needed to land and fight, thus training near Alliance became a first stop for many troops in training. Ruth secured a job on base as a secretary in the General's office. The *Alliance Times-Herald* newspaper asked Ruth to write stories about local men trained and stationed at the base as well as their later military activities, including obituaries if that became necessary. She conducted nearly a hundred military interviews, columns, and stories during that time and visited the newspaper office on a part-time basis.

With the influx of people to the Alliance area, the newspaper hired a couple of new employees to assist with the new business. One was Edwin Van Ackeren. The war and the Depression had cut supplies to the point he had to close his newspaper in Cedar Rapids, Nebraska. He moved his family to Alliance and began to work at the paper. As soon as he could see the supplies were available again and the war was over, he and another *Alliance Times-Herald* worker, Walter Schott, moved their families to North Platte to start a printing company.

The military base closed and soon Ruth was faced with a couple of personal decisions. One was a divorce and, second, Lyle had been admitted to Omaha University (now University of Nebraska at Omaha).

As a single mother in 1949, Ruth got a job in the secretary pool at the Union Pacific Railroad headquarters in Omaha. She eventually worked her way up the ladder to become the secretary for the president of the Union Pacific. Lyle graduated college in May 1953 and married October 10. She and her husband moved to Iowa.

While Ruth was officially working in Omaha, she was also still writing for *The Cattleman's Magazine*. When Robert Howard called with an interview, Ruth borrowed her father's Burlington Railroad train pass and headed for Alliance. Her parents, George S. and Clara Hendrickson Pollard, were now retired and lived in Alliance. Ruth stayed with them until her work was completed. Then borrowing her father's pass, she would return to Omaha. [The Union Pacific didn't have tracks in Alliance.]

Mr. Van Ackeren's wife had died within a year after they moved to North Platte and his three children became used to housekeepers and a single father. Young Kathy had been two and a half years old and her brother and sister were ten years older when their mother passed away. In an interview with Ruth's step-daughter, Kathy Van Ackeren Lute, now a business owner in Ogallala, she remembers she was in about the sixth grade when her father had a business trip to Omaha and had some free time, so called his friend Ruth from the old days at the *Alliance Times-Herald*, for a cup of coffee. "It took them a couple of years of getting to know each other. I was enrolled in eighth grade when they got married: August 1957," Kathy said.

Ruth moved from Omaha to North Platte. Kathy said she got along with Ruth right away. She remembered Ruth sitting in her study writing on "Hello There" columns and researching the Spade Ranch history. She laughed as she remembered telling her own three children to leave things alone in the study. "The old typewriter, all the books and stacks of research papers were always something to play with. I had to keep telling them 'don't touch anything' in that room." Kathy remembered numerous guests at their home included old friends, Robert "Bob" Howard and Lawrence Bixby.

The Van Ackeren's loved to travel. They traveled to visit their children and visited historic sites all over the country. Kathy explained, "Dad loved Jazz so they traveled to New Orleans several times. Their plans always revolved around trains. Dad didn't like to fly and they both loved trains." According to Kathy, she didn't think Ruth and Edwin wrote any travel columns to send to newspapers as was popular at the time. It was their time to get away; but, they were never too busy to find time to research a topic when it came up. Kathy said she lived in Vermont for a time. She remembered that Ruth was researching the Old Spade Ranch and had said the Richards family had moved to Nebraska from Vermont. Kathy found the cemetery where the Richards' family had several markers, and when Ruth and Edwin came to visit they took photographs of gravesites to add to the documentation.

Edwin's job printing business partner passed away. Ruth and Edwin continued with the business until the *Telegraph Newspaper* purchased it in the early 1970s.

By 1974, they moved to the Masonic Manor in Omaha. Between researching, writing, and travel there was no longer time for yard work. They lived there to the end of their lives. Edwin passed away at age seventy-two (1910-1982). Eastern Star, Nebraska Writers Guild, Nebraska Press Women and National Federation of Press Women, Omaha Chapter of Daughters of Founders and Patriots of the U.S. meetings and activities also took Ruth's time and energy.

Ruth had branched out in writing working with the Harrison Ladies Community Club to publish the history of Sioux County in 1967. Lyle and Ruth wrote a chapter for a 1980 Doubleday publication Women Who Made the West: *Heroine of Honey Creek.* There was still one story that hadn't been written.

The history of the Lakeview, Ellsworth, Alliance area, Sheridan and Cherry counties includes a shadow that has never diminished: the day the sun set on the old Spade Ranch. What was left of the ranch managed by Bartlett Richards Sr. after the government occupation dust settled was chaos.

The truth of the story involved President Theodore Roosevelt and his vision of government land, fences to provide boundaries for cattle that had been set before the Kinkaid Act of 1904 came into force, the Nebraska Land and Feeding Company, and the untimely death of its director, Bartlett Richards Sr. while he was in State of Nebraska custody in jail/hospital on charges brought by the Presidents' men.

The Richards' family had moved to California to a home they owned. The jail stay was to be for one year. While Bartlett Richards was making plans to be released from prison, he wrote his final prison letter to his wife on August 30, 1911. Shortly after the letter, his wife received word that he was gravely ill. She boarded the Union Pacific and headed for the Seventh Day Adventist Sanitarium where he had been moved at Hastings, Nebraska. While on the train she was handed a telegram from Will Comstock's wife in Hastings: Bartlett had passed away suddenly of ileitis. That was September 4, 1911.

There had been three of the Spade Ranch leadership in prison: Richards Sr., Charles C. Jameson, and Will Comstock. When the news of Richard Sr's death reached Comstock, an appeal was made that he be released from jail to assist with the funeral and business

Nebraska Historical Marker at Ellsworth, Nebraska[5]

arrangements. It was immediately granted. With the dedicated assistance of Comstock the remains of the business was handled for Mrs. Richards. For the next couple of years the Comstock and Richards' families returned to work the cattle or hayfields in the summers, living together in a house at Ellsworth. Comstock passed away in 1916. Jameson then became president of the company until his own death. Former Spade Ranch cowhand, Lawrence Bixby, was asked to manage the land by its new owners in 1924. Bixby eventually purchased the core area of the original ranch site. An Old Spade Ranch mile marker was erected by the State of Nebraska next to the Old Spade Ranch Store which can be seen today in the village of Ellsworth.

Ruth was well aware of the story, as she grew up in Lakeside and the Spade Ranch headquarters was based near Ellsworth which was only a few miles away. The town of Ellsworth, with a peak population of thirty in 1920, was located on the Chicago, Burlington and Quincy Railroad and was an early cattle shipping point. The Nebraska Land and Feeding Co., operated by pioneer cattlemen Will Comstock and Bartlett Richards and their hundred or so employees, were prime contributors to the railroad and local economy. "To some homesteaders he was a cattle baron who sought control of Sandhills land they hoped to farm. To others he was a leader of Nebraska's early livestock industry who more clearly understood the capabilities of the land."

There was another story that Ruth was aware of. The first fiction story by Mari Sandoz, Old Jules, had been published in 1935. Sandoz

(1901-1966) had been part of the Federal Writers' Project working with Rudy Umland[3] and Lowry Wimberly in Lincoln before returning to her Sandhills home when her first book was rejected. She returned to Lincoln working under funds from the New Deal working for Addison E. Sheldon,[4] and when her book sold she moved to the East Coast. It was during the years of the 20s and 30s that the literary community around the country began to embrace the progressive movements of spiritualism, regionalism, and nationalism. Sandoz fiction reflected many of the social aspects around her. The <u>Old Jules</u> publication put Sandoz on the map and she became a model for Nebraska writers. The popularity of the story made many forget that it was written as fiction. Whether the feud that she wrote about between Old Jules and Bartlett Richards was real or something from the memory of a ten-year-old girl hangs in the Sandhills shadows to this day.[4]

What was real is that Bartlett Richards Jr. was his father's son. His father died at age forty-nine. Richards Jr. was ten-years-old. Richards Jr. left the Old Spade Ranch and his family residence in California and eventually became vice president of the Acme Steele Company in Chicago. While going through old family papers at the home of his mother in 1972, Richards Jr. came across letters from his family dated from 1879 to 1911. He began to sort what he had and research facts about his family and his father's life. He had read Nellie Snyder Yost's book <u>Call of the Range</u> and wrote to ask her if she thought these new finds should be published. She encouraged him to continue his research. He also remembered a letter he had received in 1955 from Ruth Van Ackeren who had wanted to publish a book about his father's life. At that time he had replied that he didn't think there was enough information, besides the known court documents, so the project lay dormant. Now the task of writing about the truth of the story, even with the new information, seemed daunting as so many old timers and witnesses of the events had died or moved away. Richards Jr. began his rough draft and contacted all the cattlemen he could think of. With encouragement from all, he researched and wrote until his own death in the spring of 1978.

Bartlett Richards Jr., Nellie Snyder Yost, and Ruth met nearly twenty years after Ruth's original letter to Richards to review what he had written and see his newly researched materials. Ruth assisted with the editing of his manuscript, and at the time of his death took over the research and finalizing of the details of the book with Richards Jr.'s wife, Beatrice Norton Richards. The researched and well-documented result was a book about the Spade Ranch with the intent to present the truth of the story about Bartlett Richards Sr.: <u>Bartlett Richards: Nebraska Sandhills Cattleman</u>.

In 1977 Marvin Kivett, director of the Nebraska State Historical Society (NSHS), sent a rough draft of the manuscript that Bartlett Richards Jr., Nellie, and Ruth were working on to Professor James A. Rawley[6] at the University of Nebraska who was a member of the NSHS board of directors. Rawley had painstakingly researched several of his own books and now was asked to assist in the verification of this manuscript material for possible publication by the NSHS. The book was published in 1980 and the NSHS is the depository for the Bartlett Richards' papers related to the Spade Ranch. <u>Bartlett Richards: Nebraska Sandhills Cattleman</u> was met with some controversial reviews, just as Richards Sr. had been in life.

In a February1981 letter from L.G. DeLay, historian for the NSHS, to H. Nicholas Muller III editor, <u>Vermont History</u> at the Vermont Historical Society, he tried to explain some of the popular controversy: "Because Mari Sandoz, the well-known writer of historical fiction, made cattleman Richards the antagonist of her homesteader father in <u>Old Jules</u>, Richards has increasingly become one of Nebraska's most disliked figures." [4, 12]

In March 1981, DeLay wrote to Gene M. Gressley of the University of Wyoming Western History Research Center and once again tried to explain fact and fiction of history: *"Carolyn Pifer[7] (Mari Sandoz sister of Gordon, Nebraska) wrote Mrs. Van Ackeren that the book is flawed by its omissions. She has built on the myths for so long that nothing will ever shake her from believing a monumental struggle existed between Old Jules (and other assorted little Americans) and Bartlett Richards[BR]. I think I've probably looked at more stuff bearing on the Sandhills life between 1880-1912 during research over the last six years than anyone has before. My intuition tells me-given my knowledge of Richards and of human nature in general-to doubt, for example, the Mari Sandoz' tale that BR tried to run down with his buggy a crippled Old Jules. I doubt that Richard gave Sandoz much thought. I have a long incomplete list of items bearing on Jules Sandoz from NW Nebraska papers during the homesteading period. Most items view him as a comic figure and pay little attention to his posturing's. Mari's book made him the figure he is today-famous or infamous, whichever way you like him. This takes nothing away, of course, from Mari Sandoz skill as a writer of fiction."* [5]

In a November 3, 1980, letter, DeLay had written Gressley about the manuscript as the two of them were verifying facts within their respective states: *"You will notice that those with whom Mrs. Van Ackeren disagrees are not taken heavily to task—if at all. She merely gives the story as she found it, but writing, of course, as a partisan of Richards Sr."*[12]

Nebraska, Vermont, and Wyoming were key states in verification of facts for the book. Details of deals were checked and double checked, including "Bartlett's older brother, DeForest Richards, who later became governor of Wyoming, was president of the brothers' bank in Douglas and mercantile partner of C.H. King. King's grandson, Leslie L. King, Jr. of Omaha was adopted by his stepfather, grew up as Gerald Ford, and became the 38th president of the United States," said the book reviewer, Mrs. Lyle Bruere, in the *Midlands Business Journal* of March 20, 1981. [12]

Ruth was already seventy-five years old when the Richards book was completed. During the interview with Kathy Lute, she noted that it took encouragement for Ruth to begin another book. "She had all the material from all her previous research and she knew the story personally. I told her she really needed to write it." A few years later she teamed up with Robert Howard to write a sequel, <u>Lawrence Bixby: Preserver of the Old Spade Ranch</u>. It was published in 1995. Caroline Sandoz Pifer wrote the Introduction for the book and Hugh Bunnell, the longtime managing editor of the *Alliance Times-Herald,* wrote a tribute to "old Bix," Lawrence Bixby. It was printed at the end of the book. The Old Spade Ranch had come full circle again.

Whatever a reader wants to believe about the Old Spade Ranch, Bartlett Richards and the government case against him and the other men, the land itself is now part of the historic record of the Nebraska Sandhills. The memory of Old Bix, the Spade Ranch, and other ranchers in the area is continued in a small school house museum in Ellsworth owned by Bruce and Stephanie Bixby Graham.

Writing and teaching were income, but reading and history were Ruth's first loves. Later in life when Ruth gave away some of her large book collection, she wrote notes inside the books to the people she gave them to. "To Tanner Graham, one of my most cherished books" was written inside <u>An Early History of Cherry County, the story of its organization, development and people</u>. Inside her copy of the

Richards' book Ruth wrote to her friend, "To Stephanie Graham devoted historian, valued friend." Stephanie, a Bixby granddaughter, had often accompanied Ruth as she researched and wrote while she visited Alliance.

Ruth was honored for her numerous short stories and history books. For the Bartlett Richards book she received a trophy from the Cowboy Hall of Fame in Oklahoma City. For further research, some of Ruth's papers can be found at the Cattlemen Museum on the lower level of the Sandoz Museum on the Chadron

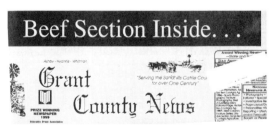

Telegram sent to Marvin F Kivett, director of NSHS, announcing National Cowboy Hall of Fame winner.[12]

State College Campus, and some of her papers and personal items are located at the Knight Museum and Sandhills Center in Alliance.

Ruth was also honored by the Nebraska Press Women with two awards for Journalism Research/Lifetime Achievement and Non-fiction: biography and history. These awards she did not see because she passed away a couple of days prior to the convention presentation. The *Grant County News* April 18, 2002, headline read: "Historian of the Sandhills' Pen is Stilled – Sandhills Author/Columnist Ruth Van Ackeren, Dies at 96." [8]

Every year the *Grant County News* and writer Sharon M. Wheelock produces "Beef Section Inside…" She continues to highlight achievements in honor of Ruth Van Ackeren and Robert "Bob" Howard, especially for their historic work with the "Hello There" columns. Several readers offered copies of the Wheelock articles to the Nebraska Authors Project® during interviews. It is obvious Ruth and Bob's work have passed the test of time through several generations of Sandhills natives.

Neighbors and friends wrote a few memories after Ruth's death in 2002. They noted that she always like to listen and discuss 'old times', history of the Sandhills area and its people. From the first remembrances of her she was liked by others and bright.

"She was a great person," said step-daughter Kathy as she explained that Lyle had passed away before Ruth and it had been Kathy that was with Ruth as she passed away. "There were always books for us to read. She had a lot of books."

Becci Thomas, Director of the Knight Museum & Sandhills Center (OpenAlliance, Nebraska), said she considered Ruth a friend. "She was a friend of my grandmother and mother. When they were gone I just continued the friendship," she continued. "Ruth would come to the Museum to do research. She was wonderful to sit and talk to. She remembered everything whether it was history or part of a conversation you had last time you talked with her.

Ruth at book signing, 1995

"The way I will always remember her is that she was always dressed well and wore pearls," said Stephanie Bixby Graham. She pulled out photo albums to show the interviewer what she meant. In each photo through the years, whether at a book signing or a simple get-together, Ruth was dressed with a pearl necklace.

"She had a good memory. You could be telling a story and get distracted in the telling and she would always know where you were in the story so you could finish it. It was amazing," Stephanie said. However, everyone seemed to agree Ruth was the best storyteller.

Perhaps Robert "Bob" Howard summed up the life of his friend the best. "She gave her life to a proficiency of writing that is rare in others." [2]

Over a dozen years after her passing, the memory of her is as clear and bright in the Sandhills as she seemed to have been in her life. N

Endnotes, Footnotes & Sources:

[1] Hansen, Nancy Sue and Dush, Barbara Ann. Nebraska Authors Volume One. "Robert 'Bob' Howard." Fullerton: D & H Adventures Publishing. 2013.

[2] Robert "Bob" Howard, former editor of *The Cattlemen Magazine,* The Nebraska Stock Growers Association, Alliance, Nebraska, interview January 2013.

[3] Hansen, Nancy Sue and Dush, Barbara Ann. Nebraska Authors Volume One. "Rudolph Umland." Fullerton: D & H Adventures Publishing. 2013.

[4] Sheldon, Addison Erwin. Nebraska Old and New. Children's textbook of history, stories and folklore, Lincoln: The University Publishing Company, 1937, 470 pp. "Old Jules" Sandoz, by Mari Sandoz, Author of "Old Jules" pp. 342-344. "Old Jules" chapter from children's textbook in appendix of this volume.

[5] Photo of Lakeside Railroad Station, 2013. Photo by Nancy Sue Hansen. Photo of NSHS marker, 2013.

[6] Hansen, Nancy Sue and Dush, Barbara Ann. Nebraska Authors Volume One. "James Rawley." Fullerton: D & H Adventures Publishing. 2013.

[7] Hansen, Nancy Sue and Dush, Barbara Ann. Nebraska Authors Volume One. "Caroline Sandoz Pifer." Fullerton: D & H Adventures Publishing. 2013.

[8] *Grant County News,* "Historian of the Sandhills' Pen is Stilled – Sandhills Author/Columnist Ruth Van Ackeren, Dies at 96," April 18, 2002.

[9] *Grant County News,* "Beef Section Inside." Vol 116, No 38 May 20, 1999 by Sharon M. Wheelock.

[10] VanAckeren, Robert M. Howard. Lawrence Bixby: Preserver of the Old Spade Ranch. Idaho: Caxton Printers, 1995.

[11] VanAckeren, Ruth and Bartlett Richards, Jr. Bartlett Richards: Nebraska Sandhills Cattlemen, Lincoln: NSHS, 1980.

[12] Bartlett, Richards Sr. and Ruth Van Ackeren files in Nebraska State Historical Society collections, Lincoln. Thanks to NSHS staff for assistance in reviewing the file and copying the correspondence for publication in this volume.

"Living with Osteoporosis: A Feature Profile, Ruth Van Ackeren, Nebraska Author" Partners in Research, Biannual newsletter Creighton University Medical Center, Omaha, Nebraska. Issue 13, Summer 2002. Reviewed June 4, 2012.

www.nebrsites.com/cemetery. Site reviewed June 4, 2012.

www.genlookups.com. Site reviewed June 4, 2012.

http://thoseoldmemories.blogspot.com. by Cheri Hopkins, Sergeant Geronimo. Reviewed 6/10/2013.

Thanks to:
Becci Thomas, Director of the Knight Museum & Sandhills Center (OpenAlliance, Nebraska), for the interviews and assistance with Museum collections, January 2013.

Stephanie Bixby Graham, Ellsworth Nebraska, The Old Ellsworth School House Museum. Interview January 2013.

Kathy Van Ackeren Lute, Trails End Gift Shop, Ogallala, Nebraska. Interview January and March, 2013.

And special thanks to (Lyle's daughter) Ruth's granddaughter , Nina Head of Omaha, for reviewing the draft of the story for accuracy and filling in the blanks with dates, and to Kathy Van Ackeren Lute for following up with the interview and passing on the information.

Nebraska Authors Book & Travel Club

Visit The Old Ellsworth School House Museum. Bruce and Stephanie Bixby Graham are curators. Stephanie says there will be a phone number on the door of the school house for Nebraska Authors Book and Travel Club visitors to call and she will give a private tour. The school house is located in Ellsworth, Nebraska. A signature from Stephanie or attach a photo of your visit to complete this box.

JEAN-BAPTIST VICTOR VIFQUAIN

Date of Birth: May 20, 1836
Location of Birth: Brussels, Belgium
Education: government military schools in Belgium graduating as Lieutenant of Cavalry illustrated history[1]
Took preemption:[2] fork of Blue River between what is now Milford and Crete, NE, Saline County, 1858
U.S. Military: Civil War: 1861 -Fifty-third New York Volunteer Infantry left as First Lieutenant &Adjutant
1862 – spring: part of expedition to kidnap Jefferson Davis in Richmond, VA. Became a prisoner of war, escaped and joined General Banks in Shenandoah
1862 – summer: became Adjutant of the Ninety-seventh Illinois Volunteer

Jean-Baptist Victor Vifquain

Infantry. After involvement in many civil war battles he was awarded by Congress with the Medal of Honor.
1891- appointed Adjutant General of the Nebraska State Militia by Governor Boyd.
1898- Spanish-American War: commissioned by Governor Holcomb as Lieutenant-Colonel of the Third Nebraska Infantry, later commissioned Colonel.
NE first Medal of Honor recipient
Date of Death: Jan. 7, 1904, NE
Buried with military honors as Brevet Brigadier General U.S.V.
Author's pen name Victor Vifquain.

Known Publications:

Vifquain Victor, Smith, Jeffrey H and Tucker, Phillips Thomas. <u>The 1862 Plot to Kidnap Jefferson Davis</u>. PA: Stackpole publishing, 1998. 182 pp. Non-fiction.

Daily State Democrat, newspaper. Established 1879. Owner, manager and editor-in chief Victor Vifquain. In 1882 Albert Watkins[3] became a partner in the publishing of the *Lincoln Daily Democrat.*

Jean-Baptiste Victor Vifquain began life as a Frenchman born in Brussels, Belgium, in 1836. When he was sixteen he was sent to the United States as a student. He returned to Belgium graduating from military schools and becoming a Cavalry Lieutenant. By 1857, he had resigned his position in his homeland and moved to Missouri. He married Louisiana native Caroline Venlemans and the two of them moved to the new territory of Nebraska in July 1858. According to a *Lincoln State Journal* newspaper article celebrating Mrs. Vifquain's 85th birthday: Victor wanted to start a Belgian colony near their homestead. They began their new life together in agricultural pursuits with crops and cattle. Caroline was the first white woman in Saline County and the couple's child the first white child. They had eight children.[4]

In the beginning there was just a freight road that passed the homestead. It was later chosen for the road to Pike's Peak and by 1861 there was a bridge across the Blue River and many travelers passed through the area. According to <u>Morton's Illustrated History of Nebraska</u>, Vifquain had a reputation of assisting settlers to come to the Republican valley. He assisted in setting them up on choice land sometimes at his expense. He said he knew that helping people would help the state and the nation and that was enough of a reward for what he had done for the settlers.[1]

Many things around the farm seemed to happen when Mr. Vifquain was away. One such time was in 1859, before their first child, when Victor was in Europe to visit his mother. The cattle came home early and there were about three hundred Indians stampeding them. "One of the Kiowa chiefs showed his crucifix to Caroline and she produced hers, and friendly relations were assured." The Vifquain's relinquished a couple of cattle to an Indian feast that night, but there was peace.

The closest neighbors were twenty-five miles from the homestead and the nearest town, Nebraska City, was seventy-five miles away, Caroline remembered in the article. She noted it didn't last long since the states of Iowa and Missouri began conscription at the time of the Civil War and those that didn't want to fight moved quickly into any land they could find, usually as squatters.

While those that did not want to fight for their country moved to the Nebraska territory, Victor Vifquain saw the world differently and traveled to volunteer in the New York Infantry before the war began. His Infantry unit was disbanded within eight months. He and three other officers from the New York Infantry went quietly to Richmond, Virginia. The idea was to kidnap the Confederacy leader Jefferson Davis and stop the Civil War. After one attempt Vifquain was captured and held as a prisoner of war. He escaped. The book he later wrote was written about this time of his life.[5]

Caroline remembered she was visiting her mother near Round Hill, Missouri, when her husband came through the area to make a quick visit with military orders to organize the ninety-second Illinois regiment at Springfield. This was just a few weeks after his return home from capture. She stayed on the homestead farm during each of his nine visits to see his family in Belgium and through each of the early military campaigns her husband ventured into. She had many memories of encounters with Pawnees and territorial Nebraska farm life to share with her husband. The family lived on the farm continuously until 1885.

Medal of Honor
Victor Vifquain[7]

Vifquain, according to <u>In Memoriam</u>[6] provided by the military at his burial in 1905, went to the front quickly with his new regiment. *"This regiment [ninety-second Illinois], soon after he joined it, was sent to the front. Its record is a part of the history of the Civil War. General Vifquain received rapid grade promotion, through the various grades until he was in command of the regiment with the rank of Colonel. He was with Burnsides at Hatteras and Roanoke, with Sherman in the campaigns of Chickasaw Bluffs and Arkansas Post, with Grant in his famous Vicksburg campaign. With Banks in the Red River expedition, with Canby in the last campaign of the Civil War, against Mobile. During the Mobile campaign he commanded a brigade, which he led in the assault upon Fort Blakesley, one of the strongest defenses of Mobile, and for gallant conduct in this charge, Congress voted him a medal of honor."*

President Lincoln also took note of his "gallant conduct and personal bravery on the field of battle" and "brevetted him, successively,

Major, Lieutenant-Colonel, Colonel and Brigadier-General. As a special mark of favor, recommended by General Canby, the President of the United States appointed him United States Commissioner to receive the parole of General Kirby Smith and his army."[5] It was October 1865 when the General was mustered out of service with the rest of the Illinois regiment[8] and returned to his homestead in the Nebraska territory.

Back with his growing family as a day-to-day farmer did not last long. In 1867. he was the democratic candidate for the office of Secretary of State of the new State of Nebraska. He became a member of the Constitutional Convention of Nebraska in 1871.

By 1879, he established the *Daily State Democrat* newspaper in Lincoln. He was the owner, manager, and editor-in-chief until he partnered with Albert Watkins in 1882 and the name changed to the *Lincoln Daily Democrat.*[3] Vifquain led the anti-monopoly forces in the state.[1]

In 1886-1887, President Cleveland appointed him Consul to Barranquilla and the Consul at Colon in South America. Two of the boys stayed behind while the rest of the family moved to South America. Caroline remembered [in the newspaper article] that Colombia, South America, "at that time was part of Panama." When the family returned they moved to Lincoln, Nebraska.

As part of the Memoriam given by the military, they remembered that "While Consul at Colon he rendered such valuable services to the Chinese Colonies in Columbia, that the Emperor of China decorated him with the order of the Double Dragon." [6]

In 1891, Nebraska Governor Boyd appointed Vifquain as the Adjutant-General of the Nebraska State Militia. According to the newspaper article, Caroline remembered that it was in 1893 that the General was appointed as "consul general to Panama from the United States, and he and Caroline did not especially enjoy life in the southern country. She was very ill part of the time, and the heat was too oppressive for comfort, and she was more than glad to get back to a more invigorating climate." After that time Caroline remained living in Lincoln as her husband traveled.[4]

As the Spanish-American War broke out in 1898 Vifquain offered his services. He was commissioned by Governor Holcomb as Lieutenant-Colonel of the Third Nebraska Infantry. Later he was commissioned as Colonel.[9] The Third Nebraska Infantry was under the command of Col. William Jennings Bryan during the Spanish-American War. The two became good friends.

When Col. Bryan resigned Vifquain took the regiment to Cuba as an occupational force following the war. It was after the peace treaty that Vifquain returned to Lincoln and retired.

He began putting the finishing touches on his memoirs. He died on January 7, 1904, before his work was published.

His writing remained a manuscript after his death, being passed down in his papers to his wife and then after her death in 1926 to their son, Blakely Marion Vifquain. The manuscript with the working title: <u>Link From a Broken Chain: Historic Reminiscences of the Civil War Relating to an Attempt to Kidnap Jeff Davis</u> was found and typed by Blakely. He donated the typed copy to the Nebraska State Historical Society on August 17, 1926. According to Jeffrey H. Smith, the general's great-great grandson, the location of the original handwritten manuscript is unknown.[5, 10]

Since the original plot was a secret endeavor, there were few that knew of its undertaking. All the participants were native born Frenchmen having migrated and readied themselves to defend their new land. Since the kidnaping did not occur, it did not make headlines; however, there were pieces in historic records that Smith and his co-editor, Phillip Thomas Tucker, could verify. Thus, the reminiscence of the kidnaping plot was found to have a historic basis while the 'swashbuckling' color and drama may be youthful memories.[5,11]

In the preface of the General's book, Smith writes that he and Tucker had earned their Ph.D's in history from St. Louis University and had already found the General in many historic accounts, including the Vifquain capture of the battle flag at Fort Blakely. Tucker had another connection, in that he lived very close to where the rebel cavalrymen were said to have captured the four Frenchmen before they could carry out their mission.

Preserving his great-great-grandfather's original work was the first concern of Smith when he and Tucker set out to edit the work for publication. Typographical and spelling errors, word changes for clarity, and re-wording long sentences and paragraphs were the primary editing tasks. Reference numbers with explanatory notes assist the reader to understand the historic context and the characters of the book.

There will be some portions of the manuscript that cannot be checked historically and thus can be enjoyed speculatively. The four

Frenchman took on the names of the characters of the popular book The Three Musketeers. Was this naming of himself as D'Artagnan and his companions as Athos, Aramis and Porthos meant as a 'cover' for their mission, or was it a romantic addition as Vifquain wrote his memoirs at the end of his life? No one may ever know. N

Endnotes, Footnotes & Sources:

[1] Morton, J. Sterling, succeeded by Albert Watkins, editor in chief; Dr. George L. Miller, associate editor. Illustrated History of Nebraska : A History of Nebraska from the Earliest Explorations of the Trans-Mississippi Region. Volume I. Lincoln : Jacob North and Co. 1906, 1907, third edition 1911. pp 429-431

[2] Olson, James C. History of Nebraska. Lincoln: University of Nebraska Press. 1966, 1955 Pre-Emption-p 89, 158. "As soon as the Indian title to a tract of Nebraska land was extinguished, it became part of the public domain and was available for acquisition by private persons. Prior to the Homestead Act of 1862, title to the public domain in Nebraska territory could be acquired by: (1) purchase under the Pre-Emption Law of 1841, by which a settler could file a claim upon 160 acres of the pubic domain and acquire title by paying $1.25 per acre at the time the land was put up for sale; (2) purchase with military bounty land warrants; and (3) direct purchase, on or after the date on which the land was put up for public auction. Had procedures in force since 1785 been followed, the settlers would not have been able to take up legal residence on the land until it was surveyed. From the beginning, however, the American pioneer had moved far ahead of the surveys, squatting on desirable tracts of land in sublime defiance of federal law; and in March, 1854, Congress, recognizing the futility of trying to hold back the squatter, provided that in certain areas, including the proposed Nebraska territory, individuals could make settlement on surveyed land and be permitted, as soon as the surveys were completed, to select the quarter section whose line corresponded most closely with the land on which they had settled…."The Pre-Emption Act of 1841, under which many of Nebraska's early territorial pioneers had secured their land, also remained in force (until its repeal in 1891)…"

3Hansen, Nancy Sue and Dush, Barbara Ann. Nebraska Authors Volume One. "Albert Watkins." Fullerton: D & H Adventures Publishing, 2013.
[4]First Saline County White Woman Celebrates Eighty-Fifth Birthday. Mrs. Caroline Vifquain. Lincoln State Journal, January 26, 1925.

[5]Vifquain Victor, Smith, Jeffrey H and Tucker, Phillips Thomas. The 1862 Plot to Kidnap Jefferson Davis. PA: Stackpole publishing, 1998. Preface.

[6]Military Order of the Loyal Legion of the United States, *In Memoriam Victor Vifquain, Brevet Brigadier General, U.S. V.* Omaha, Nebraska September 25, 1905. Circular No. 8, Series of 1905, Whole Number 228.

[7] Metal of Honor photo. Courtesy of HomeofHeroes.com .

8 Hansen, Nancy Sue and Dush, Barbara Ann. Nebraska Authors Volume One. "O.A. Abbott." Fullerton: D & H Adventures Publishing, 2013.

[9]Hansen, Nancy Sue and Dush, Barbara Ann. Nebraska Authors Volume One. "Fred R. Fairchild." Fullerton: D & H Adventures Publishing, 2013.

[10] Victor Vifquain. Nebraska State Historical Society. www.nebraskahistory.org. reviewed 11/28/2012.

[11]www.realvalue.net Victor Vifquain. Reviewed November 28, 2012 translation of a portion of the book from French with commentary that the reviewers did not know if all the facts in the book were correct, but could verify several of them.

Nebraska Authors Book & Travel Club

Visit or participate in a Civil War re-enactment in Nebraska. Provide photo of your experiences at the event.

ALBERT WATKINS

Date of Birth: Nov. 16, 1848
Location of Birth: Worcester, England
University of Wisconsin law school, 1871
Moved to NE in 1882 from IA
Date of Death: Nov. 19, 1923
Location of Death: Lincoln, NE

Albert Watkins
Editor-in-Chief of Morton's
History of Nebraska.[8]

Known Publications:

Albert Watkins became a partner in the *Daily State Democrat* newspaper edited by Victor Vifquain in 1882. The publication was renamed the *Lincoln Daily Democrat.*

Beattie, James A; Morton, J. Sterling; Watkins, Albert. School History of Nebraska. Lincoln: Western, 1920.

Morton, J. Sterling, succeeded by Albert Watkins, editor in chief; Dr. George L. Miller, associate editor. Illustrated History of Nebraska : A History of Nebraska from the Earliest Explorations of the Trans-Mississippi Region. Volume I. Lincoln : Jacob North and Co. 1906, 1907, third edition 1911.

Morton, J. Sterling, succeeded by Albert Watkins, editor in chief; Dr. George L. Miller, associate editor. Illustrated History of Nebraska : A History of Nebraska from the Earliest Explorations of the Trans-Mississippi Region. Volume II. Lincoln : Jacob North and Co. 1906.

Morton, J. Sterling, Albert Watkins, Grant L. Shumway. <u>History of Nebraska from the earliest explorations of the trans-Mississippi region</u>. Revised edition. Lincoln: Western Publishing, 1918.

Morton, J. Sterling and Albert Watkins. <u>History of Nebraska from the Earliest Explorations of the Trans-Mississippi region.</u> A revised edition. Edited and revised by Augustus O. Thomas, James A. Beattie, Arthur C. Wakeley. Lincoln, Western Publishing and Engraving Company, 1918. [History of Nebraska From the Earliest Explorations to the Present Time by Albert Watkins, Volume III First Edition. Lincoln: Western Publishing and Engraving Company, 1913].

Watkins, Albert, <u>Douglas, Lincoln and the Nebraska Bill</u> American Historical Magazine, 1908.

Watkins, Albert. <u>Outline of Nebraska History</u>. Lincoln: Nebraska State Historical Society, 1910. 45 pp.

Watkins, Albert. <u>The Evolution of Nebraska</u>. Mississippi Valley Historical Association and Nebraska State Historical Society. 1916?

Watkins wrote numerous articles for the Nebraska State Historical Society including his work on volumes 16-20 of <u>Historical Society Reports</u>. His speeches, correspondence, papers and other manuscripts related to the history of Calumet Bluff in Cedar County, settlement of Nebraska Territory, Indian problems, politics and prohibition, Civil War, Negro Question, World War I and the creation of the "Illustrated History of Nebraska" with J. Sterling Morton, C.S. Paine and others are found at the Nebraska State Historical Society Collection in Lincoln, Nebraska.

Editor extraordinary: two words to remember about Albert Watkins. His journey began when his parents immigrated from England to the United States when he was one-year-old and settled in Wisconsin. After Albert graduated from law school in 1871, he served as county superintendent in Iowa County, Wisconsin, and newspaper editor at

Mineral Point from 1874 to 1877. He moved from Wisconsin to take the newspaper editor position of the *Sioux City Tribune*. In 1882, he moved to Lincoln, Nebraska, to become a partner of General Victor Vifquain[1] publishing the *Lincoln Daily Democrat* newspaper.

It was a joint interest in tariff reform and the gold standard that created a working relationship between Watkins, J. Sterling Morton,[2] and the wing of the Democratic Party known as the Bourbon Democrats.[3] Grover Cleveland, also a Bourbon Democrat, was elected President of the United States and appointed Watkins as postmaster in Lincoln. He held the post for four years.

When Watkins continued to support President Cleveland in Cleveland's next term he was rewarded with an appointment as receiver of various failed Nebraska national banks. His principal employment between the late 1890's and 1905 was with Security Mutual Life Insurance Company as a treasurer and sometimes as an attorney. When the rise of William Jennings Bryan and his free-silver issue became popular, the Bourbon Democrats were unable to maintain a distinct Nebraska wing and Watkins joined the reorganized Democratic Party under Bryan.

Prior to the 1898 Omaha Exposition, a group of Iowans, including Clarence S. Paine,[4] began research on the "History of Nebraska." The group chose J. Sterling Morton to become the literary head of the publication. Morton turned to his old friend Albert Watkins to assist him in the editorship of the project. While the initial project was planned and begun by Morton and promoted by managing editor C.S. Paine, the bulk of the writing and editing fell to Watkins at the sudden death of Morton on April 27, 1902. Watkins worked on the three <u>Illustrated History of Nebraska</u> volumes from 1898 to 1911 with some assistance from George L. Miller[5], G.L. Shumway,[6] and others, including well-known Nebraskans who wrote special articles for the books.[2,4,5,6,7,8,9]

From 1910 until his death, Watkins held the position of Historian of the Nebraska State Historical Society, editing such works as volumes 16-20 of the *Historical Society Reports*. He wrote articles for various journals and magazines, and spoke at schools and organizations all of his Nebraska life. His insight to the history of Nebraska's formation as a state and the early years is considered distinct among his peers.[8]

In a letter from the Nebraska State Historical Society dated August 10, 1903, the curator and librarian Joy Amos Barrett wrote: *"For about eighteen months Mr. Albert Watkins has been daily at the library of the*

Nebraska State Historical Society, investigating the large amounts of material there relating to Nebraska History and writing the <u>Morton History of Nebraska</u>. I have seen much of his work and know its character very well. Mr. Watkins' sense of historical accuracy and his unexcelled command of clear and logical English have contributed to make his manuscript by far the most reliable written of Nebraska. The Morton History is a monument of careful scholarship, and my judgment is that it will be recognized as such immediately upon its publication. By ten years of work in Nebraska History in charge of the work of the Nebraska State Historical Society, I am fitted to speak in this relation and there is no reason why I should overestimate Mr. Watkin's work. I may say of his work that it is painstaking and conscientious, based upon a minute and original investigation of sources, and at the same time embodied in clear, discriminating English of great literary merit. It is historical writing of the very highest type and a credit to every one connected with the undertaking."[7,8] This concentration on detail would also give him a reputation of being overly critical and the cause of the delay in completion of the project.

From the day Watkins started his editorship of the <u>Morton History of Nebraska</u> project there were issues he had to deal with, including how to have the work published. This was a volunteer venture. There was no extra pay for the time and effort in the project. Close contact with J. Sterling Morton, the original editor in chief of the project, is described in the Morton section of this volume. None of the editors were sponsoring the published work nor did they intend to become financially responsible. Thus, the concept of writing the volumes by subscription was put into place. This was managed by C.S. Paine and the publishers; however, Watkins often became a buffer for printing and publishing issues as well as scandals which appeared when the subscriptions were sold by unscrupulous agents.

Joy Morton wrote to Albert Watkins on September 4, 1903: *"Dear Sir: Again referring to yours of August 31ˢᵗ and the letter from Jacob North & Co. of same date, and the talk we had together when you were here. After careful consideration myself and brothers have concluded that we do not care to incur any responsibility nor advance any money toward the completion of the second volume of the Nebraska History. At least not until after the first volume is out and we know how it is to be received, and whether there is any real commercial demand for that kind of a history. Yours truly,"*[8]

While the internal issues of how to finance the project and sell the volumes was being dealt with on one hand, the monumental task of sorting the materials that came in continued. Of course, there were those who were asked to send in information about themselves or their area and didn't. They were upset they weren't added. There were those who found typographical errors, and otherwise had issues with the books as time went on after the books were delivered. But there was a continuous stream of materials coming from creditable historic sources, too.

Morton had begun the research in geography of the state and the pioneers. He then had concentrated in locating the facts about how various businesses, churches, and organizations decided to move to the Nebraska Territory. He had sent letters all over the nation asking for clarification of urban legends and to separate fact from fiction for the History of Nebraska book.

One such letter had been sent to the Reorganized Church of Jesus Christ of Latter Day Saints. The Mormons had a well-worn trail through Nebraska and their wintering camps and travel through the state was to be part of the History. On September 22, 1903, Fred M. Smith, a counselor from the office of the First Presidency of the Church in Lamoni, Iowa, wrote Albert Watkins to answer a question from Watkins/Morton: *"Dear Sir: Your letter of Sept 21 addressed to President Joseph Smith was received this morning. President Smith has been in England for a month or two past, and just now is on the ocean on his return home. A few stops in the Eastern states and one or two in Canada will delay his return to Lamoni until about the 15th of October. In the meantime I shall request our Historical department to communicate with you concerning the things you desire to know and later shall turn your letter over to President Smith, when he again reaches his desk. I think it can be made quite clear to anyone who investigates the matter carefully that polygamy is a child of Brigham Young's brain, and that while it may have been hinted at in "Winter Quarters" it was not publically announced until 1852. The hand cart expedition, started, I believe, from Iowa City, where most of the hand carts were made with which Brigham Young furnished the expedition. As to numbers, our historical department may be able to give you something definite, also as to the Nebraska occupation. We shall be glad to assist you in any way that we can, and personally I shall be pleased to receive a prospectus of your coming publication, this Illustrated History of Nebraska. Trusting that we may be of service to you, and wishing to assure you that we shall be pleased to give you whatever information is at our disposal, I am, Very sincerely yours.*" Preserving history of the two branches of the reorganized church of Latter Day Saints and Utah Mormons was deemed important as it related to the Kansas-Nebraska territory.

Watkins also received letters asking if this person or that was in the book. Since Morton passed they were unsure of the continuity of the work. One letter came from the publisher Jacob E. North on July 30, 1902:"*My Dear Sir: I am aware of the fact that for the forthcoming history of Neb a biographical sketch of Dr. Miller was to have been written by our lamented friend the late J. Sterling Morton, but I think it had never been done prior to his death. I think Dr. Miller is entitled to a very prominent place in the history of this state and am anxious to know before it is too late whether he will have a proper place. Yours Truly.*" With the previous well-known occasional rift between Dr. George Miller and Morton it was a realistic question. Dr. Miller had already become an associate editor for the volumes and there were no lasting issues between them.

Some of the disapproval, which appears in the historic record regarding the writing of the <u>Morton History of Nebraska</u> volumes, comes with the fact that subscriptions were sold at the beginning of the project and it would take several years for the very detailed Albert Watkins to release the first volume to print. By then some of those who had purchased the volumes wanted their money back, or didn't remember they purchased any volumes - let alone there would be more volumes to come they were expected to pay for. And for some, they had paid more than what Mr. Paine and the editors had proposed or the publishers had received. Many letters debating the merits of these issues are found in various NSHS files and microfilm.

Mr. J.R. Thelan wrote a letter and on September 9, 1904, it was answered by Watkins: "*Dear Sir: Your favor of the 7th inst., addressed to the late J. Sterling Morton, has been received at this office, and as Mr. Morton's successor to this great trouble, I beg to say that no promises have ever been made by any on in authority as to the time when the Morton History of Nebraska would be published. Neither has anyone ever paid into the state Historical Society any money on account of this history. All financial matters in connection with this publication have been conducted by the publishers, Jacob North & Co., to whom all moneys have, or should have been, paid…*"

With C.S. Paine, Watkins faced a scam in the promotion of the books. Opportunity had been given to people to pay a certain amount for a book plate to be placed in the back of a volume or simply pay a sum to keep the research going. This was a way to generate funds prior to the publication of a volume. However, as Paine, Watkins and the publishers would find out later, at least one of their sales agents was going out and selling the plates for a much higher amount and pocketing the difference or simply pocketing the entire donation. What those buying the plates thought was that they were buying a plate and a book or that the plate cost the same for everyone. They were all surprised when the order blank came to order the book and the plate buyers thought they already had ordered, or when people who had donated funds found there was no record of their donation. Several letters back and forth to settle the scam. It was a complication for the staff.

The Hon. George A. Brooks of Bazile Mills, Nebraska, was sent a letter by Watkins dated March 27, *1906: "Dear Sir: I have yours of March 24th. Now you have started something. Immediately upon receipt of your letter I looked up the records and found that you had a $125 steel plate and several prints from the same for which you paid. But there is no record of a book order, nor that you were to have a book in connection with this plate. I have taken the matter up with Jacob North & Co., and their statement to me is that they had nothing to do with the plate business, which was then carried on by J. Clyde Lindsey, except that they required all contracts to be made payable to them so that they could make sure of having on hand the plate for use in the History..."* the letter went on to suggest options for credits or other orders and payments.

On February 3, 1908, a letter was sent to Mrs. E.M. Correll at Hebron, Nebraska, related to the third volume: *"Dear Madam: Replying to yours of the 31st ult., I beg to say that we are hopeful of being able to deliver the third volume of the Morton History without further charge. Much will depend, however, upon the honest of our subscribers. If any considerable number of them should repudiate their contracts, it would doubtless create a deficit, which I am sure no one who understands the situation, would want us to bear. Indeed, under all the circumstances, it would be altogether unreasonable. We like yourself, are citizens of Nebraska, with no other interest in this matter than to see that Nebraska has a creditable, history. To this end we have been willing, and have given freely of our time for several years, and besides have expended no inconsiderable amount of our private funds. But for us to bankrupt ourselves in order to deliver to the people more than we have agreed to deliver, would hardly be wise on our part, and would, we think, hardly be expected by the citizens who are interested in this matter…".*

J. Sterling Morton had written to Watkins at the beginning of the project regarding the University wishing to be paid for their input into the history.[2] Morton may have been surprised to read a letter dated April 26, 1906, from Edward A. Ross of the University of Nebraska, Lincoln, Political Economy and Sociology department written to Mr. Watkins: *"I have carefully examined the first volume of the <u>Morton History of Nebraska</u> and am struck with the stamp of high ability and conservatories research you have succeeding in infusing upon it. Many state histories reveal at a glance that may have been gotten up to call this <u>History of Nebraska</u>, however thanks to your capacity for taking pains and to your worked literal skill commands respect at once and is in every way a worthy memorial to the men and events that built up the commonwealth we know. You have so faithfully explored all the available material, you have so serfulously traced to its end every branch and twig of relevant inquiry that the ground you have preserved will never need to be gone over again. Your work will soon take rank as an authority and the subscribers to this work will have their satisfaction of possessing an authoratative as well as an extensively recordable history of the state. I wish for your work the source recognition among the people of Nebraska that it is certain to receive from scholars. Very sincerely yours."*

Dr. George Miller, C.S. Paine, and Albert Watkins worked with or were on the Board of the Nebraska State Historical Society (NSHS) and often had to distance their work with the NSHS from their ongoing work with the <u>Morton History of Nebraska</u> publications.

On May 26, 1908, Watkins wrote an answer to C.V. Svoboda in St. Paul, Nebraska: *"Dear Sir: Your letter of May 7, enquiring about the <u>Morton History of Nebraska</u>, and addressed to Mr. Robert Harvey, has finally reached my hands. You are in error in assuming that this History is being published by the Historical Society, and I am assured that no such representations have ever been made by anyone connected with it. The inference that it was so published is doubtless due to the fact that officers of the Historical Society have been from time to time identified with the publication. It is true that two volumes have been published and delivered as agreed. These volumes speak for themselves as to whether or not they are a 'sell'. It is also true that another volume is in course of preparation, and that we hope and expect to be able to publish it…."*

Two more issues arose: a rift occurred between the Jacob North Publishers and the <u>Morton History of Nebraska</u> project, and misinformation was out that Morton didn't write a word of the book that had his name on it. One letter to Watkins from Wm A. Saunders, Benson, Nebraska, on March 20, 1908, relayed that the *Omaha Bee* was declaring itself an authority *"that Mr. Morton did not write a line of this work. I was led to believe that it was to be an authentic history by J. Sterling Morton and other imminent authors after subscribing for the work, and finding that I had been deceived I wrote to the management asking them to cancel my order which they refused to do...."* Once again the *Bee* had tried a political ploy against three former newspaper rivals: Morton, Miller, and Watkins albeit none of them remained in the newspaper business at the time. It was not unreasonable that some people would have thought that Morton hadn't done much and they were just using his name since the books were published so long after his death. To correct the untruth about Morton not writing on the book at all, several letters were written explaining the facts. One answer to such criticism was answered by Louis Smith, the business manager on January 30, 1908.

"Dear Sir (A.G. Collins, Hebron, Nebraska): To say that we were surprised by your insulting communication of the 29th.inst., to putting it mildly. We can only attribute it to your ignorance of the facts, for we find it hard to believe that any man who is supposed to be interested in the state of Nebraska, would deliberately insult the men, who, for 11 years, have given freely of their time without hope of pecuniary reward, in the hope that the historical growth and development and the interests of Nebraska, which you in part represent, should be set forth in a creditable history of the state. That you came in contact with some of the "sharks" from whom we suffered, even more than you could possibly, is no reason why you should attempt to belittle the work which we have tried to do, and that with the ignorance of the whole matter as shown by your letter which is indeed pitiable. It will be granted that undertaking a work of this magnitude purely on a philanthropic basis, the men back of the Morton History were not always in a position to secure representatives in the field who should be above reproach, but we are the only ones who have suffered from this. More than one man made the advanced payment of $15.00, on the order of the history which never reached us, but in every case, every where that such an instance was brought to our attention the subscriber has been given credit just as though we had received the

money.

The plan on which this work was undertaken was originated and approved by the late J. Sterling Morton, Gov. Robert Furnas, G.H. Gere and others. Afterwards Dr. George L. Miller and Hon. Albert Watkins became identified with the work, and now let me tell you something, that perhaps you have forgotten in the elapse of time, or possibly the agent did not properly inform you. You should have known and doubtless were advised that there was no publishing house back of this work, and that the advanced payment of $15.00, was for the purpose of carrying the work on. Else why did you pay it? You were also informed that this money was all to go into the production of the work, and that the price had been fixed as nearly as was possible at the actual cost of producing it. In return for the advance of the money to carry it on, you were to secure the volumes at their actual cost, instead of paying a bonus to some eastern publisher. No time was fixed for the delivery of the work, and not could be, for no living person could know how much time might be required.

Talking of interest on your money, you're known as a sensible, practical man, that every day's delay in the issuance of the work as long as labor upon it was in progress, enhanced its value. Suppose we had thrown together two volumes and delivered them to you in a year, or two years, you would probably have been perfectly satisfied, but the discriminating man, the man who buys a history of a great state, not for the size, or the character of the binding, but for the historical information which it contains and the accuracy of which could not be questioned, would it be that you prefer that we could take the time necessary to make the history complete and accurate. No great historical work is anything less than a life work. Ever since this work was projected eleven years ago, a large force of people have been continually employed in searching out original material in all the archives, of the country. Upon the death of Mr. Morton, the chief editorial work was, upon the advice of his friends, placed in the hands of Dr. Albert Watkins who had, for some time previous, been employed upon the work. In order that the work might be made the memory of Mr. Morton even greater effort was made to make it as full and as reliable as possible. So, much was done, indeed as to exhaust the fund of the advanced payments and leave a large deficit. In the meantime the cost of labor and paper had so advanced that the mechanical work on the volumes, which was estimated at about $4.50, increased to $6.00 per volume. These volumes have now been issued, strictly in accordance with our contracts and while these contracts have been tested in every court of *the state, we can ill afford to engage in litigation, but we have prepared these volumes on the orders, and we must deliver them and collect the balance due, or some of the men who have been backing this are liable to be forced into bankruptcy.........."Yours truly."*

In another concern with Jacob and North, they wrote Watkins a handwritten letter and said he was stealing profits from them and the Morton Volume they published because he continued to write articles about historic things in Nebraska not in the volume. They considered such continued writing a fraud against them. Watkins and others continued to write about the history of Nebraska on issues for different audiences and viewpoints than the <u>Morton Nebraska History</u> project. The publisher continued to disagree. The second and third volumes were printed by Jacob and North, but Watkins, Miller, Paine, and Louis Smith began the Western Publishing & Engraving Co. to handle their publishing needs.

In 1912, S.C. Bassett from Gibbon wrote Watkins about a problem with the volume he had:

Dear Mr. Watkins:

Once upon a time, if my memory serves me well,

You said that if at any time I couldn't zactly tell

Where to find something I wanted in Morton's hist'ry book

Just write and you'd advise me upon which page to look.

Please, where can I find an account of the Grattan Massacre?

For I've looked till I'm all out of patience;

I've searched till I'm mad clear through'

And if you can not help me out

What in blazes am I to do?

At the time there were no indexes in the volumes so the question from Mr. Bassett was a reasonable one. A project was undertaken to create an index and on March 24, 1992, it was complete: <u>Morton & Watkins History of Nebraska Index</u>. The index was "prepared as an NYA Project by Alma F. Glade at the University of Nebraska under the supervision of Mrs. Clara S. Paine and Professor James L. Sellers."[10] This index can be found at the NSHS.

From the application for the Watkins house to be placed on the National Register of Historic Places, the role Watkins played in the publications is presented: *"Since Watkins' most lasting contribution was his role in the <u>Illustrated History of Nebraska</u>, it is important to examine both the worth of that publication, and Watkins' part in its creation. The* value of the _Illustrated History_ is acknowledged by James Olson in his _History of Nebraska_ (1955, revised ed. 1966), the current standard text on state history. Olson states "The best and most detailed account of the establishment of territorial government…[and] on the political history of Nebraska during the period of admission to the Union and establishment of state government is Morton and Watkins, _Illustrated History of Nebraska_."

According to Watkins, "_Morton envisioned only 'a brief outline of the formal history of the territory and state,' plus 'histories of counties, [and] articles on special topics, including histories of the various churches and other societies and biographical sketches…"[Editor's Preface, v. I. Illustrated History]._ Watkins, on the other hand, held firmly the option that a comprehensive and systematic history was more desirable. In the last volume Watkins changed the title of the introduction to the final volume "Author's Preface," instead of "editor's" writing in 1911. He wrote, "_When I undertook the task of constructing the text, or history proper, nothing whatever had been done toward it, so that all the preliminary research, as well as the constructive part of the work fell upon me…in fact the only material or preparation for the history which Mr. Morton turned over to me was a vast number of biographical sketches in very crude form…_" In the Morton section of this volume of Nebraska Authors there is a letter from Morton to Watkins just before Morton's death that shows a much more active Morton than this Author's Preface conveys over ten years later[2]. Regardless, Watkins legacy is with the Morton _Illustrated History of Nebraska_. At his death Addison E. Sheldon, NSHS colleague, wrote an obituary for Watkins. He noted that Watkins should be given the principle credit for the completed volumes.

According to one undated typed and hand written note, subscribers to the volumes got together to pay Watkins for work on volume three. This gift is the only known payment for work done by the volunteers. "_We, the undersigned hereby agree to pay the several amounts set out opposite our respective names for the purpose of compensating Albert Watkins for editing and compiling the third volume of the Illustrated History of Nebraska, it being understood that such work shall comprise about two hundred pages of text:…_" He had given much of his life finding and correcting the minute details of Nebraska history so no fault could be found with the finished product. His efforts are recognized by the readers of the future and the peers of the day.

Watkins at his desk[8]

NSHS made application to the National Register of Historic Places for 920 D Street, Lincoln, Nebraska, the Albert Watkins home. According to the NSHS the application was accepted; however, it is a private home and not available for visitation. The house was built in 1887 for the newspaper editor, postmaster, historian who lived and wrote there until his death in 1923 after a long illness. N

Endnotes, Footnotes & Sources:

[1] Hansen, Nancy Sue and Dush, Barbara Ann. Nebraska Authors Volume One. "Jean-Baptist Victor Vifiquin." Fullerton: D & H Adventures Publishing, 2013.

[2] Hansen, Nancy Sue and Dush, Barbara Ann. Nebraska Authors Volume One. "J. Sterling Morton." Fullerton: D & H Adventures Publishing, 2013.

[3] Definitions of terms used in Watkins' Day: According to the American Dictionary of the English Language by Noah Webster, 1828.

Bourbon Democrats, like President S. Grover Cleveland were pro-business, opposed high tariffs, free silver, inflation and imperialism. They fought for fiscal conservatism and against political corruption in all political parties, among many other public issues.

Conservative is an adjective meaning " Preservative; having power to preserve in a safe or entire state, or from loss, waste or injury."

Democrat was a noun meaning "One who adheres to a government by the people, or favors the extension of the right of suffrage to all classes of men."

Republican was an adjective referring to the noun "Republic, A commonwealth; a state in which the exercise of the sovereign power is lodged in representatives elected by the people. In modern usage, it differs from a democracy or democratic state, in which the people exercise the powers of sovereignty in person. Yet the democracies of Greece are often called republics. 2) Common interest; the public."

Progressive is also an adjective meaning "Moving forward; proceeding onward; advancing; as progressive motion or course; opposed to retrograde."

Agrarianism. It has two meanings. The *first* is a social or philosophical meaning, which briefly means that someone values rural society as superior to urban society. Thomas Jefferson represented this type of thought. The *second* is the political meaning which proposes political land redistribution from the rich to the poor, often called "agrarian reform."

[4]Hansen, Nancy Sue and Dush, Barbara Ann. Nebraska Authors Volume One. "C.S. Paine." Fullerton: D & H Adventures Publishing, 2013.

[5]Hansen, Nancy Sue and Dush, Barbara Ann. Nebraska Authors Volume One. "George L. Miller." Fullerton: D & H Adventures Publishing, 2013.

[6]Hansen, Nancy Sue and Dush, Barbara Ann. Nebraska Authors Volume One. "Grant L. Shumway." Fullerton: D & H Adventures Publishing, 2013.

[7]Morton, J. Sterling, Albert Watkins, Dr. George Miller, et. all, Illustrated History of Nebraska, Vol 1,2,3, Authors and Editors notes.

[8]Watkins, Albert. Nebraska State Historical Society Collections. Lincoln, Nebraska and NSHS website. Reviewed prior to December 15, 2012.

[9] Watkins, Albert. National Register of Historic Places Registration Form, February 24, 1989. United States Department of the Interior, National Park Service.

[10]Glade, Alma F., complier with Mrs. Clara S. Paine and Professor James L. Sellers. Morton & Watkins History of Nebraska Index. NYA Project, University of Nebraska, Lincoln. March 24, 1992.

Nebraska Authors Book & Travel Club
Visit the Nebraska State Historical Society research room. Check for hours the research room is open and ask for a tour. Have the staff person at the desk sign and date this box or have a photo taken in the lobby entry to remember your experience.

HANNIE WOLF

Hannie Wolf

Date of Birth: Dec. 30, 1925
Location of Birth: Ulm, Germany
Education: Ulm, Germany;
Denver, Colorado
Moved to Nebraska: 1940
Currently lives in Albion, NE

Known Publications:

Wolf, Hannie. Child of Two Worlds, Purcells, Inc., Broken Bow, Nebraska, 1979.

Wolf, Hannie. From the Heart - A collection of articles, essays and poems, Cover design and illustrations by Marilyn Wolf (Author's note: To my granddaughters - Natalie, Jennifer, Stephanie), 1990.

Wolf, Hannie. Life in a Nutshell, Cover design and illustrations by Natalie Wolf, age ten, printed by the *Albion News,* 1992.

Wolf, Hannie. Potpourri, printed by the *Albion News,* 1994.

Wolf, Hannie. Small Talk, cover design by the *Albion News,* 1998.

Wolf, Hannie. Roses in the Winter - A collection of articles, essays and poetry, cover design by the *Albion News,* 2000.

Wolf, Hannie. Days of Hope and Sorrow, cover design by the *Albion News,* 2000.

Wolf, Hannie. <u>As Time Goes By - A Perspective on Life</u>, cover by the *Albion News, 2002.*

Wolf, Hannie. <u>Sense and Nonsense</u>, cover design by the *Albion News,* 2004.

Wolf, Hannie. <u>Thoughts for a Year</u>, cover design by the *Albion News,* 2006.

Wolf, Hannie. <u>Journey Through Life</u>, cover design by the *Albion News,* 2007.

Wolf, Hannie. <u>Points to Ponder</u>, cover design by Big Red Printer-Columbus, 2009.

"**M**emory is the treasury and guardian of all things," was a sampling of prose Hannie Baer Wolf discovered while gathering material for her first book, <u>Child of Two Worlds</u>. Those words drive deep into the soul of this Albion, Nebraska, author.

"I am a child of two worlds, European by birth, American by choice," she reflected in her book. "My generation is known as 'the refugees.' We are the people no one wanted, the wandering Jews, the survivors of the Nazi era... The memory of my childhood is there to haunt me. Often I wonder why I survived when family and friends perished."

Born in Ulm, Germany, in 1925, Hannie describes herself as a dreamer. An only child, her life was full – trips to the parks and museums, castles and pastry shops, and going to friend's birthday parties.

She also had a passion for the written word: "I was a dreamer who enjoyed writing poetry and fiction and who vowed someday to become a writer."

Life was pleasant until Germany's new chancellor, Adolph Hitler, turned Wolf's world into endless days of terror.

"Until the Nazis came everything was normal. I had a happy childhood until Hitler came to power. It was 1933, I was eight-years-old, but I can still remember I was somewhere in the mountains with my mom on New Years over the holidays when they announced that Hitler was going to be the chancellor. My mother was horrified," Hannie vivdly remembered.

Her father's grain-dealing business began to suffer. Christians stopped doing business with him, and the Gestapo would often arrive unexpectedly to terrorize the family.

From Hannie's book: *"The Gestapo came to our apartment frequently, always at night, always unannounced. They would ring the doorbell, click their heels and search our home. Once they tore a grandfather clock apart searching for weapons. If they found something to their liking they would confiscate it with the pretext of 'putting it into safekeeping' for us. Of course none of the items were ever returned. For many years the sound of a doorbell sent shivers down my spine, and I trembled at the sight of a policeman."*

Hannie's father was eventually taken in the night to the police station to be interrogated, still wearing his night clothes. He was sent to the concentration camp in Dachau where he remained for many weeks. After Hannie's mother was able to find her father's military papers from World War I, he was released from the camp.

Again, from Hannie's book: *"From that time on he lived alone with his thoughts. Perhaps wanting to spare us the horror, he never divulged any of his experiences in the concentration camp. He took those secrets with him to the grave."*

With the onset of World War II, the family's grain business was confiscated. It was then they realized that they must immigrate to a safe country.

Their affidavit for the United States was sufficient for only three people, so Hannie's maternal Grandmother Emmy insisted on staying behind. She was to follow her later, "but that was not to be," Hannie recalled. *"On the gray, dismal morning of September 15, 1940, we bade a tearful farewell... Emmy handed me a tan leather book filled with blank spaces. She suggested that I keep a diary of my experiences. Both of us had the premonition that we would not meet again on this earth. This diary is the basis of my book."*

The diary would not be completed until November 23, 1944.

The Baers' escape took them from Berlin to Russia, then onto China, Korea, Japan, British Columbia, and finally to Seattle. When they arrived in Seattle, it was Halloween night. People on the streets and in businesses were dressed in costumes. This custom – new and frightening to the Baer family – was frightening to them upon their arrival.

Hannie recorded the forty-six day journey to America in her diary, always careful to hide it from the authorities. "Fearful that the Russian police would discover it on the train, I always kept it hidden. They might not suspect a fourteen-year-old youngster of being a spy, but I saw them arrest passengers for just such reasons, and I had no desire to land in a Russian prison."

Life continued to be difficult when they arrived in America. The country was still reeling from the Depression. The family eventually found work in Denver – Hannie as a secretary, her father as a custodian, and her mother as a dime store clerk.

The family became American citizens on May 2, 1946. The next year, Hannie married Bob Wolf – two months after having met him at a dance. The couple eventually moved to Nebraska where their son, Bill, was born. Hannie was the secretary for the family's farming and ranching business in Albion where they made their home.

Life was consumed with work and raising a family; however, writing still stirred in Hannie's dreams.

"I always enjoyed writing. My grandmother had always encouraged me, but I didn't do much of it for a long time. I was busy. It wasn't until later that a friend pushed me. She said I ought to put my diary into a book. I had to translate it. That was in the early 70s, then I wrote little books in between."

One of those "little books," titled <u>Days of Hope and Sorrow</u>," is about Hannie's grandmother who died in the war. "My grandmother was denied a visa to immigrate to the U.S. because she had no relatives to sponsor her. (The book) is the letters she sent translated from German. You don't forget your mother tongue," Hannie assured. "If you forget it, you never knew it."

Hannie never forgot her mother tongue, nor has she ever stopped writing. Now in her late eighties, she is actively involved in a monthly writers group that meets in Albion. She also writes columns that appear in Nebraska publications, and is a life member of the Nebraska Writers Guild.

In an excerpt taken from her book, "Potpourri," she writes: *"For most of my life I have been a writer. Reading and writing provided an outlet for the shy child I was. Later on my writing was confined to letter writing. To my way of thinking, a conversation over the telephone can never take the place of a penned message. My writings are derived from personal experiences, travels and day-to-day happenings."*

Hannie sometimes refers to her writing talent as a "hobby." However, that hobby has now manifested itself into twelve books, which speaks loudly for a young girl who once, "vowed someday to become a writer."

Endnotes, Footnotes & Sources:

*Beginning quote taken from Cirero 80 B.C.

Interview/photos by Barbara Ann Dush.

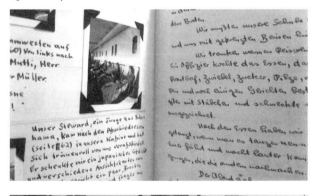

Editors Note: The Nebraska Authors Project has collected hundreds of names of Nebraska authors that fit within the stated Project criteria, however, none to-date have the last name that begins with the letter "X". Thus, this section will be set aside for authors who lived in Nebraska for less than ten years and/or wrote about a subject that includes Nebraska or issues facing Nebraskans as a major portion of their book(s).

MALCOM X

el-Hajj Malik el-Shabazz
Author's given name: Malcolm Little
Author's pen name: Malcolm X

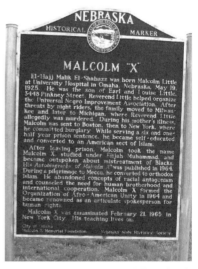

Date of Birth: May 19, 1925
Location of Birth: Omaha, NE
Lived in Nebraska about a year
Education: Lansing, Michigan
Public Schools
Massachusetts State Prision
Education System
Date of Death: February 21, 1965,
New York City, assassination

Malcolm X Nebraska Historical
Marker, Omaha.

Publications and original recordings partial list:

Malcolm X. Malcolm X on Afro-American history. Pathfinder Press, 1970. Expanded, illustrated edition. 1990, 3rd edition.

Malcolm X. By Any Means Necessary: Speeches, Interviews, n.p., 1970.

Malcolm X. <u>Two speeches by Malcolm X</u>. Pathfinder Press, 1990. 3rd edition.

Malcolm X. <u>Malcolm X talks to young people</u>. Pathfinder Press, 1989, 1969.

Malcolm X . <u>Malcolm X : a selected bibliography</u>: Greenwood Press, 1984.

Malcolm X. *The ballot or the bullet* Recording: speech Publisher: Paul Winley Records, 197? Edition: Audio cassette, Publisher: Pacifica Radio Archive, 198-?

Malcolm X. *Fire & fury : grass roots speech* Recording: speech Publisher: Paul Winley Records, 197?

Malcolm X. *Malcolm X* Recording, Publisher: Audio Fidelity, 196?

Malcolm X. *Words from the frontlines: excerpts from the great speeches of Malcolm X*
Compact disc Publisher: BMG Music, 1992.

Malcolm X. *Black man's history* Audio cassette: speech Publisher: Audio-Forum/Jeffrey Norton, 1998?

Malcolm X. *Black revolution* Audio cassette speech Publisher: Audio-Forum/Jeffrey Norton, 1998?

It was incidences at the time of his birth, in the city of Omaha, Nebraska, that would later shape the memories and emotions of the man the world remembers as Malcolm X.

Malcolm Little was the fourth of eight children in the family of Earl Little and his second wife, Louise Norton. Earl, a Baptist lay-minister, was an active supporter of the Black Nationalist leader Marcus Garvey. By all accounts Earl was outspoken in his beliefs in civil rights which often prompted death threats against him and his family.

Malcolm often retold a story his mother told him: when she was pregnant with him a hooded group of the Klu Klux Klan came to their home, showing their weapons they shouted for his father to come out. Other threats came from the white supremacist organization called the Black Legion. It was continued threats which caused the family to move from Omaha, Nebraska, to Milwaukee, Wisconsin and, when the Black Legion found them again, the family moved to Lansing, Michigan, all before Malcolm's fourth birthday. According to Malcolm, over several years three of Earl's brothers were killed, one lynched at the hands of white violence.

In 1929, Malcolm's family history shows continued harassment from the Black Legion and other white supremacist groups. Their Lansing home was burned to the ground and two years later the family was told that Earl had an accident and he was found lying across trolley tracks. At the funeral one of Malcolm's brothers was told that Earl had been helped to the tracks by a white's shovel to the back of the head. By the time Malcolm was thirteen his mother had an emotional breakdown and was committed to a mental institution. The children were split between orphanages and foster homes.

Malcolm was different than his siblings and his father, in that, he had lighter skin and a tint of red in his hair. His mother was part Scottish and he inherited these traits. The issue of skin and hair color would take on a major significance throughout Malcolm's life.

In several accounts it was noted that Malcolm Little was smart and graduated from junior high school at the top of his class. He lost interest in high school when he told his favorite teacher he wanted to be a lawyer and was told that was not a goal for someone like him. He dropped out of school.

Little made his way to Boston to live with his half-sister and became known on the streets as a petty hustler named 'Detroit Red'. By his twenty-first birthday he was in prison for burglary and sentenced to ten years. He took the time to continue his education at the prison library. He was paroled after serving seven years with a new interest in black superiority under the teachings of Elijah Muhammad the founder of the Black Muslims (the Lost-Found Nation of Islam). The organization his father had lost his life to declare alliance with had changed and Malcolm, who remembered his father teaching black pride, began to absorb the new teachings.

It was the Qadiani branch of Ahmadiyah that had attracted African Americans and Jamaican born Marcus Garvey (1887-1940). Garvey preached that blacks should become conscious of their Muslim roots and founded the Universal Negro Improvement and Conservation Association and the African Communities League (UNIA). Islam and the Koran were the alternatives to the white supremacist and Western imperialism, Garvey preached, and Malcolm's father was inspired to follow the teachings. Mosque's opened in Pittsburgh and Cleveland and the growing movement emerged with the Moorish Science Temple of America, begun in 1913 in Newark, New Jersey, as the Nation of Islam (NOI). One branch was established in Chicago, Illinois, by Elijah Muhammad and by 1934 he had taken control of the whole organization to bring internal peace.

Elijah Muhammad stated that a former leader in the movement, Wali Fard Muhammad, was a combination of Allah and Jesus. This appealed to blacks as much as the traditional Muslim beliefs in strong families and the need to abstain from drinking alcohol, eating pork, using tobacco or drugs. The members also refused to be called to military duty as the United States entered WWII, and later wars and military conflicts. Muhammad taught that white society tried to keep African-Americans from achieving any type of success. The growth of the organization was slowed during World War II, but as restrictions were lifted after the war and the Nation of Islam found a new voice, Malcolm X was appointed head of the New York Temple. According to reports the articulate, charismatic, driven new leader increased the membership of NOI from five hundred in 1952 to thirty thousand in 1963.[1] Millions more around the world would hear his teachings and continue in his inspiration, including Brazil, other countries where blacks had migrated and Africa. As membership in NOI grew so did the FBI infiltration.[2]

Malcolm later said that at this time in his life he was a follower and believed that everyone was following the teachings as closely as he and his family. He stated he had even remained celibate until his marriage to student nurse Betty (Shabazz) in 1958. He found out that his mentor had at least six women and several children which was against the teachings. Malcolm refused to cover up Elijah's deception and took a step back. He stated he felt guilty about all the members who he had led to join what he now felt was a fraudulent organization.

Malcolm "X" had retained the "X" as a last name, as was customary when an African American renounce their surname while they search for an appropriate Muslim name. It was considered that the surname was likely from a white slave master in their history and the "X" was the first step in separating themselves from that history. It was Elijah Muhammad that had assisted Malcolm to take on the "X" just as Elijah would assist Louis Walcott to become Louis X and later give him the name Abdul Haleem Farrakhan, now known as Louis Farrakhan.

It was at this time Malcolm X went on a pilgrimage to Mecca, Saudi Arabia. It was a life altering experience and he returned to the United States, as el-Hajj Malik el-Shabazz, a Sunni Muslim. He wanted to speak to all races not just to African-Americans. He resigned his position with the Nation of Islam and renounced Elijah Muhammad. He established his own Muslim sect in Harlem in March 1964 looking for common ground for problems and solutions. He found the Organization of Afro-American Unity and Muslim Mosque, Inc.

While he tried to retrace his steps and teach that cooperation was a better choice, the Elijah Muhammad's faithful tried several times to kill him and his wife and children. The FBI had information that the NOI marked Malcolm for assassination and in one public event three gunman rushed the stage where Malcolm was speaking and shot him at least fifteen times at close range.

Malcolm X Foundation Building

Twin daughters were born to the family later that year. Betty died in 1997.

The Nation of Islam remained divided by doctrine and politics until after Elijah Muhammad's death in 1975. Elijah's son attempted to take one branch and renounce the organization's former racial attitudes and previous declaration that one of the founders, Fard, was an incarnation of God. While the organization name changed to the American Muslim Mission by 1978, it would be disbanded and absorbed by the general African American Muslim community by 1985. There was one sect that maintained the original name and ideals re-creating itself with vigor in 1978, headed by the man who succeeded Malcolm X when he resigned: Louis Farrakhan.

"Malcolm X once said 'When I speak, I speak as a victim of America's so-called democracy."[3-p133]

Endnotes, Footnotes & Sources:

[1] *Malcolm X*. www.malcolmx.com. Reviewed January 2, 2012.

[2] Carson, Clayborne ; Gallen, David <u>Malcolm X : the FBI file</u>. United States Federal Bureau of Investigation. Publisher: Carroll & Graf, c1991.

[3] Ed. By the Editors of Time-Life Books. <u>People Who Shaped the Century</u>. Alexandria, Virginia: Time-Life Books, 1999, 192 pp.

Bailey, Alvin R., Jr. editor of Bibliographies of the States of the United States series, Michael L. Tate, compiler. <u>Nebraska History, An Annotated Bibliography</u>. Number 6, Connecticut: Greenwood Press, 1995, 549 pp.

Brown Reference Group Lt:, ed: Felicity Crowe, Jolyon Goddard, Ben Hollingum, Sally MacEachern, Henry Russell. <u>Modern Muslim Societies</u>. New York: Marshall Cavendish Corporation Publishers, 2011, 416 pp.

Malcolm X. www.wikepedia.org. Reviewed June 4, 2012.

Malcolm X sign at north 30th and Evans.

Nebraska Authors Book & Travel Club

Visit the prairie park behind the Malcolm X Memorial Foundation Visitor Center at 3448 Evans (north 30th & Evans), Omaha, Nebraska. Have your photo taken near the Nebraska State Historical Society Memorial Marker.

The following books are a brief list of publications about Malcolm X. The authors of these works do not meet the requirements of being born in Nebraska or lived in Nebraska for ten years. This partial list is reproduced here for your general reading or research use.

Adoff, Arnold. <u>Malcolm X</u>. Harper Trophy edition, Harper & Row, 1970.

African Islamic Mission; ECA Associates <u>Malcolm X : great Nubian quiz.</u> Publisher: African Islamic Mission, 199-?

(Malcolm X); Breitman, George. <u>Malcolm X speaks : selected speeches and statements</u>. Pathfinder Press, 1989, 1982, 1965. Publisher: Merit, 1965. Publisher: Grove Weidenfeld, 1990. Non fiction.

(Malcolm X) Breitman, George <u>By any means necessary : speeches, interviews, and a letter</u>. Pathfinder Press, 1970. Non-fiction.

(Malcolm X); Clark, Steve. <u>February, 1965, the final speeches</u>. Pathfinder Press, 1992. Non-fiction.

(Malcolm X); Carew, Jan R. <u>Ghosts in our blood : with Malcolm X in Africa, England, and the Caribbean</u>. Publisher: Lawrence Hill, 1994.

(Malcolm X); Epps, Archie C. <u>Malcolm X : speeches at Harvard</u>. Aragon House, 1991. Non-fiction.

(Malcolm X); Gallen, David. <u>Malcolm A to X : the man and his ideas</u>. Carroll & Graf, 1992. non-fiction.

(Malcolm X); Haley, Alex. <u>The autobiography of Malcolm X</u>. Audio cassette Simon & Schuster Audio, 1992.

(Malcolm X); Haley, Alex. <u>The autobiography of Malcolm X</u> . Ballantine, 1973, 1965 Publisher: Grove, 1965.

(Malcolm X); Handler, M. S; Haley, Alex. <u>The autobiography of Malcolm X</u>. Ballantine, 1992, 1965.

(Malcolm X); Karim, Benjamin. <u>The end of white world supremacy : four speeches</u> Publisher: Arcade, [1989?], 1971. Non-fiction.

Kly, Yussuf Naim. <u>The black book : the true political philosophy of Malcolm X (El Hajj Malik El Shabazz)</u>. Clarity Press, 1986.

(Malcolm X); Kopple, Martin. <u>Habla Malcolm X : discursos, entrevistas, y declaraciones</u>. Edition: Spanish language ed. Publisher: Pathfinder, 1993.

(Malcolm X); Lee, Spike; Wiley, Ralph; Haley, Alex. <u>By any means necessary : the trials and tribulations of the making of Malcolm X</u>. Publisher: Hyperion, 1992.

(Malcolm X); Perry, Bruce. <u>Malcolm X : the last speeches</u>. Publisher: Pathfinder, 1989.

(Malcolm X); Richardson, Nan; Chermayeff, Catherine; White, Antoinette. *Malcolm X speaks* out. Compact disc Publisher: Andrews and McMeel, 1992.

PBS Video *Malcolm X : make it plain* Video cassette Publisher: WGBH, 1994.

Malcolm X Memorial and prairie behind Foundation building.

LUNA ELIZABETH (STANFORD) KELLIE

Date of Birth: June 9, 1867
Location of Birth: Pipestone, MN
Education: Girls Seminary, Rockford, IL
Date of Death: March 4, 1940
Location at Death: Phoenix, AZ
Burial: Heartwell, NE

Luna Kellie ca 1892
Nebraska State Historical Society
Collection.

Known Publications:

Nelsen, Jane Taylor, ed. <u>A Prairie Populist, The Memoirs of Luna Kellie</u>. Iowa City: University of Iowa Press, 1992. 209 pp. Forward by Albert E. Stone.

Kellie, Luna, publisher. *Prairie Home/ Farmers Alliance/Industrial Union* newspaper, 1894. These are available at the Nebraska State Historical Society, Lincoln.

Jane Taylor Nelson edited Luna Elizabeth (Stanford) Kellie's autobiographical writings for her undergraduate honors thesis. Nelson presented her analysis of several of the issues presented in the manuscripts in an "Afterword" section she added to the published work.

Populist Luna Kellie was educating the rural population about farm politics before women were allowed to vote or hold office. She didn't consider herself part of the feminists movement, but believed in and acted on behalf of justices. Luna Kellie stood up for Nebraska in the late 1800's and left a foundation and spirit for generations to follow. As readers of her book find the poem/speech "Stand Up For Nebraska" the passion of her life is evident.

Luna E. Stanford was married to Canadian born James Thompson "J.T." Kellie. Luna's father had filed a homestead and timber claim in Nebraska. Luna's mother died of malarial typhoid while still in Wisconsin and her father was left to raise her siblings. Luna's father took his young family to Nebraska to secure his land. After Luna was married a while her father suggested her new family homestead in Nebraska. She, about 19 years old, and her young son boarded a train for an adventure to meet her father in a new town called Hastings. J.T. followed several months later.

She later wrote about seeing her first sod house as she arrived on the train *"Really I had thought a sod house would be kind of nice but the sight of the first one sickened me."* As she and her son arrived at the home of her father and siblings she found the dire circumstances of a two-room dugout and the neighbors just as poor as her father. What beauty she found was soon destroyed by clouds of grasshoppers that destroyed crops and gardens. While Mrs. O.C. Dake[1] served on a committee in Lincoln to assist those devastated by grasshoppers the Kellies were left with nothing but little holes in the soil full of grasshopper eggs ripening for another year of devastation. It wasn't just the spring and summer weather Luna described. During one blizzard Kellie wrote that she and her husband had to force the cattle into their two-room home to save them. The blizzard was still raging the next morning, she and her son stayed in bed to keep warm and J.T. put together some breakfast, with no milk from the cows.

J.T. and Luna had eleven children, with much of their life spent in a sod house. She wrote about the loss of two of her children. The first was Jimmie. Luna wrote that J.T. was in the field so much he didn't realize how hard his wife had to work inside the cramped quarters of the home and how hot it became in the blazing Nebraska summers. With the heat came the flies and Luna wrote that while she tried to cool off before she nursed Jimmie she found her health weaker as each week of hot weather continued. *"The cows got worse and worse acting",* and

Luna herself was unable to nourish her baby with milk. Her baby died. *"I could not allow anyone else to touch my baby and so washed dressed him for the last time putting on him a little embroidered dress and skit my mother made for me….We buried him in the yard…I suppose I might have lain and grieved myself to death had it not been for the shock about the pigs…The sow had seven fine pigs and that spring as I took delight in seeing anything grow, vegetable or animal, I rejoiced in them."*

Happy moments were the delight of the smell of new mown hay and the laughter in the rain that broke through drought, but life in the Kearney and Adams county Nebraska areas was not improving. Hand made tools and bartering were part of life. While sod busting with oxen, J.T. found rattlesnakes and experienced other hazards including life threatening injuries. But the biggest obstacle was the money system. As Crete native Fred Fairchild[2] was preparing to graduate from high school, the Kellie's lost their land and home. It was 1894. The Republican and the Democrat policies were not popular with the working citizens. The couple began to look into the activities of the Nebraska Farmers' Alliance.

Luna's memoirs were not just about the weather or the life of a wife and mother that she led on the isolated Nebraska prairie, but the oppressive circumstances industry and politics played against the people on the Great Plains and her fight to make life better for her children and her neighbors. She saw Nebraska as a whole and spent her life speaking out for the farmers and those businesses they supported. She began to write for publications in various papers on Farmers Alliance and Populist topics.

According to her manuscript a Mrs. Mazer addressed Luna with the wish that Mr. Kellie vote for more winter school days to get her boys as much education as possible. Vote? Luna became interested in politics. She approached her husband with the suggestion and his influence soon manifested results. It was discussed in the Farmers Alliance meetings and in a short time a woman, a mother of child of school age or a woman over twenty one years old who paid taxes, could vote at the school election. Meantime, any hired man over twenty-one who had been thirty days in the district could vote without any question of taxes. Luna considered this an improvement, but still not just.

"I never felt able to attend a State Alliance Meeting until January 1894. As Hastings was so close and (husband) J.T. Kellie was a delegate and wanted me to go with him I went as I was very anxious to see those

whom I felt I knew by their writings. Someone had requested me to pre-pare an article and as the Republicans were just then accusing us of slan-dering the State and hollering "Stand up for Nebraska" I took that for my subject."

Luna delivered her speech "Stand up for Nebraska' in the form of a poem. The seventh paragraph read: *"Stand up for Nebraska, In the cen-ter she lies, The most valuable jewel 'neath the fairest of skies. So favored by nature, her vile man-made laws we find of her poverty are the sole cause. Let her own her own highways and a road to the south: Stand up for Nebraska by your votes, not your mouth."*

Although she wrote articles and spoke about causes she had no "thoughts of any personal interest in the election of officers" she lat-er wrote. A member of the Kearney County delegation asked her if they could nominate her for secretary for the State organization. Her husband said she could 'do as she pleased' so she agreed without any thought that she would win. She won which she wrote left her 'fairly dazed'. She'd been local secretary but it had not been much labor, now she became devoted to new task. A room was cleared in her home and made into an office. For several years her boys daily carried the out-going and in-coming mail to meet the morning mail in town. "It was a ten-mile trip by pony and oftentimes an urgent letter from someone such as a lecturer meant yet another trip to town to catch the first train out." Keeping track of

Luna Kellie ca 1930
Nebraska State Historical Society
Collection.

records and finances consumed Luna's time, all the while still caring for a growing family.

In May 1897, while the committee considering the Trans-Mis-sissippi and International Exposition was completing their plans in Omaha for the 1898 event[3] and the scientific and economic world was unconsidered with what Nichola Tesla was doing in Colorado Springs with the transmission of electrical energy without wires and other projects,[4] Luna Kellie began publishing the newspaper *Prairie Home* to further the Alliance cause. She often worked through the night hoping to bring better conditions to future generations.

Despite Luna's best efforts and those of her family members who helped, subscribers dwindled and she gave up the newspaper. She had become physically ill and it took ten years to regain her health. She wrote her personal memoirs by hand on the back of Farmer's Alliance certificates. The 160-page manuscript became the basis for her book. She had "given up all hope of making the world any better".

Luna Kellie-the daughter, wife, mother, writer, activist and public speaker worked at building her community, her State and her nation until she was worn out. Her manuscripts, put into the book by Jane Taylor Nelson, leave a legacy of inspiration and a deep debt of gratitude owed to her by farm and ranch families and all Nebraskans for her insights into the real problems plaguing the country and her courage to do something constructive about the issues.

Endnotes, footnotes and sources:

[1] Hansen, Nancy Sue and Barbara Ann Dush, Nebraska Authors Volume One. "O.C. Dake" Fullerton: D & H Adventures Publishing, 2013.

[2] Hansen, Nancy Sue and Barbara Ann Dush, Nebraska Authors Volume One. "Fred Rogers Fairchild" "Henry Pratt Fairchild," Fullerton: D & H Adventures Publishing, 2013.

[3] Hansen, Nancy Sue and Barbara Ann Dush, Nebraska Authors Volume One. "J. Sterling Morton," "George L. Miller," "C. S.Paine," "Albert Watkins" Fullerton: D & H Adventures Publishing, 2013.

[4] Farrell, Joseph P. Babylon's Banksters, The Alchemy of Deep Physics, High Finance and Ancient Religion. Port Townsend, WA: Feral House, 2010, pp 303

Rugh, Susan Sissiors. "Review of a Prairie Populist: The Memoris of Luna Kellie" http://digitalcommons.unl.edu/greatplainsquaterly.

"Woman Well Known in Early Nebraska Politics Embarks on Second Pioneer Venture in Arizona," *Hastings Daily Tribune,* July 26, 1933, page 2.

Thank you to the Nebraska State Historical Society for permission to publish the photos. They have preserved many written items from Luna Kellie.

Thank you to Karen Buther, Adams Co. Historical Society for searching for information. Thank you to Pioneer Village in Minden for checking on materials for review. Thank you to Kari at the Stuhr Museum in Grand Island for checking on materials for review.

Nebraska Authors Book & Travel Club

Luna Kellie's manuscript describes her life in a sod house. Visit the Plainsman Museum, 210 16th Street, Aurora, Nebraska to see a re-built sod house. Call 402-694-6531 or check their website for their hours. Have a volunteer sign and date this box.

JOHN OTHO YEISER

Date of Birth: Oct. 15, 1866
Location of Birth: Danville, Fayette
County, Kentucky
Education: unknown
Moved to Ashland, NE in 1875
Date of Death: March 30, 1928
Location at Death: Omaha, NE
Burial: Red Cloud, NE

John Otho Yeiser[1]

Known Publications:

Yeiser, John O. <u>Labor as Money</u>. A story with a purpose. Presenting a practical automatic currency of stationary value. Boston : Arena Publishing Co., 1894. viii + 212 pp. Non-fiction.

Yeiser, John O. *An Argument for the best money on earth*, Omaha: s.n, 1895.[2]

Yeiser, John O. "The Abolition of Both Public and Private Property in Land and Occupancy Rights."[3]

Yeiser, John O. <u>Immortality Established through Science</u>. Omaha: National Magazine Assn., 1913. 128 pp. Non-fiction.

Yeiser, John O. *An opinion*. Omaha: National Magazine Assn., 1913.[2]

Yeiser, John O. *Death a penalty. An opinion*. Omaha: National Magazine Assn., 1914.[2]

Yeiser, John O. <u>Newspapers are common carriers of intelligence, your servants-not your masters</u>. Omaha: National Magazine Assn. 1914?[2]

Yeiser, John O. <u>Automatic elastic currency</u>. Omaha: National Magazine Assn. 1915. [2] [a portion was incorporated into <u>Debts of Today and Hell to Pay</u>.]

Yeiser, John O. <u>Evolution Proving Immortality</u>. Omaha: National Magazine Assn., 1917. 208 pp. Non-fiction.

Yeiser, John O. <u>My Country! My Congress!</u>. Omaha: National Magazine Assn., 1917. 68 p. Non-fiction.

Yeiser, John O. <u>Debts of Today and Hell to Pay</u>. Omaha: National Magazine Assn. 1918. 78 pp. Non-fiction.

Yeiser, John O. <u>Real money, just enough everywhere being a review of Mr. Yeiser's panic-proof authomatic elastic currency based on human power</u>. Omaha: National Magazine Assn, 1920. [2]

The news of the murder of President Abraham Lincoln was less than a year old when John O. Yeiser was born in Kentucky in October 1866. Six months after he was born, Nebraska was created as a state: March 1867. John was nine in 1875 when his father, a Baptist preacher,[4] moved his family to Ashland, Nebraska.[5] A year later, 1876, the family moved to Red Cloud. [6]

The 1871 election selecting Red Cloud as the county seat for Webster County had been held in the dugout home of one of the original settlers of the area: Silas Garber. He was Nebraska's governor 1875-1879. Red Cloud was a Division Center of the Burlington and Missouri River Railroad by 1879. The Yeiser family joined many other emigrants to the bustling spot on the Nebraska prairie.[7]

The news of the day, as the Yeiser family settled into the area was the soundness of the money, the weather, and sudden disasters. On November 15, 1877, an earthquake of a Modified Mercalli Intensity VII shook the state with the epicenter in Garland, Nebraska. It remains one of the major quakes of Nebraska history.[8,9] The next year a tornado in Cherry County, Nebraska, left a deposit of slime, mud, rushes, fish and turtles with "evidence that water had rushed up inclines across the prairie."[10] In 1879, a fire from a lantern explosion in Hastings, in Adams County, destroyed a block and a half of businesses. In the same year the entire town of Red Cloud was nearly destroyed.[11] The weather event is known in history as the "Great Storm of Red Cloud."[7] But it wasn't the weather that fascinated young Yeiser, it was the law and sound money.

The profession of law was an apprentice system, but who the young Yeiser worked with is currently unknown. "It is said that he was the youngest candidate ever admitted to practice law in any court of record in the United States. He began the practice when fifteen years old, being regularly admitted two years later."[3,4,12] He practiced as a lawyer in Red Cloud and Riverton.[4]

Yeiser married Hettie Skeen at Red Cloud on February 5, 1889.[3] They moved to Omaha within the year where he continued to practice law. He was twenty-three years old. They had one son, John O. Yeiser Jr., and attended the First Christian Church.[13]

The day-to-day Nebraska news of 1889 included The Olive Gang and the battle of the bridges between the Central Nebraska communities was headed to court (author Rex German[14] and the Dawson County Historical Society researched the facts years later for his book); Frank LaFlesche[15] was in his eighth year at his job at the National Bureau of Indian Affairs in Washington D.C. after the dust settled around the trial of Chief Standing Bear and the Ponca resettlement; and Ruth Van Ackeren[16] and Robert Howard[17] later wrote about the lessons learned by Sandhills and Wyoming cattlemen during their heavy losses during the winters of 1886-88 and how it affected the years that followed.

The news events fed the interest of Nebraska's youngest lawyer. Yeiser had never graduated or attended any college yet he possessed "a liberal education, acquired by private devotion to study, self-improvement, and a wide range of reading."[3] According to The Weekly Advertiser, "his private library at the time of his death, consisting of more than three thousand volumes."[4]

Regardless of his numerous political and literary activities, Mr. Yeiser's law practice remained his prime concern throughout his life. The Weekly Advertiser described Yeiser as "the Omaha attorney who was famed for his damage suits, for large sums of money, against corporations."[4] And according to a statement from the Cole-McKay Mortuary at the time of Mr. Yeiser's death in 1928, he "had litigation involving one half million dollars pending in court."[13] His "most famous cases were the 'pork and bean sandwich' suits in which he represented two sisters who asked 120 million dollars damages from the big packing companies, the Standard Oil company, the railroads, and many of the big businessmen of the country and the 'steeple shadow' case, arising from an alleged attempt to dynamite the home of Tom Dennison, political leader."[4]

Author and economist Fred Fairchild[18] was just graduating from high school when Yeiser published his interest in the labor and money system of the nation in his first book: <u>Labor as Money</u>, 1894.[19] The sound money topic was of prime concern in the writings of many, including J. Sterling Morton[20] in Nebraska City and all across the State, as bank failures had been nearly continuous since the opening of the Nebraska-Kansas Territory.

Would the money be backed by gold or silver, would banking laws change and in whose favor? What major industry besides the railroad would try to control life and land within the state? While the State of Nebraska prepared to host the 1898 Trans-Mississippi and International Exposition and Omaha Exposition to show off the upturn in Nebraska fortunes, the years of drought and heat, unemployment, low commodity prices, and high transportation costs had taken its toll.[20,21] The citizens were vocal about their financial situation, the political representation and the direction the state and the nation seemed to be headed. Numerous political parties were started in each state. Some parties would spread from state to state and sometimes their candidate would be elected; however, few were able to remain viable for more than a few years. In Nebraska the Populist Party and the Nebraska Farmers' Alliance[22] became well-organized groups for a time.[23] There was also a group called the Fusion Party.[24] The Fusion Party, technically, has several meanings around the country.[25,26] The Fusion Party became a coalition of voters with single issues who could work together for a common cause. The Nebraska Fusion Party developed platform(s) and selected candidates.[27]

Yeiser did not let his youth stop him from stepping into the Nebraska political arena. He was nominated as a Nebraska House of Representatives candidate on the Nebraska Fusion Party ticket in 1897 from Douglas County's tenth district and won his race. He became one of the youngest men elected to such an office. He was not seated as the legislature began the new session as the election certificate was delivered to his opponent. Yeiser secured his seat in the house after a protracted contest. He became a member of the constitutional amendments, militia and judiciary committees.[3,28]

According to the 1897 <u>Nebraska House Journal</u>, four men had been elected to the Nebraska House of Representatives with their results contested. As the investigations of the House concluded, it was found that bribery had been involved and three of the men had been cleared to be seated on February 1. Chief Justice A.M. Post gave J. Fitz Roberts, J.O. Yeiser, and J.H. Taylor the common oath: *"I do solemnly swear that I will support the constitution of the United States and the constitution of the state of Nebraska, and will faithfully discharge the duties of the member of the Legislature according to the best of my ability, and at the election at which I was chosen to fill said office I have not improperly influenced in any way the vote of any elector, and have not accepted, nor will I receive or accept, directly or indirectly, any money or other valuable thing from any corporation, company or person or any promise of office for any official act or influence (for any vote I give or withhold on any bill, resolution, or appropriation). So help me God."* [29]

Numerous bills were placed before the House during the session. March 4: "House Roll No. 259, a bill for an act to amend section 58, chapter 43 entitled "Insurance companies," of the Compile Statutes of Nebraska—and to repeal said section was read the third time and put upon its passage. Thereupon the Speaker stated that this bill having been read at large three different days, and the same with all its amendments having been – the question is, "shall the bill pass?" The roll was called: eleven didn't vote, 88 voted yes and Mr. Yeiser voted no. "Explanation of Vote: I believe this to be a good bill, but on account of instructions contained in the platform of my party in Douglas County which was to make no change whatever in insurance law, I am obligated to vote 'no.'" He submitted bills which were postponed and revived long after he was out of the legislature. Examples are found in the Endnotes. [30-38.] Yeiser was a man accountable to those who elected him.

The Weekly Advertiser wrote "Mr. Yeiser was a member of the state legislature in 1897 and then drew up a bill for an initiative and referendum law, said to have been the first measure of the kind to be presented a legislative body in this country. He then, also, framed a bill for a 2-cent rail fare and fought for other measures of a similar nature that were not adopted until a decade" later.[4]

"In 1897, Nebraska became the first state to provide the initiative and referendum for general use in cities. The law, sponsored by state Representative A.E. Sheldon." [39,40] The early adoption efforts were led by Walter Breen of Omaha. Breen, he became "a successful real estate salesman, secretary of the Omaha Philosophical Society,[41] and an organizer of the Populist Party of Nebraska."

Between serving in the legislature, drafting bills and maintaining a law practice, Mr. Yeiser also made time to speak to various groups. J. Sterling Morton[20] and David P. Abbott[42] were speaking to groups and working on their books which highlighted different aspects of Nebraska history. Mr.Yeiser spoke to the Omaha Philosophical Society during this time and fourteen years later, 1913, wrote a book based on the lecture he had given: Immortality Established through Science. [43]

Mr. Yeiser wrote the preface of his limited edition May 1913 publication: "This book is not a veiled argument for or against any particular church or any religious doctrine. I trust, however, it will be helpful to fundamental religion and all mankind." By November, Mr. Yeiser had to print a second edition. "The surprising demand for the first edition was such as to exhaust the same in a few weeks. It has been a pleasure to revise the manuscript, adding considerable new material, which I trust will make the volume more appreciated." Chapters reflect his thought, include the Birth of the World, Evolution of Man, Have we a Soul Now? [Is the] Soul Independent of the Body? Why a Soul Has no Pre-Birth Memory, Reincarnation Doubted and more. According to the Red Cloud Weekly Advertiser, "His early religious training kept him through life, a "fundamentalist" in religious matters and he once wrote a book Evolution Proving Immortality," in 1917.[4]

As the Nebraska Fusion Party faded, Yeiser became a Republican.[25] His second book of 1917 presented his focus: My Country! My Congress! And a year later he returned to a basic concern: Debts of Today and Hell to Pay.[44] The new debts were part of the aftermath of World War I.[18] He wrote a letter to his Fellow Citizens on page seven of the book announcing himself a candidate for United States Senator to succeed Senator Hitchcock. "I shall make this race with no partisan bitterness toward the Administration, but support its war program in the campaign as republicans have supported it in congress, because we should not fight American parties, but concentrate upon the great foreign foe and I ask for your support because this is not a democratic war, but an allied American war and a war for humanity…" He formally threw his hat into the political ring as a candidate for the United States Senate in 1922 and for Chief Justice of Nebraska in 1926.[13]

In the article about Yeiser's sudden passing *The Weekly Advertiser* wrote: "Yeiser was a candidate for district judge at the April Primary, and was the second candidate to die, District Judge Wakeley falling to his death at the court house last week," they continued. "Wednesday Mr. Yeiser, apparently in good health was at his office as usual and spent a good deal of time visiting friends, down town giving them circulars relating to his candidacy. In that circular was a phrase characteristic of him and his attitude toward life: 'Whether I win or lose, you will always find me the same old scout, happy in my citizenship among you and always glad to say, 'good morning.'"[4]

John O. Yeiser was a lawyer, author, political, economist, and populist. He was a successful contestant and servant of the people from a seat in the Nebraska House of Representatives from Douglas County, tenth district. He claimed faith in the God of Creation and His Son Jesus and spoke out showing his views of how Science and that God of Creation worked together not separately. He also did not hesitate to speak out for his country and its people against injustices and ignorance. Yeiser was sixty-one in March 1928. He died of heart trouble in his sleep.[4]

According to the Cole-McKay Mortuary[13] statement John O. Yeiser, Jr. intended to carry on the law business. Yeiser, Jr. owned WDV, an Omaha radio station becoming part of early United States broadcast history. He had also been elected by Douglas County 10th District as a Republican to the Nebraska State House of Representatives in 1921. According to various history websites the burial site of the Yeisers are unknown. However, John O. Yeiser, Sr. has a headstone in the Red Cloud Cemetery as part of a family plot with eight spaces.[45,46,47,48,49]

Red Cloud, Nebraska Cemetery[6]

John O. Yeiser 1865-1928

Endnotes, Footnotes & Sources

[1] Nebraska State Historical Society (NSHS) Collections, Lincoln, Nebraska. Thank you to the NSHS staff for assistance locating the files and permission to publish the photo for the Honorable John O. Yeiser. Reviewed November 11, 2011.

[2] www.worldcat.org. World Catalog listing of books for *John O Yeiser*. Reviewed November 11, 2011.

[3] www.usgennet.org. *Hon. John O. Yeiser State Representatives*. Reviewed August 1, 2012. This site lists a work he is writing as they complete their Nebraska State Representatives biographical history for that election cycle, however, the work is not listed in any other location: "The Abolition of Both Public and Private Property in Land and Occupancy Rights."

[4] *The Weekly Advertiser*. "J.O. Yeiser, Veteran Omaha Lawyer Dies," Red Cloud, Webster County, Nebraska, Friday, March 30, 1928, p 1- 2.

[5] Research visit to Ashland, including newspaper and review of history of the area. No records were found in the early history of the Ashland area about the family. Visit on January 7, 2013, Nancy's files.

[6] Thank you to Deb McGuire at Red Cloud City Hall for assistance in locating the family cemetery plot. Although her list had only a couple names listed it was known that more burials had been done at the site. John O. Yeiser has a marker in that family plot, but at this publication it is not yet listed in the City Hall book. Visit on March 19, 2013, Nancy Sue Hansen's files. Gravesite photo by Nancy Hansen, 2013.

[7] www.redcloudnebraska.com. Red Cloud History. Reviewed June 14, 2013.

[8] R.R. Burchett, Earthquakes in Nebraska by, Educational Circular No. 4, Conservation and Survey Division, Institute of Agriculture and Natural Resources, The University of Nebraska-Lincoln. Supported by Contract NRC 04-76-315 U.S. Nuclear Regulatory Commission, 1979. Garland, Seward County, earthquake November15, 1877.

[9] www.en.wikipedia.org/wiki. *Earthquake history in Custer County, Greeley County, Howard County and Valley County, Nebraska, USA, 1867 to 2012*. Reviewed May 2013.

[10] Betty Stevens. Shifting Winds. Nebraska's Weather Story. Lincoln: Journal-Star Printing Co. 1994, p 49.

[11] www.gendisasters.com. *Hastings, Nebraska Fire of Sept 16, 1879*. Reviewed June 14, 2013.

[12] Thank you to Brian Striman at the University of Nebraska-Lincoln Law Library Reference Desk and the staff of the Admission/Registrar Records for assistance in locating any information about lawyer John O. Yeiser. Photos were found for graduates Clint and Joseph Yeiser in 1899's, nothing found in school records for John or any relationship to the two graduates. Visit November 11, 2011, notes in Nancy Sue Hansen's file.

[13] *John O. Yeiser.* Cole-McKay Mortuary, March 30, 1928, *"Mr. Yeiser was a candidate for the United States Senate in 1922 and for Chief Justice of Nebraska in 1926. He was a republican. He was a member of the First Christian Church, His wife and their only son John O. Yeiser, Jr. of Omaha survive. The son announced he would carry on the law business. Mr. Yeiser had litigation involving one half million dollars pending in court."*

[14] Hansen, Nancy Sue and Dush, Barbara Ann. Nebraska Authors Volume One. "Rex German." Fullerton: D & H Adventures Publishing. 2013.

[15] Hansen, Nancy Sue and Dush, Barbara Ann. Nebraska Authors Volume One. "Francis LaFlesche." Fullerton: D & H Adventures Publishing. 2013.

[16] Hansen, Nancy Sue and Dush, Barbara Ann. Nebraska Authors Volume One. "Ruth Van Ackeren." Fullerton: D & H Adventures Publishing. 2013.

[17] Hansen, Nancy Sue and Dush, Barbara Ann. Nebraska Authors Volume One. "Robert Howard." Fullerton: D & H Adventures Publishing. 2013.

[18] Hansen, Nancy Sue and Dush, Barbara Ann. Nebraska Authors Volume One. "Fred R. Fairchild." Fullerton: D & H Adventures Publishing. 2013.

[19]Labor as Money. 1894. Subtitle: Presenting a practical automatic currency of Stationary value, contracting and relaxing according to the demands of the country for exchange. *Dedicated "to the members of the fifty-fourth Congress. This book is most respectfully dedicated by the author."* On page previous to the Preface *"The Question of Finance. We demand a national currency, Safe, Sound, and Flexible, issued by the General Government only, a full legal tender for all debts, public and private, and that without the use of banking corporations, a just, equitable and efficient means of distribution direct to the people (at a tax not to exceed 2 per cent per annum), to be provided as set forth in the subtreasury plan of the Farmers' Alliance,[22] or a Better System' Also by Payments in discharge of its obligations for Public Improvements."-Omaha Platform.*

[20]Hansen, Nancy Sue and Dush, Barbara Ann. Nebraska Authors Volume One. "J. Sterling Morton." C.S. Paine," "Dr. George Miller," "Albert Watkins," and "Grant Shumway." Fullerton: D & H Adventures Publishing, 2013.

[21]Hansen, Nancy Sue and Dush, Barbara Ann. Nebraska Authors Volume One. "Henry P. Fairchild." Fullerton: D & H Adventures Publishing. 2013.

[22]Hansen, Nancy Sue and Dush, Barbara Ann. Nebraska Authors Volume One. "Luna Kellie." Fullerton: D & H Adventures Publishing. 2013.

[23] Nebraska State Historical Society, on-line, *Elections in Nebraska 1886*. Reviewed March 5, 2013.

[24] www.wikipedia.org. "Fusion Party." Reviewed March 5, 2013.

[25] The Fusion Party, technically, has several meanings around the country. It was the original name of the Republican Party in Ohio in 1854. It was so named as their members were from the Free Soil Party, the Conscience Whig Party, the Know-Nothing Party and some Democrats with their focus as opposition to slavery. The Republican Party was formed and given its name in 1854 and author O.C. Dake[26] drove with a new speaker, Abraham Lincoln in Illinois, to oratory events five years later. In South Dakota the Fusion Party was formed in 1896 as an alliance between Democrats, Free-Silver Republicans and Populists who were opposed to the platform of the Republican Party.

[26] Hansen, Nancy Sue and Dush, Barbara Ann. Nebraska Authors Volume One. "O.C. Dake." Fullerton: D & H Adventures Publishing. 2013.

[27] While the Nebraska Authors Project authors were researching J. Sterling Morton[20] a letter, dated August 26, 1899, from the Peoples' Independent Party of Nebraska was found in his papers regarding the Populist, Fusion, and Republican Parties. The letter encourages Morton, as a member of the press, to write about their activities. It is published in the appendix of this volume as a historical document about the parties of the time. Mr. Yeiser was not listed in the letter, however, was active during the date(s) of the letter.

[28]Thank you to the staff of the Supreme Court Library at the Nebraska State Capitol Lincoln for assistance in finding the House Journals and making copies of the research findings. Visit June 4, 2013, notes in Nancy's files.

[29] Nebraska House Journal, 1897. pp 320-321. Reviewed June 4, 2013.

[30]Nebraska House Journal, 1897, p 628. Reviewed June 4, 2013.

[31]Nebraska House Journal 1897, pp 1271-1273, "House Roll No. 465, by Mr. Yeiser. A bill for an act requiring railroad companies to receive bicycles as baggage and transport the same for passengers without requiring the same to be crated or protected, upon the same terms and conditions and subject to the same liabilities on other baggage." It was referred after the second reading, and indefinitely postponed.

[32] Nebraska House Journal 1897, pp 1271-1273, "House Roll No 466, by Mr. Yeiser. A bill for an act requiring all owners of mortgages, real or personal, stocks, bonds, securities, commercial paper, and credits, deeds in trust, an-

nuities, franchises and royalties owned in or owing from residents of this state to schedule such property as they own, fixing the itemized value thereof, and to file the same with the county clerk; Provided, That such valuation of such property shall be the assessment of such property for taxation, providing that no action shall be maintained by the owner of such property or his assignee in any court to recover upon any such property which has not been so scheduled, and that no action shall be maintained in any court by the owner of such property, or his assignee to recover upon any such property any greater sum than that at which it was so valued." It was referred after the second reading and indefinitely postponed.

[33] Nebraska House Journal 1897, pp 1271-1273, "House Roll No. 467, by John O. Yeiser. A bill for an act fixing street railroad fares, regulating transfers from one line of street railroad to another line or branch of street railroad, and fixing a penalty for the violation of the provisions of this act." It was referred after the second reading and indefinitely postponed.

[34] Nebraska House Journal 1897, pp 1271-1273, "House Roll No. 468, by John O. Yeiser. A bill for an act defining the liability of railway corporations on account of negligence of their agents, servants, and employees in the operation of the railways in this state." It was referred after the second reading and indefinitely postponed.

[35] Nebraska House Journal 1897, pp 1271-1273, "House Roll No. 469, by John O. Yeiser. A bill for an act to vest in courts of equality the power to decree a marriage between parties who may have cohabited." It was referred after the second reading and indefinitely postponed.

[36] Nebraska House Journal 1897, pp 1271-1273, "House Roll No. 470, by John O. Yeiser. A bill for an act to add sections 904a, 904b, and 904c to chapter 1, title 30, Code of Civil Procedure Compiled Statues of Nebraska for 1891, entitled "Justices of the Peace," and providing the place where suits in justice courts may be brought and providing against assignment of choices in action for the purpose of suit in precincts where neither plaintiff nor defendant resides, and to amend sections 954, 955, 956 and 958, chapter 4, title 30, of the Code of Civil Procedure, Complied Statutes of Nebraska for 1891 relating to change of venue in justice courts, and to repeal sections 954, 955, 956, 958, 958a, 958b as now existing." It was referred after the second reading and indefinitely postponed.

[37] Nebraska House Journal 1897, pp 1271-1273, "House Roll No 471, by John O. Yeiser. A bill for an act to amend section 1076 of chapter 13 of the Compiled Statutes of Nebraska of 1895, and to repeal section 1076 as heretofore existing." It was referred after the second reading and indefinitely postponed.

[38] Nebraska House Journal 1897, pp 1271-1273, "House Roll No 472, by John O. Yeiser. A bill for an act to authorize the district judges to fix the number

and compensation of the deputy sheriffs, jailers, jail guards, and sheriff's assistants in counties constituting their respective districts and prescribing the manner of fixing the same; to amend section 3135 of chapter 28 of the Compiled statutes of Nebraska for the year 1895, and to repeal said section as now existing, and to repeal section 2850 of chapter 24 of the Complied Statutes of Nebraska for the year 1895." It was referred after the second reading and indefinitely postponed.

[39] www.iandrinstitute.org. Initiatives and Referendum history. reviewed June 14, 2013.
"*In 1897, Nebraska became the first state to provide the initiative and referendum for general use in cities. The law, sponsored by state Representative A.E. Sheldon, allowed citizens in each city and other municipal subdivisions to place initiatives and referendums on the ballot with petitions signed by 15 percent of voters. However, the law required the electorate approved to use of I & R before they could go into effect. The first cities to enable the initiative and referendum were Omaha and Lincoln in 1907. The state-level initiative and referendum were adopted in 1912. Early adoption efforts were led by Walter Breen of Omaha. Breen, a native of London, emigrated to the united States at age 17. After settling in Omaha, he became a successful real estate salesman, secretary of the Omaha Philosophical Society, and an organizer of the Populist Party of Nebraska. Direct legislation supporters, many of them prohibitionists, were thwarted by liquor interests until 1911. Support from presidential candidate William Jennings Bryan, who wrote, "I know of nothing that will do more than I&R to restore government to the hands of the people and keep it within their control," helped push an initiative and referendum law through the legislature in 1911. In 1912, Nebraska voters approved the constitutional amendment adopting I&R with 189,200 in favor and 15,315 against. One reason for the lopsided total was that the state's ratification procedure counted blank ballots as "yes" votes.*" See appendix in this volume for more about Nebraska I&R history.

[40] ballotpedia.org "The history of the Initative and Referendums. Reviewed June 13, 2013.

[41] www.wikipedia.com. *American Philosophical Society.* The American Philosophical Society was founded in 1743 in Philadelphia, Pennsylvania, by Benjamin Franklin and John Bartram as an off-shoot of an earlier club: Junto. It is considered to be the first learned society in the United States playing a role in the cultural and intellectual life of the nation for over two hundred seventy years. A museum is located at the site as a historical landmark. The Society was considered a scholarly organization of international reputation. Their aim was to promote "useful knowledge in the sciences and humanities through excellence in scholarly research, professional meetings, publications, library resources, and community outreach." The Omaha Philosophical Society was associated with the headquarters in Pennsylvania. reviewed June 14, 2013.

[42]Hansen, Nancy Sue and Dush, Barbara Ann. <u>Nebraska Authors Volume One</u>. "David P. Abbott." Fullerton: D & H Adventures Publishing. 2013.

[43]<u>Immortality Established Through Science</u>. Dedication: *"Although greatly indebted to Haeckel, Spencer, Huxley, Darwin, Buchner, Paine, Ingersoll and many other deep thinkers for part of my inspiration, I cannot dedicate this work to men who have not drawn the final conclusions from their great labors that I have reached, regardless of the profound respect I have for their ability."* "Men of the future-men who appreciate the magnitude of human life and what a wonderful thing it is to be born-men who have hope and ambition, who are not slaves of some habit of thought and who will appreciate this work-are the patrons for whom I labor and to whom I dedicate the same." P 124 *"By this process of reasoning I have not only satisfied myself that a future life is possible but the teaching of the Bible is in harmony, with such view; they strengthen each other. However any religion and any church which teaches a future life will be an aid to this sate of existence. The one which gives you the strongest conviction will be your greatest help. No new Bible, no new book of revelations, no new religion, no new church is necessary. This position is taken because I believe that the strongest physically demonstrable assurance of a future life that the Bible contains and which nature reveals is that which requires us to have faith to have eternal life."*

[44]<u>Debts of Today and Hell to Pay</u>. *"Should I have expended the money to print and give away 2,000 copies of this little book or purchased "Liberty Bonds"? I am doing both, but consider this of equal importance for the amount and a greater sacrifice. The bond money will be returned, but this is gone. I hope the expenditure will be of service to my country. I trust it will make the big subscribers, who have unselfishly and bravely invested, feel more secure and be persuaded to increase their loans to the Government and that it may induce the non-subscriber to bend every effort to do all that he possibly can. We must win this war and win it with the present system, or all is lost, but when it is won we may continue to fight for prosperity, freedom and civilization."* "Our Government debt must be paid- our private debts should also be paid. The Government obligations are staggering in amount and there is a mere pinch of gold with which to pay them." "May I explain later how the world's debts may be paid? What is being offered is no old theory-it has never been born and understood to be exploded. Please do not partially read and cast if aside with the impression you know what it is." On page 74 *"You men, who study every business detail, and who never figure on the science of money, which is the very basis of all business, will not miss a few dollars to enable your personal friends to think with you in advance upon a might question of readjustment you are about to face…use the brains God gave to meet the greatest issue of this unprecedented age, when the time is approaching for war factories to shut down, when soldiers will return out of work, and when debts and taxes fall due and hell is to pay. Sincerely, John O. Yeiser."*

[45]http://politicalgraveyard.com. *John O. Yeiser*. Reviewed 8/1/2012 recorded that burial location was unknown.

[46] Omaha Area Obit web site. Reviewed March 15, 2013 (DC: 20 June). This John O. Yeiser died June, 17 1928, at Muncie, Indiana. The author of this article did not research to see if this was Jr. or someone with the same name or Sr. with date and place of death incorrect.

[47] www.usgennet.org. <u>Nebraska Blue Book, 1920</u> *"Representatives" John O. Yeiser, Jr.*, Omaha District 10. Reviewed June 15, 2013.

[48] www.earlyradiohistory.us *June 30, 1922 Broadcast Station List*, John O. Yeiser Jr, WDV, Omaha. Reviewed June 15, 2013.

[49] http://politicalgraveyard.com John O. Yeiser, Jr. Reviewed August 1, 2012.

Nebraska Authors Book & Travel Club

Locate the most recent political platforms, local or state level, for two different political parties in Nebraska. Read them through and see if the people in positions in the State are following the platform(s) they were elected upon. Write an 'opinion' in your own words on what you find. Attach your short review experience opinion with this autograph box.

PATRICIA J. YOUNG

Patricia J. Young, 2012, Arkansas[1]

Date of Birth: Sept. 17, 1930
Location of Birth: farm, Calloway, NE
Education: Completed the first eight grades at country school
Graduated Calloway High School, 1948
Received the 3rd year elementary school teaching certificate
Currently lives between Arkansas and Calloway

Known Publications:

Young, Patricia J., Frances Engle Marks. Tears on Paper: the history and life stories of the orphan train riders. Idaho: Rathdrum publishers. 1990

Young, Patricia J., Jackie Young. Grandma's Favorites. Kearney: Morris Press.

Young, Patricia J., Nice 'N Naughty E-Mails. Self publish, n.d.

"Worth Repeating" columns in the weekly newspaper *Callaway Courier*.

"I was just watching a documentary on educational television about something called the Orphan Train. I was touched by the story of the little boy in the program: *Home At Last*," Patricia said. "I wrote to every newspaper in Nebraska asking if there were more children like him in Nebraska and the letters started to pour in. I had no idea what I was getting into."

The letters turned into interviews and then into her first book in 1990: <u>Tears on Paper</u>. "I didn't coin the term, 'Tears on Paper.' An Orphan Train Rider, Mary Tenopir, was asked what it felt like to be an orphan train Rider and Mary said, 'Tears Can't be Put on Paper.' That seemed to be a good summary for our book and we used it," Patricia explained.

Patricia J. Young, 2012[2]

Frances Engle Marks is the co-author Patricia was referring to as 'we'. "I have never met her," she said. "She lived in another state and had a word processor. I would interview the Orphan Train Riders and send her the tapes and notes and she would type them and send them back to me. She lives in Canada now."

The Orphan Trains steamed throughout the Midwest and Great Plains States from 1853 to 1929, many of them stopping in Nebraska. "It was the people and their stories, in those letters I got, that inspired me to find out the history and interview as many people as I could," Patricia said. Roughly 250,000 babies and children were sent out from the East Coast from different agencies to families in mid-America. Most were sent from the Children's Aide Society and the Catholic Foundling Home.

"Mary Ellen Johnson founded the Orphan Train Heritage Society of America in 1986. She lived in Springdale, Arkansas, so the headquarters was there," Patricia continued. "The organization hosted events nationally for families of Orphan Train Riders and assisted with tracing families. Nebraska and Minnesota usually have had the largest number of attendees." The Nebraska Orphan Train Riders also have events. The first Nebraska reunion was held in 1962 in Grand Island and have continued each year.

"The organization is an important link for the history of the Orphan Train and for the riders themselves. Some of the riders have never told their families, it is important to me that these riders come forward and tell their stories for their families and for the history of United States," Patricia said.

She continued, "These people have bonds which we will never experience nor truly feel. How some can remember the train ride and the anticipation of a new home in a new land with new parents or the horror of being separated from your brothers and sisters maybe never to see them again is amazing. Some remember standing on a stage and having people look you over to see if they wanted you for their little boy or girl, or worst of all, if no one wanted you and you had to be put on the train and go to the next stop."

There is controversy about the use of Orphan Trains today just as there was when the trains began. In June 1986, a lady wrote in the *Smithsonian* magazine "When I first read the records of what happened to the children on the Orphan Trains I was haunted by the feelings these children must have had. It seemed frightful, but when I looked at the conditions they were living in, I came to see that the placing program was a good one. Most of the children had better lives then if they would have stayed on the streets of New York," Patricia quoted the article.

She stated that the National Orphan Train Museum and Research Center is now part of the National Orphan Train Complex located in a remolded Union Pacific Railroad Depot in Concordia, Kansas. There is now a merger of the Orphan Train Heritage Society of America (OTHSA) and the National Orphan Train Complex (NOTC).

When asked if there was someone special among the riders, Patricia immediately said Mary Tenopir. "Her story is in the book. She is known for her work with the Nebraska Orphan Train Riders." And, as it turns out, was part of the cast of the TV documentary filmed at Stuhr Museum in Grand Island, Nebraska, that Patricia had seen so many years before. "She gave me many names of folks I visited and interviewed for the book," Patricia said.

"Then I met Fred Swedenburg from the Children's Aide Society. He became a good friend with a lot of information and new resources. There is not one person more special than any other," Patricia said confidently, "but I do have to mention Father Paul Fangman who was at every reunion. He was an interesting person. He was an Orphan Train Rider and always come to the reunions ready to give mass."

Patricia thought for a moment and then said, "There is a song they sing together at the reunions called <u>An Orphan's Prayer</u>. It is a ballad by Vera Kinter. The music is by one of the orphans, Marian Christiansen. It starts 'Why, oh why was I an orphan, No parents had I or family tree'. I'll send you a copy and maybe you can reprint it with this story". [see appendix of this volume].

There is one regret that Patricia still shakes her head about. "I was just getting started in getting all this information and I talked to a lady that said she was one of the children survivors from the Titanic. She had been taken to the Children's Aid Society and sent out on the Orphan Train," she said. Patricia was skeptical. "The woman kept telling me that there was something in a bank box that she would show me. Well, I didn't go to see her right away, but I did look up the names of the Titanic survivors and her name wasn't there. Then I studied up on the Titanic and found that it was mainly the wealthy that had their names listed on the records and there really were other survivors." By the time Patricia had done her background work, she was no longer able to contact the woman. "That is one missed story I will always regret," Patricia said.

Patricia explained that most of the riders she met along the way had "done without, made the best of what they had realizing they didn't have to be like their parents and most of them were over achievers because of it."

"There is one thing I will say about the riders I have met over the years," Patricia said. "Not one of them talk about their 'bad' life or 'abuse' that some of them endured as an excuse. They all wanted to excel and show that they were good people and intelligent." She went on to explain that many of these children, most smaller in stature than children around them, were treated as less intelligent and social outcasts even among their own siblings. Many of the riders have kept their background quiet as they didn't want to be teased and looked down on anymore. But over the years these riders have been found to be productive members of society and are now even putting the fact they were riders on their tombstones."

How productive did Patricia find the riders to be? Page twenty-nine of her book gives an example: "A Governor of a state, a Governor of a Territory, John Green Brady of Alaska, and Andrew Burke of North Dakota - two members of Congress, two District Attorneys, two sheriffs, two mayors, a Justice of the Supreme Court, four judges, two college professors, a cashier of an insurance company, twenty-four clergymen, seven high school principals, two school superintendents, and auditor-general of a state, nine members of the State legislatures, two artists, a senate clerk, six railroad officials, eighteen journalists, thirty-four bankers, nineteen physicians, thirty-five lawyers, twelve postmasters, three contractors, ninety-seven teachers, four civil engineers, and any number of business and processional men, clerks, mechanics, farmers and their wives, and others who filled honored positions plus four army officers and seven thousand soldiers and sailors."

Patricia explained that Frances was in charge of distribution of the book when it was completed and found that libraries were interested in purchasing the book. "There are many libraries that have the book because of her efforts," Patricia acknowledged. "We have never put our book into any contests or anything. We just wanted to tell the story, it is about them – the rider: not about us as the interviewers, typists, compliers."

The book was self-published and sold out quickly. They were talked into printing a second edition and that is sold out, too. "If anyone has a copy they don't need any more there are people who write me all the time for a copy and I don't have any. I sold or gave away all of my copies and even this first edition I had to buy at a library sale." The

Still writing, Patricia, Calloway, 2012[2]

library had two copies and was selling one and Patricia just happened to see it. She has a list of people waiting for copies of the book.

"We won't be re-printing it again. We have two printings out there now. There are a lot of books about the Orphan Train Riders now. In fact, there is one seven volume set. It is great." A list of materials, books, and history of the Orphan Trains can be found at www.orphantraindepot.com and, of course, at the museum in Concordia, Kansas.

"I still get letters from people I met while working on our book. There are a lot of new people, too. The stories and history of the Orphan Train Riders will not be forgotten and the contribution to Social History will not be forgotten as we continue to tell the stories and begin to find this history in our school books. I have saved all the correspondents, tapes, and interviews. When I stop my writing and corresponding I'll probably give that history to the Research Center in Kansas."

As to other books, Patricia and a sister-in-law Jackie Young made a family cookbook with drawings of all their grandmothers and used these drawings with their favorite recipes: <u>Grandma's Favorites</u>. It was published in Kearney, Nebraska at Morris Press. She also has a limited edition book titled <u>Nice 'N Naughty E-Mails</u> which she published a few years ago. The collection came from her gleaning of the web for her newspaper column "Worth Repeating," found weekly in the Callaway newspaper. "The column is meant to be light and funny. I put together jokes and funny stories I find." Patricia admits she loves poetry and sometimes a lyric or two will find its way into her articles, too.

Laughter: "Worth Repeating" [2]

While the stories of the riders of the Orphan Train are not poetry, they do tell a rhythmic whistle-stopping history of America and its children.

Endnotes, Footnotes & Sources:

[1]Thanks to Patricia and LeRoy Young for the interview, photos and correspondence.

[2] Interview notes in Nancy's files. Photos by Nancy at Calloway interview, 2012.

Nebraska Authors Book & Travel Club

Signature or take time to reflect on the first memories you have of your parents, grandparents, aunts, uncles, cousins and siblings. Write the memories down on paper (or computer). Add to these memories the sounds, smells and visuals in colors and seasons as you continue to reflect on them. Write the happy and the sad or scary times. Orphans, foster, or adopted children have pieces of memories just as children with one or both of their natural parents. Don't make up stories to fit the blanks in a memory, write the memory and at some point it will come together. Keep your memories as part of your heritage.

ORVILLE HERMAN ZABEL

Date of birth: Sept. 1, 1919
Location of birth: Western, NE
Education: Western H.S.-1937
A.B. 1941;
UN-L, M.A 1942
attended graduate school Univ of
Wisc.
University of Nebraska, Ph.D.
1955.
What NE town call home:
Fremont
Military: U.S. Army Air Corp.
WWII,
Air Force Reserves retired:
Colonel 1980
Date of death: Aug. 30, 1985

Dr. Orville H. Zabel, 1985

Known Publications:

Zabel, Orville Herman. Church and State in Nebraska 1854-1950: a study of the legal relationship. Ph.D. Thesis University of Nebraska, Lincoln 1954. (God and Caesar in Nebraska. A study of the legal relation-ship of church and state, 1854-1954. Published by various institutions and used as a textbook.)

Johnson, Edgar Nathaniel, Orville Herman Zabel. Study Guide for an Introduction to the History of the Western Tradition. Ginn Publication, Boston, 1959. Vol 1, 2.

Zabel, Oville Herman. "College Professors-As Viewed from the Other Side of the Desk". *Midland Viewpoint*, Midland College, February, 1959.

Zabel, Orville Herman. "To Reclaim the Wilderness: The Immigrant's Image of Territorial Nebraska." *Nebraska History*, December, 1965. (Vol 46, No 4), pp 315-324.

Zabel, Orville Herman. "Review of Wilderness Kingdom: Indian life in the Rocky Mountains, 1840-1847 by Nicolas Point," S.J. Sun Newspapers, November 21, 1967, p 11-A.

Zabel, Orville Herman. Review of "Vision for a Valley: Olof Olson and the Early History of Lindsborg" by Emory Lindquist (1970). *Journal of the Illinois State Historical Society*, summer, 1972.

Zabel, Orville Herman. Review of "Swedes in Chicago: A Demographic and Social Study of the 1846-1880 Immigration" by Ulf Beijbom (1971), *Journal of the Illinois State Historical Society*, Vol 67, No. 3, 1974.

Zabel, Orville Herman. "Community development: Another look at the Elkhorn Valley." *Nebraska History,* fall, 1973 (Vol 54, No 3), pp 383-398.

Zabel, Orville Herman. The bicentennial and the lively experiment. *International Catholic Review: Communio.* Summer, 1976 (Vol 3, No. 2). 151-164.

Zabel, Orville Herman. "History in Stone: The Story in Sculpture on the Exterior of the Nebraska Capitol" *Nebraska History*, fall 1981 (Vol 62, No. 3), pp 285-372. (This article received the James L. Sellers Award for the best article in Nebraska History by the Nebraska Historical Society.)

A Translation of the Annales of Lambert of Hersfeld (1073-1077)
Lambert, von Hersfeld, Zabel, Orville Herman; Ernstmeyer, M.S. published 1942, M.A. Thesis UN-L

Zabel, Orville Herman. "Nebraska" entrees in Americana Encyclopedia Annual, 1970, 1971, 1973, 1975, 1976, 1977, 1978, 1979, 1980, 1982, and 1983.

It was a continual love of education and history which propelled Dr. Orville H. Zabel through teaching at two post high school institutions in Nebraska and writing numerous articles, booklets, and study guides. His Ph.D. dissertation was reproduced at numerous institutions and used as a textbook resource. It is still used today as a basis to show changes and history of church and state issues.

Zabel's foundation for the love of history seems to have come, in part, from knowing his own family history. According to *The Midland* April 28, 1967, article "Zabel Family History Marks Excitement; Indian Scares, Steamboat Rides Common," Zabel had paid attention to stories his German grandparents told about the world around them and their reactions to the events from emigration. Weaving first hand stories into a history courses may have included a Nebraska dugout home, near famine with only pumpkins to eat one winter, and his maternal grandfather's Civil War experiences fighting with the Illinois military before moving to Saline County, Nebraska. According to quotes from those who knew Dr. Zabel, he was insistent that students knew more than dates and places in history: "Students need to know why the dates are important." He used his own experiences to inspire students to understand history for themselves.

Dr. Zabel gave an address to the Midland College Faculty Workshop in February 1959. From the *Midland Viewpoint* publication of the

speech, Zabel gave insight into his beliefs: "... *Besides, a spirit (college spirit) tied exclusively to athletics is very insecure indeed, for it may fade when the promising quarterback chooses some other school...I suggest, ...the faculty is most responsible for that intangible thing we call "spirit"...If this assumption about the importance of the faculty in* [Midland Viewpoint] *producing a college spirit is valid, one may justly ask 'What professorial characteristics help to provide a real school spirit?' My observations suggest that such characteristics may be placed into three overlapping categories: a professor should be a human being; a professor should be a student; and a professor should be a teacher.*" Perhaps it was this belief which his life put into action that produced the headlines "Professor 'inspires' students" from the October 12, 1985, *The Midland.*

Zabel was "drafted early in World War II. He had a bachelors and masters in political science and history so he went into Officers Training," said his son Robert during a phone interview for the story. "He served as a 2nd Lieutenant in Florida, Oklahoma, Indiana, and Nebraska among other sites. I remember him as a captain."

It was after his World War II experiences, his business administration courses at Harvard while stationed in the Army Air Corp in the area, and his attending classes at the University of Wisconsin that he was hired by Midland Lutheran College in Fremont. He finished his PhD in 1955 at the University of Nebraska. He served as Midland's Dean of Men and Chairman of the Division of History and Social Sciences, full-time, 1948-1967.

He became the sponsor of the International Relations Club (I.R.C.) in 1948 during his first year teaching at Midland. He was instrumental in organizing the National Association of International Relations Clubs, and served seven years as National Advisor for American I.R.C. By 1965 the local club was recognized as one of the nation's outstanding clubs. Midland held two national and one regional conference for the American I.R.C.

He left Midland College in 1967 to join the history department at Creighton University in Omaha where he retired as Professor Emeritus in 1983. He received the Kennedy Teaching Excellence Award in 1975 which is awarded yearly by the student body. Zabel returned to Midland Lutheran College in Fremont to teach part time 1982-85. He received the Zimmerman Distinguished Professorship 1983-84 and 1984-85.

Zabel also continued to serve in the Air Force Reserves completing active duties in Washington, D.C., the Air Force Academy and other locations. "I remember he would

Orville H. Zabel, 1967

have a couple of weeks of active duty with the specialization in Intelligence," son Robert recalled. He retired at the rank of Colonel. His family remembers the focus he had in assisting recruits who wanted to attend the Air Force Academy as some of his final military duties. "He worked with the recruit and the Congressional representatives to get their appointments," Robert added.

There were two educational focuses of interest outside of the

Dr. Zabel and student Walter Haag discussing the Air Force, cira 1967

traditional classroom in which Zabel also had popular roles. He was active in the United Methodist Church, and served in leadership roles in his local congregation and within the Nebraska Methodist Synod. He was a certified lay minister who often was a guest minister in Methodist and other protestant churches. He was also passionate, and a popular speaker, about the Nebraska Capitol. His award winning writings remain a viable resource regarding the sculpture on the exterior of the capitol.

Orville Zabel was married to Irene Matzke Zabel for forty-five years. They had three sons. At his death he was returned to Western, Nebraska, in Saline County, to be buried near the farm where he was born. N

Endnotes, Footnotes & Sources:

The Midland and the *Midland Viewpoint* publications, Midland Lutheran College, Fremont, Nebraska.

Zajicek Funeral Home, Wilber-Western, Nebraska, memorial leaflet.

Thanks to the library staff at Midland Lutheran (College) University, Fremont, Nebraska: Barbara Coke, Director Barbara Dean, and Dr. Thomas Boyle, Kelly Johnson. And to Nate Neufind, the Director of Communications of Midland University, for permission to re-publish photos.

Special thanks to Willie and Cloe Zabel, Lincoln, son of the late William Zabel, grandson of Orville for answering our letter sent to see if the addressee was related to Orville and referring us to Robert "Bob" Zabel, Minneapolis, and Jim Zabel, Chicago, sons of Orville and Irene.

Nebraska Authors Book & Travel Club

Visit Midland Lutheran University Campus. Have a photo taken of yourself at a Midland event or while walking the campus.

DARRYL FRANCIS ZANUCK

Date of Birth: Sept. 5, 1902
Location of Birth: Wahoo, NE
NE towns called home? Wahoo/ Oakdale
Education: Elementary/military school, CA
Oakdale, NE until age 14
Military: Private First Class, 34th US National Guard WWI, 1916-1919
& Colonel in Signal Corp, WWII, 1942-43
Date of Death: Dec 22, 1979
Location of Death: Palm Springs, CA
Author's pen names: Gregory Rogers, Melville Crossman, Mark Canfield

Darryl Francis Zanuck

Known Publications:

Zanuck, Darryl F. wrote for the *A.E.F. newspaper*, and *The Stars and Stripes*.

Zanuck wrote several short stories and articles including "The Man Who Lived Time" and hundreds of television and movie scripts.

Zanuck, Darryl F. <u>Habit</u> and other stories: A thrilling yarn that starts where fiction ends and life begins. Los Angeles: Time-Mirror, 1923, 311 pp.

According to the front page story of the Wahoo, Nebraska, newspaper announcing Darryl Francis Zanuck's death, "He stood 5 ft. 6 ¾ inches tall, weighed 142 pounds and embodied what may be nature's ultimate effort to equip the species for outstanding success. Zanuck was endowed with a tough-mindedness, talent, an out-sized ego, and a glutton's craving for hard work. These qualities made him a leader for a quarter of a century."[1] Who was Darryl F. Zanuck?

Zanuck was a powerful Hollywood, California, movie producer for almost fifty years. According to the newspaper article, he supervised more than 1,500 motion pictures. He co-founded 20th Century Studios in 1933. It merged with Fox Studios and Zanuck became CEO. The beginning of that career was in Nebraska.

Iowan Frank Zanuck married Louise Torpin of Oakdale, Nebraska, in the early 1890s. They managed the La Grande Hotel in Wahoo, Nebraska, which was owned by Henry Torpin, Louise's father. The couple had two sons. Donald was born in 1893 and Darryl was born in a second floor room at the Hotel in 1902. Donald died in El Paso, Texas, a year later, 1903, after being kicked by a horse. According to records at the Saunders County Museum in Wahoo, Frank apparently became a gambler and drinker. Louise divorced Frank and took their son to Glendale, California, where she thought she could recover from tuberculosis. She married Joseph/C.C. Norton who was abusive to both Louise and Darryl. Zanuck was sent off for elementary education at a military school. He constantly skipped school and went to the movies. He had his first movie role at age seven as an Indian maiden in a western.

When Zanuck was thirteen he was sent to Oakdale to live with his grandfather. By all accounts Zanuck idolized his grandfather Henry Torpin. Torpin, a wealthy businessman and land owner, told his grandson wild west stories and introduced him to outdoor life. Zanuck loved hunting, riding horses, and learned polo. He later traveled the world taking part in sports using the skills his grandfather taught him.

Zanuck World War I[3]

Although Zanuck loved his grandfather he considered World War I more exciting. He lied about his age, and joined the army at age fourteen. He was sent to Camp Cody, Deming, New Mexico, with the 34th (later 37th) Division 109 Sanitary Train as a Private First Class, National Guard. He was sent to New Jersey, and then shipped to Europe where he saw brief action in Belgium. According to museum files, he neither fired a shot nor reached German soil, but did receive two non-combat related wounds. He sent letters about what he saw in Europe home to his grandfather. He was mustered out of the Army in September 1919. He went briefly to Oakdale, Nebraska, and then moved to Los Angeles with aspirations to become a writer.

He worked as a long-shoreman at the San Pedro waterfront and became a lightweight fighter. According to reports, he was knocked out in his first bout in the ring. He began a business called the Darryl Poster Service which featured outdoor advertising. He sold some short stories to a magazine and adapted some stage plays for the screen. Sometimes he wrote under a pen-name. He had three names he used to submit stories: Gregory Rogers, Melville Crossman and Mark Canfield. He became a gag writer and then moved up to screen writing. He wrote his novel: <u>Habit</u>.

In 1923 he began work for Harry and Jack Warner of Warner Bros. Studio. During his first year he wrote twenty scripts for about $125.00 a week. The majority of them were for the popular dog star, *Rin Tin Tin*. From screen writer to head of production at age twenty-five, Zanuck's successes already included some of the Charlie Chaplin movies.

He married Virginia Fox, an actress in movies with Buster Keaton and the Keystone Cops. They were married by a Justice of the Peace on January 24, 1924, and remained married to each other until death.

Zanuck and the Warner Studios were pioneers creating features involving talking sequences in their movies. Zanuck supervised *The Jazz Singer* with the popular Al Jolson, which became the first movie using the new techniques. Zanuck took the new techniques and turned out *Little Caesar, Public Enemy*, and the 'gangster' films of the 1920s, including the James Cagney films.

In 1933 Zanuck left Warner Brothers Studios and co-founded 20th Century Studios, which quickly merged with Fox Studios becoming the 20th Century Fox Studios. They were responsible for many movies with memorable stars such as Shirley Temple, Eddie Robinson, Marilyn Monroe, Betty Grable, Tyrone Power, and Dick Widmark to name a few. Movies included: *The Grapes of Wrath* (1940), *How Green Was My Valley* (1941), *Winged Victory* (1944), *The Razor's Edge* (1946), *Gentlemen's Agreement* (1947), and *Viva Zapata!* (1952).

Darryl Zanuck with his daughter Darrylin (R) and Shirley Temple (L).

From 1942-43, Zanuck joined other Americans in WWII. He served as a Colonel in the Signal Corp. first being sent to London as Chief U.S. liaison to Britain film units. He also filmed fighting in Algeria and Tunis and numerous other outposts. When his deployment ended he returned to Hollywood, maintaining his powerful status during the so-called Golden Age of Hollywood. He continued to make movies with new techniques, technologies and twenty-hour work days. Many of his movies were considered social conscious pictures dealing with controversial topics like racism, semitism, and mental illness.

It was President Woodrow Wilson that Zanuck admired for his contributions to world peace after World War I. After WWII Zanuck felt the public was ready for a serious theme: a biography of Wilson. Despite the historic opposition[2] to WWI from Nebraska Senator Norris and others, Zanuck felt that the movie would be an honor to the spirit of the country and Nebraska should present the world premiere of *Wilson*. On October 10, 1944, a train carried stars Betty Grable, Bette Davis, Dana Andrews, Gene Tierney, Joan Fontaine, Tyrone Power, and Jennifer Jones along with the Zanuck family from Hollywood to Omaha for the premiere event. *All About Eve* (1950) gave Bette Davis and Zanuck awards.

In 1957, he stepped down from the helm at 20th Century Fox to start his own company: DFZ Productions. He spent a lot of time in

Europe over the next few years while his family remained in the United States. The results of his previous European adventures were films such as *Island in the Sun* and *The Longest Day*. According to museum notes, Zanuck often made films he wanted to make rather than what the critics or the public wanted to see. *The Longest Day* was one of those films. It was telling the story of war from the viewpoints of those who took part in it. He used his personal contacts from his service in WWII to secure, on loan, authentic WWII military equipment and personnel for the movie. The World Premiere was in Paris with Charles de Gaulle, the entire French Cabinet, NATO Commanders, and the diplomatic corps as guests.

In the meantime, 20th Century Fox was headed toward bankruptcy with only one unfinished picture, *Cleopatra*, and one hit 30-minute TV series: *Dobie Gillis*. Zanuck returned to the United States and to 20th Century Fox in 1962 to make *Cleopatra* a box office smash, produce a half-dozen new TV hits, and create the movie *Hello Dolly*. It was a new beginning. In 1971, he was elected president emeritus of the studio. He had three Oscars and three Irving S. Thalberg Memorial awards voted by the Academy of Motion Picture Arts and Sciences for the "Most Consistent High Quality of Production Achievement". Most of all he had produced numerous movies whose names and stars many movie and television fans still know today.

Zanuck didn't forget he was from Nebraska. According to the Wahoo newspaper article, when "solicitations were being made for the construction of the Veterans Memorial building Darryl Zanuck sent his contribution of $1,000 and a large water-color portrait of himself." Later when Luther Junior College needed choir robes he had his designers create a design for them. He received an honorary doctorate degree from the University of Nebraska and in turn issued an invitation to Wahoo residents to" visit him and his studio sometime". The invitation stood until he retired.

Darryl and Virginia had three children. Richard Darryl Zanuck was born in 1934 and followed in his father's footsteps producing movies at 20th Century Fox. He was responsible for movies like: *The Sting*, *The Sound of Music*, *MASH*, *Jaws*, *Cocoon*, *Driving Miss Daisy*, and *Charlie and the Chocolate Factory*. Daughter Susan, born in 1933, died in 1980. Daughter Darrylin, born in 1931, became active in preserving her father's memory and legacy. Both Virginia and Darrylin were in regular correspondence with Nebraskans, especially the Wahoo

Woman's Club. The family sent a trophy from the movie *David and Bathsheba* to the Club for display.

According to the Wahoo newspaper article, "He is quoted as saying: I don't want to sound immodest, but a lot of that Golden Age of Hollywood was of my own making. And while I don't live in the past, I'm proud of what I did. If I had another chance, I'd do it the same way. Hell, every man is a captive of his own nature, his own talents. I was never much of a writer. I left school at the end of the eighth grade. But I was always a prolific and creative idea man."

Controversial to some during his life, the research shows there is controversy about his death as well. The on-line encyclopedia Wikipedia says Zanuck was a long time cigar smoker and died of jaw cancer. According to the Wahoo newspaper article, he died after suffering a stroke while recovering from a bout with pneumonia. Either way, it was just before Christmas 1979 when he died.

Zanuck's daughter Darrylin provided many of her father's plaques, an Oscar and papers now housed on the first floor at the Saunders County Museum in Wahoo. Among the hundreds of memoirs are thank yous to both Mr. and Mrs. Zanuck, such as the 1947 presentation for a donation to Darryl as a "Construction Engineer of the House of Magic otherwise known as the Shriners Hospital for Crippled Children in Los Angeles" and a plaque received by Virginia: "*The Gold Circle of California, an organization dedicated to furthering the highest principles of the good in California recognizes as a member Mrs. Darryl Zanuck one of California's most distinguished and dedicated citizens. Signed Ronald Reagan, Governor and John Wayne, Chairman. 1970-1971, 1972-1973.*"

There have been several books and television documentaries about Darryl F. Zanuck. One book about his life may be of interest: Rudy Behlmer published a selection of his letters and memoranda in <u>Memo from Darryl F. Zanuck: the golden years at Twentieth Century-Fox</u>. Grove Publishers, 1993. Other books for consideration are one by Mel Gussow in 1971, <u>Don't Say Yes Until I Finish Talking: A Biography of Darryl F. Zanuck</u>; <u>Zanuck: the Rise and Fall of Hollywood's Last Tycoon</u> by Leonard Mosley, 1984 and Stephen M. Silverman, 1988, <u>The Fox That Got Away! The Last Days of the Zanuck Dynasty at Twentieth-Century Fox</u>.

Next time you see the credits roll as that old television show or movie begins you might consider giving it a fresh look, remembering it was how a Nebraskan saw the world, produced and programmed it, and sent it back to you for entertainment. N

Endnotes, Footnotes & Sources:

[1] *Wahoo, Nebraska, Newspaper.* "Famous Son, Darryl F. Zanuck, Dead at 77." Front page, December 27. 1979.

[2] Hansen, Nancy Sue and Dush, Barbara Ann. Nebraska Authors Volume One. "Frederic Babcock." Fullerton: D & H Publishing, 2013.

[3] Saunders County Historical Society, Wahoo, Nebraska photo collection permission to publish all photos with this story.

www.wikipedia.com. *Darryl F. Zanuck*. Reviewed April 2013.

Thanks to Janet Maly and staff at the Wahoo Public Library for help with background for this story.

Special thanks to Erin Hauser, Curator of the Saunders County Historical Society in Wahoo, Nebraska.

Nebraska Authors Book & Travel Club

Visit the first floor exhibit at the Saunders County Historical Society County Museum, Wahoo, Nebraska. Check www.saunderscountymuseum.org for hours of operation. Attach a ticket or have a museum staffer sign and date this box.

Appendix

Note of Thanks:

Special thanks to Mary Dohmen, Karen Meyer, Susan Peterson, and Jan Shull for their assistance in proof reading this volume during different stages of completion.

Special thanks to our families for time we spent going over transcripts and copies of research and formulating thoughts for stories when we could have been doing something with them.

Thanks to Jeri at Copycat in Grand Island who came to our rescue when we didn't have the correct program to complete the formatting for printing, and to Jan at Henderson Service Press for waiting as we changed our proposed date of publication more than once.

Special recognition to those authors before us, who accumulated names and stories about authors of their day, giving us the opportunity to put all the lists together and, at some point, produce a work on the subjects these authors wrote about. The goal is to present Nebraska in history.

Additions and corrections and Index to Volume One

Care has been taken to prevent typographical errors and mislabeling of photos as much as possible. However, if an error has been made in the substance of information in a story, a misspelling or mislabeling, please understand that it was not intentional. Contact D & H Adventures Publishing at P.O. Box 112, Fullerton, Nebraska 68638 with the information you wish to have reviewed for an error. If an error is found it will be acknowledged by making the correction in the next printing and by printing it in the Index Volume which is planned after about 130 stories have been written.

Each index will list subjects accumulated in the previous volumes for those who wish to use the information for study of Nebraska history. The Index Volumes will have one set of stories with the accumulated index and be presented and sold as any other volume.

Bone Creek Museum of Agrarian Art, David City, Nebraska

In an interview trip to David City Nancy introduced Barb to the Bone Creek Museum as they were ready to leave town; it was a relaxation side trip for the day. The trip accordingly provided two authors: Guenther and Nichols. The Nebraska Authors Project® decided to highlight at least one museum or similar facility in each volume. The first volume highlights Bone Creek Museum of Agrarian Art in David City, Nebraska.

The Bone Creek Museum is attempting to move from their store front location near downtown David City to a building of their own which will display more agrarian art especially of Nebraska, Mid-west and Great Plains Artists. Amanda Mobley Guenther wrote a book for the Museum for a Dale Nichols art exhibition and the proceeds assist in the building program.

Volume One highlighted both the Guenther book and Nichols books for your enjoyment. Many other artists are displayed at the Museum and there are other books about Nebraska artists which will be presented in other volumes about Nebraska Authors. Enjoy Bone Creek Museum of Agrarian Art in David City and perhaps their dream of building their own facility will become a reality for us all.

Daddy, Tell Me A Story

by

GEORGE L. JACKSON

Drawings by
MILDRED PALMGREN
and WALTER THOMAS

Pioneer Publishing Company
Kearney, Nebraska

Introduction

To Parents, Teachers, and others who
may be interested in,

"WHY JOHNNY CAN'T READ"

For a number of years we have been reading and hearing about "Why Johnny Can't Read." Of course, a few of those who look on the bright side of things, or those whose experiences have been happy, contend that in fact Johnny *can* read.

And it seems agreed that those who contend that "Johnny Can't Read" do not in fact brand him as an absolute illiterate. Rather, it is a matter of comparing Johnny, – who seems to be somewhere between the fifth and eighth

9

grades, — with his father, grandfather, and great-grandfather when they were about his age and in the same grades in school.

Here indeed the vast majority seems to agree that Johnny compares unfavorably with his preceding generations. Considering the technological advances that have been made in all other fields of endeavor, this situation seems strange. The question is, — what has happened here?

A few of us hardy old timers, — with whom Johnny is being compared, — can look back upon our childhood at the turn of the century and recall what we were given to read and how well we did it.

We had first, second, third, and fourth readers. Kindergarten had not yet been imported from Germany. In the first grade we learned the alphabet. We recited the letters and sang them until we could say our A B C 's. We "sounded out" the new words in our reader, and then we spelled them over and over again. By the end of the year we had

mastered a hundred or so small words which we could read or spell at the drop of a hat. We could also write them, and we had learned to count to one hundred.

The second, third, and fourth readers were progressively more difficult but were built exactly on the first-reader foundation. We were drilled on phonics and sounded out the new words. If we were still baffled we would hold up our hands and "ask teacher." We were drilled in spelling. This was climaxed by the Friday afternoon "spell-downs."

By the fourth grade we were taking grammar with its diagramming of sentences and learning about nouns, pronouns, verbs, adjectives, adverbs and prepositions. Spelling drill continued. Tough words were showing up but we had to stick with it until we could master such words as Massachusetts, assafoetida and orthography. We not only knew the spelling of this last word, but we also knew its meaning, and we had been eternally drilled on all its phases. We knew about synonyms, antonyms, and homonyms. There were lists of these in our speller, so we could recognize them and know what to do about them when we found them in our reading.

In the fourth grade we would go through one publisher's Fourth Reader. In the fifth grade we would take another publisher's Fourth Reader, or perhaps just go through the same book a second time. These fourth readers contained such gems as *Crossing the Bar*, *Thanatopsis*, and *Washington's Farewell Address*. These books were printed with small type, about like that used in newspapers, and there were few, if any, pictures in them. It is quite likely that a book like this would seem formidable to most of our present fourth graders.

Having completed the Fourth Reader, — the subject of reading was behind us. It was assumed without further concern that now we could read. So during the sixth, seventh, and eighth grades we were studying "Literature." Our texts here were a series of pamphlets, *Evan-*

geline, *The Merchant of Venice*, *Julius Caesar*, etc. The Shakespearian plays were straight from the author and with no editing for juveniles. We struggled through them and still know, over a half century later, the general themes of the stories. These were not easy. They were not intended to be easy. We were the "big kids" in school. *Chicken Little* and *The Three Bears* were far behind us.

When we were through the eighth grade the vast majority had graduated. We, like our fathers, went out into the world. We could read, write and figure well enough to build railroads from coast to coast, build vast cities, industries, and financial institutions. We invented automobiles, electric lights, and thousands of other things that are taken today for granted. Why could the sixth to eighth graders, — or that equivalent in schools which were not graded, — from the times of Washington, Lincoln, Ford and Edison read, write, and figure so well that the country grew faster and became more prosperous than any other nation in a similar span in history?

This question brings us to the heart of our problem, — "Why can't Johnny read, or write, or spell, or figure like the old timers could do when they were his age?" Is his time being wasted?

Indeed many educators agree that it is being wasted, — that it must be wasted. The law will not permit Johnny to go out into the world to be a full-time hand at fourteen like his grandfather did. So there is nothing to do but keep "educating" him until another four years have gone by and he is through high school. So he is deliberately slowed up in the elementary grades, and the years are padded out with such things as physical education, band, cheer leading, and baton twirling.

Paul Woodring writing in the Saturday Review states, "For the past year we have been trying to find, for our readers, a definitive article, written by someone able to stand above the fray, survey the

facts calmly, tell us what it is all about, and advise parents, teachers, and school board members regarding what steps might be taken to improve the teaching of reading."

The answer of many to this plea is simple. If it is really desired that the Johnny of today read as well as the Johnny of old, the remedy is "put on the pressure." Quit talking about "What steps might be taken," — but give him the works like great-granddad got his. But to many moderns this would be bitter medicine. So it is a matter of paying the price or leaving the merchandise on the shelf.

Another angle in the controversy is the matter of practice material. From civil-war times to recent years there was very little supplemental reading material. But nonetheless the people read exceedingly well, — well enough to build a nation such as was never built before.

Grandfather devoured any reading material at hand. Favorites were the historical novels of G. A. Henty and the inspirational ones of Horatio Alger. Children like to read so librarians and book publishers say "Give them books." Books pour out by the millions but still Johnny isn't doing so well.

While we are groping for answers Ada Campbell Rose in an article in the Saturday Evening Post stops us cold with an article entitled *Are Children's Books Trash?* Mrs. Rose was for twenty-one years the editor of Jack and Jill, the Curtis magazine for children, so we assume that she speaks with some authority. She begins, — "If you're wondering why your child won't read these days, take a look at what he's offered."

"Fancily packaged and fancily priced, more than 200,000,000 juvenile books are sold each year. Most of them I submit, don't have enough between their covers to nourish the mind of a gnat. — There is a serious question in my mind as to whether some of these current products are, indeed, books — especially

in the elementary age group. Pictures, montages, bad free verse or abstract art, perhaps, but not books. A caustic father I know has a more accurate description. He calls them 'decorative garbage'."

She deplored the cutting down and regurgitating of the classics, — and when she turned to new fiction she found the results even more deplorable. "Nothing," she says, "approaching a literary style is attempted, and any plot — or none at all — seems to suffice. There is little suspense, emotion, or portrayal of character. — Mediocre books pour off the presses with tedious regularity." She further states, "One new title which a ten-year-old friend of mine read from cover to cover in exactly six minutes, cost $5.95."

Well!! Perhaps we who sell books and publish educational materials had better take another look!

Okay. We have looked. Many books are cracker jacks, and we are proud to recommend them. But, alas, too many are only pictures. Bright and shiny pictures on every page, — but very little to read. And no plot, — no visual writing. Why visual writing when every sentence is illustrated?

This is picture writing. The Indians used picture writing. The ancient Egyptians used picture writing. Perhaps this is one of the keys to our puzzle. We are trying to teach Johnny to read by having him practice on pictures.

Perhaps, Mrs. Rose has led a new horse to our door. We propose to saddle him and see if we can ride. Herewith we offer the first in a series of books for children to read, — books for readers, — not picture lookers. There will be books with stories, complete with plot and characterization, that children can read for fun. There will be books to tell facts. There will be books containing old classics, — not "cut down and regurgitated."

Do you think that we can ride this horse? Well, help us into the saddle, — then watch our dust!

18

∏EBRASKA PLASTIC∫

Irrigate with
the NEW, IMPROVED
'RAINBOW'
TINTED RED
SIPHON IRRIGATION TUBES

'RAINBOW' PLASTIC DAMS

DAM MATERIAL IN ROLLS

RAINBOW TUBES

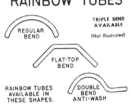

REGULAR BEND

TRIPLE BEND AVAILABLE (Not Illustrated)

FLAT-TOP BEND

RAINBOW TUBES AVAILABLE IN THESE SHAPES.

DOUBLE BEND ANTI-WASH

Plastics for Agriculture and Industry

np NEBRASKA PLASTICS, Inc.

The Originators and Manufacturers of Plastic Siphon Irrigation Tubes : Phone 500

Nebraska Plastics advertisement, 1952,
Siphon Irrigation Tubes.

Correspondence to J. Sterling Morton, Arbor Lodge
as Newspaper Editor

OFFICERS

J. H. EDMISTEN, *Chairman.*
E. W. NELSON, *Secretary.*
S. J. KENT, *Treasurer.*

CANDIDATES

SILAS A. HOLCOMB, *Supreme Judge.*
EDSON RICH, *Regent of University.*
JOHN L. TEETERS, *Regent of University.*

HEADQUARTERS

OF THE

Peoples' Independent Party

OF NEBRASKA.

EXECUTIVE COMMITTEE

First Dist.—W. G. SWAN, Tecumseh.
Second Dist.—C. A. WHITFORD, Arlington.
Third Dist.—J. C. SPRECHER, Schuyler.
Fourth Dist.—W. A. WAGNER, Beatrice.
Fifth Dist.—J. R. THOMPSON, Grand Island.
Sixth Dist.—JOHN MILLER, Kearney.

August, 26, 1899

Windsor Hotel, Lincoln, Nebraska,

My dear Sir.—

Every true member of the People's Independent Part of
Nebraska, as well as every true member of the People's Party in
other states, became a populist by and through study and investigation. Every true populist is a man of convictions and has the
courage of his convictions. There was a time when to be a populist
required courage and self possession in order to withstand the
taunts and jeers of the multitude who followed blindly at the beck
and call of a few scheming politicians who had nothing in common
with those they led. In those days, the politicians scoffed at
the People's Party, its members and the principles set forth; called
populists "wild-eyed, fanatical, soreheads, demagogues and like
epithets; and denounced their principles as "dangerous, Chimerical,
and a menace to the existing order of things". And the unthinking
multitude, taking the cue from their leaders, made personal attacks
upon the members of the People's Party, knowing nothing about its
principles. The politicians recognized the justice and truth in
the principles enunciated in the platform of the People's Party,
but knew too well that a general knowledge and acceptance of such
principles by the people, would leave them, Othello - like, " their
occupation gone" Hence, they bitterly denounced men who had the
hardihood to stand up for principle rather than for men; and, for
want of argument to combat them, scoffed at and ridiculed the
truths upon which populism has its foundation. And so long as the
multitude did not read the truth, they, too, scoffed and ridiculed.

But a great change has come over the multitude —— and greater
changes are yet to come. Truth is mighty and must prevail.

To Oratory much, but to the press more, belongs the honor for
having wrought this transformation. In many localities where
eight years ago populism was nearly synonymous with imbecility—
or worse —— it is now considered not only respectable, but the very
essence of truth and justice. Without the elements of truth and
justice, populism could not endure a day in the broad glare of
publicity it now enjoys. Without the aid of the Press —— and
especially the country press —— populism would not to day be per-
meating all political parties, for even the republican party is
compelled to recognize some of its truths.

We, your committee have ever recognized the power of the
Press. We have known for years the great influence wielded by the
country newspapers, whether for weal or woe depending upon whether

truth or error was advocated. In campaigns gone by more or less
effort has always been made by the Populist State Central Committee
to keep in touch with all the wide awake, earnest papers in the
state, and it is interesting to note that results were always most
satisfactory when the Committee's relations with the newspapers
were most close and cordial.

That results in the forthcoming campaign may be a triumph
for the fusion forces of reform, your committee have decided to
create a department to be devoted wholly to aiding the reform newspapers of Nebraska in every available manner to spread the light;
to furnish these newspapers any and all information regarding state
affairs, matters of public record at the capital, and progress of
the campaign in other parts of the state. This department will be
under the supervision of Charles Q. De France, who has had considerable experience in newspaper work and is thoroughly familiar
with the state records at the capital.

In order that the most effective work in this line may be
done, the committee would esteem it a favor if you would place upon
your mailing list, say until November 20, the name and address!

    C. Q. De France,
      Press Department,
      People's Independent Com.
      Box 1520, Lincoln.

(This address, however, may be abbreviated to suit your convenience.)

Mr. De France, beginning with next week, expects to mail you a
weekly letter touching upon the campaign and political matters
generally. This can be used or not as you prefer. It may be run as
one article, or cut up and used in paragraphs, or the idea may be
used in your own language --- all that the committee desire is to
assist you whatever they can in giving your readers the truth.

You no doubt understand that the committee have meager facilities
for keeping tab on what the republican country papers have to say
politically, and would be glad to have you call to the attention of
Mr. DeFrance, giving clipping if practicable, any article emanating
from a republican paper, which in your judgment, requires explanation and investigation of records and books not easily accessible
to you. He stands ready to attend promptly to all such matters, and
will take great pleasure in doing whatever he can for you.

May we expect an early response from you, with such suggestions as you may deem proper?

      Yours for victory,

                                Chairman.

  Secretary.

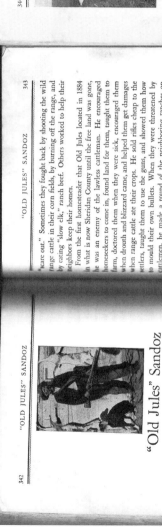

"Old Jules" Sandoz

By Mari Sandoz, Author of "Old Jules."

WHEN "Old Jules" Sandoz was twenty-five, he drove his wagon up the Niobrara into the wild, free country of northwest Nebraska. He found deer in the brush patches, a dark cloud of wild ducks in the sky, and soil that was deep and black: a fine place to build a home and a community of free men. He began to bring in settlers at once.

But there were already a few ranchers along the streams. Some of them recognized the rights of the homesteaders. Others refused to give up the free range. Settlers were threatened and their horses shot, their soddies were often torn down by cowboys in the night, and their frame shacks dragged into gullies with lariats or burned to the ground. Here and there a homesteader was found shot through the back and the murderer was never caught. Many deserted their new homes. But in every place there were a few settlers who would not

scare out." Sometimes they fought back by shooting the wild range cattle in their corn fields, by burning off the range, and by eating "slow elk," ranch beef. Others worked to help their neighbors keep their homes.

From the first homesteader that Old Jules located in 1884 in what is now Sheridan County until the free land was gone, he was an enemy of the lawless cattleman. He encouraged homeseekers to come in, found land for them, taught them to farm, doctored them when they were sick, encouraged them when drouth and blizzard came, and helped them get damages when range cattle ate their crops. He sold rifles cheap to the settlers, taught them to use the guns, and showed them how to mould their own bullets. When they were threatened by cattlemen, he made a round of the neighboring ranches on his Indian pony, his rifle across his saddle before him, and did a little target shooting in sight of the cow hands. He could throw sand from a bare spot the size of a tablecloth as far as he could see it or drop a coyote in his tracks a quarter of a mile away. His settlers were not molested.

Because no one dared face the rifle of the crack shot of the range, cattlemen tried to drive him out of the country by less dangerous means. For fifteen years Old Jules was dogged by arrests and lawsuits on one excuse or another, not hard to find because he had a violent temper. Four times he was put in jail and released. His brother was shot by a cattleman-hired killer. Old Jules his brother was never caught without his rifle, even in his orchards.

After years of protest to Washington, Old Jules and others like him found a sympathetic president in Theodore Roosevelt. He had been a cattleman. He ordered the fences down from around the free land. He forced charges against dozens of ranchers for dishonest land filings and for threatening the

SETTLERS TAKING THE LAW IN THEIR OWN HANDS *Butcher Photo Co.*

settlers. But the cattlemen were powerful. Witnesses were bought off or vanished. Jules Sandoz and his buckskin team with his surveying outfit under the seat, his rifle between his knees, drove over the ranch country for months with government agents collecting evidence. He made many trips to Omaha as government witness in the federal court. Finally, even the power of the big cattle kings could no longer delay the case. Many were fined while some were sent to the penitentiary.

Old Jules lived to see many of his penniless homesteaders become wealthy farmers and stock growers. Recognition came at last for his work in horticulture. In 1931, his portrait was hung in the Nebraska Hall of Agricultural Achievement.

TOPICS AND ACTIVITIES

1. What do you think of "Old Jules"?
2. How was his faith in western Nebraska rewarded?
3. Why had the cattle kings fenced around the free land?
4. Is it true that there was no place for a weak man in the Old West

Sheldon, Addison E. Nebraska Old and New Children's textbook of history stories and folklore. Lincoln: the University Publishing Co. 1937, 470 pp.

Permission to republish these three pages from the Nebraska State Historical Society, 2013.

Initiatives & Referendum (I & R) Notes

Nebraska allows initiative and referendums at both the state and local level.

"In 1897, Nebraska became the first state to provide the initiative and referendum for general use in cities. The law, sponsored by State Representative A.E. Sheldon, allowed citizens in each city and other municipal subdivisions to place initiatives and referendums on the ballot with petitions signed by fifteen percent of voters."[1] Omaha and Lincoln enabled the law in 1907, and the state level in 1912.

The Weekly Advertiser, Red Cloud, wrote: "Mr. Yeiser was a member of the state legislature in 1897 and then drew up a bill for an initiative and referendum law, said to have been the first measure of the kind to be presented a legislative body in this country. He…fought for other measures of a similar nature that were not adopted until a decade later."[2]

"The early adoption efforts were led by Walter Breen of Omaha. Breen, a native of London, emigrated to the United States at age seventeen. After settling in Omaha, he became a successful real estate salesman, secretary of the Omaha Philosophical Society, and an organizer of the Populist Party of Nebraska. Direct legislation supporters, many of them prohibitionists, were thwarted by liquor interests until 1911. Support from presidential candidate William Jennings Bryan, who wrote, "I know of nothing that will do more than I&R to restore government to the hands of the people and keep it within their control." helped push an initiative and referendum law through the legislature in 1911."[1]

"The state's most famous initiative was a 1934 constitutional amendment that created the nation's only unicameral state legislature. U.S. Senator George Norris, a New Deal Republican who is best known for his bill creating the Tennessee Valley Authority, led the unicameral campaign on the grounds that a two-house system was outdated, inefficient, and unnecessary. The vote was sixty percent in favor and forty percent against."[1]

[1]*Initiative* & Referendum, www.landrinstitute.org
From Initiative & Referendum Institute at the University of Southern California.

[2]*The Weekly Advertiser*. "J.O. Yeiser, Veteran Omaha Lawyer Dies," Red Cloud, Webster County, Nebraska, Friday, March 30, 1928, p1- 2.

An Orphan's Prayer

This ballad and its music is dedicated to all the Orphan Train orphans who came westward to find homes and families between 1853 and 1929.

Most of them were from the New York City area where the unwanted children found shelter temporarily in foundling homes.

During those years a hundred thousand of the children, transported on specially equipped trains, found loved ones to adopt them in the heartland of America. They found loving families, good homes and life with God's watching over them.

This ballad is true and was written with God's guidance and love.

Sincerely,
Vera G. Kinter
Marian Christiansen

Music by
MARIAN A. CHRISTIANSEN
Lyrics by
VERA KINTER

Chorus
Moderately

Why, oh, why was I an or - phan, No par - ents had

I or fam - i - ly tree. Child - ren in - a

found - ling home, were my on - ly fam - i - ly.

AN ORPHAN'S PRAYER

$2.75

A ballad by
VERA KINTER

Music
by one of
the orphans,
MARIAN CHRISTIANSEN

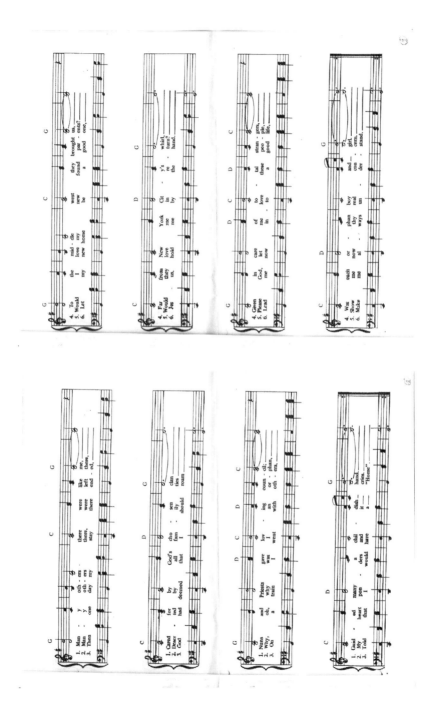

405

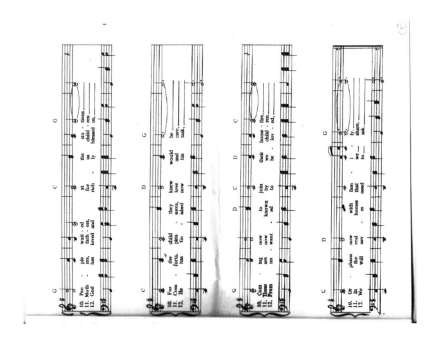

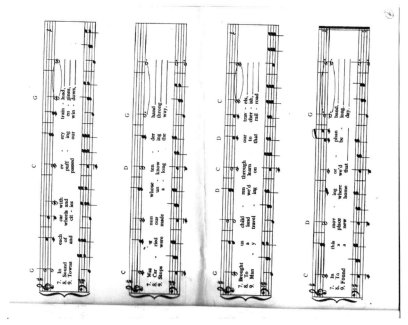

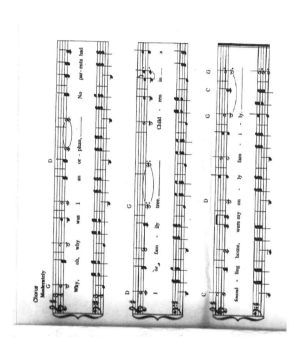

Nebraska Authors Book and Travel Club Polices

As noted in the *Introduction,* Barb and Nancy decided they wanted to encourage readers to participate in Nebraska life as the authors they were writing about had done. Numerous discussions between the two authors were focused on how to remember the past culture(s) of the state as well as participate and build the future through understanding Nebraska history.

It was decided that at the end of each story there would be an autograph box. Book signings will be scheduled and readers can bring their book to a signing and each author present at that signing can sign the box after their story. The autograph boxes also include activities which represent some interest of that author. Traveling to the area where a particular author called home, for at least part of their life, or taking part in or witnessing an event the author would have understood, would provide readers the option to see where history took place as well as participate, in some cases, in history being made. Usually if an author signs his or her box the activities listed in the box are not required to be completed to become part of the Nebraska Authors Book and Travel Club. It is an either-or activity.

When all the boxes are signed and dated or otherwise have the activities completed, contact D & H Adventures at P.O. Box 112, Fullerton, Nebraska 68638 to check the schedule of the authors to see when they will be in your area to review your activities and signatures. Specific information will be given at that time. In the meantime:

1) Please do not contact the authors these stories are written about at their homes or businesses for signatures in the autograph box. There will be signing dates around the state for you to visit with the authors and they can sign your book at that time. You can purchase their book(s) at that time, if they have not sold out. If you cannot get to a signing or not all the authors are present at the book signing(s), you attend their activities in which you can participate in lieu of the signature.

2) When you visit a location around the state please remember no litter and other environmental courtesies. There will be others who visit the location after you and will want a peaceful, beautiful visit for themselves.

3) Remember that the Nebraska Authors Project® wants you to remain safe and enjoy your travels around the state. No liability for your travels rests with the Nebraska Authors Project® or anyone associated with the publication as the activities are options for you.

4) As you plan your trip to the area noted in the autograph box, remember it is only one stop and there are other sites and adventures for you in that area.

5) Autograph boxes with non-travel writing suggestions are meant for your thoughts and how you and your life has been part of the building of the nation. We do not have to read each item, except the travel log story, as they are personal to you and your family(s).

6) When you have completed the fifty-two autograph boxes and contacted the Nebraska Authors Project,® you will be invited to an event with the authors and receive a Volume One Club Membership suitable for framing. At the time of this publication not all the prizes have been finalized so look forward to some surprises.

The Volume One authors and the Nebraska Authors Book and Travel Club look forward to meeting you.

Nebraska Authors Books and Travel Club Map for volume one

NEBRASKA

410

NEBRASKA AUTHORS Book and Travel Club: Volume One

Autograph box activity as related to a map of Nebraska[1]

Each author has been given a number which is placed in the vicinity of the location where the Book and Travel Club activity is located. Please use a Nebraska map with marked highways and distances for preparing your travel plans. This map is to give a summary of the where the activities are located not as an exact reference. Enjoy your visit(s) and be safe.

The top three columns of author's activities are designed to be done in your home, on your travels or anywhere in the state where the activity is scheduled.

[1] map modified from exhibit in Van Ackeren, Ruth and Bartlett Richards Jr. Bartlett Richards: Nebraska Sandhills Cattleman. Lincoln: Nebraska State Historical Society, 1980.

3- Frederic Babcock
28- Fern Nilson
29- Tom Osborne
41- Rudolf Umland
49- John Yeiser
50- Patricia Young

1- David Abbott
2- Othman Abbott
4- Bone Creek Museum of Agrarian Art, Amanda Mobley Gunther
6- Mary Connelly
7- O.C. Dake
8- Barbara Ann Dush
9- Dixie Eckhoff
10- Genevieve Eppens
11- Fred Rogers Fairchild
12- Henry Pratt Fairchild
13- Rex German
14- James Griess
15- Laurel Haymart
16- Robert Howard

5- Margaret Cannell
39- Isabella Taves
44- Victor Vifquain

17- Virginia Inness,
18- Maxine Isackson
19- George Jackson
20- Carl Jennings
21- J. Martin Klotsche,
22- Dorthy Koepke
23- Francis LaFlesche
24- William Lawrence
25- George Miller
26- J Sterling Morton
27- Dale Nichols
32- Caroline Sandoz Pifer
34- Daniel Quinn
35- James Rawley
36- Arthur Riedesel

30- Jim Overturf
31- Clarence S. Paine
33- Amil Quayle

37- Grant Shumway
38- Don Strinz
40- Billie Thornburg
42- Emily Jane Uzendoski
43- Ruth Van Ackeren
45- Albert Watkins
46- Hannie Wolf
47- Malcolm X
48- Kellie, Luna/Jane Taylor Nelson
51- Orville Zabel
52- Darryl Zanuek

How to order more books

If you have access to the internet, check our website: www.dandhadventurespublishing.com or place your order on a separate piece of paper with all the information.

1) Print your first and last name.

2) Print your full address and zip code.

3) Print the address where you want the response from the Nebraska Authors Project® to be sent if different than the address in #2.

4) Print phone number in case we have questions.

5) Print your e-mail if you have a question which may be answered via e-mail nancy@dandhadventurespublishing.com or barbara@dandhadventurespublishing.com

6) Check the website for the current price of the book and shipping information or mail us a request for the information.

7) If you have a school class, book club, or similar group who would like to sell the book as a fundraiser, please contact the Nebraska Authors Project® for information.

8) If your business would like to carry the book for sale in your store, please contact the Nebraska Authors Project® for information.

9) Send a check or money order for your payment to the address below. Your item(s) will be shipped when the check clears.

Thank you.

Mail to: The Nebraska Authors Project®
D & H Adventures Publishing
P.O. Box 112
Fullerton, Nebraska 68638

Add a Nebraska Book or Nebraska Author to our list

As was discussed in the *Introduction,* a compiling of names of authors is being conducted for Nebraska. For the list "A" the author has to have been born in Nebraska and/or lived in the state for at least ten years. For list "B" the author has to have 1) lived in Nebraska for less than ten years, but write about Nebraska issues, people, or places or 2) have never lived in Nebraska, but write about Nebraska issues, people, or places.

If you participate in a book signing conducted by the Nebraska Authors Project,® the current list of authors that has been compiled to date will be available for you to see if you or your Nebraska author is on the list. If it is and you have updated information from what is available on the list, there will be a form on-site for you to provide the information to the Nebraska Authors Project.® If the author is not on the list or a published book is omitted from the list, there will be a form on-site for you to provide the information to the Nebraska Authors Project.®

If you are unable to attend a book signing or other event sponsored by the Nebraska Authors Project® where the current list of authors is available, you can contact the Project at "Authors List," P.O. Box 112, Fullerton, Nebraska 68638 with the information. Please provide your name, address, and phone number so the material you send may be verified with you if we have questions. Thank you.

We will accept new entries until July 1, 2014. After that time the collection will be readied for distribution via the best modes of publication at that time.

About the authors

1980 *Brown County Gazette,* Indiana Sports Editor

Nancy Sue Hansen was born and raised on a farm in Hamilton County, Nebraska. She has a Bachelor of Science degree with a major in Vocational Allied Health Occupations Education, minor in coaching from the University of Nebraska-Lincoln. While completing her student teaching and throughout the next few years she had a journalism career working in sports, especially professional basketball in Kansas City and on the East Coast. She completed her Masters in Science at Indiana University at Bloomington, worked in Washington D.C. and a few other states before returning to Nebraska. Beginning a consulting business in the late 1980's for business and education she researched, taught and wrote on various topics initially based in Lincoln. In addition to her early training in both medical and holistic health she retained a love of history and education. She has participated in politics, Junior Chamber of Commerce Board of Directors, and 4-H club activities. Nancy continues taking advanced coursework toward specialization in Nebraska History. She has one daughter.

Author, Listen with the Heart, 2004.

Barbara Ann Dush was born in Genoa, Nebraska, and raised on a farm near Clarks, Nebraska. She graduated from Central Community College-Platte Campus, majoring in communications. This opened the door to a career in journalism, and a job at the *Nance County Journal* in Fullerton where she continues to work. Dush has won numerous awards from the Nebraska Press Women, the National Federation of Press Women (NFPW), Society of Professional Journalists, and has twice won the Jim Raglin award. In 2004, she was the first woman from Nebraska to win the first place Sweepstakes Award from the NFPW, and was named the Nebraska Press Women Communicator of Achievement in 2008. Dush has served in several capacities on the board of the Nebraska Press Women and currently serves as secretary. She has also served on the Nebraska Womens Commission, and is currently serving on the NFPW Board as an Appointed Director on her fourth term. She and her husband, Albert Micek, have four daughters.

"*One fact seems to have emerged clearly out of the present world confusion. It is that we are engaged in a decisive struggle between those who want to remain free and those who are determined regardless of cost to enslave the human spirit.*"

Dr. J. Martin Klotsche, *Educational Leadership*. March 1951.

"*An Orphan Train Rider Mary Tenopir, was asked what it felt like to be an Orphan Train Rider and Mary said, 'Tears can't be put on paper.' That seemed to be a good summary for our book and we used it.*"

Patricia Young from her 1990 book.

He told them that through his experiences he found that "*Looseness with the truth, or if you will allow me to be blunt, just plain dishonesty, threatens to undermine our very system of government and of commerce. It is not confined to just one part; indeed all three major parties practice deception on the voter. And it is time we called them to account.*"

William H. Lawrence, speech to Lincoln High School graduates 1971.

"*In 1920 Fred [Fairchild] had published an article proposing a restructuring of the post war, World War I, tax system. The public was calling for the repeal of the excess tax which had been enacted during the war. Fred proposed that the government could expect reasonable revenue with justice to the differing classes of taxpayers by changing the tax codes to make corporations exempt from paying taxes on their income, and spreading the payment through the dividends to the stockholders to pay the taxes.*"

Dr. Fred Fairchild as Yale Professor.

In Jan. 1940 the Birth Control Federation of America (BCFA) had their annual meeting entitled *"Race Building in a Democracy"*. Dr. Henry Fairchild, in his luncheon address noted that the conference *"showed how close the two great movements of eugenics and birth control had come in working together and they were 'almost indistinguishable'."*

Dr. Henry Fairchild, Professor New York University.